Democratic Phoenix
Reinventing Political Activism

Conventional wisdom suggests that citizens in many countries have become disengaged from the traditional channels of political participation. Commentators highlight warning signs that include sagging electoral turnout, rising antiparty sentiment, and the decay of civic organizations. But are these concerns justified?

This book compares systematic evidence for electoral turnout, party membership, and civic activism in countries around the world and suggests good reasons to question assumptions of decline. Not only is the obituary for older forms of political activism premature, but new forms of civic engagement may have emerged in modern societies to supplement traditional modes. Political participation appears to have evolved over the years, in terms of the agencies, the actions used for political expression, and the political actors that participants seek to influence. The process of societal modernization and rising levels of human capital are primarily responsible, although participation is also explained by the structure of the state, the role of agencies, and social inequalities.

Pippa Norris is the McGuire Lecturer in Comparative Politics at the John F. Kennedy School of Government, Harvard University. Her work focuses on forms of political communication, elections, and gender politics. She has published more than two dozen books, including two companion volumes to this one, *A Virtuous Circle: Political Communication in Postindustrial Societies* (2000) and *Digital Divide: Civil Engagement, Information Poverty, and the Internet Worldwide* (2001), also published by Cambridge University Press.

Democratic Phoenix

Reinventing Political Activism

PIPPA NORRIS
Harvard University

CAMBRIDGE
UNIVERSITY PRESS

PUBLISHED BY THE PRESS SYNDICATE OF THE UNIVERSITY OF CAMBRIDGE
The Pitt Building, Trumpington Street, Cambridge, United Kingdom

CAMBRIDGE UNIVERSITY PRESS
The Edinburgh Building, Cambridge CB2 2RU, UK
40 West 20th Street, New York, NY 10011-4211, USA
477 Williamstown Road, Port Melbourne, VIC 3207, Australia
Ruiz de Alarcón 13, 28014 Madrid, Spain
Dock House, The Waterfront, Cape Town 8001, South Africa

http://www.cambridge.org

First published 2002

Printed in the United States of America

Typeface Sabon 10/12 pt.   *System* QuarkXPress [BTS]

A catalog record for this book is available from the British Library.

Library of Congress Cataloging in Publication data
Norris, Pippa.
Democratic Phoenix : reinventing political activism / Pippa Norris.
p. cm.
Includes bibliographical references and index.
ISBN 0-521-81177-5 (hardback) – ISBN 0-521-01053-5 (pbk.)
1. Political participation.   2. Political parties.   3. Elections – turnout.
4. New social movements.   I. Title.
JF799 .N67 2002
323'.042 – dc21   2002020164

ISBN   0 521 81177 5   hardback
ISBN   0 521 01053 5   paperback

Contents

Tables

Figures

Preface

It is widely assumed that citizens in many countries have become disengaged from the conventional channels of political participation. This book compares systematic evidence for electoral turnout, party membership, and civic activism in countries around the world and suggests good reasons to question popular assumptions of pervasive decline.

Before proceeding to articulate this argument, so that the wary might be warned before proceeding further, we should note that interpretations of the contemporary state of political participation can and often do fall into multiple potential traps.

One is the danger of mythologizing a romantic Golden Age when all the town hall meetings were packed, all the voting booths were overflowing, and all the citizens were above average.[1] It is all too easy to equate change with decline. Familiar patterns of our parents' and grandparents' generations are regarded nostalgically as the norm, in a misty-eyed Jimmy Stewart small-town-America sort of way. But change can simply mean adaptation to circumstances.

Ethnocentrism is another common danger. The bulk of research on political participation originates in America, and it is sometimes assumed that political fashions are like the export of McDonald's, Nikes, or Levis, so that patterns that first emerge in the United States (or even in California) will probably become evident later among other Western publics. Yet in this regard, as in many others, as Lipset suggests, there may well be American exceptionalism. The individualistic values and particular constitutional structures created at the founding of the United States set a specific cultural milieu, so that civic ills do not necessarily creep north over the Canadian border, let alone spread widely like a virus throughout Western political systems.[2] Particular circumstances, particular historical legacies, and particular institutional structures may block generalized contagions.

Another potential obstacle concerns partial perspectives. Political science has experienced growing fragmentation and intellectual specialization; as

Almond pointed out, like Rattigan's actors, we are increasingly "sitting at separate tables."[3] As a result, research on older mainstream channels of participation, such as elections and political parties, often fails to be integrated into work on new social movements and transnational policy networks. Students of political behavior decry eroding party membership, while elsewhere international relations scholars celebrate the flowering of a cosmopolitan civic society. Psephologists mourn half-empty ballot boxes, while communications scholars herald the rise of internet activism. A wide-ranging voyage drawing upon multiple subareas and many countries is needed to develop a more comprehensive and balanced perspective, even if breadth comes at the inevitable expense of some loss of depth.

Outdated theoretical frameworks are another barrier. We are often imprisoned by the uncritical inheritance of concepts for studying political participation arising from the early classics of the 1960s, but as curiously old-fashioned today as the stump speech, the railway whistle-stop tour, and the "I Like Ike" campaign button. We need to build on the past and honor the intellectual foundations that we inherit. Yet overreliance on traditional frameworks can blind us to modern forms of civic engagement that are symbolized today by events on the streets of Seattle, Gothenberg, and Genoa, and the wide repertoire of activities engaged in by environmentalists, peace protestors, human rights advocates, and women's groups. These dimensions of participation need to be captured, as well as the way that the more conventional activities of parties and elections function, evolve, and adapt in transitional and consolidating democracies such as Russia, Mexico, and South Africa.

Accounts can also exaggerate the value of participation. Viewed through a Schumpeterian lens, democracy involves three core components: the existence of widespread political rights and civil liberties such as freedom of expression and association, party competition in the pursuit of office, and opportunities for citizens to vote at regular intervals to elect their leaders. As such, opportunities for participation by all citizens are a necessary but far from sufficient condition for democracy. Multiple institutions need to be working effectively to channel citizen's voices into representative government, and to ensure that the participation is meaningful rather than merely symbolic. Nor is greater participation by itself necessarily a sign of democratization in the absence of other important safeguards; mass demonstrations on the streets of Iraq, high electoral turnout in Belarus, and plebiscitary rallies in Pakistan have been utilized to legitimize the rule of authoritarian regimes and radical antidemocratic factions.

Data limitations are yet another major barrier. Studies of trends in political participation are restricted by the availability of longitudinal time-series aggregate and cross-national survey data. Until recently, this has produced a systematic bias toward studying postindustrial societies in Western Europe and the United States. Most series of survey data date back no further than the 1970s or 1960s. The number of confounding factors that can complicate the analysis once we start to compare many different regions and types of states around the world can lead to the familiar difficulty of too many variables and too few cases (nations). The "most similar" research design, which focuses on a few countries sharing similar democratic political systems, cultural histories, and historical legacies, has many well-established advantages. Qualitative case studies provide richness and depth. Yet this approach is also limited, particularly in how far those who know only democracies can ever hope to understand democracies. This is akin to feminist strategies claiming that we can understand gender best by focusing on women, rather than comparing similarities and differences between the sexes. In formal terms, the danger is to bias the inferences that can be drawn. We need to understand the process of democratization, not just for its own sake, but also because understanding the path traveled by transitional and consolidating democracies generates important insights into established democracies. The flowering of the third wave of electoral democracies since the early 1970s, and the wider availability of new sources of cross-national survey data since the 1980s, help to illuminate how far we can generalize from the comparative laboratory of older democracies to patterns evident elsewhere around the world. Recent decades have generated a flourishing range of regional studies on the transition and consolidation of democracies in Latin America, Central and Eastern Europe, Asia, and sub-Saharan Africa, which can be integrated and synthesized to help clarify the broad trajectory of world trends. We can start to "turn proper names into variables."[4] Globalization has gradually transformed world politics, but comparative politics has been relatively slow to adapt to the new reality by becoming more global in its research designs.

Given these multiple difficulties, many wiser heads might have been deterred from proceeding. Nevertheless, the topic appeared too important, and the current systematic evidence too flimsy, to allow the conventional wisdom to occupy center stage unchallenged. My previous books had circled around issues of political participation, but the time seemed ripe for a more direct approach.

This book owes many debts, as ever, to friends and colleagues. The idea for the study originated over lunch with Lew Bateman, whose constant support at Cambridge University Press has proved invaluable. It received early encouragement that I should proceed, despite the difficulties, in conversations with Russ Dalton, Jan Van Deth, Ronald Inglehart, Jane Mansbridge, David Marsh, Ian McAllister, Joseph Nye, Robert Putnam, Ben Reilly, Marian Sawer, Sidney Verba, and Paul Whiteley. The book got under way during a visit to the Research School of the Social Sciences at the Australian National University, and I would like to thank colleagues there, especially Ian McAllister and Marian Sawer, for their generous and congenial hospitality. I am also most grateful to all those who went out of their way to provide feedback on initial ideas, or to read through draft chapters and provide chapter-and-verse comments, including Andre Blais, Ivor Crewe, Mark Franklin, Michael Lewis-Beck, Peter Mair, and Susan Scarrow. The first section, on turnout, would not have been possible without the data kindly provided by International IDEA in Stockholm, especially the help of Bengt Sond-Saverland and Maria Gratschew. Subsequent analysis was heavily dependent on the World Values Study, and I owe a large debt of gratitude to the principal investigator, Ron Inglehart, for collecting and sharing this invaluable data set. Data and literature for specific chapters were collected by research assistants at the John F. Kennedy School of Government, including Josh Good, Rob Hanna, Sarah Herrup, and Andrea Stephanous. I would like to thank the panel discussants and colleagues who commented as draft papers were presented at professional meetings, including the Midwest Political Science Association in Chicago, the Political Studies Association of the UK, the European Consortium of Political Research, and the ESF Conference on Social Capital at Exeter University, as well as at the University of Oslo, the University of Orebro, and the Universidad Internacional Mendez Pelayo in Santander. Lastly, this book would not have been possible without the encouragement and stimulation provided by many colleagues and students at the Joan Shorenstein Center on the Press, Politics and Public Policy and the John F. Kennedy School of Government, Harvard University.

Cambridge, Mass.
November 2001

INTRODUCTION

The Decline and Fall of Political Activism?

The conventional wisdom suggests that in the late twentieth century many postindustrial societies experienced a tidal wave of citizen withdrawal from the traditional channels of political participation. Symptoms of this malady include sagging electoral turnout, rising antiparty sentiment, and the decay of civic organizations. Concern about these issues has been expressed in public speeches, leader columns, and academic studies. These voices are heard most commonly in the United States, but similar echoes resonate in many other democracies. But are these fears justified? This book is the last of a trilogy considering related facets of this phenomenon. The first, *A Virtuous Circle*, developed a critique of the media malaise thesis, demonstrating that attention to the news media was positively, not negatively, linked to political participation. *Digital Divide* explored the potential of the internet for civic engagement, and examined how new opportunities online facilitate a more level playing field for challengers and opposition movements with technical skills and know-how.

Building upon this foundation, this book suggests reasons to question and revise popular assumptions of a contagious plague of citizen apathy. In particular, three core claims are advanced, demonstrated, and defended to show that the obituary for civic activism is premature.

First, the study documents mixed trends during the second half of the twentieth century in electoral turnout, party membership, and voluntary associations, not a steady secular erosion. Chapters will demonstrate that voting participation has been stable in established democracies during the postwar era, not in free fall, while by contrast growing literacy, education, and wealth in developing societies have generated rising turnout. Official estimates confirm that party membership has ebbed since the early 1980s in Western Europe, it is true, but at the same time there has been growth in newer democracies such as Slovakia and Hungary. Secularization has shrunk the pool of regular churchgoers in Catholic and Protestant Europe, and modernization undercuts religious faith. Yet despite the rise of the service economy, trade union membership shows a mixed trend across Europe over the last fifty years, not a consistent slump. Moreover, post-industrial societies, where traditional agencies have become less popular, have seen the rise of alternative avenues through protest politics, reinventing activism. Demonstrations, signing petitions, and consumer boycotts have become far more common since the mid-1970s. Engagement in new social movements, exemplified by environmental activism, has flowered in afflu-ent nations. In sum, indicators point more strongly toward the evolution, transformation, and reinvention of civic engagement than to its premature death. The evidence remains more limited than would be desirable in the best of all possible comparative analyses, but nevertheless it is sufficiently robust and reliable across different independent indicators to debunk some common myths.

Second, the book examines survey evidence available for many countries around the world in the mid-1990s wave of the World Values Study to analyze who votes, who joins parties, and who belongs to civic organiza-tions. Conventional explanations of political participation commonly focus on social inequalities of class, education, age, gender, and ethnicity, as well as on cultural attitudes such as political interest and confidence. Yet these factors are insufficient by themselves to explain the marked contrasts in national levels of political activism. It is also important to take account of the broader context set by societal modernization, institutional design, and mobilizing agencies. In particular, the early stages of the modernization process generate rising levels of human capital (education, literacy, and wealth) that are strongly related to many dimensions of citizen activism, although this is a curvilinear pattern that tapers off after a certain point (thereby solving the so-called puzzle of electoral participation). This broader context shapes and mediates the impact of social structure and cultural attitudes on civic engagement.

Lastly, multiple newer channels of civic engagement, mobilization, and expression are rapidly emerging in postindustrial societies to supplement traditional modes. Political participation is evolving and diversifying in terms of the *who* (the *agencies* or collective organizations), *what* (the *reper-toires* of actions commonly used for political expression), and *where* (the *targets* that participants seek to influence).[1] Admittedly, it is difficult to sub-stantiate this argument with the limited evidence available. Nevertheless, this claim seems both important and persuasive. Protest politics did not dis-appear with afghan bags, patchouli oil, and tie-dyed T-shirts in the sixties; instead, it has moved from margin to mainstream. New social movements, transnational policy networks, and internet activism offer alternative avenues of engagement. The politics of choice appears to be replacing the politics of loyalties. It follows that studies of political participation focus-ing exclusively on conventional indicators, such as trends in electoral turnout in the United States and party membership in Western Europe, may seriously misinterpret evidence of an apparent civic slump. Political energies have diversified and flowed through alternative tributaries, rather than simply ebbing away.

Before proceeding to articulate these arguments, we need to summarize the standard textbook case for civic decline, outline the revisionist interpretation presented in this book, and then describe the comparative framework, the main sources of evidence, and the overall plan of the book.

The Case for Civic Decline

There is widespread agreement among varied democratic theorists, ranging from Jean Jacques Rousseau to James Madison, John Stuart Mill, Robert Dahl, Benjamin Barber, David Held, and John Dryzak, that mass participation is the lifeblood of representative democracy, although conceptions differ sharply over how much civic engagement is either necessary or desirable.[2] On the one hand, theories of "strong" democracy suggest that citizen activism is intrinsically valuable. Mill argued that by actively participating in the civic life, rather than allowing others to make decisions in their own interest, people learn and grow. In this view, involving the public can make better citizens, better policies, and better governance. On the other hand, Schumpeterian democrats believe that the essential role of citizens should be relatively limited, confined principally to the periodic election of parliamentary representatives, along with the continuous scrutiny of government actions.[3] Nevertheless, even this minimalist view sees voting participation as one of the essential features of representative government, alongside many other institutional safeguards.

Opportunities for widespread public engagement in public affairs, making all voices count in the policy-making process, are not sufficient in themselves to ensure that representative democracies work effectively. Nondemocratic regimes well understand the symbolic power of legitimating events, as demonstrated by pro-government rallies organized by the police and military in Nigeria, plebiscitary elections in one-party predominant states such as Singapore, Algeria, and Belarus, and anti-American protests mobilized by ruling elites in Iraq. In elections during the 1990s in Uzbekistan, Angola, and Equatorial Guinea, all governed by nondemocratic regimes, over 87 percent of voters flocked to the polls.[4] By itself, public participation does not guarantee the workings of representative democracy. Arguably, it is not even the most pressing challenge facing many transitional and consolidating democracies. But at least some minimal opportunity for electoral choice is one of the necessary but not sufficient conditions for Schumpeterian democracies. Widespread disengagement from civic life is problematic if political participation functions as a mechanism to hold elected officials to account, to articulate and express public demands and grievances, and to train and educate future political leaders. There should be concern if lack of participation undermines confidence in the legitimacy of representative governments, drains the lifeblood from the more fragile democracies, and reinforces social inequality and the disadvantages facing poorer groups, women, and ethnic minority populations already at the margins of power.

The standard view emphasizes a familiar litany of civic ills that are believed to have undermined the democratic channels traditionally linking citizens to the state. Elections are the most common way for people to express their political preferences, and the half-empty ballot box is taken to be the most common symptom of democratic ill health.[5] The idea of representative democracy sans parties is unthinkable, yet studies of party organizations suggest the desertion of grassroots members, at least in Western Europe, during recent decades.[6] An extensive literature on partisan dealignment has established that lifetime loyalties anchoring voters to parties have been eroding in many established democracies, contributing to sliding turnout and producing a more unstable electorate, open to the sway of short-term forces.[7] Political mobilization via traditional agencies and networks of civic society, such as unions and churches, appears to be under threat. Structural accounts emphasize that union membership is hemorrhaging due to the decline of jobs in manufacturing industries, changing class structures, flexible labor markets, and the spread of individualist values.[8] Theories of secularization, deriving originally from Max Weber, suggest that the public in modern societies has been abandoning church pews for shopping malls.[9] The bonds of belonging to the plethora of traditional community associations and voluntary organizations may be becoming more frayed and tattered than in the past.[10] Putnam presents the most extensive battery of evidence documenting anemic civic engagement in America, displayed in activities as diverse as community meetings, social networks, and association membership.[11] Surveys of public opinion suggest that growing public cynicism about government and public affairs has become pervasive in the United States, at least before the events of 9/11, while citizens have become more critical of the institutions of representative government in many other established democracies.[12]

Given the weight of all this accumulating evidence, the conventional perspective suggests that traditional political activities that arose and flourished during the late nineteenth and early-twentieth centuries peaked during the postwar era and have waned in popularity since. Common activities for our parents and grandparents, such as attending party conferences, union branch meetings, and town hall rallies, may appear as musty, quaint, and outmoded to the internet generation as the world of eighteenth-century Parisian political salons, nineteenth-century Yorkshire rotten boroughs, and early twentieth-century Chicago party machines. The conventional wisdom has set policy alarm bells ringing from Washington, D.C., to Brussels and Tokyo, although prognostications differ about "what is to be done," because there is far greater consensus about the diagnosis of the symptoms than about the cure.[13]

Elsewhere, there are obvious grounds for greater optimism. The last quarter of the twentieth century witnessed a dramatic expansion of free elections worldwide. Countries as diverse as the Czech Republic, Mexico, and South Africa celebrated a political renaissance. Since the onset of the "third wave" in 1974, the proportion of states that are at least electoral democracies has more than doubled, and the number of democratic governments in the world has tripled.[14] Many hoped that these developments would deepen and enlarge the opportunities for citizens to become engaged in public affairs and governance. Yet even here, there remain multiple problems in civic life. In many states, the establishment of free and fair elections has not been accompanied by the robust institutionalization of democracy through more effective party competition, freedom of expression and association, respect for justice and the rule of law, guarantees of human rights, and government transparency and accountability. Many newer democracies, such as those in the Andean region, have developed the architecture of competitive electoral institutions but failed to create the supporting foundations of vibrant civic societies, while deep-rooted political mistrust is apparent throughout Latin America, creating the danger of occasional reversions to authoritarian rule.[15]

Countervailing Trends and Forces

Yet despite the conventional wisdom, there are good reasons to question popular assumptions that civic decline has become pandemic throughout the older democracies, and that it has failed to flourish and take root in the stony and uncertain ground of the newer democracies. Not all indicators, by any means, point toward consistent and steady secular deterioration across all dimensions of political activism. Instead, after a few minutes' thought, even the most casual observer of current events will quickly identify many complex contradictions, crosscurrents, and anomalies. In the U.S. presidential election of 2000, for example, many commentators deplored the fact that only half of the American electorate voted, despite the tightest presidential contest in forty years, the importance of the outcome, and the three billion dollars spent on the campaign. Yet a year later, the dramatic events of the destruction of the World Trade Center generated a coast-to-coast outpouring of patriotic displays, from flags to army volunteers, a flowering of community giving, from an estimated one billion dollars in charitable donations to lines of volunteers at blood banks, and a massive resurgence of the news audience.

Similar counterflows are found elsewhere. The UK general election of June 2001 prompted a pervasive mood of campaign apathy, the lowest turnout since the First World War, and hemorrhaging party membership, generating official government reports on how to improve voter participation.[16] Yet in recent years not all of the British public has been disengaged; instead, there have been multiple demonstrations, blockades, and direct-action protests by disparate groups concerned about animal rights, genetically modified food, road development plans and fuel taxes, the rights of Muslim citizens, and the state of race relations. Across the Channel, France has often seen similar outbreaks exemplified by port blockades by fisherman, farmers dumping manure on the steps of the French parliament, violent anti-globalization protests against McDonald's, and massive anti–Le Pen rallies. U.S. air strikes on Afghanistan triggered daily street protests stretching from Jakarta, Nairobi, and Karachi to Belfast, Berlin, and Boston.

Moreover, protests are not merely symbolic politics; they can have critical consequences. In Belgrade, an estimated half-million opposition supporters took to the streets in a general strike demanding the resignation of President Milosevic, leading to his downfall and eventual trial before an international court in The Hague. In the Philippines, a peaceful uprising of people power on the Manila streets – a melange of lawyers and students, businessmen and middle-class housewives – caused the abrupt ejection of President Estrada from power. Similar manifestations disrupted Argentinian politics following the banking crisis. The young are assumed to be politically lethargic. Yet anticapitalist demonstrations among this generation have rocked summits of world leaders from Seattle to Quebec, Gothenberg, and Genoa, forcing reconsideration of issues of debt repayment by poorer nations.

The major examples of counterbalancing tendencies come from protest politics, but in certain circumstances even traditional electoral channels have proved remarkably popular. In August 2001, for example, East Timor's first free elections since independence from Indonesia and Portugal generated long lines at the polls, and 91 percent of electors voted. In June 1999, 89 percent of South Africans cast a ballot in parliamentary elections. In 1998, despite violence and intimidation during the campaign, the Cambodian general election saw lengthy queues at polling stations, 94 percent turnout, and a strong challenge to the governing party.[17] Voting apathy is not universal.

These phenomena may or may not be related. But taking them together, even the causal observer would acknowledge that the pervasive idea that the public has become disengaged from every form of civic life oversimplifies a far more complex and messy reality. These anecdotal observations suggest that it is time for a more thorough reexamination of the systematic evidence, with a mind open to findings running counter to the conventional view.

To consider these issues, the first aim of this book is to examine the standard claim of a pervasive, long-term erosion of political activism experienced in many countries around the world during the postwar era. Although such a trend is often widely assumed, in fact the evidence of secular decline often remains scattered and patchy; consistent and reliable longitudinal trend data is limited; and most previous systematic research has been restricted to case studies of particular countries, particularly the United States, and comparative evidence among established democracies in Western Europe, making it hard to generalize more widely. Given these limitations, this study aims to update the analysis and to examine the broader picture of trends in recent decades where evidence is available across many nations.

The second major aim of the study is to analyze and explain the variations in levels of electoral turnout, party membership, and civic activism in countries around the world today. There are substantial contrasts among contemporary societies. For example, in national elections held during the 1990s, electoral turnout remained remarkably high (over 85 percent) in democracies as diverse at Iceland, South Africa, and Uruguay, but it fell below 50 percent in the United States, Jamaica, and Switzerland.[18] As subsequent chapters demonstrate, there are similar cross-national divergencies in many other common dimensions of civic life, including the membership of parties, religious organizations, and trade unions, as well as the propensity to protest through demonstrations, strikes, and boycotts. In seeking to explain these national differences, the book focuses on modernization theories, suggesting that long-term processes of societal and human development (including rising levels of literacy, education, and wealth) are driving patterns of political participation. But rather than adopting a monocausal theory, the study also explores how far levels of activism are shaped by political institutions and the structure of the state, mobilizing agencies such as parties, unions, and churches, social inequalities in resources, and cultural attitudes held by groups and individuals.

Lastly, the conclusion aims to reflect more generally on the nature of political participation and on whether the standard indicators used to monitor civic energies are capable of capturing alternative forms of political expression and activism through new social movements, transnational policy networks, and internet channels. If modes are evolving, then political science may be in danger of lagging behind. The heart of this book therefore explores whether many common dimensions of political participation have eroded during the late twentieth century, as many assume, analyzes the reasons for cross-national patterns of civic engagement in many countries, and considers the consequences for democratic governance.

Comparative Framework

This study seeks to understand these issues by comparing countries around the globe, maximizing the advantages of the "most different" comparative strategy.[19] Much existing research on political participation is based upon the United States, as well as on established Western European and Anglo-American democracies. Yet it is not clear how far we can generalize more widely from these particular countries. Patterns of participation that gradually evolved with the spread of democracies in the mid nineteenth and early twentieth centuries, following the long-term process of industrialization, are unlikely to be the same as those found in Latin American nations that have experienced authoritarian regimes and military rule, or in Central European states that have lived under Communist Party hegemony. If distinctive historical experiences have made their cultural mark on these nations, in a path-dependent pattern, they may continue to influence patterns of political activism today.

Moreover, as the earliest comparative studies have long stressed, political systems offer citizens widely different structures of opportunity to become engaged in their own governance.[20] In pluralist societies such as the United States, for example, voluntary organizations, professional associations, and community groups commonly mobilize people into politics, with the church playing a particularly important role.[21] In Western Europe, by contrast, mass-branch party organizations often play a stronger role. And in many developing societies, such as the Philippines and South Africa, grassroots social movements draw people into protest politics and direct action strategies. In short, patterns of activism in both Western Europe and the United States may prove atypical of the range of transitional and consolidating democracies in Latin America, Central and Eastern Europe, Asia and sub-Saharan Africa.[22]

Given these considerations, this study follows the well-known conceptualization of Przeworski and Teune in adopting the "most different systems" research design, seeking to maximize contrasts between a wide range of societies in order to distinguish systematic clusters of characteristics associated with different dimensions of political activism.[23] Clearly, there are some important trade-offs involved in this approach, notably the loss of the richness and depth that can come from case-study comparison of a few similar countries within relatively similar regions. A broader canvas increases the complexity of comparing societies that vary widely in terms of cultural legacies, political systems, and democratic traditions. Yet the strategy of attempting a worldwide comparison, where data is available, has multiple advantages. Most importantly, the global framework allows us to examine whether, as theories of societal modernization claim, patterns of political activism evolve with the shift from traditional rural societies, with largely illiterate and poor populations, through industrial economies based on a manufacturing base, with a growing urban working class, to postindustrial economies based on a large middle-class service sector.

The approach adopted in this study maximizes the comparison of nations at many different levels of societal modernization today, including some of the most affluent countries in the world (including Sweden, Germany, and the United States), those characterized by middle-level human development and transitional economies (typified by such nations as Taiwan, Brazil, and South Africa), as well as poorer rural societies, such as India and China. Some states under comparison are governed by authoritarian regimes, while others have experienced a rapid consolidation of democracy within the last decade. Today the Czech Republic, Latvia, and Argentina are ranked as being just as "free" as Western European nations with long traditions of democracy, such as Belgium, France, and the Netherlands.[24] The approach adopted here follows in the footsteps of Verba, Nie, and Kim's seminal seven-nation study published in 1978, which compared participation in Austria, India, Japan, the Netherlands, Nigeria, the United States, and Yugoslavia, although the current research benefits from the easier availability of data and compares many more nations, allowing more reliable cross-national generalizations.

Classification of Nations

Countries were classified for analysis according to levels of human development. The Human Development Index produced annually by the UNDP provides the standard measure of societal modernization, combining levels of literacy and education, health, and per capita income. This measure is widely used, and it has the advantage of providing a broader indicator of the well-being of a society than simple levels of economic income or financial wealth. The only alteration made here to the standard UNDP classification is that nations ranking highest in human development were subdivided into "*postindustrial* societies" (the most affluent states around the world, ranking 1–28, the highest HDI scores in the UNDP index, and mean per capita GNP of $23,691) and "*other highly developed* societies" (ranked 29–46 by the UNDP, with mean per capita GNP of $9,006). This subdivision was selected as more precise and consistent than the conventional use of OECD member states to define industrialization, since a few OECD member states such as Mexico and Turkey have low development, although in practice most countries overlap.[25]

Over the years there have been many attempts to gauge levels of democracy, and the Gastil index measured annually by Freedom House has become widely accepted as one of the standard measures of democratization. Freedom House provides an annual classification of political rights and civil liberties around the world. For this study, the history of democracy in each nation-state worldwide is classified based on the annual ratings produced from 1972 to 2000.[26] An important distinction is drawn between thirty-nine *older democracies*, defined as those with at least twenty years' continuous experience of democracy (1980–2000) and a current Freedom House rating of 2.0 or less, and forty-three *newer democracies*, with less than twenty years' experience of democracy and a current Freedom House

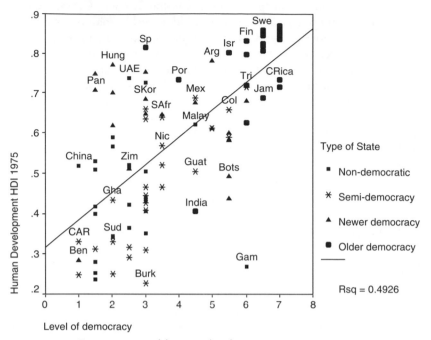

FIGURE I.I. Democracy and human development, 1975.

rating of 2.5 or less. Following the Freedom House rankings, other countries were classified based on the most recent ratings (1999–2000) into *semi-democracies* (which are often referred to as "partly free," "transitional," or "consolidating" democracies) and *non-democracies* (which includes a wide variety of regimes lacking political rights and civil liberties, including military-backed dictatorships, authoritarian states, elitist oligarchies, and ruling monarchies). The Appendix lists the classifications of countries used throughout the book, based on these measures.

In practice, it remains difficult to disentangle the complex relationships between human and political development. In the early literature, many researchers argued that the modernization process was closely related to the spread of democratization.[27] Figure I.I illustrates the strength of this association in the mid-1970s, and the strong correlation (R = .49) during this era shows that most countries clustered in a predictable pattern around the regression line. Even so, there were a few outliers with relatively high levels of human development and yet restricted political rights and civil liberties, such as the communist governments in Romania and Hungary and the dictatorial regimes in Spain and Chile, as well as some poorer countries with democratic governments, such as India, Papua New Guinea, and

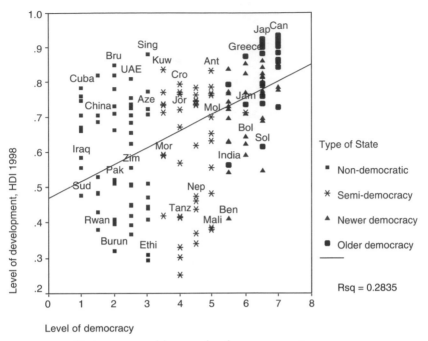

FIGURE 1.2. Democracy and human development, 1998–9.

Botswana. Yet this general relationship between democracy and development altered significantly in later decades, following the "third wave" revolutions in Central and Eastern Europe, Asia, and Latin America. Figure 1.2 illustrates the nature of this association across all of the nations under comparison in the late 1990s. The figure shows a greater scatter around the line, especially among semi-democracies and non-democracies. This association has important implications for attempts to disentangle the relationship of human and democratic development, and for the classifications used in the analysis. All of the older democracies except India are relatively affluent and modern societies, and almost all of the newer democracies are also moderately developed societies. Nevertheless, there is a wide distribution of semi-democracies and non-democracies by level of human development, as shown by the stark contrasts between affluent Bahrain, Brunei Darussalam, and Singapore, on the one hand, and the poorer societies of Rwanda, Burundi, and Sudan, on the other. As discussed in the next chapter, the modernization process brings greater education, literacy, and affluence, which are associated with mass participation in democracy, but outliers such as India and Singapore illustrate that there can be important exceptions to this pattern.

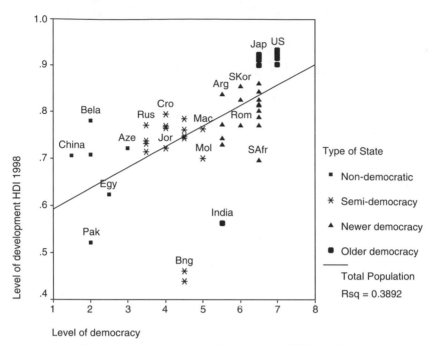

FIGURE 1.3. Democracy and human development, WVS nations, 1998–9. *Note*: Positions of the societies as compared in the World Values Study, mid-1990s.

Sources of Evidence

The study adopts a multimethod research design, drawing upon aggregate data for 193 independent nation-states derived from many sources, such as levels of electoral turnout monitored from 1945 to 2000 by the International Institute for Democracy and Electoral Assistance (IDEA), information on membership in trade unions collected by the International Labour Organization, data on secularization from the *World Christian Encyclopedia*, and so on. Much of the analysis is based on survey data from the three-wave World Values Study (WVS) of public opinion conducted in almost seventy societies during the early 1980s, the early 1990s, and the mid-1990s. Figure 1.3 displays the distribution of the societies that can be compared using just the third wave of the World Values Study, conducted in the mid-1990s, including fifty-three countries from different global regions at all levels of human and democratic development. This source provides the broadest cross-national survey data currently available, including measures of voting participation, political discussion and interest, social trust, membership in voluntary organizations and political parties, willingness to engage in political protest, and a wide range of values, attitudes, and standard background variables. Where appropriate, the book also draws on many other sources of public opinion surveys for time-series and cross-national data, such as the 1973–6 Political Action survey, the International Social Survey Program (ISSP) conducted in the mid-1990s, and the fifteen-nation Eurobarometer (1970–2000).

Plan of the Book

Analytical Framework
Chapter 2 outlines the analytical and conceptual framework for explaining patterns of political participation, and considers why the process of societal modernization may have transformed many key dimensions of civic engagement. The discussion is grounded within broader theories of political participation drawn from classic landmarks in the literature from Almond and Verba (1963) onward, especially the typology of multidimensional participation developed by Verba and Nie (1972) and by Verba, Nie, and Kim (1978), the research on protest potential developed by Barnes and Kaase (1979), work on social movements by Tarrow (1992) and others, studies of transnational advocacy networks by Keck and Dinneck (1998), and theories of social capital following Putnam (2000). The core model outlined in this chapter combines five factors that can help explain patterns of participation: the *level of societal modernization* in each country, the *structure of the state*, the role of *mobilizing agencies*, the *resources* that individuals bring to the process, and the *motivation* that draws citizens into civic affairs.

Electoral Turnout
The book then turns to examine electoral turnout as the most common form of conventional participation, though also one of the least demanding. Chapter 3 maps national patterns of electoral turnout as a proportion of the voting-age population (Vote/VAP) worldwide, and compares trends during the last fifty years, based on the analysis of national election results from International IDEA. Patterns are compared across traditional, industrialized, and postindustrial societies as well as across different types of political system, including older and newer democracies, semi-democracies, and authoritarian regimes. Based on modernization theories, the chapter explores whether broadly similar trends in turnout are found among nations at roughly similar levels of human development. The study confirms that electoral participation dropped in the United States from 1945 to 2000, but it also shows that, contrary to much popular speculation, there was a significant fall in turnout during the same period in only ten other postindustrial societies (including Australia, Canada, Austria, New Zealand, Switzerland, and France). Most Western nations show a pattern of

stability or trendless fluctuation during the second half of the twentieth century, while a few, such as Sweden, Greece, and Israel, have seen rising electoral participation during this era. A modest dip in turnout was experienced during the 1990s across Western Europe, but this returned levels to the status quo ante found during the postwar decade. A broader comparison of worldwide trends during the second half of the twentieth century reveals that almost twice as many countries have seen rising as opposed to falling turnout, with steady gains in many developing societies in Latin American, such as Mexico, Brazil, and Chile, as well as among smaller states in the Pacific and Caribbean regions.

Yet even among relatively similar types of society, such as Switzerland and Sweden, or the United States and the United Kingdom, there remain substantial contrasts in how many citizens vote. Chapter 4 examines institutional explanations for these differences. Structural variables can affect the costs of participation, such as the time and effort required to cast a ballot, and the anticipated benefits of participating, including the symbolic and instrumental rewards of voting. Based on a soft version of rational choice theory, the study assumes that, ceteris paribus, people will be more likely to vote where costs are low and the benefits are high – for example, in close parliamentary contests in majoritarian electoral systems, where even a few votes can determine which party enters government. The chapter analyzes the role of the direct institutional factors, such as the use of compulsory voting and the facilities for casting a ballot, and indirect institutional variables, including the type of electoral system. The chapter concludes that, after controlling for levels of human and democratic development, political institutions and rules still matter. Voting participation is maximized in elections using proportional representation, with compact electoral districts, regular but relatively infrequent national contests, competitive party systems, and presidential contests. Legal rules also count, such as the year when woman were first enfranchised and the use of literacy requirements. Moreover, institutions and rules matter more for turnout than do specific voting facilities, such as the registration process.

Chapter 5 goes on to analyze motivational and resource-based explanations of electoral participation, drawing upon the International Social Survey Program data in twenty-two nations, to see how far cross-national patterns of turnout can be accounted for by the role of structure, culture, and agency. Structure involves the impact of patterns of inequality, including the major social cleavages of gender, class, race/ethnicity, and generation. Culture includes a variety of attitudes, such as support for democracy, satisfaction with government performance, political interest, efficacy, and trust, and the strength of partisan loyalties, as well as broader traditions determined by religious, colonial, and communist legacies. Agency concerns the way in which social networks such as unions, churches, and community associations draw citizens into public life. The study confirms the importance of all these factors in predicting turnout, even after controlling for human development and the broader institutional context.

Political Parties

Part II turns to consider cross-national differences in support for the institution of political parties, and whether there has been a widespread erosion of membership and activism. Parties traditionally represent one of the central organizations linking citizens and the state, and in established democracies any partisan decline may have significant consequences for how far citizens can influence governments. Party organizations are compared in the light of debates about the erosion or transformation of party support.[28] Chapter 6 sets out Duverger's ideal type of mass-branch parties, where parliamentary leaders rely on a broad base of active members in local areas, and an even wider circle of loyal voters in the electorate. The study then examines trends from the early 1980s to the mid-1990s, along with cross-national patterns of party membership and activism, using the World Values Study. This survey data is compared against estimates of party membership derived from official party records in Western democracies. The results show that patterns of party membership vary considerably cross-nationally, even within similar types of society and global regions. Rather than a consistent slump in membership, the evidence suggests a more complex pattern, with party support growing in some newer democracies, even if there has been a slump in many Western democracies.

Chapter 7 explains reasons for the cross-national differences in party membership, establishing that modernization processes, in particular the spread of electronic media, are important factors driving this process. Party membership is usually greatest in societies with low diffusion of the broadcasting media. This suggests that parties make the most effort to mobilize and retain grassroots activists where traditional face-to-face campaigning predominates, but that parties face lesser incentives to recruit members where alternative channels of mass communication allowing them to connect directly with voters are easily available. Moreover, organizational networks and political interest are stronger predictors of individual party membership than the standard social factors such as gender, age, class, and education.

Social Capital and Civic Society

Part III focuses on debates about the role of civic society, generated by the work of Putnam and others.[29] Chapter 8 considers theories of social capital. Putnam's definition has two components: associational activism and social trust. The study compares alternative measures of belonging to many common types of voluntary associations, social clubs, and civic organizations. The study concludes that social trust, but not associational activism, is strongly related to levels of human and democratic development.

Chapter 9 examines whether traditional agencies of mobilization, such as trade unions and religious organizations, have weakened over the years because of long-term secular and structural trends, and considers how far these agencies boost levels of political participation. The chapter concludes that, far from showing a uniform secular trend, union density has varied substantially in Western Europe during the postwar period, with some nations experiencing falling membership but others remaining stable, and yet others managing to recruit new members and boost their rolls. By contrast, secularization does receive confirmation from the available data on church attendance in Western Europe, with a fall found during the last thirty years in most countries, although from varying levels.

Chapter 10 analyzes new social movements and protest politics, building upon work on "unconventional" participation by Barnes and Kaase and others.[30] The study examines where protest activism is most prevalent, comparing societies by levels of human and political development, and whether the social background of the protest population has "normalized" in terms of gender, class, generation, and race/ethnicity. New social movements are exemplified by environmentalism, so countries are compared to see whether environmental activists are particularly inclined toward protest politics. The chapter discusses the role of the internet in facilitating transnational advocacy networks – concerning such issues as human rights, conflict resolution, women's equality, environmental protection, and trade/debt – that transcend national borders. The concluding chapter draws together the major findings of the book and considers their implications for changing patterns of civic activism, for broader normative theories of democracy, and for understanding the voice of citizens in the democratization process worldwide.

2

Theories of Political Activism

The first task is to see whether there has been a systematic weakening of the channels of electoral, party, and civic activism. The second is to examine the most plausible explanations to account both for differences among nations and for trends over time. The most common explanation for long-term developments in political participation comes from *modernization theories* advanced by Daniel Bell, Ronald Inglehart, and Russell Dalton, among others, suggesting that common social trends – such as rising standards of living, the growth of the service sector, and expanding educational opportunities – have swept through postindustrial societies, contributing to a new style of citizen politics in Western democracies.[1] This process is believed to have increased demands for more active public participation in the policy-making process through direct action, new social movements, and protest groups, while weakening deferential loyalties and support for traditional hierarchical organizations and authorities such as churches, parties, and traditional interest groups.

By contrast, *institutional accounts* emphasize the way in which the structure of the state sets opportunities for participation, exemplified in arguments by Powell and by Jackman that electoral laws, party systems, and constitutional frameworks help explain differences in voting turnout among nations.[2] Trends in participation can also be accounted for by changes in the rules of the game, such as the expansion of the franchise and reforms in campaign spending laws. *Agency theories*, exemplified by Rosenstone and Hansen,[3] focus on the role of traditional mobilizing organizations in civic society, notably the ways in which political parties, trade unions, and religious groups recruit, organize, and engage activists. Putnam's account, emphasizing the role of social capital, also falls into this category.[4] Lastly, the civic voluntarism model, developed by Verba and his colleagues, emphasizes the role of social inequalities in *resources* such as educational skills and socioeconomic status, and *motivational* factors such as political interest, information, and confidence, in explaining who participates.[5]

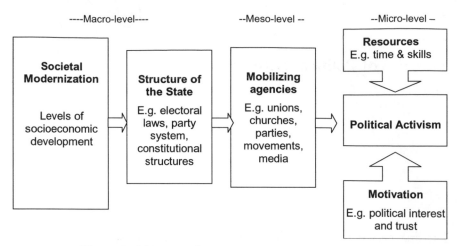

FIGURE 2.1. Theoretical framework.

In the light of these theories, the challenge is to try to sort out the relative importance of each of these factors. Figure 2.1 illustrates the core analytic model used in the book.

Societal Modernization

The central claim, and indeed the seductive appeal, of modernization theories is that economic, cultural, and political changes go together in predictable ways, so that there are broadly similar trajectories, which form coherent patterns, even if particular circumstances mean that what occurs in any given society cannot be predicted exactly. Modernization theories are rooted in the sociological classics of Max Weber and Emile Durkheim. These accounts became increasingly popular during the late 1950s and early 1960s in much of the literature on socioeconomic development and democratization, popularized in the work of Seymour Martin Lipset, Daniel Lerner, W. W. Rostow, Karl Deutsch, and Daniel Bell, among others.[6] Lipset's core thesis was that growing wealth, education, urbanization, and industrialization were the social foundations for democracy and for mass participation in the political system.[7] This theory subsequently became unfashionable, in part because democracy failed to take root in many Asian and Latin American nations that had experienced rapid economic development during the 1960s and 1970s, such as Brazil, Chile, the Republic of Korea, and Taiwan. Critics lambasted the ethnocentric assumptions of linear "progress" toward a Western model of democracy, as well as the economic determinism inherent in early, cruder versions of the thesis.[8] It appeared that many of the central tenants of modernization theory – such as the automatic link assumed between progress toward scientific rationality and the decline of religiosity – turned out to be rather simplistic, with counter-secularization trends and religious revivals occurring among conservative, orthodox, and traditionalist movements in some postindustrial societies as diverse as the United States, Israel, and Japan.[9]

In recent decades, the emergence of "third-wave" democracies has spurred fresh interest in reexamining the association between socioeconomic development and the process of democratic transition and consolidation. Nonlinear theories of cultural modernization have experienced a revival in political science, fuelled largely by the work of Ronald Inglehart,[10] while Alex Inkeles and Anthony Giddens have offered alternative interpretations about the consequences of modernity in affluent nations.[11] "Modernization" refers to a multitude of systemic-level trends – social, economic, demographic, and technological – transforming the structure of societies from rural to industrialized, and from industrialized to postindustrial. In turn, these developments are believed to exert a decisive influence upon the process of democratization, including the political attitudes and participatory behavior of citizens.

Modernization theories in the work of Daniel Bell run along the following lines.[12] Traditional societies are characterized by subsistence livelihoods largely based on farming, fishing, extraction, and unskilled work, with low levels of literacy and education, predominately rural populations, minimum standards of living, and restricted social and geographic mobility. Citizens in rural societies are strongly rooted to local communities through ties of "blood and belonging," including those of kinship, family, ethnicity, and religion, as well as long-standing cultural bonds. The shift from traditional to industrialized society concerns the move from agricultural production to heavy manufacturing, from farms to factories, and from peasants to workers. This phase occurred in Britain during the mid to late eighteenth century, then spread during the nineteenth and early twentieth centuries throughout the Western world. The familiar litany of social changes that accompanied these economic developments includes:

- The population shift from rural villages to metropolitan conurbations;
- Growing levels of education, literacy, and numeracy with the spread of basic schooling;
- Occupational specialization and the expansion of working-class employment on heavy industry, manufacturing, and processing;
- The rise of the urban bourgeoisie and the decline of landed interests;
- Rising standards of living, increased longevity, and expanding leisure time;
- The greater availability of the print media, and growing access to movies, radio, and television;
- The growth of Weberian bureaucratization and reliance on legal-rational authority in government;
- The development of the early foundations of the welfare state;

- The shift from extended to nuclear families and the entry of more women into the paid workforce.[13]

The early studies suggested that the key stage involved the move from agricultural processing to industrial production, but the subsequent literature emphasized that a further distinct stage can be distinguished, as a nonlinear process, in the rise of advanced industrialized or postindustrial societies. For Daniel Bell, the critical tipping point was reached when the majority of workers had moved from manufacturing into the service sector, producing a far more educated, skilled, and specialized workforce employed in sectors such as finance and banking, trade, insurance, and leisure, as well as in science and technology.[14] This development is conventionally understood to have started in the most affluent parts of the Western world after the Second World War, a process that continues to spread and expand. This stage is fuelled by multiple developments, and the ones most commonly highlighted include:

- The rise of the professional and managerial occupations in the private and public sectors;
- Rapid technological and scientific innovation;
- The process of globalization breaking down the barriers of the nation-state;
- Economic growth generating an expanded middle class, rising standards of living, and growing leisure time;
- Increased levels of human capital and cognitive skills generated by wider access to university education;
- Growing equality of sex roles in the home, family, and workplace, and the rise of women in the paid labor force;
- The shift in the mass media from broadcasting toward more specialized narrowcasting in the digital age;
- The growth of immigration across national borders and the rise of multiculturalism;
- The move from ascribed occupational and social roles given at birth toward achieved roles derived from formal educational qualifications and careers;
- Greater social and geographic mobility;
- The diffusion from urban areas to suburban neighborhoods;
- The weakening of the bonds connecting the extended family, and changing patterns of marriage and divorce;
- The process of secularization weakening religious ties.

There is a broad consensus that common socioeconomic developments have been sweeping across many societies, although alternative interpretations continue to dispute the exact timing and the appropriate weight to be given to different components. There remains considerable controversy, however, surrounding the *political* consequences of these changes, in particular the impact of human development on democratization and civic engagement. One difficulty is that the abstract concept of "societal modernization" encompasses so many different dimensions of social change that it can be a kind of Rorschach test, where different theorists see whatever they want to see. Social change contains crosscutting developments, some of which could possibly depress activism, while others seem likely to encourage civic engagement. As Brody points out, there is a puzzle at the heart of claims about the political impact of human development, since many of the factors most closely associated with societal modernization should push electoral turnout upward – rising levels of literacy, education, leisure, and affluence, the expansion of the professional middle class, and the movement of women from the home into the paid workforce.[15] Growing levels of human capital, in particular, should plausibly serve to buttress and strengthen citizen participation: Studies have long established that education, and the cognitive skills that it provides, is one of the factors that most strongly predict individual political activism.[16]

At the same time, certain other social trends associated with postindustrial societies may tug in the contrary direction – such as individualism, secularization, and suburbanization. In particular, modernization theories suggest that long-standing and stable orientations rooted in traditional habits and affective loyalties are likely to be replaced by more instrumental motivations, weakening stable links to traditional institutions such as parties, unions, and churches. The population shift from rural areas and cities toward more anonymous and atomistic suburbs may have contributed to the dilution of traditional community associations. Industrialization generated the trade union movement that organized and mobilized the manual working class, but economic shifts toward the service sector have shrunk manufacturing and processing industries in the rust belt – the Detroit auto production lines, the Ruhr steel mills, the Glasgow shipyards – depleting the number of blue-collar workers, eviscerating working communities, and possibly diluting union membership. Theories of partisan dealignment argue that, compared to the 1950s and 1960s, contemporary citizens in postindustrial societies have become less strongly anchored to political parties, and there is considerable evidence that the bonds of social class exert a weaker impact on voting choices.[17]

The claim that secular trends in postindustrial society may have caused public engagement in civic affairs to flow through alternative channels remains controversial. Some indicators point in this direction: For example, the most comprehensive recent survey of political participation in the United States, by Verba, Schlozman, and Brady, reported that the modest drop in voting turnout since the 1960s has not been accompanied by a general decrease in political activism; instead, Americans have become *more* engaged in contributing money to campaigns and in contacting officials.[18]

Time devoted to voluntary activities such as attending campaign and party meetings had been replaced by checkbook contributions to candidates and causes. Secular social trends can be expected to produce citizens with improved cognitive and political skills, and with the financial resources and time that facilitate political engagement. Education and socioeconomic status, in particular, have long been regarded as among the most significant determinants of civic engagement. Verba, Nie, and Kim suggest that these long-term developments in society generate the motivation and resources for mass political engagement, as citizens become more aware of the wider world of politics, as they acquire norms of civic engagement, and as they develop the cognitive and organizational skills needed for political activity.[19]

Along similar lines, Richard Topf presented one of the most thorough recent examinations of participation in Western Europe from 1959 to 1990, and he found that, while electoral turnout had remained stable, forms of political participation beyond voting had been rising dramatically, especially among the younger generation of well-educated citizens.[20] Topf concluded that alternative forms of public participation in Western Europe might have been altering, not simply eroding. Bernhard Wessels compared sixteen industrialized nations, based on the 1990 WVS, and found a positive relationship between membership in social and political organizations and indicators of modernity, such as growing levels of urbanization, education, and the size of the service sector.[21] Russell Dalton has also suggested that participation in citizen-initiated and policy-oriented forms of political participation – including citizen action groups, communal participation, and direct democracy methods – is increasing, producing new challenges for the traditional institutions of representative democracy.[22] Sidney Tarrow argues that modern societies have seen a rise in volunteerism and networks of social activists who often vigorously challenge power holders and political authorities, a development that has proved healthy for democratic states: "Social activism is not dead: it has evolved into a wider variety of forms."[23]

Moreover, Ronald Inglehart has developed the strongest case that social trends in postindustrial societies have fuelled a revolution in cultural values, especially among the younger generation of well-education citizens, who have less interest in the old left-right issues of the economy and greater concern about the postmaterialist agenda of quality of life issues such as the environment, gender equality, and human rights. Inglehart suggests that support for traditional hierarchical and bureaucratic organizations such as parties and churches has declined, but that the younger generation in affluent societies has become increasingly active in politics via new social movements and transnational advocacy networks, with a rise during the 1980s in political interest and discussion, petition signing, and willingness to demonstrate and engage in boycotts: "As we shall see, though voter turnout has stagnated (largely because of weakening political party loyalties), Western publics have *not* become apathetic: quite the contrary, in the last two decades, they have become markedly more likely to engage in elite-challenging forms of political participation."[24] Yet despite the range of voices expressing the view that dimensions of public activism are evolving in postindustrial societies, the evidence supporting the transformationist case remains far from watertight, and the declinist thesis continues to hold sway as the conventional wisdom. If the modernization process has altered patterns and modes of political participation, then we should find parallel trends evident during the postwar period among similar types of Western societies. Moreover, if the process of societal modernization has gradually transformed electoral turnout, party membership, and civic activism, then this should be evident today in significant contrasts among the traditional, industrialized, and postindustrial societies compared in this study.

The State Structure

The socioeconomic context, like an inevitable tide sweeping across the globe, represents one plausible determinant of the dimensions of political participation, but much comparative research also highlights the importance of political institutions. The structure of opportunities for civic engagement within each society may be shaped and influenced by the state and the constitutional rules of the game, such as the type of majoritarian or proportional electoral system, the levels of competition and fragmentation in the party system, and the degree of pluralism or corporatism in the interest-group system, as well as by overall levels of democratization and by the existence of political rights and civil liberties. The role of the state is likely to prove particularly important in explaining differences in patterns of participation among societies at similar levels of development – for example, levels of party membership and electoral turnout in Australia, Britain, and the United States.

The role of the state structure is perhaps most easily illustrated in accounting for cross-national differences in electoral turnout. Direct factors most proximate to the act of casting a ballot include the legal regulations and administrative arrangements within each country, the qualifications for citizenship and the franchise, the efficiency of registration and balloting procedures, the use of compulsory voting laws, the ease of obtaining absentee and postal ballots, the frequency of electoral contests, the number of electoral offices and referendum issues on the ballot, whether voting day is a national holiday, and so on.[25] For example, Wolfinger and Rosenstone concluded that if U.S. registration laws were similar to those common in Europe, then turnout in American presidential elections would increase by about 9 percent.[26] To these must be added the impact of *indirect* structural factors, including many broader constitutional arrangements setting the rules of the game. These include factors such as whether the electoral system is proportional, mixed, or majoritarian; whether the election is presidential or parliamentary; the type of party system (in terms of the number of electoral and parliamentary parties and their ideological distribution); and the levels of electoral competition.[27] If institutional theories are correct, then we should find that the structure of the political system plays an important role in shaping dimensions of mass participation, such as cross-national levels of turnout, as well as patterns of party activism and association membership.

The stability of political institutions appears to make this account less plausible as an explanation of change over time, yet alterations in the performance of political institutions can offer important insights here. For example, if party systems gradually become less competitive, because incumbents build safer majorities in electoral constituencies, then this provides less incentive for citizens to cast a vote. Minor innovations such as the adoption of "motor voter" registration in the United States,[28] and the occasional introduction of major constitutional reforms, such as the switch between majoritarian and proportional electoral systems in the early 1990s in New Zealand, Japan, and Italy, also provide case studies or natural "pre- post" experiments monitoring the impact of changes in the rules of the game on levels of electoral turnout, holding the culture and societal structure relatively constant.[29]

Mobilizing Agencies

By contrast, organizational theories give greater weight to the role of agencies and social networks engaged in activating citizens, including parties, unions, churches, voluntary associations, and the news media.[30] Even within relatively similar groups of countries, such as Anglo-American majoritarian democracies and consociational political systems in the smaller European welfare states, there can be very different levels of group mobilization produced by civic organizations. Rosenstone and Hansen exemplify this approach in the United States: "We trace patterns of political participation – who participates and when they participate – to the strategic choices of politicians, political parties, interest groups, and activists. People participate in politics not so much because of who they are but because of the political choices and incentives they are offered."[31]

Traditional accounts of representative democracy regard political parties as the main channels linking citizens' demands to the state,[32] and political scientists such as E. E. Schattschneider have concluded that "modern democracy is unthinkable save in terms of political parties."[33] Parties can serve multiple functions at the mass level: simplifying electoral choices, educating citizens, and mobilizing people to vote, as well as articulating and aggregating political interests, coordinating activists, recruiting political candidates and leaders, organizing parliaments, and allocating government offices.[34] Political parties have long played a vital role in organizing and mobilizing supporters, encouraging peripheral groups of citizens to turn out on polling day via "get out the vote" drives, generating volunteers for campaign work such as canvassing and leafleting, providing organizational skills for members and activists, and facilitating an important channel of recruitment into elected office.[35] Kitschelt argues that this process is likely to prove particularly important where mass-branch labor and social democratic parties employ electoral strategies and engage in party activities designed to encourage working-class participation.[36]

Moreover, agency-based explanations may provide important insights into short-term changes in participation, such as changes in levels of electoral turnout affecting established democracies. If the linkage mechanisms have weakened, so that agencies are no longer so capable of mobilizing voters, then this could be expected to lead to greater electoral disengagement. Dalton and Wattenberg present clear systematic evidence for the widespread erosion of partisan identification across postindustrial societies during the postwar era.[37] Weakened long-standing loyalties connecting supporters and parties have been widely regarded as contributing to a wearing down of electoral participation. Wattenberg's comparison of nineteen OECD states demonstrates a 10 percent average fall in turnout from the 1950s to the 1990s, a pattern that he attributes to weakening party membership and declining partisan loyalties among the general public in established democracies.[38] Gray and Caul suggest that the strong historic links between trade unions and the Social Democratic, Labour, and Communist Parties have been particularly important in encouraging working-class voters to turn out, and that this process has weakened over the years in postindustrial societies due to the shrinkage of the manufacturing base, the decline in union membership, as well as weaker links between unions and parties of the center-left.[39] Along similar lines, the long-term process of growing secularization and emptying churches may have shrunk the mass basis of support for Christian Democratic parties in Western Europe.[40]

Other important agencies believed capable of encouraging political engagement include community groups, voluntary associations, and social networks, all of which can help draw neighbors, friends, and workers into the political process.[41] Most recently, Robert Putnam's account of the role of voluntary associations, in studies of both the United States and Italy, has proved widely influential.[42] According to Putnam's theory of social capital, all sorts of voluntary associations, community groups, and private organizations providing face-to-face meetings contribute to a rich and dense civic network, strengthening community bonds and social trust. Some organizations may be explicitly directed toward politics, while others are recreational clubs, ethnic or religious groups, neighborhood organizations, work-related associations such as professional, business, cooperative, and

union groups, and so on. The core claim is that the denser the linkages promoted by these heterogeneous organizations, the more "bridging" social
trust will be generated that facilitates cooperative actions in matters of
common concern, acting as a public good that affects even those who do
not participate directly in the networks. Putnam's work has stimulated a
growing debate about how far the theory of social capital can be applied
to comparable societies beyond the United States, and the evidence from
case studies seems to suggest the existence of varied patterns in Britain,
Japan, Germany, and Spain.[43]

Pluralist theories give an equally important role to intermediary groups,
with the competition between groups seen as vital to providing checks and
balances in a democracy. Such groups include trade union, business, and
professional associations, welfare and charity organizations, civic and community groups, and educational, art, and cultural social clubs.[44] The term
"interest group" conventionally refers to more formal organizations that
are either focused on particular social groups and economic sectors – such
as trade unions and business and professional associations (the NAACP, the
American Medical Association) – or on more specific issues such as abortion, gun control, and the environment. Often traditional interest groups
have well-established organizational structures and formal membership
rules, and their primary orientation is toward influencing government and
the policy process and providing direct services for members – for example,
trade union negotiations over pay levels in industry, or the provision of
informational networks for professional associations. Some develop an
extensive mass membership base, while others are essentially lobbying
organizations focusing on insider strategies, with little need to maintain a
larger constituency.[45] By contrast, new social movements, exemplified by
the civil rights and antinuclear movements of the 1950s, and the counterculture environmental and women's movements of the 1970s, tend to have
more fluid and decentralized organizational structures, more open membership criteria, and to focus on influencing lifestyles and achieving social
change through direct action and community building as much as by formal decision-making processes.[46] Transnational advocacy networks bring
together loose coalitions of these organizations under a common umbrella
organization that crosses national borders. If organizational theories are
correct, and these claims can be generalized across different societies, then
we should be able to establish a significant relationship between the strength
of party, church, unions, and voluntary associations, indicated by levels of
mass membership and/or activism, and levels of electoral turnout, as well
as other indicators of campaign work and civic participation.

The news media may also play an important role as a mobilizing agency.
During the last decade, a rising tide of voices on both sides of the Atlantic
has blamed the news media for growing public disengagement, ignorance
of civic affairs, and mistrust of government. Many, such as Cappella and

Jamieson, believe that negative news and cynical coverage of campaigns and policy issues on television has turned American voters away from the electoral process.[47] Yet, as argued elsewhere, extensive evidence from a battery of surveys in Europe and the United States casts strong doubt upon these claims.[48] Instead, contrary to the media malaise hypothesis, use of the news media has been found to be positively associated with multiple indicators of political mobilization. People who watch more TV news, read more newspapers, surf the net, and pay attention to campaigns have consistently been found to be more knowledgeable, trusting of government, and participatory. Far from being yet another case of American "exceptionalism," this pattern is found in Western Europe *and* the United States.[49]

Social Resources and Cultural Motivation

Even within particular contexts, some individuals are more actively engaged in public life than others. At the individual level, studies focus upon patterns of resources that facilitate political action and are at the heart of the civic voluntarism model.[50] It is well established that education is one of the best predictors of participation, furnishing cognitive skills and civic awareness that allow citizens to make sense of the political world.[51] The central claim of the widely accepted socioeconomic model is that people with higher education, higher income, and higher-status jobs are more active in politics. The resources of time, money, and civic skills, derived from family, occupation, and association membership, make it easier for individuals who are predisposed to take part to do so. "At home, in school, on the job, and in voluntary associations and religious institutions, individuals acquire resources, receive requests for activity, and develop the political orientations that foster participation."[52] Moreover, since resources are unevenly distributed throughout societies, these factors help to explain differences in political participation related to gender, race/ethnicity, age, and social class.

As well as the skills and resources that facilitate civic engagement, participation also requires the motivation to become active in public affairs. Motivational attitudes may be affective, meaning related to the emotional sense of civic engagement – for example, if people vote out of a sense of duty or patriotism – or instrumental, driven more by the anticipated benefits of the activity. Many cultural attitudes and values may shape activism, including the sense that the citizen can affect the policy process (internal political efficacy) and political interest, as well as a general orientation of support for the political system, including belief in democracy as an ideal, confidence in the core institutions of representative democracy, such as parliaments and the courts, and satisfaction with the performance of the government. Ever since *The Civic Culture*, political cynicism has been regarded as one plausible reason for declining activism. Since many Americans lost faith in government at roughly the same time that the fall in turnout occurred, these factors were commonly linked by contemporary commentators, who believed that a "crisis of democracy" occurred in Western nations during the late 1960s and early 1970s.[53] In postindustrial nations elsewhere, declining trust and confidence in government has also fuelled widespread concern. As Putnam, Pharr, and Dalton summarized the contemporary scene, while seeing no grounds to believe in a fundamental crisis of democracy: "There is substantial evidence of mounting public unhappiness with government and the institutions of representative democracy throughout the trilateral world."[54]

Many are concerned that widespread mistrust of government authorities in the mainstream culture may foster a public climate that facilitates the growth of antistate movements and, at the most extreme, the breakdown of the rule of law and sporadic outbreaks of domestic terrorism by radical dissidents – whether the bombing of abortion clinics in America, threats of biological terrorism in Japan, the assassination of elected officials in the Basque region, violent racist incidents in France and Germany, heated ethnic/religious conflict in Sri Lanka, or splinter terrorist groups sabotaging the peace process in Northern Ireland and the Middle East. Imported terrorism, exemplified by the destruction of the World Trade Center, can be attributed to other causes. Although many suspect that there is a significant connection between mistrust of authorities and radical challenges to the legitimacy of the state, it is hard to establish the conditions that foster the beliefs and values of extreme antistate groups, since insulated minority subcultures such as neo-Fascist and anti-Semitic groups can flourish even in the most tolerant and deeply rooted democratic societies. In terms of conventional politics, systematic empirical analysis has often failed to establish a strong connection at the individual level between general feelings of political trust and conventional forms of participation, such as levels of electoral turnout in the United States, Britain, Germany, and France.[55] Much commentary assumes that if people have little confidence in the core institutions of representative democracy, such as parliaments and the legal system, they will be reluctant to participate in the democratic process, producing apathy. But it is equally plausible to assume that political alienation could mobilize citizens, if people were stimulated to express their disaffection, throw out office-holders, and seek institutional redress.[56]

Conclusions

Many theories in the literature can help explain cross-national differences in how and why citizens get involved in public affairs. Rather than relying on an oversimple monocausal explanation, the challenge is to understand the relative importance of each of these factors and the interactions among them. The underlying social and economic forces are entered first in subsequent models, such as macro levels of human development, measured by rates of literacy, education, and income (per capita GNP). Aggregate levels of political rights and civil liberties, and the institutions associated with the structure of the state, are subsequently analyzed. The strength of mobilizing organizations is entered next, followed by individual resources and motivation. Based on this approach, we can start by examining postwar trends in voting turnout to see whether there is convincing evidence of a long-term secular slide in electoral participation in industrialized societies, as many claim, and to monitor patterns of turnout in developing nations around the globe.

PART I

THE PUZZLE OF ELECTORAL TURNOUT

The report of my death was an exaggeration.

Mark Twain (1896)

3

Mapping Turnout

Electoral turnout is one of the most common indicators used to gauge the health of democracy, and many worry that conventional participation via the ballot box is plummeting in affluent societies, providing a danger signal for deeper troubles. If so, the reasons for this phenomenon remain a puzzle. The evidence for decline appears clearest in the United States, producing studies of *The Disappearing American Voter* and *Why Americans Still Don't Vote*.[1] Detailed analysis of the American electorate by Miller and Shanks provides convincing evidence from the series of U.S. National Election Studies of persistent generational differences in turnout, with the post–New Deal generation least likely to cast a ballot, a pattern that has significant implications for the future of American democracy through the process of demographic replacement.[2] Putnam couples the fall in American voting participation during the postwar era with a battery of evidence showing the broader erosion of civic mobilization in America since the 1960s and 1970s, indicated by the decline in formal attendance at political rallies and speeches, working for a political party, and writing to Congress, as well as in activism within informal associations in the local community.[3]

Yet if historical experiences have produced widespread civic apathy among the postwar generation in America, it remains unclear whether these patterns are distinctive to the United States. Comparative studies continue to debate whether analogous trends are evident in other established democracies. Analysis of trends in electoral turnout in Western Europe from the end of World War II until around the end of the 1980s, by Topf and by Andweg, suggests that levels of participation in these countries were relatively constant and stable during these decades.[4] More recent research, however, indicates that this pattern may have changed during the last decade, although, if so, the extent of any fall should not be exaggerated. International IDEA found a slight slippage in average levels of voting within thirty-six established democracies, from a high of 74 percent in the 1970s down to 71 percent in the 1990s, and a similar-sized downturn in elections held around the globe.[5] Reviewing the evidence across Western Europe, Mair concluded that electoral turnout, which had been fairly stable in every decade since the 1950s, dropped by about 5 percent more or less consistently across fifteen countries during the 1990s.[6] Others confirm this general decline, estimating that the size of the slump in established democracies may be 10 percent over the last forty years.[7] Less is known about cross-national patterns of turnout in local and regional elections, or in referenda and initiatives, although it is well established that levels of participation are usually lower in these contests than in general elections.[8] What is clear is that the erosion of voter participation evident over the last twenty years in direct elections to the European Parliament has caused alarm among politicians in Brussels, Strasbourg, and Luxembourg as further evidence that the public is becoming disenchanted with the European Union. The level of voting plummeted to just under half (49.2 percent) of all European citizens in June 1999, compared with almost two-thirds (63 percent) of the electorate two decades earlier.[9] Fewer studies have compared changes in voter participation in nonindustrialized countries, in part because the new democracies that flowered during the early 1990s have held too few national elections to allow trends to be analyzed with any reliability. But the broadest comparison, in a report published by International IDEA, found that developing countries had experienced steadily rising levels of electoral participation over the last fifty years, a pattern most evident in Latin America.[10] Initial indications therefore suggest that the scenario may be rosier in the developing world. Nevertheless, there is growing suspicion and accumulating evidence that, at least in postindustrial societies, "something is rotten in the state of electoral participation," generating heated debate about the *cause* of any decline.

Theories of Societal Modernization

As discussed in the previous chapter, many factors may contribute to this process, including changes affecting the structure of the state, the role of mobilizing agencies, and the motivation that draws citizens into public affairs. Modernization theories are most commonly evoked in global comparisons, emphasizing the impact of socioeconomic development.[11] These accounts, with intellectual roots stretching back to Marx and Weber, suggest that changes to the economic structure of production are at the root of social relations, cultural shifts, and political development. If the claims of modernization theory are true, then even if countries start at different levels of civic engagement, broadly similar trends in turnout should be apparent over time across similar types of societies.

Modernization theories suggest that the early stages of the industrial revolution, with the shift in production from agriculture toward manufacturing, generate the social preconditions underlying democratic participation. These include:

- Greater literacy, education, income, and wealth;
- Growing urbanization and suburbanization;
- The expansion of access to mass communication media such as newspapers, radio, and television;
- The rapid expansion in the size of the working class;
- The rise of the professional, managerial, and intellectual bourgeoisie;
- The development of mass-based urban organizations to mobilize these citizens, including social democratic parties, trade unions, workers' cooperatives, charitable organizations, and municipal associations.

Although there continues to be considerable dispute in the literature, a series of comparative studies, based on both cross-sectional and time-series analysis, has confirmed that economic development is strongly and significantly related to the process of democratization.[12] Research has also established a more direct association between modernization and participation; for example, an earlier aggregate-level cross-national comparison of twenty-nine democracies by Powell found a positive curvilinear relationship between economic development (logged per capita GNP) and turnout.[13] Many individual-level studies of participation have confirmed a strong link between educational background and the propensity to vote, with the effect occurring, as Verba, Schlozman, and Brady suggest, through the way that education effects the intervening role of political attitudes by boosting political interest, information, and efficacy.[14] If the relationship between socioeconomic development and democratization operates in a linear fashion, as the early accounts of the late 1950s generally proposed,[15] and as many assume implicitly today, then, ceteris paribus, rising levels of modernization (such as the continued expansion of college education) should be associated with steadily growing levels of civic engagement, in the trajectory sketched in Model A (see Figure 3.1).

Yet, as discussed in the previous chapter, nonlinear theories of cultural modernization have experienced a revival in political science, fuelled largely by the work of Ronald Inglehart,[16] while Alex Inkeles and Anthony Giddens have offered alternative interpretations of the consequences of modernity in affluent nations.[17] According to the seminal account offered by Daniel Bell, the process of industrialization and modernization should not be understood as a linear process, if the rise of postindustrial societies marks a distinct stage of development characterized by the shift in production from manufacturing industry toward the service sector, from working-class urban communities toward the spread of middle-class suburbs, from bonds of blood and belonging within the extended family toward the traditional nuclear and then single-parent families, from traditional sex roles toward growing gender equality in the home and the paid workforce, from ascribed

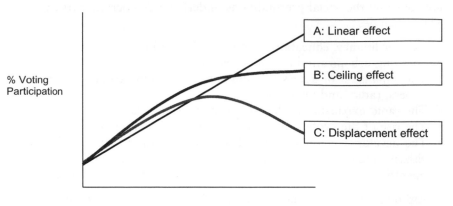

% Voting
Participation

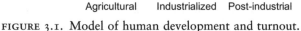

Agricultural   Industrialized   Post-industrial

FIGURE 3.1. Model of human development and turnout.

roles toward achieved status, owing to social and geographic mobility, from
collective agencies such as unions and the safety net of the postwar welfare
state toward greater individualism, from more homogeneous societies
bounded by national borders toward multicultural ones characterized by
ethnic diversity and the global flow of migrants, and from low levels of literacy toward growing human capital, with education generating more cog-
nitively skilled citizens.[18] There are therefore multiple secular trends that,
sociological theories suggest, go together in predictable ways associated
with socioeconomic development.

If we assume that postindustrial societies are a distinct last stage, then
there are two alternative trajectories that can be envisaged for how this
process can affect patterns of political participation. Jackman examined the
general relationship between economic development and democratization,
and concluded that there is a "ceiling" effect, so that the shape of the relationship should be understood as curvilinear.[19] Along similar lines, if rising
levels of literacy, numeracy, and education are at the heart of the developmental process, generating the cognitive skills, civic awareness, political
interest, and practical knowledge that facilitate following public affairs in
the news and casting a ballot, then once primary and secondary education
become universal throughout society, further development may have no
additional effects on expanding turnout. If this proposition is true, then we
might expect that the relationship between socioeconomic development and
civic participation will produce a plateau, with postindustrial societies
experiencing a fairly stable pattern or trendless fluctuation in turnout over
time, depending upon particular circumstances and events (illustrated in
Model B).

Alternatively, many theories of modernization suggest that new forms of
engagement may displace traditional activities, producing declining turnout

in postindustrial societies (shown in Model C). For reasons discussed in Chapter 1, the second stage of development, as the most affluent countries move from industrial towards postindustrial societies, may have altered many traditional agencies, modes, and issue agendas, and the scope of political participation. If there is a trade-off involved between newer and older activities, because of limited time and energies, then this may simultaneously reduce traditional forms of activism, such as voting turnout, while expanding newer forms of engagement, such as internet discussion groups and direct action strategies. Inglehart presents the strongest case that younger, well-educated generations in Western societies are increasingly disenchanted with state-oriented forms of participation through traditional bureaucratic agencies, such as voting for established parties in parliamentary elections, and are instead channeling their energies into ad hoc coalitions of new social movements and transnational advocacy networks concerned with issues such as human rights, gender equality, and environment protection.[20] Theorists offer many reasons why declining turnout may relate to enduring developments associated with the move from industrial toward postindustrial society, including the rise of post-materialist values (as Inglehart suggests), the breakdown of dense social networks and bonds of belonging to local communities (as Putnam argues), the weakening of traditional grassroots campaign organizations and get-out-the-vote drives by unions (as Gray and Caul contend), and the process of partisan dealignment (as Wattenberg claims).[21]

To summarize, all of the modernization theories claim that we should expect to find a consistent *rise* in turnout among developing societies experiencing the early stages of industrialization, characterized by growing levels of education, literacy, and wealth. At the same time, there is less agreement about the impact of development upon the third stage of the modernization process: "*Ceiling effect*" theories expect to find a flattened, stable plateau in turnout once the effects of secondary education and literacy become almost universal throughout societies, while "*displacement*" theories suggest that there may be a consistent and significant glacial erosion of electoral turnout, if there is a trade-off between the time and energies devoted to older and newer forms of participation. These propositions can be tested by comparison of trends during the last fifty years in traditional, industrialized, and postindustrial societies that have held elections throughout this period, as well as by cross-national analysis examining the factors most closely associated with turnout in the 1990s.

Gauging Voting Turnout

The impact of socioeconomic development on electoral participation can be analyzed drawing upon the data set provided by International IDEA, which provides the most comprehensive record of turnout in national elections that is currently available.[22] This data set covers 1,620 national-level elections held from 1945 to 2000 in all 193 independent nation-states worldwide, including 1,218 parliamentary and 402 presidential contests. Since there was a high correlation between the series, and the average turnout in presidential elections (61 percent) was fairly similar to that in parliamentary contests (64 percent), these series were merged in this chapter, in order to increase the number of cases for analysis in each country. The next chapter goes on to consider the impact of presidential and parliamentary institutional arrangements on voting participation, alongside other variants such as electoral and party systems.

Measuring Turnout

Electoral turnout has commonly been measured in two different ways. *Turnout as a proportion of the registered electorate* can be calculated as the number of votes divided by the number of citizens who are legally registered to vote (referred to briefly as Vote/Registered). This measure can be misleading, however, in situations with a restricted franchise, for example, if only men are eligible to vote, as in Kuwait, or if only whites can vote, as was the case under apartheid in South Africa, since in these countries official estimates of turnout can be relatively high even if the voices of all women or of ethnic majorities are excluded.[23] Citizenship rights embodied in electoral laws often routinely exclude certain categories such as stateless aliens and illegal immigrants, the poorer homeless and transient populations lacking a permanent residence, those who moved and thereby changed districts after the register was compiled, felons and bankrupts, those resident abroad, those in mental institutions, and others deemed ineligible to cast a ballot. A comparison of sixty-three democracies found an overwhelming majority restricted the right to vote of mentally deficient people and set the minimum voting age at eighteen. There was little agreement about other conditions, however, such as whether the right to vote should be limited to national citizens or granted to all residents, whether there should be a country or an electoral-district residency requirement, whether electors living abroad should retain the right to cast a ballot, and whether prison inmates, those on parole, and those with a felony record should have the right to vote.[24] Moreover, even among those who are legally eligible, the efficiency of the registration process can vary substantially, which can systematically bias the accuracy of any comparison. A poorly administered registration system that excludes many eligible citizens, such as the many African-American eligible citizens who were automatically purged from the Florida electoral rolls in Miami-Dade County without adequate background checks during the 2000 U.S. presidential contest, can still produce an official record showing relatively high turnout.[25]

For all of these reasons, it is more satisfactory to compare *turnout as a proportion of the voting-age population* (referred to briefly as Vote/VAP), representing the number of valid votes (discarding spoiled ballots) divided by the size of the population over the minimum legal voting age, whether enfranchised and registered or not. This measure also has certain potential problems, since it depends upon the accuracy of the population count and updating of projections made on the basis of the official census data. It also includes groups legally ineligible to cast a ballot, such as resident aliens, felons, and immigrant populations lacking full citizenship rights, and it excludes citizens resident abroad. Legal reforms, such as the extension of the franchise to women or eighteen-year-olds, can produce sharp changes in levels of turnout as a proportion of the voting-age population. McDonald and Popkin argue that the use of this measure as the official standard by the U.S. Bureau of the Census needs to be replaced by an estimate of the voting-eligible population (Vote/VEP) that automatically excludes groups who are legally restricted from participation.[26] Although Vote/VAP provides a conservative measure of electoral participation, it has become the standard measure adopted in cross-national research, as it provides a more consistent yardstick for comparing societies than the alternatives, since the exclusion of certain voting-age population groups varies among countries. Moreover, the extension of the franchise to all adult residents living within a nation-state is an important indicator of the democratic quality of elections. The difference between Vote/VAP and Vote/Registered is indicative of the legal restrictions on eligibility for citizenship and of the practical efficiency of the registration process. This difference varies substantially among countries; for example, in the 1990s it was 61.8 percent in Kuwait and 17.4 percent in the United States, compared to 2.2 percent in the UK.[27] If some countries restrict citizenship more than others, it is important to highlight this practice. This study therefore reports turnout based on Vote/VAP, unless otherwise indicated.[28]

Time Series

The end of the Second World War provides an appropriate starting point for the series, given the immense social disruption caused by the Great Depression of the pre-war era, the civilian displacement during the war, and the establishment of new democratic constitutions after 1945 in Germany, Japan, and Italy. Any interpretation of trends remains heavily dependent upon the selection of starting and ending points for the time series, for example, our understanding of changes in levels of the misery index or the Nasdaq 500. The importance of examining long-term trends can be illustrated by the United States, which has experienced successive waves of mobilization rather than a simple linear decline.[29] Many studies, such as that by Teixeira, analyze American turnout from the early 1960s onward, suggesting on this basis that voting participation has declined fairly steadily in successive presidential elections, from 62.8 percent of the voting age population in 1960 down to 50.2 percent in 1988.[30] Although there are occasionally longer series, many of the key trends in political participation documented by Putnam are also based on analyses starting in the 1960s or early 1970s, because this is when much of the systematic survey data first become available.[31] One problem is that if this period represented a temporary peak in American civic engagement, because of the "hot button politics" produced by the mélange of civil rights, the war on poverty, the Vietnam War, and the counterculture student and feminist movements, then any longitudinal analysis starting in the mid-1960s may provide a misleading impression of enduring trends. Moreover, the choice of 1960s as the starting point for the series is also problematic because, as Burnham argues, American turnout throughout the twentieth century displays stepped shifts that are at least partially explained by the extension of the legal franchise, such as the introduction of the female suffrage in 1920.[32] The expansion of the U.S. voting-age population through the Civil Rights Act in 1965, combined with the lowering of the minimum voting age from twenty-one to eighteen in 1971, expanded the voting-age population to include younger citizens and African Americans, both groups with lower-than-average participation rates, and thereby depressed Vote/VAP.[33] A glance across the series of American elections since 1932, illustrated in Figure 3.2, shows that the 1960 Kennedy–Nixon election occurred during a period of greater-than-average participation. American electoral turnout subsequently fluctuated, increasing in campaigns such as the Bush–Clinton–Perot contest in 1992, while returning in the 2000 presidential election to just over half (50.5 percent) of all Americans of voting age, about the same levels found earlier in the 1932 and 1948 elections.[34] Accordingly, systematic analysis needs to take advantage of the longest time-series data that are available in order to provide a reliable guide to the landscape, and this study examines trends during the last fifty years.

The comparative framework used for the classification of nations is the one discussed in Chapter 1. The level of electoral participation should not be understood as an automatic indicator of the democratic quality of these contests. Some nations under comparison, such as Canada and Norway, are established democracies, characterized by the existence of widespread political rights and civil liberties, regular rotation of parties in government, and

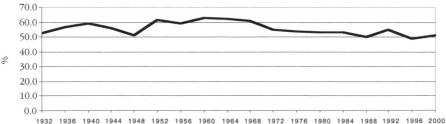

FIGURE 3.2. U.S. turnout, 1932–2000 (presidential Vote/VAP). *Source*: U.S. Census Bureau, 1932–96; see note 5 for estimate of turnout in 2000.

multiple opportunities for participation. Other states, such as Greece, India, Chile, and Paraguay, have had more checkered histories, with periods when normal democratic practices were suspended. In yet others, such as Burma and Zimbabwe, elections have been held under nondemocratic regimes with evidence of widespread corruption, voter intimidation, and outbreaks of violence at polling places. In these states, as under pre-war Fascist regimes, elections may serve a purely symbolic function, with state propaganda mobilizing mass turnout designed to legitimize the governing authorities in the eyes of the world, and the outcome may be discounted if unfavorable to the ruling elites. Lastly, many states in Central and Eastern Europe, Latin America, and Asia are transitional and consolidating democracies with steadily rising levels of political freedom in recent decades. Rather than assuming any automatic relationship, we will explore the association between levels of turnout and the process of democratization later in the book.

To remove fluctuations and "noise" produced by individual results, the average turnout (Vote/VAP) for each election was summarized by decade and displayed for each nation in graphs illustrating trends. To test more systematically for the significance and direction of any trends, and to see whether certain specific elections were outliers causing fluctuations to the overall pattern, OLS regression analysis models were run for each country, with year regressed on Vote/VAP.[35] The models provide a more reliable estimate than examining the difference in mean turnout per decade, used in previous studies, given that countries around the world have different starting and ending dates for analysis, with many newer democracies achieving independence and holding free and fair elections only in the 1980s in the Asia-Pacific region, and in the 1990s in postcommunist states.

Core Hypotheses

To recap the logic of the research design, and to state the core hypotheses more formally, in interpreting patterns that may be attributable to the process of societal modernization per se, such as the impact of growing levels of education and affluence associated with socioeconomic development, the most general claim is that we should expect to find broadly similar trends among nations at roughly similar levels of socioeconomic development. More specifically, all of these modernization theories predict that (Hypothesis 1) *turnout will increase significantly during the first stage of modernization as agricultural societies move toward becoming industrialized states*, with the shift from farms to factories, from peasants to workers, and from villages to cities, mainly because of sharply rising levels of literacy, education, and wealth, growing urbanization, and the growth of collective agencies of mobilization for the working class. At the same time, there are alternative interpretations of patterns evident among postindustrial societies. Ceiling effect theories predict that (Hypothesis 2) *turnout can be expected to stabilize as industrialized societies become postindustrial*, with a plateau. Alternatively, displacement effect theories suggest (Hypothesis 3) that *turnout can be expected to decline as industrialized societies become postindustrial*, as traditional forms of engagement are displaced by newer modes. The shift from factories to offices, from blue-collar jobs to white-collar careers, from cities to suburbs may be expected to erode the older forms of linkage between citizens and the state, while generating newer agencies and modes of activism among the younger generation of well-educated citizens. Lastly, (Hypothesis 4) if we establish a null relationship, that is, if dissimilar trends in turnout are evident among societies at similar levels of socioeconomic development, then this strongly suggests that we should search for other explanations, including those already discussed in Chapter 2, such as the impact of state structures, the direct role of mobilizing agencies, and changes in cultural attitudes.

Trends in Turnout Worldwide

Rising Turnout in Developing Societies?
Table 3.1 and Figure 3.3 illustrate the main trends in voter participation in all national elections held from 1945 to 2000, broken down by type of society. They lend initial support to the first claim of all modernization theories: *The results illustrate the dramatic growth in turnout evident among high and medium development nations*, with average voting participation surging from 1945 to 1950, then again during the 1970s, before reaching a plateau of about two-thirds of the voting-age population during the 1990s. The regression analysis models confirm that the rise among all of these countries was both strong and significant over the last fifty years. By contrast, the models show that similar trends were not apparent among the poorest group of societies, which experienced no such change.

Stable or Falling Turnout in Postindustrial Societies?
"Ceiling effect" theories predict that postindustrial societies, far from experiencing further gains, will have fairly stable patterns of participation, and the graph illustrating trends in these countries broadly confirms this thesis. The most affluent nations experienced a slight rise in turnout to the 1950s, a steady plateau across the 1960s to the 1980s, and, as others have reported, a modest slippage during the 1990s. The regression coefficient for changes in turnout among the group of postindustrial societies confirmed a slight fall, but this proved statistically insignificant across the whole series. There is no support here for the displacement thesis, suggesting that the post-industrial societies have experienced a consistent long-term erosion in voting turnout, although clearly if the decline found in the 1990s continues on its downward slope then this could change in the future. If we compare levels of electoral turnout today, there is a sharp contrast among the different types of society: About three-quarters of the voting-age pop-

TABLE 3.1. *Changes in turnout by type of society, state, and region,*
1945–2000

	Mean Turnout, 1990s[a]	Change, 1945–2000 (B)	Sig.	Number of Elections
Type of society				
Postindustrial	72.7	−.017	.673	495
Other high development	68.4	.494	.000	186
Medium development	63.8	.435	.000	755
Low development	51.3	.029	.864	142
Type of state				
Older democracies	72.7	.024	.519	613
Newer democracies	69.1	.427	.000	399
Semi-democracies	55.7	.418	.000	423
Non-democracies	58.6	.401	.026	156
Global region				
Central and Eastern Europe	67.4	−1.668	.005	97
Arab States	56.2	−.423	.065	63
Pacific	73.1	−.343	.023	90
North America	50.2	−.171	.067	59
Sub-Saharan Africa	55.5	.002	.866	191
Western Europe	75.5	.005	.422	282
Scandinavia	80.8	.006	.120	101
Asia	70.4	.386	.000	147
Latin America	62.2	.494	.000	572
Total	64.5	.728	.000	1620

[a] Average valid vote as a percentage of voting-age population in national-level parliamentary and presidential elections held during the 1990s. Calculated from the International IDEA database *Voter Turnout from 1945 to 2000*. www. idea. int.
For details of the classification of political systems and types of socioeconomic development, see the Appendix.
Source: Calculated from the International IDEA database *Voter Turnout from 1945 to 2000*. www. idea. int.

ulation (73 percent) participated at the ballot box during the 1990s in the most affluent nations, in contrast to 68 percent in high development countries, 64 percent in medium developed states, and just over half (51 percent) in the poorest societies. Postindustrial societies thus still continue to have substantially higher average turnout than poorer countries, but the gap between the richest and the next-richest nations has closed dramatically during the second half of the twentieth century.

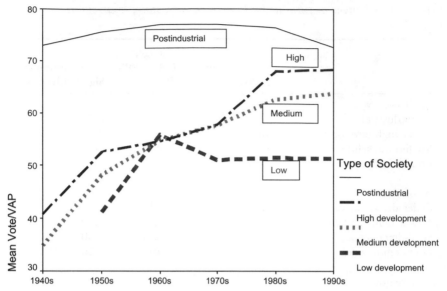

FIGURE 3.3. Turnout trends per decade by type of society, 1945–2000. *Note*:
Turnout is calculated as the number of valid votes cast as a proportion of the voting-
age population in all parliamentary and presidential elections. For details of the classification of type of society, see the Appendix. *Source*: Calculated from International
IDEA database *Voter Turnout from 1945 to 2000*. www.idea.int.

Turnout and Democratization

The comparison of turnout by type of political system sheds further light on
these trends. Based on the Freedom House index, countries were classified
into older democracies, newer democracies, semi-democracies, and non-
democracies (see Appendix). There is obviously considerable overlap among
different types of states and levels of human development, since most established democracies are also among the most affluent countries in the world.
Nevertheless, as discussed in Chapter 1, there are also some important
outliers, and the overall relationship between human development and
democratization has weakened during the last thirty years. Although about
three-quarters of the older democracies are postindustrial societies, eleven
established democracies have high or medium levels of economic development. Many developing island microstates that were former British colonies
have been long-standing democracies with a history of free and fair elections,
competitive parties, and effective parliamentary institutions, such as the
Bahamas, Barbados, and Trinidad and Tobago. Costa Rica, Dominica,
Mauritius, and Kiribati can also be counted as consolidated democracies.
There is also the exceptional case of Singapore, one of the richest societies
in the world that remains nondemocratic, as well as semidemocratic and
nondemocratic affluent states such as Kuwait, Bahrain, Antigua and

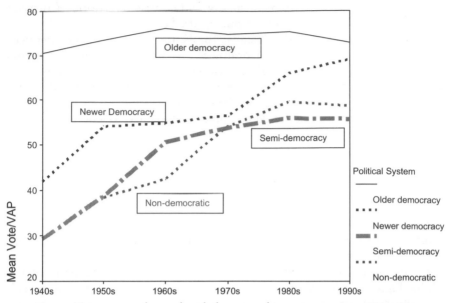

FIGURE 3.4. Turnout trends per decade by type of state, 1945–2000. *Note*: Turnout is calculated as the number of valid votes cast as a proportion of the voting-age population in all parliamentary and presidential elections. For details of the classification of political systems, see the Appendix. *Source*: Calculated from International IDEA database *Voter Turnout from 1945 to 2000*. www.idea.int.

Barbuda, and the Brunei Darussalam, all characterized by high human development coupled with a poor record of political rights and civil liberties.

The comparison of the visual trends in Figure 3.4, and the results of the regression analysis, indicate that there was no significant change in electoral participation among all older democracies during the entire postwar era. The average vote in older democracies rose slightly during the 1940s and 1950s, then largely stabilized, with about three-quarters of the voting-age population participating from the 1960s to the 1980s, before a sharp decline, by 7 percent on average, during the 1990s. This provides independent confirmation that the fall noted by Mair in fifteen Western European countries at the end of the twentieth century is found in a wider range of older democracies. The recent slide deserves further exploration, since it was both relatively sharp and also uncharacteristic of established democracies, given the previous pattern of glacial constancy. Moreover, the decline was experienced during a decade marked by considerable prosperity in most Western democracies, indeed the longest peacetime boom that America has experienced. Nevertheless, despite the fall during the 1990s, it should be stressed that average trends across the whole series since 1945 have proved stable. Although there has been a recent dip, there has not been, as many popular commentators assume, a steady and consistent erosion of turnout across *all* established democracies during the last fifty years.

Moreover, contrary to the declinist thesis, the last half of the twentieth century witnessed a steady and dramatic rise in electoral turnout across all other nations around the globe holding parliamentary elections. This pattern includes many newer democracies that have emerged from the early 1970s onwards, as well as elections held by semi-democracies and by nondemocratic regimes. In newer democracies, competitive elections have been decisive in determining the parties in power, but nondemocratic regimes have also held symbolic elections, banning opposition movements, in the attempt to legitimate the regime and mobilize popular support behind the government, such as in Burma and Zimbabwe.

Regional Trends

Even if there are similarities among societies at similar levels of development, due to path-dependent historical experiences and cultural traditions, there could still be important differences between different parts of the globe. Figure 3.5 breaks down the turnout trends by global region, revealing substantial geographic variations. A relatively flat plateau is displayed across Scandinavia and Western Europe, with North America showing the temporary peak in the 1960s mentioned earlier, followed by the return to the status quo ante. By contrast, over the last half-century Asia and Latin America, which experienced rapid economic growth, also show dramatic steady *gains* in levels of electoral turnout, with mean turnout more than doubling in Latin America. The regression models confirm the significance of the gains achieved in both regions.[36] Following the checkered and uncertain history of democracy in the region, sub-Saharan Africa shows a sharp rise in turnout during the 1950s, during the initial period of decolonization, followed by trendless fluctuation in subsequent decades.[37] In the postcommunist world, Central and Eastern Europe made some gains in their first free and fair elections held during the 1990s, but then dropped significantly in successive contests, although again it is still too early to identify the subsequent trajectories.[38] Lastly, the Pacific region and the Middle East display erratic patterns, in large part because elections have spread to a far broader range of nations in each region, many without any history of democratic elections. The broad swings behind the smoothed curves illustrate the deviations from the mean, with the sharpest contrasts evident in the Arab states and in the Asia and Pacific regions. By contrast, Latin America and Scandinavia show far more homogeneous patterns, and hence fewer differences between countries across these regions.

National Trends

These patterns can be broken down more finely to examine trends in turnout within each country. Figure 3.6 shows the change in the mean

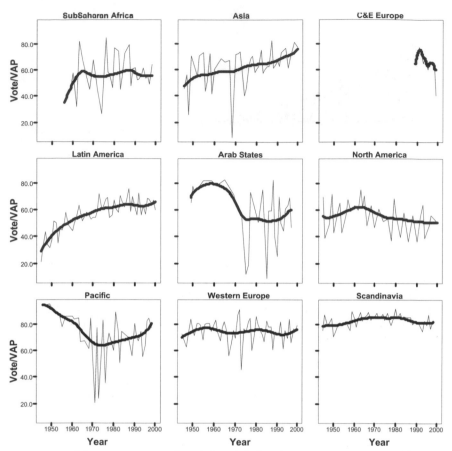

FIGURE 3.5. Mean turnout per decade by global region, 1945–2000. *Note*: Turnout is calculated as valid votes cast as a proportion of the voting-age population in all parliamentary and presidential elections. The curve-fit line displays smoothed trends across elections. *Source*: Calculated from the International IDEA database *Voter Turnout from 1945 to 2000*. www.idea.int.

turnout from the 1950s to the 1990s, indicating the larger increases among some developing nations that held elections during both periods, as well as the fall among other developing societies. This replicates previous studies, but the comparison of the means can prove misleading, since the choice of starting and ending decades is arbitrary, and different cut-off points (such as the 1960s and the 1970s) would produce different patterns. Moreover, this approach excludes postcommunist nations and many other newer democracies that held their first free and fair elections only during the last decade.

For more reliable comparison, regression models were run for all countries around the globe that held parliamentary or presidential national

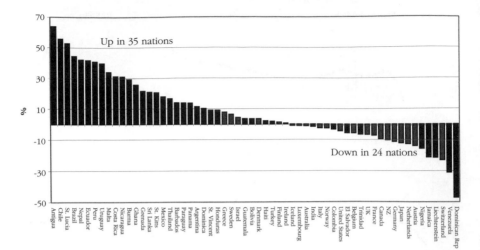

FIGURE 3.6. Change in mean turnout, 1950s and 1990s. *Note*: Turnout is calculated as the number of valid votes cast as a proportion of the voting-age population in all parliamentary and presidential elections. The columns represent the
change in mean turnout per country for all elections held in the 1950s and the 1990s.
For details of the classification, see the Appendix. *Source*: Calculated from the International IDEA database *Voter Turnout from 1945 to 2000*. www.idea.int.

elections from 1945 to 2000, in order to analyze the direction and significance of any changes in turnout over time. Out of 191 independent nation-
states worldwide, according to the International IDEA database, 185 held
at least one election, and 156 held at least two elections, during this period.
Although regression models were run for all countries with at least two
elections, Table 3.2 reports only the models that proved statistically significant, and Table 3.3 summarizes the overall patterns. The results show
that out of all countries that held more than one national election, almost
three-quarters (72 percent) experienced stability or trendless fluctuation in
turnout over time. Nevertheless, forty-three countries, or about one-quarter
of all nations holding a series of elections, did experience a significant
change in voting participation during the last fifty years. In total, the overall
news is largely positive: Twenty-seven countries (representing 14 percent of
all nations around the world) registered a significant surge in electoral participation during this period. By contrast, only sixteen nations experienced
a significant fall in voting turnout over the whole time series.

   Providing further confirmation of the basic claim of modernization
theory, the growth in voting participation is most notable in developing
countries throughout Latin America where electoral democracies were
being consolidated – such as in Nicaragua, Peru, Chile, Uruguay, and Peru
– although elsewhere more people were going to the ballot box in devel-

TABLE 3.2. *Significant changes in turnout by nation, 1945–2000*

Decreased Turnout (16 nations)			Increased Turnout (27 nations)		
Nation	B	Sig.	Nation	B	Sig.
Georgia	−13.02	.007	Benin	11.08	.013
Slovakia	−8.56	.031	Chile	9.37	.000
Senegal	−7.22	.041	Nepal	8.23	.015
Croatia	−6.50	.000	Antigua & Barbuda	7.55	.001
Seychelles	−5.88	.000	Uruguay	6.35	.000
Dominican Republic	−3.93	.000	Peru	6.25	.000
Switzerland	−2.58	.000	Nicaragua	5.35	.000
France	−0.93	.000	Vanuatu	5.00	.028
New Zealand	−0.82	.001	St. Lucia	4.99	.000
Austria	−0.77	.005	Brazil	4.56	.000
Netherlands	−0.68	.025	Solomon Islands	3.95	.052
Canada	−0.56	.011	Papua New Guinea	3.88	.021
Monaco	−0.45	.025	Malta	3.64	.000
United States	−0.42	.016	Djibouti	3.62	.026
Australia	−0.26	.014	Costa Rica	3.45	.000
Liechtenstein	−0.24	.000	Ecuador	3.39	.000
			Grenada	2.68	.005
			Egypt	2.64	.026
			St Kitts & Nevis	2.62	.009
			Thailand	2.61	.000
			Nauru	2.42	.028
			Bahamas	2.29	.017
			Argentina	1.96	.000
			Mexico	1.35	.006
			Greece	0.98	.006
			Israel	0.73	.020
			Sweden	0.48	.025

Note: The OLS regression coefficients (unstandardized betas) estimate the direction and significance of any changes in turnout over time. Turnout in each country was measured as the number of valid votes as a proportion of voting-age population (Vote/VAP) in all national-level parliamentary and presidential elections held from 1945 to 2000. Regression models were run for all independent nation-states worldwide that held more than one election during this period (N = 156), and only those with significant trends are displayed. The remainder produced a pattern of trendless fluctuation or stable turnout.

Source: Calculated from the International IDEA database *Voter Turnout from 1945 to 2000*. www. indea. int.

oping countries as diverse as Nepal, Thailand, and Egypt. Table 3.3 summarizes the pattern, confirming that rising turnout during the last fifty years was by far the most common in high development societies such as Chile, the Bahamas, and Uruguay; one-third of the nations in this category experienced growing voter participation. In the category of medium

TABLE 3.3. *Significant changes in turnout by type of society, 1945–2000*

	Postindustrial Societies		Other High-development Societies		Medium-development Societies		Low-development Societies		All Societies	
	Percent	N	Percent	N	Percent	N	Percent	N	Percent	N
Increasing	15%	(4)	33%	(6)	19%	(15)	10%	(3)	17%	(27)
Stable	56%	(15)	50%	(9)	76%	(62)	87%	(26)	72%	(113)
Decreasing	30%	(8)	17%	(3)	4%	(4)	3%	(1)	10%	(16)
Total	100%	(27)	100%	(18)	100%	(81)	100%	(30)	100%	(156)

Note: See Table 3.2 for analysis and methodology. The figures represent the proportion of nations in each category of increasing, stable, or decreasing electoral turnout, 1945–2000 (with the number of nations in parenthesis). Turnout in each country was measured as the number of valid votes as a proportion of voting-age population (Vote/VAP) in all national-level parliamentary and presidential elections held from 1945 to 2000. Regression models were run for all independent nation-states worldwide that held more than one election during this period (N = 156), and those with significant increases or decreases are counted above. The remainder produced a pattern of trendless fluctuation or stable turnout.

Source: Calculated from the International IDEA database *Voter Turnout from 1945 to 2000*. www. idea. int.

development, one-fifth of the countries had rising turnout levels, including Mexico, Egypt, and Papua New Guinea. By contrast, one in ten of the poorest nations, such as Nepal and Benin, experienced a rise in turnout. As noted earlier, there is a distinct regional effect in the data, since most countries with rising levels of turnout are in Latin America. Yet the overall pattern is not wholly consistent, since during the same period a few developing nations saw a significant fall in turnout, including Georgia, Croatia, and the Dominican Republic, all characterized by moderate levels of economic growth, as well as Senegal, among the poorest nations. The time-series models therefore serve to provide further confirmation of the proposition that the shift from agricultural to industrialized societies is associated with growing electoral participation, which suggests that we need to look more closely and systematically at what it is about the modernization process that may be driving rising turnout, particularly the role of education, wealth, and literacy, through cross-sectional analysis of patterns during the 1990s.

The pattern is more complex and difficult to interpret in affluent nations. The results provide some limited support for the displacement theory that postindustrial societies have seen some turnout decline over time: Out of the twenty-seven postindustrial societies under comparison, eight (33 percent) found voters deserting the polls during these years, including Austria, France, Switzerland, and the Netherlands in Western Europe, as well as four Anglo-American democracies – Australia, Canada, the U.S., and New Zealand. The graphs in Figure 3.7 illustrate the steady erosion in

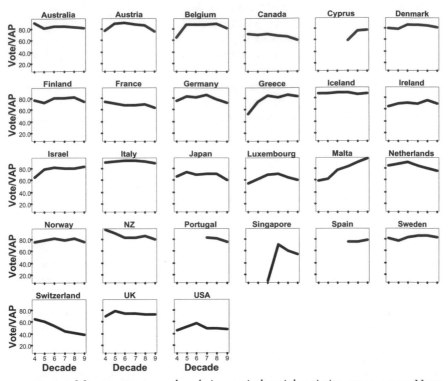

FIGURE 3.7. Mean turnout per decade in postindustrial societies, 1945–2000. *Note*: Turnout is calculated as the number of valid votes cast as a proportion of the voting-age population in all parliamentary and presidential elections. For details of the classification, see the Appendix. *Source*: Calculated from the International IDEA database *Voter Turnout from 1945 to 2000*. www.idea.int.

Vote/VAP that is consistent in every decade in Switzerland, and the more recent falls in France, Austria, and New Zealand. The pattern in the United States confirms a statistically significant erosion of turnout from 1945 to 2000, although the size of the coefficient remains modest, and the graph confirms the 1960s apex. It is also true, as Mair reported, that turnout does dip in twenty out of twenty-seven industrialized societies during the 1990s, but this decline is not large enough to register as statistically significant across the whole series of postwar elections. Moreover, the fact that this fall occurred during the last decade, but not earlier, strongly indicates that it cannot be accounted for satisfactorily by glacial social trends associated with the modernization process, such as patterns of suburbanization and secularization, and that we need to search elsewhere for the answer to this puzzle. The overall pattern was also not wholly consistent, because there was rising turnout in a few postindustrial societies as well, shown in Sweden, Israel, Greece, and Malta. Thus the erosion in electoral participation found in the U.S. during the last fifty years is evident in almost one-third of the comparable postindustrial societies elsewhere, but the extent of this phenomenon, and indeed the size of the fall-off, should not be exaggerated. *The evidence points more clearly and consistently toward a "ceiling effect,"* as the majority of postindustrial societies experienced stability or trendless fluctuation over time, according to the regression models. Despite popular assumptions, and much political concern, growing electoral disengagement actually remains far from the norm among all Western publics. The reasons for the diverging patterns found among similar types of postindustrial society, such as the timing of legal reforms expanding the franchise to eighteen-year olds, or changes in voting registration procedures – the end of compulsory voting in the Netherlands, for example – will be explored in depth in subsequent chapters.

Figure 3.8 shows more detailed trends in turnout averaged by decade since the war in each of the thirty-one developing societies that have had at least one election per decade from the 1950s to the 1990s, for comparison of changes over time among the same universe of nations. The graphs confirm that in many Latin American and Caribbean countries – such as Brazil, Chile, Peru, Ecuador, and Uruguay – the process of socioeconomic development during the postwar era has been strongly associated with a substantial and persistent increase in electoral turnout. A few countries in the region, such as the Dominican Republic, display a sharp fall, while Bolivia, Colombia, and Venezuela show a curvilinear pattern. Although there are some general tendencies, the variations among similar societies at roughly similar levels of socioeconomic development suggest that we need to look for additional explanations if we are to understand these trends fully, such as the historical development of democratic reforms and the role of political institutions in each country.

Explaining Turnout in the 1990s

Yet if modernization does widen electoral participation in developing countries, we still need to understand more fully why this is the case. The reasons may be complex, since the process of modernization involves multiple interrelated social developments that are difficult to untangle. Moreover, the impact of many trends can be expected to be lagged, producing changes as new generations enter the electorate. As the last step in this process, however, we use regression analysis models to explore some of the factors underlying the relationships that we have shown, in particular the role of levels of education, literacy, and population size in predicting mean levels of turnout during the 1990s across all countries, with controls for the region and the democratic history of the country, using a summary Freedom House index for 1972–2000 to measure the tradition of political rights and civil liberties. Table 3.4 shows the results of the analysis and confirms the overwhelming importance of primary, secondary, and tertiary education in pre-

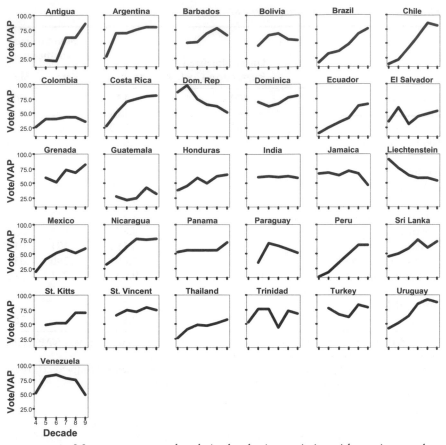

FIGURE 3.8. Mean turnout per decade in developing societies with continuous elections, 1945–2000. *Note*: Turnout is calculated as the number of valid votes cast as a proportion of the voting-age population in all parliamentary and presidential elections. For details of the classification, see the Appendix. The comparison includes all developing societies that held at least one national election per decade, 1945–2000. *Source*: Calculated from the International IDEA database *Voter Turnout from 1945 to 2000*. www.idea.int.

dicting levels of turnout. This is by far the most significant variable in the equation, and once this is entered, literacy per se does not emerge as important, nor does the size of the population. In addition, the democratic history of the country proves to be significant, suggesting that explanations based on socioeconomic development alone need to be counterbalanced by others emphasizing the role of political factors. The regional patterns show that Scandinavia, Western Europe, and Asia emerge with higher-than-average levels of turnout, even after controlling for socioeconomic development.

TABLE 3.4. *Models predicting turnout, 1990s*

	Unstandardized Regression Coef. B	St. Error	Standardized coefficients Beta	Sig.
Education	.402	.134	.497	.002
Literacy	.065	.118	.097	.539
Population size	.001	.000	−.022	.788
Democratic history	.044	.023	.265	.054
Region				
Middle East	−5.339	6.179	−.090	.389
North America	−5.318	9.935	−.049	.594
Central and South America	5.948	5.741	.133	.302
Africa	7.051	5.840	.186	.230
Asia	12.781	5.198	.291	.015
Western Europe	14.972	7.001	.290	.035
Scandinavia	18.072	9.031	.211	.048
Adjusted R²	.272			
Constant	14.8	13.811		.283

The models present the result of OLS regression analysis with mean turnout (Vote/VAP) in the 1990s in 126 nations as the dependent variable.
Education: Combined primary, secondary, and tertiary gross enrolment ratio (percent), 1998.
Literacy: Percent adult literacy rate 1998 (age 15 and above).
Population size: In millions, 1998.
Sources:
UNDP. 2000. *Human Development Report 2000*. New York: Oxford University Press.
Democratic history: The sum of the Freedom House Index, 1972–2000. Calculated from *Freedom around the World*. www.freedomhouse.org.
Regions: Coded as dummy variables, with Central and Eastern Europe excluded.

The overall model explains 27 percent of the variance in turnout, also indicating that we need many other institutional factors, as we shall see in the next chapter, to produce a more comprehensive explanation of cross-national differences in voting patterns.

Conclusions: The Role of Societal Modernization

So far, we have made some progress in understanding the role of socioeconomic development on electoral participation and, by implication, on the broader process of democratization as well. Modernization theories are seductive intellectually because of the claim that economic, cultural, and political changes go together in predictable ways, so that there are broadly similar trajectories, which form coherent patterns. Modernization accounts suggest that economic shifts in the production process underlie changes in the political superstructure, in particular, that rising levels of education, literacy, and wealth in the transition from rural subsistence economies to industrialized nations generate the conditions favoring rising voting participation. When citizens are given opportunities to express their political preferences through the ballot box, then the first stage of industrialization can be expected to foster electoral turnout, as well as broader aspects of civic engagement such as the growth of party and trade union organizations. The evidence presented in this chapter suggests three broad conclusions:

1. The study largely confirms the modernization thesis: During the last fifty years, *countries with rapid human development have experienced substantial growth in electoral turnout*, especially in Asia and Latin America.
2. Interpretation of the data to clarify trends in electoral participation within the world of postindustrial societies is more difficult, but overall the evidence suggests that *there is a ceiling effect in the impact of human development*. In particular, once primary and secondary education become ubiquitous throughout the population, producing the basic cognitive skills that facilitate civic awareness and access to mass communications, then further gains in the proportion of the population attending college and ever-rising levels of personal wealth, income, and leisure time do not, in themselves, produce further improvements in electoral participation.
3. At the same time, the more pessimistic view that postindustrial societies are inevitably experiencing a secular erosion of civic engagement and voting participation seems to be exaggerated. Overall, the majority of these nations saw a long-term pattern of trendless fluctuation or stability in electoral participation, and only eight postindustrial nations have experienced a significant decline in turnout over successive decades since 1945. While there is good evidence that there has been a slight short-term fall in voting participation during the 1990s across many postindustrial societies, the timing of the shift means that this cannot plausibly be attributed to the sort of glacial socioeconomic trends, such as suburbanization and secularization, that are at the heart of modernization theories.

Nevertheless, there remain considerable contrasts between countries at similar levels of development – for example, between Switzerland and Sweden, the United States and Italy, Mexico and South Africa. The reasons for this remain to be explored further, as we turn to the role of political institutions and mobilizing agencies in promoting electoral turnout.

4

Do Institutions Matter?

Modernization theories emphasize the role of long-term social forces sweeping like tsunamis across the ocean, transforming civic engagement and democratic states around the globe in their wake. Yet despite the attractive appeal of these accounts, it is also well established that levels of electoral participation can vary substantially, even among societies at relatively similar levels of socioeconomic development – the contrasts, for example, between the United States and Germany, Hungary and Poland, Colombia and Uruguay. A glance at the results of parliamentary elections worldwide during the 1990s reveals stark contrasts in the number of citizens casting their votes at the ballot box (see Figure 4.1). Over 90 percent of the voting-age population (VAP) participated in Malta, Uruguay, and Indonesia, compared to less than a third in Mali, Colombia, and Senegal. Even within the more limited universe of established democracies, all relatively affluent societies, during the 1990s turnout in parliamentary elections ranged from over 80 percent in Iceland, Greece, Italy, Belgium, and Israel to less than 50 percent of the voting-age population in the United States and Switzerland.

Ever since the first classic studies of nonvoting by American political scientists Charles Merriam in 1924 and Harold Gosnell in 1930, and by the Swedish sociologist Herbert Tingsten in 1937, comparative research has sought to understand the reasons for these cross-national differences.[1] Many studies trying to explain variations among established democracies have emphasized the importance of the institutional and legal arrangements for registration and voting, which affect the costs and benefits of electoral activism. Powell compared turnout in twenty-nine democracies, including the effects of the socioeconomic environment, the constitutional setting, and the party system, and he established that compulsory voting laws, automatic registration procedures, and the strength of party-group alignments boosted turnout, while participation was depressed in cases of one-party predominant systems allowing no rotation of the parties in

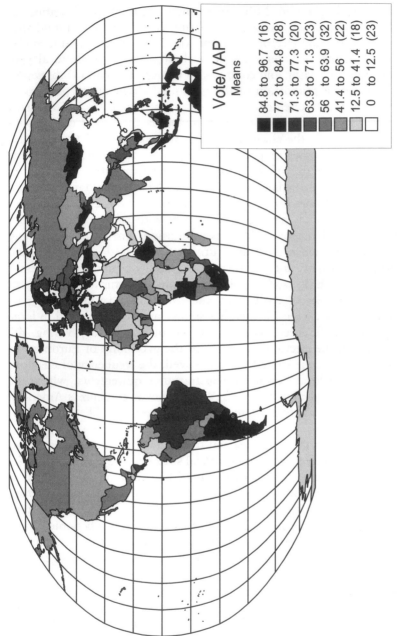

FIGURE 4.1. Turnout, 1990s. *Source:* International IDEA database *Voter Turnout from 1945 to 2000.* www.idea.int.

government.[2] Jackman and Miller examined electoral participation in twenty-two industrialized democracies during the 1980s and found that political institutions and electoral laws provided the most plausible explanation for variations in voter turnout, including levels of electoral proportionality, multipartyism, and compulsory voting.[3] Blais and Dobrzynska analyzed voters as a proportion of the registered electorate in parliamentary elections in ninety-one democracies from 1972 to 1995 and reported that multiple factors influenced turnout, including the use of compulsory voting, the voting age, the electoral system, the closeness of the electoral outcome, and the number of parties, as well as levels of socioeconomic development and the size of the country.[4] They concluded: "Turnout is likely to be highest in a small, industrialized, densely-populated country, where the national lower house election is decisive, voting is compulsory and the voting age is 21, having a PR system with relatively few parties and a close electoral outcome. All these conditions are never met in any specific instance but when most are, turnout can exceed 90 percent, and when most conditions are not met, turnout may easily be under 60 percent." Franklin, van der Eijk, and Oppenhuis compared turnout for direct elections to the European Parliament and found that variations in participation among the fifteen EU member states could be attributed in large part to systemic differences, notably the use of compulsory voting, the proportionality of the electoral system, and the proximity of European to national elections.[5] In the United States, as well, the frequency of elections combined with the legal hurdle of registration requirements, where the onus lies with the applicant, have long been believed to depress American turnout, the latter generating attempts at partial reforms like the "motor voter" initiative.[6]

It follows that even if common social trends have been sweeping across traditional, industrialized, and postindustrial societies, the way in which the public responds to these developments could plausibly be conditioned by the institutional context of elections and how these arrangements structure the costs and opportunities of electoral participation in these countries. Political institutions are often regarded as largely stable phenomena and therefore unable to account for fluctuations in levels of turnout, but the way in which they operate may be subject to significant changes over time, such as reforms expanding the franchise to women and younger groups of voters; the abandonment of restrictive practices such as poll taxes, property qualifications, and literacy requirements; changes in the laws governing compulsory voting; the increased frequency of contests due to developments such as the introduction of direct elections to the European Parliament, the use of referendums, and devolution to regional bodies; and changes in patterns of party competition, such as the shift toward catch-all center-left parties, the rise of the Greens, and the collapse of unreconstructed communist parties. Case studies within particular countries can also provide important insights into the impact of these developments. Major constitutional reforms during the 1990s provide "before and after" natural experiments monitoring the impact of institutional changes on levels of electoral turnout, holding the culture and social structure relatively constant within each country – for example, when New Zealand adopted the mixed member system of proportional representation, when Italy moved toward a more majoritarian electoral system, and when the UK abandoned the classic Westminster system for everything except contests for the House of Commons and local elections.[7]

Many previous studies have been limited to established democracies. Building on this literature, we can explore whether political institutions have similar effects on voting participation in a wider range of countries around the globe, including transitional and consolidating democracies. Institutional structures can be subdivided into three major categories. *Political institutions* include the broad arrangements in the political system that can shape the decision whether to turn out, including levels of competition in the party system, the basic type of electoral system used by each nation, and whether the contest is for legislative or presidential office. *Legal rules* determine who is eligible to cast a ballot, including the regulations governing compulsory voting and the legal qualifications for voting in terms of age, literacy, and gender. Lastly, *voting facilities*, such as the use of proxy or postal ballots, influence the costs of registration and voting. The multivariate models developed in this chapter analyze the impact of these arrangements on turnout, controlling for levels of socioeconomic and democratic development, as the broadest context affecting the decision to vote or not to vote.

Motivational Theories

Why would institutions be expected to affect turnout? The motivational theory developed in this chapter suggests that the structural context shapes the incentives to participate at the ballot box by influencing electoral costs, electoral choices, and electoral decisiveness.

Electoral Costs

Electoral costs concern the time, energies, and informational demands required to register and cast a ballot. The difficulties of voting can be reduced by the widespread availability of special arrangements for mobile populations, such as mail, proxy, absentee, and overseas voting, as well as polling facilities for the elderly and disabled in nursing homes and hospitals, and elections held on a weekend or holiday rather than on a workday. Registration procedures can be an important hurdle. In many countries such as Britain, Sweden, and Canada, registration is the responsibility of the government, conducted via a door-to-door canvas or annual census, so most eligible citizens are automatically enrolled to vote. In others such as the United States, France, and Brazil, citizens have to apply to register, often well ahead of the election, and complicated, time-consuming, or restrictive practices can depress participation levels.[8] Under other regimes, voters can be deterred by far more serious barriers, such as in Pakistan, Zimbabwe, and Indonesia, where citizens face the threat of intimidation, violence, and coercion at polling places. Standard rational choice theories suggest that, all other things being equal, the deterrent of higher costs reduces electoral participation.

Electoral Choices

Electoral choices are determined by the options available on the ballot, notably the range of parties and candidates contesting elected offices and the policy alternatives listed for referenda issues. Elections can be classified as competitive, semicompetitive, or controlled contests.[9] Of the 191 nations under comparison, 24 have held no competitive elections (defined as those contested by more than one party) during the postwar era. One-party elections were organized in the Stalinist Soviet Union to demonstrate unanimous consent for the governing regime, but the Communist Party restricted even the minimal competition among candidates. The ability of organized opposition parties to contest elections continues to be limited under many authoritarian regimes, where parliamentary assemblies function primarily to legitimize the government, although various candidates can run for office – for example, in Bhutan, Cuba, Vietnam, Qatar, Bahrain, Burma, Liberia, Swaziland, and Iraq. In semicompetitive elections, there is a genuine contest for power between major parties, but certain opposition groups are legally banned, such as the fundamentalist Islamic Salvation Front in Algeria and the Kurdistan Workers Party in Turkey. By contrast, competitive democratic elections let voters choose among two parties, two-and-a-half parties, moderate multiparty systems, and polarized multiparty systems. In Israel, for example, the May 1999 elections to the 120-member Knesset returned 17 parties, and no single party won more than 14 percent of the popular vote. In the Ukraine, thirty parties and party blocks contested the 1998 parliamentary elections, and as a result eight parties were elected via party lists and seventeen won seats via the single-member districts, along with 116 independents.[10] Rational choice theories suggest that in general, all other things being equal, the greater the range of choices available on the ballot, the more voters will find a party, candidate, or referendum issue that reflects their viewpoint, and the stronger will be the incentive to vote.

Electoral Decisiveness

Yet there may well be a trade-off between electoral choices and electoral *decisiveness*, or the political benefits anticipated from casting a ballot in determining the composition of parliament and government, the legislative and public policy agenda, and the outcome of referendum issues. Standard rational choice theories suggest that in elections that are anticipated to be close – on the basis of past results, opinion polls, or media commentary – voters are likely to feel far greater incentive to get to the polls than in those where the outcome appears to be a foregone conclusion. Hence, for example, British studies have found that the closer the difference between the major parties in the national share of the vote, the greater the level of electoral participation during the postwar era.[11]

The motivational theory developed in this chapter suggests that the incentives motivating electors to cast a ballot represent a product of electoral *costs* (of registering and voting), electoral *choices* (how many parties are listed on the ballot) and electoral *decisiveness* (how far votes cast for each party determine the outcome for parliament and government). If voters face restricted options, so that they cannot express support by choosing a party that reflects their views, then this is likely to discourage participation. And if casting a ballot expresses support for a party, candidate, or cause, but makes little difference to the composition of parliament or government, to the policy agenda, or to the outcome of specific referenda or initiatives, then again this reduces the marginal value of the vote, and therefore the instrumental incentives associated with voting.

What remains unclear from previous studies is the relative importance that citizens give to electoral costs, electoral choices, and electoral decisiveness in weighing the decision whether to participate. It may be, for example, that elections can be very costly (for example, with multiple complex referendum issues on the ballot creating high information hurdles) but that citizens may still participate if the result is expected to be decisive (a closely balanced result, for example, or one that is important to the interests of voters). Moreover, the link between the broader institutional context and how voters perceive and weigh the costs, choices, and decisiveness of elections is poorly understood. The motivation of individual voters can also be influenced by many other factors discussed in the next chapter, such as mobilization efforts by particular parties, groups, and community networks; political attitudes such as a sense of political efficacy, trust in government, civic duty, and interest in current affairs; as well as individual-level resources such as education and income. Nevertheless, rational choice accounts suggest that the institutional context plays an important role in structuring voters' choices, and we can test the evidence for these claims.

Institutional Models Explaining Turnout

In order to examine the impact of political institutions, a series of multivariate models are developed using OLS regression analysis. The dependent variable is turnout measured by Vote/VAP in 405 national parliamentary and presidential elections held during the 1990s in all of the countries under comparison worldwide where we have consistent indicators. For comparison with the previous chapter, Model A in Table 4.1 first entered levels of human development and democratization, without any institutional factors, with these factors alone explaining 18 percent of the variance in turnout. Model B then adds two sets of factors: the main political institutions and the legal rules commonly thought to influence voter participation, for reasons to be discussed in detail later. The *institutional* factors include the basic type of electoral system, the size of electoral districts, the frequency of national elections, whether the contest was presidential or parliamentary, and the type of party system. Model B then also tests for the impact of *legal rules* determining the eligibility to vote, including the use of compulsory voting, the age at which citizens are eligible to vote, the length of time that women have been enfranchised, and the use of any literacy requirements. After including these structural factors, the overall level of variance explained by the model (shown by the R2) rises from 18 percent to 29 percent. This suggests that Model B improves the goodness-of-fit, although considerable variance remains to be explained. Let us consider these results in terms of each of the structural factors that can be expected to influence turnout.

The Impact of Political Institutions

Electoral Systems
Ever since the seminal work of Maurice Duverger (1954) and Douglas Rae (1971), a flourishing literature has classified the main types of electoral system and sought to analyze their consequences.[12] Systems vary according to a number of key dimensions, including district magnitude, ballot structure, effective thresholds, malapportionment, assembly size, and the use of open or closed lists. The most important variations concern electoral formulas that determine how votes are counted in order to allocate seats. There are four main types: *majoritarian* formulas (including second-ballot and alternative voting systems), *plurality* formulas (e.g., first-past-the-post), *semiproportional* systems (such as the cumulative vote and the limited vote), *proportional representation* (including open and closed party lists using largest remainders and highest averages formulas, the single transferable vote, and mixed-member proportional systems).

Previous studies have commonly found that the type of electoral formula shapes participation, with proportional representation systems generating higher voter participation than majoritarian or plurality elections.[13] This pattern seems well supported by the evidence in established democracies, although the exact reasons for this relationship remain unclear.[14] Motivational explanations focus on the differential incentives facing citizens under alternative electoral arrangements. Under majoritarian systems such as first-past-the-post, used for the House of Commons in Westminster and the

TABLE 4.1. *Explaining turnout in national elections, all countries in the 1990s*

	Model A: Socioeconomic Development				Model B: Development plus Institutions			
	b	(s.e.)	St. Beta	Sig.	b	(s.e.)	St. Beta	Sig.
Constant	45.675	(5.822)		***	76.767	(12.635)		***
Development								
Human development	0.035	(.006)	.314	***	0.021	(.007)	.190	**
Level of democratization	0.954	(.329)	.162	**	0.839	(.329)	.143	**
Political institutions								
Electoral system					2.652	(1.025)	.130	**
Mean population per MP					−.0009	(.000)	−.095	*
Frequency of national elections					−3.471	(.557)	−.337	***
Predominant party system (1 = yes)					−3.977	(2.467)	−.076	
Fragmented party system (1 = yes)					−6.228	(3.766)	−.076	
Presidential (1) or Parliamentary (0) contests					4.541	(1.767)	.115	**
Legal rules								
Age of voting eligibility					−.991	(.620)	−.070	
Length of women's enfranchisement					.191	(.052)	.192	***
Use of compulsory voting					1.964	(2.106)	.043	
Literacy requirements					−20.686	(6.173)	−.146	***
Number of elections	405				405			
Adjusted R^2	.182	(16.7)			.294	(15.5)		

Vote/VAP is measured as the number of valid votes as a proportion of the voting-age population in 405 parliamentary and presidential national elections held in 139 nations during the 1990s. The figures represent unstandardized regression coefficients (b), standard errors, standardized beta coefficients, and significance, with mean Vote/VAP as the dependent variable. * $p < .05$, ** $p < .01$, *** $p < .001$

Human development: Human Development Index 1998 combining literacy, education, and income, UNDP.
Level of democratization: Freedom House Index in the year of the election. Combined reversed fourteen-point scale of political rights and civic liberties. Freedom House, www. freedomhouse. org.
Electoral system: See Table 4.2. Majoritarian/plurality (1), semi-proportional (2), PR (3).
Party system: See Table 4.3. Predominant party system where the party in first place gets 60 percent of the vote or more. Fragmented party system where the party in first place gets 30 percent of the vote or less.
Compulsory voting: See Table 4.4 for countries.
Source: Calculated from the International IDEA database *Voter Turnout from 1945 to 2000*. www. idea. int.

United States Congress, supporters of minor and fringe parties with geographic support dispersed widely but thinly across the country, such as the Greens, may feel that casting their votes will make no difference to who wins in their constituency, still less to the overall composition of government and the policy agenda. The "wasted votes" argument is strongest for safe seats where the incumbent party is unlikely to be defeated. By contrast, PR elections with low vote thresholds and large district magnitudes, such as the party list system used in the Netherlands, increase the opportunities for minor parties with dispersed support to enter parliament even with a relatively modest share of the vote, and therefore increase the incentives for their supporters to participate. This proposition can be tested using the IDEA handbook by classifying nations around the world into three categories: PR, semi-PR, and plurality/majoritarian electoral systems.[15] Table 4.1 shows that, even after controlling for levels of development, the basic type of electoral system is a significant indicator of turnout, with PR systems generating higher levels of voting participation than plurality/majoritarian systems.

Since the type of electoral system can be understood best as a categorical rather than a continuous variable, Table 4.2 provides further details about the impact of different electoral systems on average levels of voter turnout during the 1990s, measured in the standard way by vote as a proportion of the voting-age population (Vote/VAP) and, for comparison with some previous studies, by vote as a proportion of the registered electorate (Vote/Reg). The results without any controls confirm that average turnout (using either measure) was highest among nations using proportional representation, namely, party list and the single transferable vote electoral systems. By contrast, voting participation was fairly similar across majoritarian, plurality, and semi-PR systems, with turnout across all of these systems about 7.5 to 11 points less than under PR. These findings suggest that the basic type of electoral system does shape the motivation to participate, but that the key distinction is between PR systems and all others.

Electoral Districts

Many other aspects of the electoral system may possibly shape voter participation – such as the ballot structure, the use of open or closed party lists, and levels of proportionality – but district magnitude, and in particular the population size of the average electoral district, can be expected to be especially important, since this may determine the linkages between voters and their representatives. It has long been suspected that there is a relationship between the size of a country and democracy, although the reasons for this association remain unclear.[16] It is possible that the smaller the number of electors per member of parliament, the greater the potential for constituency service and for elected representatives to maintain com-

TABLE 4.2. *Electoral systems and turnout, 1990s*

Type of Electoral System	Mean Vote/VAP, 1990s	Mean Vote/Reg, 1990s	Number of Elections
Majoritarian			
Alternative vote	65.5	92.9	2
Two-round "runoff"	58.5	65.0	21
All majoritarian	**59.1**	**67.6**	23
Plurality			
First past the post	61.2	67.7	43
Block vote	56.5	70.9	9
All plurality	**60.4**	**68.3**	52
Semiproportional			
Parallel	63.5	69.0	19
Single Nontransferable vote	52.6	59.8	2
All semiproportional	**62.5**	**68.1**	21
Proportional			
Mixed-member proportional	66.6	71.9	7
List PR	70.0	74.7	59
Single transferable vote	83.4	81.7	2
All PR systems	**70.0**	**74.6**	68
All	64.4	70.8	164

Mean Vote/VAP is measured as the number of valid votes as a proportion of the voting-age population in all nations worldwide that held parliamentary elections during the 1990s.
Mean Vote/Reg is measured as the number of valid votes as a proportion of the registered electorate in all nations worldwide that held parliamentary elections during the 1990s.
The classification of electoral systems is based on Andrew Reynolds and Ben Reilly. 1997. *The International IDEA Handbook of Electoral System Design.* Stockholm: IDEA, Annex A.
Source: Calculated from the International IDEA database *Voter Turnout from 1945 to 2000.* www. idea. int.

munication with local constituents, and therefore the higher the incentive to turn out based on any "personal" vote.[17] Voters may not be able to shape the outcome for government, but in smaller single-member or multimember districts they may have greater information, familiarity, and contact with their elected representative or representatives, and therefore they may be more interested in affecting who gets into parliament.[18] The simplest way to measure this is to divide the number of seats in the lower house of the legislature into the total population of each country. There are considerable cross-national variations in the average number of electors per representative depending upon the size of the population and the number of seats in parliament, ranging from India, with 1.7 million electors per member of the Lok Sabha, down to about 5,500 electors per MP in the Bahamas, Malta, and Cape Verde. The results in Table 4.1 confirm that the size of electoral districts did indeed prove to be a significant predictor of turnout, in a negative direction, with smaller districts generally associated with higher voter participation.

Frequency of Contests

The frequency of elections has also been thought to be important for participation, because this increases the costs facing electors and may produce voting fatigue. Franklin and colleagues have demonstrated that the closeness of national elections immediately before direct elections to the European Parliament is a strong predictor of turnout in European elections.[19] The cases of Switzerland and the United States are commonly cited as exemplifying nations with frequent elections for office at multiple levels, as well as widespread use of referenda and initiatives, and both are characterized by exceptionally low voter participation among Western democracies.[20] California, for example, has primary and general elections for local and state government, including judicial, mayoral, and gubernatorial offices, congressional midterm elections every two years for the House and Senate, presidential elections every four years, as well as multiple referendum issues on the ballot, all producing what Anthony King has termed the "never-ending election campaign."[21] If the frequency of elections generates voter fatigue, the increase in contests associated with the growth of primaries in the United States after 1968, the introduction of direct elections to the European Parliament in 1979, and contests for regional bodies following devolution and decentralization in countries such as Spain, France, and the UK, could help to explain any decline in turnout in recent decades. A simple measure of electoral frequency can be calculated using the number of national-level parliamentary and presidential elections held during the decade of the 1990s; the measure ranges from only one contest in a few semi-democracies up to seven or more elections in the United States, Ecuador, and Taiwan. It should be noted that this measure provides the most consistent and reliable cross-national indicator that is available, although it is likely to represent a conservative estimate, since it does not count many other types of contest held during this decade, including national and local referenda and initiatives, pre-nomination primaries, and European, regional/state, and local contests. The results in Table 4.1 confirm that the frequency of national elections was strong and significant, in a negative direction: The more often national elections are held, the greater the voter fatigue. This result is likely to provide important clues to some of the sharpest outliers in turnout, such as Switzerland and the United

States, both among the richest and most developed countries on Earth, yet characterized by relatively low (and falling) levels of voter participation.

Party Systems and Electoral Competition

The type of party system and the levels of electoral competition are likely to be closely related to the basic type of electoral system, although there is not a perfect fit. Ever since Duverger, it has been well known that the plurality method of elections favors two-party systems, by systematically over-representing the largest party when translating votes into seats.[22] Lijphart's comparison of thirty-six established democracies demonstrates that as disproportionality rises, so the effective number of parliamentary parties falls.[23] Yet there are a number of important exceptions to this rule, with plural societies such as Papua New Guinea and India characterized by multiple parties in majoritarian electoral systems, and Malta and Austria having two-party and two-and-a-half party systems despite PR elections. There are many mechanical variations among PR systems, and the use of high voting thresholds (as high as 10 percent in Turkey) can prevent the election of smaller parties.[24] The levels of fragmentation, polarization, and competition in the party system also reflect the existence of cleavages in plural societies, including divisions of class, religion, ethnicity/race, language, and region.

Intuitively, it would seem likely that in elections expected to be close, citizens would feel greater incentive to participate, and parties would feel greater incentive to mobilize supporters to get them to the polls. Patterns of electoral competition can therefore be expected to influence voter turnout, but there is little agreement in the literature about the exact nature of this relationship, or about how best to gauge competition. Some suggest that the greater the range of alternative parties listed on the ballot, stretching from the nationalist far right through the moderate center to the post-communist left, the more people are stimulated to vote.[25] This claim assumes that wider electoral choices across the ideological spectrum mean that all sectors of public opinion and all social groups are more likely to find a party to represent their views, preferences, and interests. Yet a counterargument is heard from those who suggest that the higher the level of party fragmentation, the higher the probability of coalition government, the smaller the share of votes cast that determines the formation of government, and therefore the lower the inducement for electors to turn out.[26] As Jackman has argued, voters in multiparty systems that produce coalitions do not directly choose the government that will govern them; instead, they vote for the parties in the legislature that will select the government that will determine the policy agenda. Under multiparty coalitions, voters appear to be offered a more decisive choice among policies, whereas in fact they are offered a less decisive one.[27] The most important proposition based on the motivational theory already discussed is that under conditions of free and fair elections, all other things being equal, we would expect to find a curvilinear relationship between the *effective number of electoral parties* and *levels of voting turnout*. More parties running for office simultaneously increases electoral choice, but also decreases electoral decisiveness. Patterns of electoral competition can be gauged in many ways, but the share of the national vote for the strongest party provides a simple and effective summary indicator. In highly fragmented party systems, such as in Israel, the Netherlands, and the Ukraine, the strongest parliamentary party in each election commonly wins less than a third of the popular vote. At the other extreme, predominant one-party systems characteristically have a winning party with vote shares of 60 percent or more, as in the case of Singapore.

Table 4.1 confirms that both predominant party systems and fragmented party systems are characterized by lower-than-average levels of turnout, although in the multivariate models the difference was significant only at the .10 level. Yet the measurement of party competition employed in the study could be seen to be somewhat arbitrary. To explore these results in more detail, Table 4.3 and Figure 4.2, without any prior controls, confirm the curvilinear pattern as expected. Turnout was lowest where the party in first place swept up 60 percent or more of the vote, indicating an election with a predominant party and single-party executive facing a weak and ineffective opposition in parliament. In such situations, the marginal value of each vote appears lowest, owing to the predictable outcome, and parties may make less effort to mobilize supporters. Turnout rises steadily with a more evenly balanced vote share, before dropping again where the winning

TABLE 4.3. *Party competition and turnout in parliamentary elections, 1945–2000*

Share of the Vote Won by the Party in First Place	Mean Vote/VAP, 1990s	Mean Vote/Reg, 1990s	Number of Elections
More than 60%	55.8	69.7	130
50 to 59.9%	62.5	73.4	188
40 to 49.9%	73.5	79.5	287
30 to 39.9%	73.0	78.0	168
Less than 29.9%	64.2	73.5	120
All	67.5	75.9	876

Mean Vote/VAP is measured as the number of valid votes as a proportion of the voting-age population in all nations worldwide that held parliamentary elections from 1945 to 2000.
Mean Vote/Reg is measured as the number of valid votes as a proportion of the registered electorate in all nations worldwide that held parliamentary elections from 1945 to 2000.
Source: Calculated from the International IDEA database *Voter Turnout from 1945 to 2000*. www.idea.int.

party gets 30 percent or less of the vote, indicating a highly fragmented multiparty system and coalition government.

The evidence suggests that people are likely to be most discouraged from voting in predominant one-party systems, such as the extended rule of the Liberal Democratic Party in Japan, the Christian Democrats in Italy (1945 to 1980), and the PRI in Mexico (from 1929 until 2000), where the same party is returned to government over successive elections, and the polarized and fragmented opposition remains unable to mount an effective challenge.[28] Under this type of competition, voters may have the choice of many parties listed on the ballot, but in practice these options are fairly meaningless, as supporters of opposition parties are unable to "throw the rascals out" and displace the governing regime. Turnout is also slightly lower than average in fragmented multiparty systems, typified by parliamentary elections in Switzerland and the Netherlands, which maximize electoral choice but simultaneously reduce the decisiveness of the electoral outcome for government. Voters can choose from among multiple options, and as a

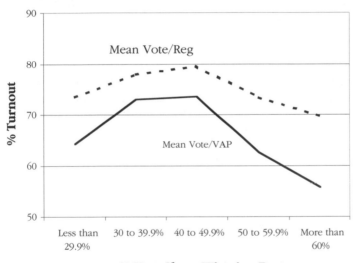

% Vote Share Winning Party

FIGURE 4.2. Party competition and turnout. *Note:* The figure shows the mean turnout in 876 parliamentary elections held from 1945 to 2000 against the vote share of the winning party. *Mean Vote/VAP* is measured as the number of valid votes as a proportion of the voting-age population in all nations worldwide that held parliamentary elections from 1945 to 2000. *Mean Vote/Reg* is measured as the number of valid votes as a proportion of the registered electorate in all nations worldwide that held parliamentary elections from 1945 to 2000. *% Vote Share Winning Party* is calculated for the party in first place in each parliamentary election from 1945 to 2000. *Source:* Calculated from the International IDEA database *Voter Turnout from 1945 to 2000.* www.idea.int.

result they may well influence the composition of parliament by electing members from minor and fringe parties, but at the same time their votes will have less impact on which parties enter government, and therefore on which parties determine the policy agenda. In the most extreme case, in Switzerland, the four largest parties have formed the same broad coalition government for almost the entire postwar era.

By contrast, participation is likely to be higher in elections with more competitive party systems. Two parties vying for power in a unitary parliamentary government, typified by Westminster (in the 1950s and 1960s), Barbados, and New Zealand (until 1993), usually produce a decisive electoral outcome and, by definition, regular rotation of government and opposition parties in power. Where two fairly evenly divided major parties compete for marginal seats, the "winners' bonus" or "manufactured majority" characteristic of majoritarian and plurality electoral systems means that a modest tremor in the popular vote can trigger a dramatic shift in parliamentary seats. In such systems, like a finely balanced mechanism, even a small swing in electoral support may change the party that forms the government. Two-party systems usually offer voters clear and simple choices between two alternative sets of public policies, and this pattern of competition also forces parties to maintain their core base and to compete for the "swing" votes in the center. Moderate multiparty systems, typified by Germany and Norway, are characterized by more than two and less than five or six parliamentary parties. This pattern of competition provides voters with a range of electoral choices, although at the same time these systems decrease the decisiveness of the electoral result and the salience of casting a ballot, as the outcome is more likely to produce coalition governments resting upon negotiations among parties rather than the share of the vote and seats.

Presidential versus Parliamentary Executives

Another constitutional factor commonly believed to influence the motivational incentives to turn out concerns the power of the office and, in particular, whether there is a parliamentary or presidential system of government. *First-order elections* are the most important national contests, including legislative elections in countries with parliamentary systems of government and presidential contests in countries with strong presidencies. By contrast, *second-order* elections are all others, including state, provincial, and local contests, referenda and initiatives, and direct elections to the European Parliament among the fifteen EU states.[29] In parliamentary systems, the head of government (the prime minister, the premier, the chancellor) is selected by the legislature and can be dismissed by a legislative vote of no confidence. In presidential systems, the head of government is popularly elected for a fixed term and is not dependent upon the legislature.[30] Rational choice theory suggests that the incentive to vote is likely to be greatest for the most salient elections determining the composition of government, so that in countries with presidential systems of government where elections for the president and legislature are held on separate occasions – the midterm elections in the United States, for example – more people are likely to participate in executive than in legislative contests. Where presidential and parliamentary elections are held on the same date, there is likely to be no substantial difference in levels of turnout in the two types of contest. The result of the analysis presented in Table 4.1 confirms that, overall, presidential elections produced significantly greater turnout than parliamentary contests.

The Impact of Legal Rules

Direct arrangements more closely related to legal eligibility include restrictions of the franchise based on age, gender, and literacy, along with the use of compulsory voting laws.

Eligibility for the Franchise

The minimum age at which people qualify to vote is important, since in most Western European countries for which we have survey data the young are consistently less likely to vote than older groups, and similar patterns are well established in the United States.[31] Ceteris paribus, we would expect to find that the lower the age at which citizens are eligible to vote, the lower the turnout. Blais and Dobrzynska confirmed that, all other things being equal, turnout is reduced by almost two points when the voting age is lowered by one year.[32] Latin American states were the first to lower the voting age from twenty-one to eighteen, beginning in the nineteenth century, and it was only in the 1970s that the United States and Western European countries followed suit.[33] Today the minimum voting age is usually eighteen to twenty years old, although it varies in a few of the countries under comparison. Four nations set eligibility below eighteen, including fifteen years old in Iran and sixteen in Brazil. By contrast, eighteen nations set the qualifying age above twenty, ranging from twenty-one years old in Nicaragua up to twenty-eight in Algeria. Yet the results of the analysis in Table 4.1 show that the age of voting eligibility was unrelated to turnout, probably because most countries now use fairly similar age brackets.

Restrictions on the franchise vary from one country to another, such as the disenfranchisement of felons, bankrupts, resident aliens, and groups such as the mentally incapacitated.[34] Waves of immigration or increases in the prison population can have an important dampening effect on Vote/VAP. In the United States, the claim of steadily declining turnout since 1972 has been challenged as an artificial product of the rise in the number of ineligible voters (due to increased numbers of resident aliens and felons in prison or on probation), swelling the size of the voting-age population.[35] One of the most important restrictions concerns the use of literacy requirements for voting, a fairly common practice in the Americas in the past, which served mainly to disenfranchise the less educated and ethnic minority groups. These requirements were gradually abolished during the postwar period in Venezuela (1946), Bolivia (1952), the United States (1965), Chile (1970), Ecuador (1978), Peru (1980) and Brazil (1985).[36] Where enforced, these requirements can be expected to have depressed the number of eligible voters, and the abolition of the requirements should have served to boost Vote/VAP. Table 4.1 confirms that a residual of these regulations remains, so that turnout is significantly lower among the few countries that still employ this practice.

The enfranchisement of women has had a dramatic impact on electoral participation. Only four countries enfranchised women before the start of World War I: New Zealand in 1893, Australia in 1902, Finland in 1907, and Norway in 1913. Women had attained the suffrage by the end of World War II in 83 nations, and in 171 nations in total by 1970. In another twenty nations this occurred even later, for example, in 1971 in Switzerland, 1976 in Portugal, 1980 in Iraq, 1984 in Liechtenstein, and 1994 in Kazakhstan; and today women continue to be barred from voting in Qatar, Saudi Arabia, Oman, and the United Arab Emirates.[37] The first election after women are first enfranchised has usually seen a sudden drop in overall levels of Vote/VAP, as older generations of women who had never participated before suddenly become eligible to vote, followed by a slow recovery in rates of turnout. In the United States and Britain, for example, women were first enfranchised in the early 1920s, and the first election afterward saw an immediate sharp drop in overall turnout. Subsequent decades saw a slow and steady increase in levels of female turnout until the early 1980s, when women come to participate at similar, or even slightly higher, levels than men. Similar patterns have been found elsewhere.[38] The residual effect of this pattern is found more widely; countries that enfranchised women prior to 1945 had average turnout (Vote/VAP) of 69 percent in the 1990s, compared to 61 percent for countries that granted women the vote in the postwar era. Nor is this simply due to a close association between women's rights and overall levels of democracy. In the multivariate model in Table 4.1, the difference proves to be strong and significant; even after controlling for all other factors, including general levels of political rights and civil liberties, countries that enfranchised women earlier tend to have higher turnout today than those that reformed their systems in more recent decades.

Compulsory Voting

The use of compulsory or mandatory voting laws can be expected to have an obvious impact on turnout, although the strength of the effect depends upon how strictly such regulations and any associated sanctions are implemented and enforced.[39] In practice, legal rules for voting may be de jure or de facto. The most common legal basis is statutory law, although the obligation to vote may also be rooted in constitutional provisions.[40] Implementation ranges from minimal de facto enforcement to the imposition of various sanctions. Fines are most common, as in Brazil, Egypt, and Luxembourg, although other punishments include the denial of official documents such as passports, identity cards, drivers licenses, and government benefits, used in Italy and Greece, and even occasionally the threat of imprisonment (up to six months in Cyprus) as a criminal offence. The effectiveness of any legal penalties is dependent upon the efficiency of the prior registration process and, where the initiative falls upon the elector, whether there are fines or other penalties associated with failure to register. Where implementation is loosely enforced, the impact of any mandatory regulations has to operate largely through the impact of the law on social norms, similar to the effect of no parking restrictions on city streets.

Mandatory voting regulations may be genuine attempts to increase public involvement in the political process, or they may be employed by less democratic regimes to compel the public to vote, in the attempt to legitimize one-party contests. Even in democratic states, the use of legal regulations may have unintended consequences for participation, since it may reduce the incentive for parties to organize and mobilize their heartland supporters to get them to the polls.[41] Worldwide, twenty-three countries currently use compulsory voting in national parliamentary elections, including seven older democracies such as Australia, Belgium, Greece, Luxembourg, and Italy. In addition, this practice is used for national elections in a few provinces in Austria (in Styria, Tyrol, and Vorarlberg) and in Switzerland (in Schaffhausen), and until 1970 the Netherlands also used such regulations. Voting is also mandatory in many Latin American countries at different levels of democratization, and is used by nondemocratic regimes in Singapore and Egypt.[42]

Most previous studies have found that compulsory voting is associated with higher turnout, but these have been limited mainly to established democracies, most of which are in Western Europe. Table 4.1 demonstrates that in national elections held worldwide, the use of compulsory voting proved to be unrelated to actual turnout, whereas, by contrast, Table 4.5 confirms that among established democracies, the use of compulsory voting regulations proved to be both strong and significant. To explore this difference further, Table 4.4 shows the levels of turnout in the 1990s found in all twenty-three countries worldwide with compulsory voting regulations, broken down by type of democracy. The results show that in older democracies there is indeed a positive relationship; voting levels as a proportion of the voting-age population are 7.7 percent higher in nations using mandatory voting laws, and are a remarkable 14.2 percent higher in terms of vote

TABLE 4.4. *Compulsory voting and electoral turnout, 1990s*

	Mean Vote/VAP	Mean Vote/Reg	Number of Nations
Older democracies			
Compulsory	79.4	86.9	7
Noncompulsory	71.7	72.7	32
Difference	**+7.7**	**+14.2**	39
Newer democracies			
Compulsory	67.7	75.8	9
Noncompulsory	69.3	73.9	31
Difference	**−1.6**	**+1.9**	40
Semi-democracies			
Compulsory	53.9	60.6	5
Noncompulsory	56.6	67.0	40
Difference	**−2.7**	**−6.4**	45
Non-democracies			
Compulsory	40.9	70.6	2
Noncompulsory	61.8	67.8	38
Difference	**−20.9**	**+2.8**	40
All			
Compulsory	65.9	75.4	23
Noncompulsory	64.2	70.0	140
Difference	**+1.9**	**+5.4**	163

Mean Vote/VAP is measured as the number of valid votes as a proportion of the voting-age population in all nations worldwide that held parliamentary elections during the 1990s.

Mean Vote/Reg is measured as the number of valid votes as a proportion of the registered electorate in all nations worldwide that held parliamentary elections during the 1990s.

Compulsory voting: The following twenty-three nations were classified as currently using compulsory voting, with the types of democracy as shown in the Appendix.

Older democracies: Australia, Belgium, Costa Rica, Cyprus, Greece, Italy, and Luxembourg.

Newer democracies: Argentina, Bolivia, Chile, Dominican Republic, Ecuador, Liechtenstein, Panama Canal Zone, Thailand, and Uruguay.

Semi-democracies: Brazil, Guatemala, Honduras, Peru, and Venezuela.

Non-democracies: Singapore and Egypt.

Source: Calculated from the International IDEA database *Voter Turnout from 1945 to 2000*. www.idea.int.

as a proportion of the registered electorate. Where these laws exist in established democracies in Western Europe, the Asia-Pacific region, and South America, the registered electorate – the group that is most obviously subject to any sanctions – is far more likely to cast a ballot. Yet in all other types of political system, the result is very different, with Vote/VAP actually slightly lower among newer democracies and semi-democracies with mandatory laws, and far lower in Egypt and Singapore, the only two non-democratic states with mandatory regulations and at least semicompetitive elections.

There may be a number of explanations for this intriguing finding. First, it may be that the law is enforced more strictly and the registration processes are more efficient in the older democracies, so that voters face stronger negative incentives to participate. In addition, it may be that the impact of mandatory laws depends primarily upon broader social norms about the desirability of obeying the law and those in authority, which may prove stronger in established democratic states in Western Europe than in many Latin American cultures. Lastly, it may be the case that newer democracies characterized by low electoral turnout are more likely to introduce laws in the attempt to mobilize the public, but that without strict implementation these laws prove ineffective correctives. Without further research, these possible reasons have to remain speculative, but they may help to account for some of the striking differences in the impact of compulsory voting laws in different types of political system, and they suggest the need for caution in generalizing from established democracies to other nations.

The Impact of Voting Facilities

Turnout may also be affected by administration of registration procedures and facilities for voting that alters the costs for certain groups, such as the use of absentee, advance, overseas, and postal ballots, proxy votes, the distribution of mobile polling facilities for special populations such as the elderly, infirm, and disabled in nursing homes and hospitals, and polling scheduled for weekend or holidays rather than workdays.[43] The analysis presented earlier covers all countries under comparison. By contrast, given the limited availability of information about voting facilities, Table 4.5 is restricted to seventy national elections held during the 1990s in twenty-five older democracies. Similar steps are followed within this smaller group of elections: Model A focuses on *voting facilities*, including the use of automatic or voluntary registration processes, the number of polling days, the use of rest days or workdays for polling, postal voting, proxy voting, special polling booths, transfer voting, and advance voting, with controls for socioeconomic and democratic development. Model B examines the role of political institutions and legal rules for these older democracies. Model C presents the combined impact of all factors under consideration. All models control for levels of socioeconomic development and democratization, which, in contrast to the worldwide comparison, prove to be largely

TABLE 4.5. *Explaining turnout in twenty-five older democracies in national elections held during the 1990s*

	Model A				Model B				Model C			
	B	(s.e.)	St. Beta	Sig.	B	(s.e.)	St. Beta	Sig.	B	(s.e.)	St. Beta	Sig.
Constant	98.6	(40.70)		**	40.5	(44.2)			11.707	(79.18)		
Development												
Human development	−.051	(.040)	−.12		−.076	(.036)	−.39	*	−.071	(037)	−.35	
Level of democratization	2.237	(2.26)	.17		3.576	(1.86)	.28		.506	(2.23)	.04	
Political institutions												
Electoral system					2.952	(1.87)	.19		8.345	(2.68)	.55	**
Pop. per MP					−.0262	(.00)	−.56	**	−.0449	(.000)	−.11	
Frequency of election					−1.386	(.871)	−.18		−4.00	(1.33)	−.53	**
Presidential election					4.042	(2.95)	.11		3.812	(2.79)	.10	
Fragmented party system					3.546	(4.16)	.09		−4.001	(5.07)	−.11	
Legal rules												
Age of voting eligibility					3.630	(2.14)	.14		5.718	(3.99)	.22	
Length of women's enfranchisement					.416	(.078)	.54	***	.322	(.095)	.42	***
Use of compulsory voting					10.413	(2.75)	.34	***	14.874	(3.53)	.49	***

Voting facilities						
Automatic registration	6.326	(3.33)	.22	-4.373	(5.49)	-.16
Number of polling days	-12.19	(3.49)	-.65 ***	.696	(6.03)	.04
Polling on rest day	7.201	(3.44)	.24 *	-8.947	(5.08)	-.30
Postal voting	1.226	(3.21)	.04	-5.436	(3.38)	-.20
Proxy voting	-11.55	(3.50)	-.40 **	5.603	(4.98)	.19
Special polling booths	1.070	(3.92)	.03	6.904	(3.11)	.23 *
Transfer voting	3.675	(3.34)	.13	5.037	(3.00)	.18
Advance voting	1.785	(3.44)	.06	-3.597	(3.13)	-.12
Number of elections	70		70		70	
Adjusted R2	**.339**	**(11.16)**	**.687**	**(7.68)**	**.735**	**(7.06)**

Vote/VAP is measured as the number of valid votes as a proportion of the voting-age population in seventy parliamentary and presidential national elections in twenty-five older democracies during the 1990s. The figures represent unstandardized regression coefficients, standard errors, standardized beta coefficients, and significance, with mean Vote/VAP as the dependent variable. * = p < .05 ** p < .01 *** p < .001.

Human development: Human Development Index 1998 combining literacy, education, and income, UNDP.

Level of democratization: Freedom House Index in the year of the election. Combined reversed fourteen-point scale of political rights and civic liberties. Freedom House, *www.freedomhouse.org*

Electoral system: See Table 4.2. Majoritarian/plurality (1), semi-proportional (2), PR (3).

Party system: See Table 4.3. Fragmented party system where the party in first place gets 30 percent of the vote or less.

Compulsory voting: See Table 4.4. All Voting Facilities: Coded Yes (1) No (0).

Source: Calculated from the International IDEA database *Voter Turnout from 1945 to 2000. www.idea.int.*

insignificant predictors of voter participation among this smaller group of postindustrial societies sharing similar levels of economic development and an established tradition of political rights and civil liberties.

Registration Processes

The facilities for registration and casting a ballot are commonly expected to affect turnout. The evidence that the registration process matters is most persuasive in comparisons of regulations that vary within the United States. Rosenstone and Wolfinger examined the difference in turnout between those states with the easiest registration requirements, for example, those such as North Dakota that allow registration at polling places on election day, and those with the strictest requirements. Their estimates suggest that if all American states had same-day registration, this would provide a one-time boost in turnout of about 5 to 9 percent.[44] Since their study in the 1970s, many states have experimented with easing the requirements, through initiatives like "motor voter" registration (where citizens can register to vote at the same time that they complete the form used for motor vehicle registration), with limited effects on voter participation.[45] Some states such as Oregon have also experimented with postal voting. The 1993 National Voter Registration Act requires all states to make voter registration available at motor vehicle bureaus, as well as by mail, and at various social service agencies, and it also forbids removing citizens from the rolls simply for not voting. Nevertheless, as the Florida case in the 2000 presidential contest vividly illustrated, the efficiency of the registration and voting procedure at state level can leave much to be desired. Studies suggest that easing voter registration processes has slightly improved American voter turnout, with a one-time bump when new processes are introduced, but that the impact is not uniform across the whole electorate; it has had the most impact in increasing participation among middle-class citizens.[46]

Yet the comparative evidence is less well established. Studies have long assumed that voluntary registration procedures, where citizens must apply to be eligible to vote, are an important reason why American turnout lags well behind many comparable democracies.[47] In countries with application processes, including the United States, France, and Australia, prospective voters must usually identify themselves before an election, sometimes many weeks in advance, by registering with a government agency. In other countries, the state takes the initiative in registering eligible citizens, through an annual census or similar mechanism. But what is the impact of this process? Katz compared the electoral regulations in thirty-one nations and found that nineteen used an automatic registration process, while twelve registered citizens by application.[48] The analysis of electoral participation based on this classification of countries suggests that the registration hurdles may be less important than is often assumed, since average Vote/VAP proved to be identical in the two types of system.[49] Contrary to the conventional wisdom, the results in Table 4.5 confirm that the use of automatic or voluntary registration procedures was unrelated to levels of turnout in established democracies.

Polling Facilities

In terms of other voting facilities, most countries hold their elections on a single day, usually on the weekend, which makes it easier for employed people to visit a polling station. In a few countries, however, elections are spread over more than one day; in India, for example, where there are more than 600 million voters and some 800 thousand polling stations, balloting takes place on a staggered basis during a month across the whole country. In addition, there are important variations in the use of absentee, overseas, postal, and advance ballots, proxy voting, and in whether polling stations are distributed widely throughout the community for groups who might otherwise have difficulty in getting to the polls, such as the population in residential homes for the elderly and hospitals, and military personnel posted overseas.[50] Franklin compared average turnout from 1960 to 1995 in parliamentary elections in twenty-nine countries and found that compulsory voting, Sunday voting, and postal voting facilities all proved to be important predictors, along with the proportionality of the electoral system, although not the number of days that polls were open.[51] Model A in Table 4.5 shows that after controlling for levels of development, only polling on a rest day provided a significant boost to turnout in established democracies; by contrast, the use of proxy voting and the number of days that the polling stations were open proved to be negatively associated, perhaps because countries concerned about low turnout try to increase the opportunities to get to the polls. Other special voting facilities all proved to be unrelated to turnout. Overall, the comparison of older democracies found that after controlling for levels of development, the role of voting facilities (in Model A) proved to explain far less variance in electoral participation than the role of institutions and legal rules (in Model B). The final equation in Model C included all of the structural and developmental factors, successfully explaining almost three-quarters of the variance in turnout among established democracies.

Conclusions: Structural Contexts and Voting Participation

Rational choice theories suggest that the primary incentives facing citizens in national elections may be understood as a product of the electoral *costs* of registering and voting, the party *choices* available to electors, and the degree to which casting a ballot determines the composition of parliament and government. The costs include the time and effort required to register and to vote, any legal sanctions imposed for failure to turn out, and the frequency with which electors are called to the polls. All other things being equal, among affluent societies we would expect that turnout would be higher in political systems that reduce the costs of voting, such as those with automatic processes for maintaining the electoral register, and electoral arrangements that maximize party competition but that also maintain a strong link between voters' preferences and the outcome for parliament, for government, and for the policy agenda.

The main findings in this chapter can be summarized as follows:

1. In multivariate models analyzing turnout in national elections around the world during the 1990s, after controlling for levels of human and political development, *political institutions and legal rules proved to be strongly and significantly associated with voter participation.*

2. In the worldwide comparison, all other things being equal, among the *political institutions* that matter, voting participation is likely to be maximized in elections using proportional representation, with small electoral districts, regular but relatively infrequent national contests, and moderately competitive party systems, and in presidential contests.

3. In terms of the *legal rules*, the worldwide comparison showed that voter participation tended to be lower in countries that had enfranchised women more recently and that employed literacy requirements, although the age of voting eligibility and the use of compulsory voting made no significant difference to turnout.

4. Although the comparison is limited to established democracies, the evidence shows that the broader context of *political institutions and legal rules influence turnout more strongly than specific voting facilities*, such as registration processes, transfer voting, and advance voting, all of which proved insignificant.

5. Lastly, in national elections held *in established democracies the use of compulsory voting regulations was an important indicator of higher turnout, whereas this was not found among the broader comparison of elections worldwide.* Although it cannot be proved here, the reasons for this difference probably concern the efficiency of the system of electoral registration and sanctions for nonvoting, as well as cultural traditions concerning obeying the law.

It is well established that even within particular political systems, some groups and individuals remain far more likely to participate than others. Some people may choose to vote under any circumstances, for largely affective reasons, such as a general sense of civic duty, or to express support for a party or cause without any hope of electoral gain, even if other instrumental citizens are motivated by the rational trade-off between electoral costs, electoral choices and electoral decisiveness. We therefore need to turn from the structural context to examine the motivation and resources that help to explain why some people have higher civic engagement than others.

5

Who Votes?

Institutional explanations focus on the structure of opportunities surrounding electoral turnout. Yet even within the same country there are often substantial gaps between rich and poor, young and old, as well as between college graduates and high school dropouts. Accounts based on structure, culture, and agency have commonly been offered to explain why people participate at the ballot box. *Structural* accounts stress social cleavages, such as those of age, gender, and class, which are closely related to civic resources such as time, money, knowledge, and skills. *Cultural* explanations emphasize the attitudes and values that people bring to the electoral process, including a sense of civic norms, political interest, and party identification. *Agency* accounts stress the role of mobilizing organizations such as get-out-the-vote drives and social networks generated by parties, trade unions, voluntary organizations, and community associations. In short, these explanations suggest that people don't participate because they can't, because they won't, or because nobody asked.

This chapter seeks to disentangle the relative importance of these factors in determining who votes. Evidence is drawn from the 1996 Role of Government III survey conducted in twenty-two countries by the International Social Survey Programme (ISSP). Given the importance of economic development and institutional contexts that has already been established, it is important to compare turnout in a wide variety of nations. The ISSP survey covers newer electoral democracies at different stages of the consolidation process, including the Czech Republic, Hungary, and the Russian Federation, as well as long-established democracies scattered across the globe, such as the United States, Japan, and Norway. The comparative framework includes presidential executive systems based on majoritarian elections, such as the United States and Russia; "Westminster" majoritarian parliamentary democracies such as Britain, Canada, and Australia; larger Western European states such as France, Spain, and Italy; and smaller welfare-state parliamentary democracies with consociational power-sharing arrangements, coalition cabinets, and proportional representation electoral systems, exemplified by Sweden and Norway. At the time of the survey, Bulgaria and Latvia had per capita GDP of less than $2,500, compared to Canada, Norway, and the United States, some of the richest nations around the world (UNDP 2000).

Equally important, the comparative framework includes leader and laggard countries in electoral participation. Turnout is measured as a proportion of the voting-age population that reported voting in the election prior to the survey in the mid-1990s. As shown in Table 5.1, turnout ranged from about 90 percent or more in New Zealand, Italy, Australia, and Israel down to less than two-thirds in Japan, the United States, and Poland. The reported levels of turnout measured by the ISSP survey were usually higher than the actual aggregate vote estimated by International IDEA, on average by about 6 percent. This is a well-known pattern. Studies in the United States, Britain, and Sweden have found that, probably out of a sense of what represents socially desirable behavior, the public usually overreports or exaggerates voting behavior, as revealed when survey responses of reported behavior are validated against the electoral register.[1] Recalled turnout is also prone to misremembering, since in some countries the ISSP survey was conducted two or three years after the previous general election, and people may have confused whether they had voted in national elections or in subsequent local, state, or regional contests. Yet there was a strong correlation ($r = 0.773$ p. < 0.001) between the reported and actual levels of turnout at the national level, which suggests that although there may be a systematic tendency to overreport, it is not clear that the public consistently exaggerates more in one country than in another.[2]

The series of multivariate models developed in Table 5.2 uses logistic regression to analyze voting turnout. Given the importance of levels of development and the institutional context in each country, established in previous chapters, Model A first enters these controls.[3] Model B then tests for the effects of *structural* variables, including income, education, and age. The pooled sample includes all countries, and then similar models are run with the results broken down by nation. Model C then adds two blocks of factors, the role of *mobilizing agencies*, such as union membership, and the effect of *cultural attitudes and values*, such as interest and efficacy. After including all of these factors, the overall level of variance explained by the model (shown by the R^2) rises from 10 percent to 34 percent. This suggests that the final model, incorporating institutional and individual-level variables, provides a more satisfactory explanation of voting turnout. Let us consider the reasons for these results and how these factors help to unlock the mystery of the simple decision to vote or not to vote.

Structural Accounts

The process of casting a ballot is one of the most common forms of political participation in democracies, and also one where the individual

TABLE 5.1. *Proportion of VAP who reported voting in the previous national election*

	Date of Prior Election	Date of f/w	Type of Election	Percent Vote/VAP ISSP 1996 (i)[a]	Percent Vote/VAP IDEA (ii)[b]	Difference (i) – (ii)
New Zealand	1996	Apr–Aug 1997	House of Rep.	93.3	83.0	+10.3
Italy	April 1996	Oct 1996	Camera dei Deputati	92.1	87.3	+4.8
Israel	May 1996	1996	Knesset	90.1	84.7	+5.4
Australia	March 1993	1996	House of Representatives	89.1	83.4	+5.7
Sweden	September 1994	Feb–May 1996	Riksdag	85.9	83.6	+2.3
Cyprus	1996	1996	Parliament	84.2	75.9	+8.3
Norway	Sept 1993	Feb–Mar 1996	Stortingsvalget	83.3	74.5	+8.8
Ireland	November 1992	1996	Dail	82.9	73.7	+9.2
Czech Republic	May 1996	Oct–Dec 1996	Sněmovna Poslanců	82.2	77.6	+4.6
Canada	October 1993	Nov–Dec 1996	House of Commons	80.9	63.9	+17.0
Britain	April 1992	May–Jul 1996	House of Commons	80.3	75.4	+4.9
Slovenia	Dec 1992	Dec 1995	Drzavni Zbor	80.3	85.5	–5.2
France	May 1995	Oct–Dec 1997	First ballot presidential	79.5	72.3	+7.2
Russia	1996	Apr 1997	Presidential	77.8	67.5	+10.3
Germany	October 1994	Mar–May 1996	Bundestag	77.3	72.4	+4.9
Bulgaria	April 1997	Feb–May 1997	Narodno Sobranie	74.8	81.0	–6.2
Latvia	1995	Sept 1996	Saeima	74.5	50.6	+23.9
Spain	June 1993	Jan 1996	Congress	74.4	76.8	–2.4
Hungary	May 1994	Oct 1996	National Assembly	68.0	68.3	+0.3
United States	Nov 1992	Feb–May 1996	Presidential	65.6	55.2	+10.4
Japan	July 1993	July 1996	Diet	65.1	66.2	–1.1
Poland	Sept 1997	Oct–Dec 1997	Sejm	53.6	52.0	+1.6
ALL				78.8	73.2	+5.6

[a] (i) = The proportion of the voting-age population (VAP) in each country who reported voting in the last national election prior to the survey.
[b] (ii) = the aggregate Vote/VAP as recorded by International IDEA.

Sources: Role of Government Survey III, 1996, International Social Science Program; International IDEA database *Voter Turnout from 1945 to 2000.* www.idea.int.

TABLE 5.2. *Models explaining turnout*

	Model A			Model B			Model C		
	B	(s.e.)	Sig.	B	(s.e.)	Sig.	B	(s.e.)	Sig.
Development									
Human development	9.940	(2.243)	***	16.599	(2.329)	***	29.593	(2.606)	***
Level of democratization	.347	(.057)	***	.555	(.060)	***	1.053	(.068)	***
Institutions									
Electoral system	-.017	(.158)		.148	(.036)	***	.212	(.040)	***
Population per MP	.000	(.000)	***	.000	(.000)	***	.000	(.000)	***
Frequency of national elections	-.006	(.053)		.095	(.055)		.363	(.062)	***
Length of women's enfranchisement	.009	(.002)	***	.004	(.002)	*	.003	(.002)	
Use of compulsory voting	2.234	(.149)	***	2.934	(.165)	***	2.239	(.166)	***
Legal voting age	-.342	(.062)	***	-.570	(.066)	***	-.605	(.071)	***
Party system	.447	(.439)		-1.357	(.477)	**	-2.962	(.517)	***
Structure									
Age (*logged years*)				4.272	(.140)	***	3.968	(.151)	***
Gender (*male = 1*)				.040	(.044)		-.161	(.049)	***
Education (*seven-point scale*)				.295	(.019)	***	.203	(.021)	***
Income (*household income*)				.000	(.000)	***	.000	(.000)	***

	Model 1	Model 2	Model 3	
Agency				
Union membership (*1 = member*)			.559	(.064) ***
Religiosity (*six-point scale of church attendance*)			.056	(.015) ***
Party affiliation (*1 = yes*)			1.693	(.054) ***
Culture				
Political interest (*five-point scale*)			.257	(.026) ***
Internal political efficacy (*ten-point scale*)			.077	(.014) ***
Political trust (*ten-point scale*)			.038	(.013) **
Constant	−3.294	−11.668	−24.079	
Nagelkerke R²	.099	.200	.339	

Note: The table lists unstandardized logistic regression coefficients, standard errors, and significance, with reported voting turnout as the dependent variable in twenty-two nations (N = 16,353). * p < .05, ** p < .01, *** p < .001

Human development: Human Development Index: *Human Development Report 2000.* New York: United Nations Development Program.

Level of democratization: Mean Freedom House Index of political rights and civil liberties, 1996. *www.freedomhouse.org.*

Electoral system: See Table 4.2. Majoritarian/plurality (1), semiproportional (2), PR (3).

Party system: See Table 4.3. Logged percentage vote for the party in first place.

Compulsory voting: See Table 4.4. Yes(1), No (0).

Frequency of national elections: Mean number of national elections (parliamentary and presidential) in the 1990s.

Length of women's enfranchisement: Years.

Legal voting age: Age qualified to vote.

Structural factors and mobilizing agencies: See Table 5.4.

Cultural attitudes: See Table 5.5.

Source: Role of Government III survey, International Social Survey Program 1996.

benefits are minimal but the collective outcome is important in determining the outcome for party government and in communicating voter preferences to leaders. The act of voting typically makes fairly modest, although not negligible, demands on citizens. In electoral democracies, the most important include gathering and processing the information required to make a choice from among competing parties, multiple offices, and issue referenda listed on the ballot, as well as the time and effort required to establish the location of the polling place and to get to the polls on election day.

The costs of voting can vary substantially based on institutional factors such as the frequency of elections, the levels of office, and the number of choices on the ballot, as well as the availability and complexity of information sources available via the mass media.[4] Voting can make relatively few demands: For example, in postwar British general elections, held every few years, most citizens faced a relatively simple choice between the two or three parliamentary candidates representing the main parties competing in their constituency, with information provided via the partisan-leaning national press, and beyond this there were only local elections. By contrast, today British citizens face far more elections (at regional and European levels, as well as occasional referendum campaigns), a choice of candidates from far more parties, and a slightly more complex voting process (with different electoral systems operating for bodies like the European Parliament, the Scottish Parliament, and the House of Commons).[5] Americans commonly face far greater demands than most Europeans due to the sheer number and frequency of U.S. primary and general elections (for presidential, congressional, gubernatorial, state, municipal, and judicial offices), multiple referenda and ballot initiatives in states like California, the rise of the "permanent campaign," as well as relatively weak partisan cues guiding choices in many candidate-centered races, with information conveyed by the news media fragmented into a multichannel environment and a largely metropolitan press.[6] Voters face even more complex electoral choices in newer democracies such as Russia, where multiple personalist parties are often weakly institutionalized, with few clear programmatic differences. Members of the Duma often switch allegiances, partisan identification is largely absent, the public strongly mistrusts politicians, and information conveyed by television news is rarely balanced.[7]

Structural explanations emphasize that social and demographic inequalities – based on educational qualifications, socioeconomic status, gender, and age – lead to inequalities in other civic assets, such as skills, knowledge, experience, time, and money. Possession of these assets makes some better placed than others to take advantage of the opportunities for participation. Resources are perhaps most obviously useful in fostering more demanding forms of activism, exemplified by the value of social networks in campaign fund raising, the need for leisure time to volunteer in a community association, the asset of a flexible career for the pursuit of elected office, the advantages of communication skills in producing the local party newsletter, and the organizational abilities that help to mobilize social movements. But these resources can prove important in voting turnout as well.

Age

Age, one of the most fundamental predictors of political participation, has long been found to influence electoral turnout as well as patterns of party membership, involvement in voluntary organizations, and engagement in group activity. The most thorough study of generational trends in the United States, by Miller and Shanks, emphasizes that a long-term secular trend has generated turnout decline, with the post–New Deal generation consistently less likely to vote than their parents or grandparents. This phenomenon was not a product of life cycle or aging, they suggest, but rather represents an enduring shift among the generation who first came to political consciousness during the turbulent politics of the 1960s. The long-term slide in American turnout, they suggest, can be attributed to the process of generational replacement, not to a fall in the propensity of the older generations to turn out.[8] More recently, Bob Putnam has presented a formidable battery of evidence illustrating lower levels of civic engagement among the postwar generation, including electoral participation.[9] Yet it is not clear whether this pattern is peculiar to the United States, or if similar developments are evident elsewhere. The most thorough comparative study, by Richard Topf, compared the propensity to vote by birth cohort across sixteen Western Europe nations from the 1960s to the early 1990s. The results confirmed that younger Europeans were consistently less likely to cast a ballot than older cohorts. Nevertheless, it is not clear whether this is a generational or a life-cycle effect, since Topf established that this generation gap was already evident in the earliest available surveys for the 1960–5 period, and that the size of the gap had not expanded over time. In Western Europe, it could be that the pattern reflects life-cycle experiences, as younger people settle down in a community, buy homes, start families, and establish clearer partisan identities over successive elections, rather than distinct generational experiences that affected the civic attitudes of those growing up during the Depression years of the interwar era or during the affluent 1950s and 1960s.[10] A more recent report comparing youth turnout in fifteen Western European states, by International IDEA, found that electoral participation was usually lowest among those under thirty, but this pattern did vary substantially by nation. The generation gap proved to be minimal in Belgium and Italy (which use compulsory voting) and in Sweden, and highest in Ireland, France, Finland, and Portugal.[11]

To explore this further, turnout in the pooled sample was broken down by age group. The overall pattern proved to be curvilinear, with a sharp

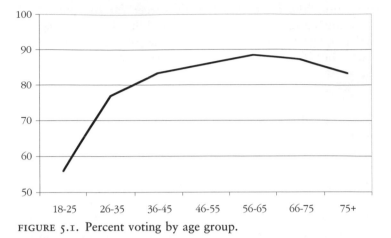

FIGURE 5.1. Percent voting by age group.

rise in participation among those under thirty, a plateau evident among the
late middle-aged, and a slight fall again among the elderly (see Figure 5.1).
Given this curvilinear pattern, logged age was entered into the models, and
the results of the regression analysis in Table 5.2 confirm that logged age
was significant, even with the standard controls; indeed, age proved to be
one of the strongest predictors of turnout in the study. Moreover, when the
pooled sample was broken down, this pattern was found in every nation
except one (Australia, with compulsory voting). In general, just 55 percent
of those under twenty-five voted, compared to 88 percent of the late middle-
aged, by far the largest participation gap found for any demographic or
social group in the study.

Gender

The earliest studies of voting behavior in Western Europe and North
America established that gender was one of the standard demographic and
social characteristics used to predict levels of civic engagement, political
activism, and electoral turnout, alongside age and education.[12] In the late
1970s, Verba, Nie, and Kim concluded: "In all societies for which we have
data, sex is related to political activity; men are more active than women."
The study established that these gender differences persisted as significant
even after controlling for levels of education, institutional affiliations such
as trade union membership, and psychological involvement in politics.[13] In
recent decades, however, the orthodox view that women are less active
has been challenged. More recent studies by Christy and others have found
that traditional gender differences in voting participation diminished during
the 1980s and 1990s, or even reversed, in many advanced industrialized
countries.[14] In the United States, for example, in every presidential election

since 1980 the proportion of eligible female adults who voted has exceeded the proportion of eligible male adults who voted, and the same phenomenon is found in nonpresidential midterm elections since 1986.[15] Evidence suggests that by the mid-1990s the traditional gender gap in electoral turnout had become insignificant in many postindustrial societies, although there were still fewer women than men participating in postcommunist societies.[16]

The results in Table 5.2 show that when entered in Model B using the pooled sample, gender failed to prove a significant predictor of electoral participation. A similar pattern was replicated when the pooled sample was broken down by country. Overall, 79 percent of men reported voting compared to 78 percent of women. However, gender did became significantly associated with turnout when interacting with mobilizing agencies and cultural attitudes in Model C. This pattern suggests that, in many societies, long-term secular trends in social norms and in structural lifestyles, fuelled by generational change, may have contributed to removing many factors that had inhibited women's voting participation in the past; but there are complex interaction effects at work here. Women, especially among the older generation, continue to prove slightly less interested in conventional politics than men, as well as being less likely to join trade unions, although they are more faithful in church attendance. It is these crosscutting secondary characteristics that explain any residual effects of gender on turnout, rather than gender alone.

Socioeconomic Status
Many studies have found that socioeconomic inequalities are among the strongest predictors of individual turnout. In one of the earliest studies in the 1950s, Seymour Lipset noted that income, education, and occupational class were closely associated with voting turnout in many countries.[17] Education is widely believed to facilitate the acquisition of civic skills, competencies, and knowledge that lead to political participation. Education is thought to furnish citizens with a wide variety of assets that may be useful in politics, as in life, such as the cognitive skills to make sense of current events in the mass media, the verbal and written skills essential to political communication, and the basic understanding of civics and public affairs that facilitates further campaign learning. Educational attainment is strongly related to subsequent socioeconomic inequalities in the workforce. Professional and managerial careers bring higher financial rewards, more flexible control of time, and more leisure hours, all of which can contribute to civic engagement.

The evidence that education, income, and class matter for turnout is most extensive in the United States. Research by Verba and Nie, as well as by Wolfinger and Rosenstone, has demonstrated that socioeconomic status, measured by a combination of education, occupation, and income, strongly fostered voting in American campaigns.[18] Teixeira found that turnout gaps by education and occupational class had widened in the United States from the 1960s to the late 1980s.[19] The most recent research by Verba, Schlozman, and Brady confirms that the turnout disparities by income have not faded over time: Half of those Americans with family incomes under $15,000 cast a ballot, compared to 86 percent of those with incomes of $75,000 and over.[20] Yet it is not clear whether these inequalities necessarily function in the same way in other countries. Verba, Nie, and Kim's classic seven-nation study established that disparities in participation by socioeconomic status were stronger in the United States than in most of the other societies under comparison. Moreover, the study found that differences of wealth and education helped to predict activities such as political discussion and interest far more than voting turnout; Verba and his colleagues attribute this pattern to the strong impact of institutional constraints and mobilizing agencies on electoral participation.[21] Bingham Powell's cross-national research also found that educational attainment exerted an effect on turnout that was far stronger in the United States than in the eight other postindustrial nations under comparison. One reason for this, suggested by Verba, Nie, and Kim and by Bingham Powell, is that the relationship between class and voting may be conditioned by the role of parties and voluntary organizations in mobilizing groups of supporters: "Group-based forces embodied in institutions such as parties and organizations can modify the participation patterns that one would have if only individual forces were operating."[22] Piven and Cloward present perhaps the strongest argument that if American parties were to target policy initiatives and get-out-the-vote drives toward poorer inner-city neighborhoods and ethnic minorities, then voters would respond.[23] Subsequent research has tended to confirm the conclusion that patterns in the United States differ from those in other mature democracies, where long-established social democratic and labor parties, founded by the trade union movement at the turn of the century, organize and mobilize working-class communities. The United States is, after all, exceptional in lacking a major socialist party of the left, as well as a strong movement for organized labor. In Britain, Heath and Taylor found that the indicators of social class, housing tenure, and education had only a limited association with turnout, and that the context of the election proved more significant, particularly the closeness of the race.[24] The most detailed study of turnout in the EU member states, by Richard Topf, established that from the 1960s to the early 1990s, educational attainment had a minimal effect upon voting turnout: "In general, West European citizens of low and high levels of education are equally likely to vote in national elections."[25]

So how far do educational inequalities predict voting behavior outside of the United States? The initial results of the regression analysis in Table 5.2 show that education was significant across the pooled sample of twenty-two nations, even after controlling for general levels of development and the institutional context. If the highest and lowest levels of educational attainment are compared, turnout proved to be 10 percent lower for those with minimal educational attainment (those who failed to complete primary school) than for college graduates (see Table 5.3). Yet when this pooled sample was broken down by country, running logistic regression models, the impact of education proved significant in just under half of the nations under comparison, including the United States, Japan, Norway, Ireland, and Cyprus, and in four postcommunist societies (Russia, Poland, Hungary, and the Czech Republic) (see Table 5.4). Yet, as Topf established earlier, education failed to predict turnout throughout most of Western Europe. In many postindustrial societies such as France, Sweden, and Britain, once basic levels of literacy and schooling become ubiquitous throughout society, education fails to influence voting turnout. The pattern among newer democracies in Central and Eastern Europe may be attributable to the failure of the reconstructed communist parties to mobilize their base during the elections of the mid-1990s, as well as to disillusionment among poorer sectors of the population who lost out in the early stages of the transition toward democracy.[26] It remains to be seen whether this pattern will continue in subsequent elections in the region.

Structural explanations suggest that the main reason why social and demographic inequalities are important for turnout is that they lead to differentials in civic assets such as skills, experience, time, and financial resources. Money – measured by household income – plays a *direct* role in certain types of campaign activities, such as cash donations to candidates, parties, and issue causes. The unequal distribution of financial resources throughout society helps to explain inequalities commonly found in political participation. Moreover, the role of money in politics may have increased in recent decades. Many observers have pointed to the shift away from traditional toward modern and postmodern campaigns, with the decline in voluntary labor drawn from the party membership and the growth of full-time professional "hired guns" such as pollsters, campaign managers, and press officers, along with a reliance on mediated channels rather than on face-to-face doorstep campaigning.[27] It is generally believed that this development has increased the costs of electioneering, and the U.S. is widely said to exemplify this trend, although systematic evidence supporting this proposition across many countries is hard to establish.[28] Yet irrespective of organizational developments, at the individual level the resources of money, such as levels of household income, are unlikely to have a strong *direct* effect on the propensity to turn out. In any well-administered process, with multiple points of access, the financial expense of traveling to the polling place is usually minimal. But household income can be expected to influence turnout *indirectly* in an important way, as an important indicator of socioeconomic status. The regression results of the

TABLE 5.3. *Social background and turnout*

	Percent Voting	Voting Gap, Lowest to Highest	Sig.
Age group			
18–25	55.1		
26–35	75.6		
36–45	82.2		
46–55	84.4		
56–65	87.5		
66–75	86.7		
76+	83.1	32.4	***
Gender			
Men	79.3		
Women	78.4	0.9	
Income			
Highest quintile	84.4		
Lowest quintile	74.8	9.6	***
Education			
Lowest: incomplete primary	76.5		
Primary	76.4		
Secondary incomplete	78.5		
Secondary completed	77.1		
Semi-higher	81.0		
Highest: University graduate	86.0	9.5	***
Work status			
FT employment	79.9		
PT employment	82.7		
Unemployed	66.4		
Student	54.0		
Looking after the home	80.1		
Retired	85.0		
Social class			
Working	75.3		
Middle	85.3	10.0	***
Trade Union			
Member	86.3		
Nonmember	77.1	9.2	***
Religiosity			
Never attend religious services	77.5		
Church once a week	82.4	4.9	***
All	78.8		

Note: The figures represent the proportion who reported voting in each social group, without any controls. Social class is defined by the respondent's occupation. The significance of group differences is measured by ANOVA. $^*p < .05$, $^{**}p < .01$, $^{***}p < .001$.

Source: International Social Science Program: Beliefs in Government Survey 1996 (N = 26,852).

TABLE 5.4. *Social background and turnout by nation*

	Age (logged)	Gender	Education	Income	Nagelkerke R²
United States	***		***		.242
Slovenia	***				.221
Cyprus	***		*	*	.218
Canada	***				.206
Hungary	***		***	*	.189
Japan	***		**		.163
Russia	***		***	***	.159
Poland	***		***	***	.158
Britain	***				.151
New Zealand	***	*		**	.145
Germany	***			***	.131
Norway	***		**	**	.125
Australia				*	.110
Sweden	**			***	.105
Czech Republic	**		*		.083
Ireland	***		*		.076
France	***				.072
Bulgaria	***	*			.047

Note: Logistic regression models were run in each country, including logged age (in years), gender (male = 1, female = 0), education (seven-point scale), and income (continuous scale), with reported turnout as the dependent variable. For details of the codings, see Table 5.3. This table shows just the significance of the logistic regression coefficients in each country. The overall fit of the model, showing the strength of the social factors on turnout, is summarized by the Nagelkerke R² (N = 14,437). $*p < .05$, $**p < .01$, $***p < .001$.

Source: Role of Government III survey, International Social Survey Program, 1996.

pooled sample in Table 5.2 confirm that family income was significantly related to turnout, even with the usual prior controls. Overall, 84 percent of those falling into the top quintile of family income voted, compared to 75 percent of those in the bottom quintile. The size of the gap mirrored exactly that found for social class, when respondents were classified by their occupational status. When broken down by nation, income differentials proved significant for electoral participation in about half of the nations under comparison, including some of the older democracies, such as Australia and Norway, as well as the newer democracies, such as Russia and Poland.

Another resource related to occupational status is leisure time, which is regarded as a particularly valuable asset for traditional forms of campaigning, including attending local party meetings, volunteering to help canvass or deliver leaflets, and persuading others how to vote, as well as following the election more passively in the mass media and turning out to vote on polling day. Certain institutional contexts can reduce the role of time: namely, how many days and hours the polling stations are open, whether polling is held on a rest day or a work day, and the availability of alternative ways to cast a ballot, such as postal voting. Ipso facto, the less demanding the conditions, the less the time factor functions as a constraint. As shown earlier in Chapter 4, aggregate turnout was affected by holding the election on a rest day and the availability of proxy voting. In terms of micro-level explanations, time is a resource that is relatively evenly distributed across the population, although certain groups generally have more leisure hours and flexibility in their use of time than others, namely the population that is not constrained by full-time employment. Table 5.3 confirms that there was indeed slightly higher-than-average turnout among part-time workers, the retired, and those looking after the home, although the pattern had complex crosscutting cleavages, because turnout was extremely low among the unemployed and students. More direct measures of available leisure hours are necessary in order to examine this further, and to explore the role of time resources on participation in different nations. Therefore, of the structural variables, age provides the strongest predictor of who votes in almost all nations, while education and income also proved to be significant in the pooled models, although not in every country under comparison.

Agency Accounts

In addition, the organizational perspective has long stressed the role of *mobilizing agencies*. Rosenstone and Hansen emphasize the electoral functions of party and candidate organizations, group networks such as churches, voluntary associations, and trade unions, social networks of families, friends, and colleagues, and the role of the news media.[29] Putnam has argued that the decline of dense networks of local associations and community organizations has reduced social capital and contributed to a long-term erosion of American turnout among the postwar generation.[30] Verba found that churches and voluntary organizations provide networks of recruitment, so that those drawn into the political process through these associations develop the organizational and communication skills that facilitate further activity.[31] In the United States, studies by both Aldrich and Wattenberg suggest that the decline of party organizations, and their replacement by entrepreneurial candidates, have been critical to this process.[32] Studies by Leighley and others have argued that the main reason for socioeconomic disparities in turnout is that poorer groups are often demobilized by lack of electoral competition in the American party system.[33] Powell has also suggested that the relationships between socioeconomic characteristics and electoral participation are not automatic; instead, they are largely conditioned by the linkages between social groups and parties. Where the working class is strongly mobilized by parties of the left, they may turnout at levels similar to those of middle-class populations.[34]

More direct evidence for the role of mobilizing agencies will be considered in subsequent chapters, when we examine the role of activism and membership in parties and groups in greater depth, but in this analysis we can provide a more limited test of the effects on turnout of union membership, religiosity (how often people attended church services), and party identification (how close people felt to a party). This does not tell us what these organizations do, for example, how actively union organizers and church leaders mobilize their members during election campaigns. Nor can we disentangle reciprocal patterns of causality from the available cross-sectional survey evidence – whether people who join these organizations are civic-minded and may also have a propensity to cast a ballot, or whether membership in these organizations helps to foster community networks, social contacts, and social trust that encourage broader aspects of electoral participation. Nevertheless, the survey evidence provides at least some limited insight into the strength of the association between mobilizing agencies and electoral turnout.

The result of the pooled analysis in Table 5.2 confirms the significance of linkages with mobilizing agencies, even with the standard controls. In general, 86 percent of those who belonged to trade unions voted, compared to 77 percent of nonmembers. There was also slightly higher-than-average turnout among the most regular churchgoers (82 percent) compared to those who never attended religious services (77 percent). But, not surprisingly, party identification provided the strongest association with electoral participation:[35] Eighty-seven percent of those who could name a party affiliation voted, compared to 56 percent of those who could not. The size of the participation gap was rivaled only by that produced by age. When broken down by type of party, those who supported parties of the far left proved to be slightly more strongly motivated to vote in the countries under comparison, although the difference across party types was not substantial. Subsequent chapters will consider the role of mobilizing agencies in stimulating political participation more generally and, in particular, the profile of party members and activists.

Cultural Accounts

Ever since Almond and Verba's *Civic Culture* (1963), studies have stressed the importance of political attitudes and values learned through the early socialization process.[36] These have been conceptualized and measured in many ways: Almond and Verba emphasized the role of subjective competence; Barnes and Kaase used political efficacy to explain protest activism; while many others have stressed the role of political interest.[37] More diffuse support for the political system has also been thought to be related to political participation.[38] Political cynicism, lack of trust and confidence in government, has been regarded as one plausible factor depressing activism. Since the rising tide of political cynicism in the United States occurred during roughly the same period as the fall in turnout, these trends are commonly linked by popular commentators. Nevertheless, systematic analysis has failed to establish a causal connection at the individual level between feelings of political trust and electoral turnout in the United States.[39] Indeed, contrary to the conventional wisdom, the most thorough study of participation in Britain found that the most cynical were actually more politically engaged than the average citizen across a range of activities, including voting.[40] Much commentary assumes that if people don't have confidence in the core institutions of representative democracy, such as parliaments and the legal system, they will be reluctant to participate in the democratic process, producing apathy. But it is equally plausible to assume that alienation from representative democracy could mobilize citizens, if people are stimulated to express their disaffection, throw out officeholders, and seek institutional redress.[41]

The result of Model C, entering the cultural variables into the regression model, with the standard controls, confirms the close association between political interest and turnout. Overall, 91 percent of those who were "very interested" in politics cast a ballot, compared to 58 percent of those who were uninterested (see Table 5.5). Being stimulated and motivated to follow current events is related to willingness to take a more active role. Moreover, the political efficacy scale, measuring the degree to which people felt they were well informed about public affairs and were competent to participate, was also significant, suggesting that education may play an indirect role by boosting confidence. The more limited indicators of political trust were also significant, although more weakly linked to participation. Initial models also tested the effects of general satisfaction with democracy, but this proved insignificant and was dropped from the analysis. The analysis suggests that even after controlling for prior institutional, structural, and agency factors, cultural attitudes remain important in motivating people to get to the polls, but of these political interest is the most strongly related to turnout.

Conclusions

While the institutional context set by electoral laws and voting procedures is clearly important in determining some of the major cross-national variations in electoral participation, individual-level factors remain important in explaining who votes within particular societies. The main findings in this chapter can be summarized as follows.

TABLE 5.5. *Political attitudes and turnout*

	Percent Voting	Voting Gap, Lowest to Highest	Sig.
Party identification			
Party affiliation	87.3		
No party affiliation	56.3	31.0	***
Party support			
Far left	90.7		
Center left	88.6		
Center, liberal	82.4		
Right, conservative	88.8		
Far right	85.3		***
Political interest			
Very interested	91.2		
Not at all interested	57.9	33.3	***
Political trust scale			
Elections make government pay attention			
Strongly agree	84.9		
Strongly disagree	67.2	17.7	***
Politicians try to keep their election promises			
Strongly agree	78.3		
Strongly disagree	77.0	1.3	
Political efficacy scale			
Understanding of issues			
Strongly agree	87.9		
Strongly disagree	60.3	27.6	***
Information about politics and government			
Strongly disagree	84.4		
Strongly disagree	69.7	15.1	***
All	78.8		

Note: The figures represent the proportion in each group who reported voting. The significance of group differences are measured by ANOVA. $^* p < .05$, $^{**} p < .01$, $^{***} p < .001$ Respondents were asked to express agreement or disagreement on a five-point scale with the following statements:
Political trust scale:
"*Elections are a good way of making government pay attention to what people think.*"
"*People we elect as politicians try to keep the promises they made during the election.*"
Political efficacy scale:
"*I feel that I have a pretty good understanding of the important political issues facing the country.*"
"*I think most people are better informed about politics and government than I am.*" (reversed)
Source: International Social Science Program: Beliefs in Government Survey 1996 (N = 26,852).

1. Even after controlling for levels of development and the institutional context, *structure, agency, and culture still played an important role in predicting micro-level turnout.*

2. Among the structural factors, *age provided the strongest predictor of who votes,* in a curvilinear pattern. The youngest cohorts were by far the least likely to vote, and the late middle-aged were most engaged. Moreover, the age profile of voters was evident in every country except for Australia, which uses compulsory voting.

3. In addition, *education and income also proved to be significant in the pooled model,* although when broken down by country there differentials proved to be important only in about half of the nations considered.

4. *Gender displays a more complex pattern,* since by itself it is no longer significantly related to turnout in the pooled model, but it becomes significant when interacting with other factors such as political interest and union membership.

5. *Agency explanations were further confirmed, with union membership, church attendance, and party identification all associated with turnout,* as expected. Chapter 9 considers the reasons for this pattern in more depth.

6. Lastly, *cultural attitudes and values also proved important,* particularly political interest, which was closely associated with turnout, even with prior controls.

While this furthers our understanding of macro and micro explanations of turnout, it remains an open question at this stage how far we can generalize from these patterns to other types of political participation. In a long series of studies, Verba and his colleagues have argued persuasively that various forms of activism make different demands on skills, money, and time, so that political participation can best be understood as a multidimensional phenomenon.[42] That is, people who vote are not necessarily involved in other dimensions, such as party work and community activism. Turnout is different from other activities, such as regularly donating money to campaigns, organizing demonstrations, mobilizing on the Internet, and contacting elected representatives. There are different costs and benefits associated with different dimensions of participation. Based on the findings in this chapter, we therefore need to go further in order to understand more fully activism in parties and civic societies, how this in turn affects electoral turnout, and the multiple channels of participation beyond the simple act of voting.

PART II

POLITICAL PARTIES

6

Mapping Party Activism

Parties serve multiple functions: simplifying and structuring electoral choices; organizing and mobilizing campaigns; articulating and aggregating disparate interests; channeling communication, consultation, and debate; training, recruiting, and selecting candidates; structuring parliamentary divisions; acting as policy think tanks; and organizing government. Not only are parties one of the main conduits of political participation, they also serve to boost and strengthen electoral turnout. If mass membership is under threat, as many suspect, this could have serious implications for representative democracy. The first part of this chapter outlines theories of how party organizations respond to changes in their electoral environment and considers the implications that flow from this understanding. The chapter then looks at evidence for trends and patterns of party membership in the 1990s, comparing estimates based on official party records in the United States and Europe to survey data for fifty-nine countries from the World Values Study. On this basis, Chapter 7 goes on to examine the reasons why people join parties, based on the factors considered in earlier chapters, including the impact of societal modernization and political institutions at the national level, and the role of structure, agency, and culture in drawing individual citizens into public life.

Theories of Party Organization Change

In order to understand their role and functions, following the convention established by V. O. Key, parties can be divided into three hierarchical components: parties-in-elected-office, parties-as-organizations, and parties-in-the-electorate.[1] Parties continue as vital sinews connecting the organs of government, particularly binding together the executive and legislature.[2] Yet many suggest that accumulating indications of partisan decay are becoming clear elsewhere.[3] Throughout established democracies there is now overwhelming evidence of a glacial erosion of partisan identification in the electorate, not covered by this study, which has reduced the proportion of habitual loyalists in the electorate who support their party come rain or shine.[4] In addition, there is growing evidence that parties in established democracies face contracting membership rolls, which is considered to be an indirect indicator of eroding activism.[5] If so, the typical party organization may be weakening at the middle level, limiting opportunities for political participation, undermining civic society, and lessening the accountability of leaders to followers.

Historical and institutional accounts suggest that many specific factors may affect this process of party organizational change. For example, studies examining the radical overhaul and modernization of the British Labour party during the 1990s point to their experience of repeated electoral defeats, the selection of party leaders committed to reform, such as Smith, Kinnock, and Blair, and the party's internal power balance.[6] In other countries, specific crises such as the corruption scandals in Italy and Japan during the early 1990s have triggered the collapse of the party system, and a major overhaul of the party machinery for those surviving the fallout. American parties were transformed during the post-Watergate early 1970s by legal reforms governing campaign funding and the wider use of state primaries for candidate selection.[7] In this view, particular circumstances explain different party organizational structures within any country; Panebianco suggests that the historical conditions of its birth often stamp a particular organizational structure on a party, and there can be a time lag as institutions respond slowly to changes in their environment.[8] Today, Christian Democrats and Social Democrats, Greens and Facists, Labour and Conservative Parties continue to bear the imprint of their origins. By contrast, modernization theories and sociological explanations give greater emphasis to long-term secular trends in the underlying social structure, notably the erosion of the working-class and trade union base for parties of the left, and how far parties respond strategically to these developments.[9] In this view, while particular events may be important in specific cases, the more general catalysts underlying structural change relate primarily to the linkage functions that party members perform in connecting leaders with the electorate.[10] Party organizations gradually react to the broader changing circumstances of election campaigns and, in particular, the primary function of party members as channels of political communication connecting citizens and their elected representatives.

Mass-Branch Party Organizations in Older Democracies
In the postwar era, Duverger described the classic ideal of mass-branch parties: parliamentary leaders were based on a larger circle of engaged grassroots membership and an even broader base of loyal voting supporters.[11] This extra-parliamentary structure had evolved in Western Europe with the expansion of the franchise; more and more electors needed to be

contacted in traditional campaigns, well beyond the number who could be reached via the poll book lists maintained by electoral agents and individual candidates. Labor-intensive socialist parties lacking financial resources, exemplified by the German SPD, relied on volunteer networks of community supporters for contacting and mobilizing voters during election campaigns. In return for their work, the structure provided members with opportunities for direct involvement in internal debates about party policies and principles at local and regional levels, culminating in regular national conventions. Collective decisions eventually became embodied in a manifesto that set out the official party platform and bound the hands of government. Moreover, where local channels of recruitment prevailed, candidates for elected office were selected by, and thereby accountable to, party members, and ultimately to constituents. In this model, the role of activist foot soldiers was to carry out the hum-drum local party work: attending branch and regional meetings, donating money, signing petitions, passing motions, acting as local officers and campaign organizers, displaying window posters and yard signs, helping with door-to-door canvassing and leafleting, training and selecting candidates for office, attending the national party convention, and assisting with community fund-raising events – in short, making tea and licking envelopes. The motivation for getting involved in party work has been explained as the product of three types of reward: *ideological* incentives (the achievement of gaining collective goals and giving expression to deeply held beliefs), *outcome* incentives (the rewards that come from achieving certain personal goals, such as expanding social networks, getting a patronage job, or becoming an elected representative), and *process* incentives (derived from the inherent interest and stimulus of being politically active).[12] Of these, mass parties are heavily dependent upon the ideological rewards that come from working together to achieve certain common principles and ideals.

Not all parties, by any means, met this model, even in postwar Western Europe, although Duverger believed that this model would gradually spread through "contagion of the left." By contrast, Duverger also described other types of party organization, including "caucus-cadre" models of shifting "top-down" parliamentary factions, with leaders selected by smaller circles of acolytes, local notables, and financial backers, with a minimal role for a wider membership and formal organizational structure.[13] Caucus-cadre organizations are essentially based on political elites, usually created within parliament. The United States has moved from caucus-cadre party machines toward direct primary elections for candidate selection, bypassing any substantial and ongoing policy role for party members.[14] Duverger also identified militia structures adopted by extreme right-wing parties during the interwar years and by the communists, characterized by a hierarchical top-down command structure with supporters enrolled upon military lines. Nevertheless, the model of the mass-branch party has proved to be a widely influential ideal type, and in this context declining party membership within democratic societies has commonly been regarded as prima facia evidence of an erosion of the channels of political participation.[15] Proponents argue that this type of organization facilitates internal party democracy, encourages stability and continuity, since loyalty is directed toward the broader organization rather than to particular leaders, and promotes linkages between civic society and the state, particularly thick networks among voters, local activists, parliamentary representatives, and party leaders in government.

Understood in this way, the mass-branch party model can be seen as an appropriate organization for the age of "traditional" face-to-face campaigns. Because of institutional inertia, residual organizational structures often persist well after their original functions disappear. The initial structure creates institutional "stakeholders" who are interested in preserving the status quo. But theories of political communication suggest that this structure, and the role of party members in particular, may have become outdated during the era from roughly the mid-1950s to the early 1990s, which was characterized by the rise of "modern" campaigns in established democracies.[16] Just as Bagehot distinguished between the "dignified" and the "efficient" parts of the British constitution,[17] so in the modern campaign, members may have become more part of the "symbolic" than the "effective" channels of party communication. This does not mean that local activists have become irrelevant to fund raising, mobilizing supporters, and generating turnout in local campaigns, as they still play a role, but simply that this has gradually become less significant than it was during the traditional era prior to television.[18] Many accounts have described how Western European parties evolved from the 1950s onward toward an organization less reliant upon volunteer grassroots activists and the wider circle of loyal lifetime supporters in the electorate, and more dependent upon television for communication, state subsidies for resources, and paid professionals for advice.[19] Argument continues to surround the best way to describe this organizational structure; in the 1960s, Kirchheimer saw this trend as the growth of the "catch-all" party that abandoned its ideological anchors in helter-skelter pursuit of electoral gain.[20] Epstein, influenced by the loose decentralized structure of American parties, characterized the key developments as the rise of the "electoral-professional" party.[21] More recent work by Katz and Mair has depicted the most important developments as the rise of the "cartel" party that derives its financial resources and related services from the public purse, with the spoils divided among those parties already in parliament.[22] In the light of changes in campaigning, Duverger's ideal of the mass-branch party dependent upon a volunteer "tea-and-envelope" brigade may be limited to characterizing, and perhaps romanticizing, a particular organizational structure evident in Western European and in older democracies shaped by its culture, such as Australia and New Zealand, during a period running roughly from the expansion of the franchise and the growth of social democratic and labor parties at the turn of the century, to the rise of the television age in the mid to late 1950s.[23]

For proponents of the mass-branch party structure, if there are low and declining levels of party membership and activism in older democracies, this could seriously reduce civic engagement. If parties today have shrinking membership rolls, *and* if parties provide minimal opportunities for those who do join to shape party policy and to select party leaders, this limits the role of these organizations as channels of conventional political participation. Moreover, if parties have weakened as institutions this also reduces their other functions: mobilizing agencies in civic society, simplifying electoral choices, and boosting turnout. This may prove particularly problematic for social equality if left-wing parties are no longer capable of activating and channeling the political energies of poorer groups and peripheral communities already at the margins of power. Party efforts to contact, persuade, and mobilize voters can have considerable effect on turnout in local, state, and national elections, particularly for social groups otherwise least likely to participate, by fostering social connections and providing electoral information.[24] Representative democracy without parties is unthinkable, and representative democracy with minimal party membership is clearly weakened in certain important respects.

Party Organizations in Newer Democracies

The literature has been heavily influenced by the experience of Western European and Anglo-American older democracies, where the historic roots of most major party organizations were established as the franchise expanded during the late nineteenth and early twentieth centuries, the pre-television era. Yet the Duverger model of mass party organizations has often failed to take root elsewhere. In newer democracies in middle-income countries, party organizations developed in a context where television was already widely available. In Latin America, for example, despite the spread of free and fair elections since the early 1990s, and the growth of multiparty systems, party organizations often remain poorly institutionalized. In institutionalized systems, party organizations generally have as their defining features regularized procedures, relatively cohesive structures, stable roots in civic society, and an independent resource base.[25] By contrast, parties in Latin America commonly reflect personal support for particular leaders or parliamentary factions based on the division of the spoils of patronage and clientelism, rather than being founded on coherent programmatic party platforms, a core set of well-defined ideological principles, and a stable mass-branch organizational structure. In presidential elections, such campaign organizations are ideally suited to candidates launching personal leadership appeals directly through television advertising, with fund raising conducted through affiliated groups and personal backers, rather than working through decentralized membership structures and programmatic party appeals. Lack of institutionalization is even clearer in many African states, which achieved independence later than those in Latin America. African parties are often based on informal personal and lineage-based clientalistic networks and ethnic identities, rather than on clear programmatic identities and institutional structures.[26] In consolidating democracies in Central and Eastern Europe, some parties can trace their lineages back to the interwar era, but both older and newer parties have difficulty in attracting members, since partisanship continues to be associated with the corruption and malpractice of the old Communist Party.[27] Party building among local neighborhoods, workplace and welfare associations, and housing communities often proved difficult during the 1990s, an era of rapid social and economic transformation. The remnants of communist parties in Eastern Europe, reflecting long-standing cultural traditions, may function more as "top-down" electoral and fund-raising machines dominated by the leadership than as channels of "bottom-up" internal debate and political accountability.

Finally, there are various nondemocratic regimes with progressively more restrictive practices.[28] These include *hegemonic* party systems or one-party predominant systems, in which opposition parties are legal but have limited opportunities to compete for government office;[29] *authoritarian* regimes, in which most forms of political organization (except for the ruling party) are banned; and *totalitarian* regimes, in which all forms of autonomous political organization and basic civic and political liberties are repressed, and the governing party maintains power based on control of the military and civilian bureaucracy. Under nondemocratic regimes, leaders often use patronage, corruption, and intimidation to motivate local party supporters and as a means to exert control over the general population.[30] Under the more restrictive regimes, party membership may be relatively widespread, but membership functions essentially as a top-down mechanism of control rather than as a genuine form of bottom-up political participation that allows activists to influence the policy process, hold political leaders to account for their actions, and remove them if necessary.

The debate about the role and function of party organizations raises large and complex theoretical issues about the role of parties in democracy that are well beyond the scope of this limited study, but here we can examine a series of specific questions related to the role of parties as channels of political activism. In particular, *is there good evidence that party membership has eroded consistently across established democracies in recent decades*, as so often is assumed? And *what is the pattern of membership and activism in other types of political system*, including newer democracies, semi-democracies, and non-democracies? Evidence is derived from the official party records in twenty Western societies, and these estimates are compared to survey evidence from the World Values Study from the early 1980s to the mid-1990s. On this basis, the next chapter goes on to examine the factors that can best explain activism through partisan channels.

Estimated Patterns and Trends in Official Membership Rolls

Are there convincing grounds to believe that party membership has fallen across many established democracies, or are commentators being seduced by romantic myths of a Golden Age of mass parties? One important source of data is the official figures or estimates of membership compiled by parties. Although they are commonly used, it should be noted that these aggregate numbers can be crude and unreliable, particularly where parties exaggerate their support, or where central record keeping is simply inefficient or erratic. Ironically, attempts to create more accurate registers may produce an apparent decline in the rolls. As voluntary organizations, parties are rarely obliged to maintain public records. In decentralized parties, there may be no available estimates of national figures. The meaning and definition of "membership" also varies in different countries; for example, in the United States it is commonly understood to be the party affiliation declared by electors when they register to vote, whereas in Norway and in the British Labour Party, card-carrying membership requires payment of at least a minimum annual subscription. Indirect party membership via affiliated organizations such as trade unions and churches also complicates the comparison. Nevertheless, even if flawed and inflated, these official records provide the best estimates available at the national level. Two measures of party "density" can be compared: trends over time in the *absolute* number of members and, given population changes, the *relative* party membership expressed as the percentage of the total electorate who are members (M/E).

Using the most thorough comparative project, the Party Organization Study, Katz and Mair analyzed official membership figures for Western Europe from the 1960s through the end of the 1980s.[31] The study concluded that any apparent fall in the raw membership numbers was, in fact, highly uneven. In Sweden, for example, membership had remained roughly stable, and in a few nations, including Germany and Belgium, the total number of members had even grown from 1960 to the late 1980s, while often contracting elsewhere in Western Europe. More recent analysis by Mair and Biezen has extended the estimates from the early 1980s to the end of the 1990s, providing the most authoritative and reliable source. Trend analyses of these figures indicate considerable variations from one country to another (see Table 6.1). In thirteen long-established European democracies, Mair and Biezen found that the absolute number of members has fallen consistently, sometimes substantially, as in France, Italy, and the UK.[32] Along similar lines, Scarrow compared aggregate party enrollment from the 1950s to the mid-1990s in sixteen established democracies and

TABLE 6.1. *Trends in estimated official party membership, 1980–2000*

Country	Period	Party membership as a Percentage of the Electorate, Late 1990s	Percent Change[a]	Change in Numbers of Members	Change in Numbers as Percentage of Original Membership
France	1978–1999	1.6	−3.48	−1,122,128	−64.59
Italy	1980–1998	4.0	−5.61	−2,091,887	−51.54
United States	1980–1998	1.9	−2.20	−853,156	−50.39
Norway	1980–1997	7.3	−8.04	−218,891	−47.49
Czech Rep	1993–1999	3.9	−3.10	−225,200	−41.32
Finland	1980–1998	9.6	−6.09	−206,646	−34.03
Netherlands	1980–2000	2.5	−1.78	−136,459	−31.67
Austria	1980–1999	17.7	−10.82	−446,209	−30.21
Switzerland	1977–1997	6.4	−4.28	−118,800	−28.85
Sweden	1980–1998	5.5	−2.87	−142,533	−28.05
Denmark	1980–1998	5.2	−2.16	−70,385	−25.52
Ireland	1980–1998	3.1	−1.86	−27,856	−24.47
Belgium	1980–1999	6.5	−2.42	−136,382	−22.10
Germany	1980–1999	2.9	−1.59	−174,967	−8.95
Hungary	1990–1999	2.1	+0.04	+8,300	+5.02
Portugal	1980–2000	3.9	−0.29	+50,381	+17.01
Slovakia	1994–2000	4.1	+0.82	+37,777	+29.63
Greece	1980–1998	6.8	+3.58	+375,000	+166.67
Spain	1980–2000	3.4	+2.22	+808,705	+250.73

[a] The percentage change in party membership is measured as a proportion of the electorate. All estimates of change are made for the specified period.

Source: Peter Mair and Ingrid van Biezen. "Party membership in twenty European democracies, 1980–2000." *Party Politics*, 7:1 (2001).

confirmed a fairly general picture of diminishing mass membership in these countries, whether measured in absolute or standardized terms: "Overall the decline is too general, and in many cases too steep, to dismiss as either an administrative artifact or as the product of country-specific effects."[33]

At the same time, the Mair and Biezen estimates suggest that the number of party members rose in "third wave" Mediterranean democracies, including Portugal, Greece, and Spain, as well as in postcommunist Hungary and Slovakia. The contrasting trends in long-established and newer democracies are striking and important for the insights they may provide about developments around the globe. In addition, official figures on relative party membership during the late 1990s highlight substantial variations across the twenty nations. Austrian parties are closest to the ideal of "mass" parties, with party membership of over one million, meaning that about one in five citizens are members. Membership as a percentage of the electorate is also relatively high in Finland and Norway; this ratio is lowest in the UK and France.

Yet the official records cannot tell us how we should interpret the causes of this phenomenon and its consequences for democratic participation. Four limitations, in particular, should be noted. First, as with any trend analysis, the selection of starting and ending points is critical. It is unclear whether the 1950s and 1960s represent an artificially high point in the postwar decade; if so, subsequent patterns may represent a return to the status quo ante. As Scarrow points out, mass-membership parties have not been the norm for most democracies in the twentieth century. Both before and after the 1950s, parties have shown an uneven pattern of commitment to enlisting supporters in permanent organizations.[34] In addition, and even more importantly, little evidence is available to monitor whether trends in party *activism* have fallen since midcentury in parallel with membership, or whether the main decline has been in the more peripheral supporters who were never deeply involved in the day-to-day functions of the party. Studies from many nations indicate that activists in local branches represent a minority of all members.[35] This pattern was confirmed by the World Values Survey in the mid-1990s, where roughly a third of those who said they were party members reported being active. Therefore, the core workers may persist, perhaps because of their greater ideological commitment to partisan causes and core principles, even if fringe supporters melt away.

Moreover, the impact of any fall in membership upon the structure of the party remains unclear. The shrinkage of the grassroots base is often assumed to produce greater centralization of power within party organizations, as the leadership becomes less constrained by a mass movement. But, as Tan suggests, this relationship could be contingent upon many other developments, such as party traditions and ideologies, the rules of leadership selection, and the size of the party, rather than being an automatic process.[36] Parties with large memberships, such as the Chinese Communist Party, can be highly centralized and hierarchical, while minor and fringe parties with relatively few activists, such as the Belgian and British Greens, may prove to be extremely participatory, decentralized, and democratic, in part because they have a greater incentive to attract and retain supporters.

Lastly, the official membership rolls cannot tell us who joins parties, or indeed anything more about the political attitudes, experience, and behavior of party workers. Therefore, the available official membership data, while indicating a decline in the relative number of party members in established democracies since the 1950s and 1960s, is unable by itself to resolve the meaning of these developments or to provide insights into their underlying causes.

Estimated Patterns and Trends in Survey Data

Alternative estimates of party membership and activism are available from surveys, although this source too is not without its flaws. In particular, cross-national survey data gauging membership trends is relatively scarce, and even more limited outside a limited range of established democracies. If only 5 to 10 percent of the electorate join parties, then too few members can be identified for subgroup analysis from the standard national election surveys. Also, notions of what it is to be a "party member" or "activist" may differ cross-nationally, limiting consistent comparisons. Where official membership is only loosely defined – for example, in newer parties in sub-Saharan Africa and Asia which have not developed a formal bureaucratic organization and official rule book – many people may associate "party members" with "party supporters" or even "party loyalists." Similar problems of cross-national comparability plague official party records, where membership rules may be relatively strict or lenient. What can be said is that despite these real limitations, where survey data is available, it can reveal important information about the background, characteristics, and motivations of party members, as well as distinguishing between self-reported passive followers and core activists. Most importantly, surveys allow us to move beyond the description of trends to plumb the reasons why people join parties.

The most systematic and comprehensive cross-national study, by Widfeldt, monitored trends in party membership based on Eurobarometer surveys from the 1960s to the early 1990s in ten Western European countries.[37] The results confirmed that party membership levels in these countries were generally fairly low, varying between 5 and 10 percent of the population. Moreover, in Western Europe, although there was no precipitate drop, party membership tended either to contract slightly during this period or, at best, to be stable. Rather than confirming the idea that parties faced an acute crisis, Widfelt concluded that the evidence raised questions about how well parties in established democracies were functioning as participatory channels.

Evidence concerning a broader range of countries is available from the World Values Study (WVS), ranging from some of the most affluent nations, such as the United States, Japan, and Norway, to some of the poorest, such as Nigeria, India, and China. Unfortunately, not all nations were included in each wave of the survey, and there are some important differences in the wording of questions over time, making it difficult to examine comparable trends over each successive wave of the survey. Nevertheless, we can examine comparative cross-national patterns using the 1995 WVS, which monitored whether respondents were active members, passive members, or not members in a range of voluntary associations in civic society, such as labor unions, charitable groups, and environmental organizations, as well as in political parties. For the cross-national comparison, the categories of "active" and "passive" members were merged in the preliminary analysis to facilitate comparison with the earlier figures based on membership data, since party records do not distinguish between core activists and more peripheral members. To check reliability, the official estimates of relative party membership were compared to the survey estimates in the twenty nations included in both sources. Overall, the survey suggests that 7.9 percent of the adult population were party members in the mid-1990s, a figure marginally higher than that estimated from official party records in the late 1990s (5 percent), but one reasonably similar given the different time periods, definitions, and measures involved.

Cross-national Patterns

The results of the comparison shown in Table 6.2 provide independent confirmation, as Mair and Biezen reported, that levels of party membership differ substantially among Western democracies, and moreover that the

TABLE 6.2. *Trends in party membership, early 1980s to early 1990s (percent)*

	Early 1980s	Early 1990s	Change
Finland	3.2	14.3	+11.1
Iceland	11.3	15.2	+3.9
South Korea	2.6	6.5	+3.9
United States	11.3	15.0	+3.7
Netherlands	7.6	10.1	+3.5
Mexico	2.3	5.6	+3.3
Belgium	2.8	5.8	+3.0
Canada	5.9	7.8	+1.9
Norway	13.3	13.9	+0.9
Britain	4.6	5.0	+0.4
France	2.7	3.1	+0.4
Japan	3.3	3.3	0.0
Denmark	6.6	6.5	−0.1
West Germany	8.1	7.6	−0.5
Ireland	4.4	3.9	−0.5
Italy	6.4	5.3	−1.1
Northern Ireland	2.9	1.6	−1.3
Spain	3.8	1.9	−1.9
Sweden	15.0	10.3	−4.7
Argentina	7.9	2.0	−5.9
All	*6.3*	*7.2*	*+0.9*

Note: "Please look carefully at the following list of voluntary organizations and activities and say which, if any, do you belong to?" The figures represent the proportion who "belong to a political party."

Source: World Values Study.

variations in membership are even greater in other countries around the globe. Overall, in the twenty societies under comparison, party members constituted about 6 to 7 percent of the adult population, representing a substantial number and translating into millions of citizens in these nations. But the estimate disguises considerable cross-national differences. Among long established democracies, for example, in the early 1990s membership was most common in the Scandinavian countries, despite evidence that membership has fallen in this region.[38] Many Western European countries fell in the middle of the spectrum, with between 5 and 10 percent of the public joining parties, along with the Anglo-American nations. By contrast, relatively few citizens joined parties in Spain, Northern Ireland, France, and Japan.

Equally important, and contrary to popular commentary, Table 6.2 suggests that at least in the short term, party membership has not slumped consistently across all nations during the 1980s. Instead, in eight countries, including Sweden, Spain, and Argentina, it fell, while in a few others membership stayed stable; it even rose slightly in eleven nations, such as Iceland, South Korea, and Mexico. The difference between the estimates of official party membership and those derived from the WVS survey data could be attributed to the slightly different time periods under comparison, the selection of the countries, or alternatively to some of the flaws and limitations in the official membership records and the survey data already noted.[39] It is possible that a longer-term slide in membership in established democracies occurred during the late 1950s and early 1960s, accompanying the rise of modern campaigns in the television age, well before the first wave of the World Values Study in the early 1980s. What the broader analysis suggests, however, is that although parties have commonly experienced a short-term erosion of membership in some established democracies since the early 1980s, the picture shows considerable variability, with strong contrasts among different societies. Such apparently contradictory shifts during this decade suggest the impact of particular political events on party fortunes, such as specific election victories or defeats, changes in the party leadership, and membership drives, which can boost or depress voluntary activism and grassroots support, rather than the influence of secular trends such as spreading disillusionment with partisan politics.

Even greater contrasts in the popularity of partisan politics are apparent globally, as shown in Table 6.3. In the mid-1990s, party membership lagged behind in many postcommunist societies, especially in Poland, Ukraine, Russia, Moldova, and Belarus. In the Soviet Union, party workers under the old regimes were manipulated by both patronage and coercion as a way to legitimate the Communist Party, artificially inflating the figures, which subsequently plummeted with a prevailing mood of antipartyism.[40] The pattern in Albania and Montenegro during this period may be a residue of the old practices. Many of the newer democracies in

TABLE 6.3. *Levels of party membership, mid-1990s (percent)*

South Africa	44.1	Finland	9.8
Nigeria	43.4	Australia	9.6
Albania	33.7	Turkey	8.8
Dominican Rep	33.4	West Germany	8.6
Mexico	23.3	Spain	8.1
Montenegro	22.9	Philippines	7.8
Macedonia	21.3	Czech Rep	6.7
Bangladesh	18.9	Slovakia	6.7
India	18.6	Japan	6.5
Switzerland	16.9	Azerbaijan	6.3
Uruguay	16.2	Bulgaria	5.7
Peru	15.7	Slovenia	4.7
Chile	15.6	Georgia	4.5
Norway	15.5	East Germany	4.1
Sweden	15.1	El Salvador	3.7
Brazil	14.3	Hungary	3.4
China	14.2	Latvia	3.3
Venezuela	13.8	Lithuania	3.2
New Zealand	13.3	Moldova	2.9
Romania	11.9	Estonia	2.0
South Korea	11.8	Russia	1.9
Serbia	11.4	Belarus	1.8
Colombia	11.2	Ukraine	1.6
Argentina	10.1	Poland	1.1

Note: "Now I am going to read off a list of voluntary organizations; for each one, could you tell me whether you are an active member, an inactive member, or not a member of that type of organization?" The figures represent the proportion of "active or passive party members." It should be noted that the questions used in successive waves of the WVS survey were equivalent but not identical, and the change in wording makes it difficult to compare estimates in this table with Table 6.2.
Source: World Values Study.

South America and Asia fall in the middle of the party spectrum. By contrast, the two African states (South Africa and Nigeria) display exceptionally strong levels of mass membership in the early to mid-1990s, as do China, India, Bangladesh, Mexico, and the Dominican Republic.

We need to interpret this data with caution, as there are many reasons why these figures may prove unreliable or exaggerated, including the problems of conducting survey fieldwork among poorer, illiterate rural populations. There are particular difficulties in eliciting honest responses to political questions among those living under regimes lacking a tradition of free speech and open criticism of the ruling party. When asked in surveys, people living under these regimes may report relatively high levels of party membership, if the question is regarded as a test of loyalty to the regime, such as displays of the national flag and levels of turnout in one-party states, even if in fact few are voluntarily engaged, and some who declare overt support may even be actively hostile to the dominant party. This problem may create systematic bias in responses in nondemocratic regimes. In addition, as discussed earlier, the cross-national comparisons may not be comparing like with like, where "belonging to a party" means a paid-up card-carrying member in organizations with formal rules and regulations, as in the British Labour party, and just an unofficial party supporter in another, for example, registered Republican voters in America. Thus the South African figure may reflect the public's overwhelming approval of Mandela's post-apartheid ANC and enthusiasm for the new democracy, rather than any more formal sense of joining a party.[41] In African states, party membership also carries considerable patronage benefits, including access to jobs, health care, and educational opportunities. Different cultural meanings of "party membership" also create difficulties in interpreting the official membership records in cases where rules differ (as well as in comparing parties within any particular country). Given these limitations, these preliminary estimates need to be treated with due skepticism until they receive independent corroboration, especially in non-democracies; nevertheless, the figures confirm considerable variation in patterns of party membership around the globe, and the reasons for these differences are worth exploring further. Levels of modernization, political institutions, the role of mobilizing agencies such as unions and churches, and differences in social resources and cultural attitudes could all play a role.

Trends in Campaign Activism
It is far more difficult to establish whether changes in party membership actually make a decisive difference in the strength of party activism, or indeed in broader indicators of the proportion of citizens who are prepared to invest their time and energies in supporting candidates and parties during campaigns. We lack any systematic cross-national evidence that measures trends in campaign activism. The best we can do is to examine trends within particular countries where national election studies have monitored long-term developments. In particular, we can focus on the United States, which can be taken to exemplify some of the most advanced developments in the professionalization of modern campaign techniques. If these developments have reduced grassroots campaign activism, it should be apparent in this country. The American National Election Study (NES) includes a battery of items monitoring whether Americans have become less engaged in common electoral activities, such as donating money and attending meetings (see Table 6.4). The evidence during the last half-century across the long series

TABLE 6.4. *Trends in campaign activism, United States, 1952–2000 (percent)*

Year	Persuade	Meeting	Party Work	Button	Donate
1952	27.5	7.0	3.2		4.2
1956	28.3	7.0	3.2	15.5	9.8
1960	33.5	8.3	5.6	20.9	11.6
1964	31.4	8.7	5.2	16.5	10.7
1968	32.9	9.1	5.8	14.8	9.0
1972	31.6	8.9	5.0	14.0	10.4
1976	36.8	6.3	4.5	7.6	16.2
1980	36.1	7.5	3.6	6.7	8.0
1984	32.4	7.8	4.1	9.2	7.8
1988	28.9	7.2	3.3	8.7	8.7
1992	37.4	8.0	3.4	11.2	7.2
1996	28.5	5.8	2.7	10.2	8.6
2000	35.1	5.5	2.8	10.0	6.6

Note: The proportion of the American electorate who carried out these activities during the presidential campaign. The items measure talking to others for or against a candidate (persuade), attending a candidate or party meeting (meeting), working for a candidate or party (party work), displaying a campaign button (button), and donating money to a candidate or party (donate).

Source: National Election Survey (NES), 1952–2000.

of presidential elections shows that the proportion of Americans who persuaded others how to vote by discussing the candidates, arguably the least demanding form of participation, remains fairly high, and the pattern shows trendless fluctuation over time rather than a secular decline. This closely follows trends in the other indicators of campaign interest observed elsewhere.[42] The sharpest drop is in the proportion of Americans wearing a button or displaying a bumper sticker, both minor activities that have become unfashionable. Since the sixties, there has also been a modest long-term decline in activism within parties, reflecting the erosion of grassroots party organizations, although the proportion of party workers active today is similar to the situation in the 1950s. As Rosenstone and Hansen have found, the proportion of Americans engaged in other types of campaigning remains fairly stable, such as those contributing money or going to a political meeting.[43] Despite concern about declining civic engagement, the erosion of parties, and dramatic changes in the nature of American elections, levels of campaign activism have been remarkably constant over the last fifty years.

Conclusions

Many believe that parties are contracting at the middle level, in particular, that citizens are deserting grassroots activity and are no longer volunteering for the usual functions of organizing and mobilizing party support, debating party policy, selecting candidates, and maintaining ongoing links between party leaders in government and their local supporters during the interelectoral period as well as during campaigns. Yet rather than any "crisis" in party organizations, or even a more steady erosion, the evidence in this chapter suggests four core findings:

1. First, aggregate evidence based on official records suggests that patterns of party membership vary substantially cross-nationally, even among Western democracies.
2. Both the trends in estimated official party membership from 1980 to 2000, and the WVS survey estimates during the 1980s, suggest cross-national variations in trends in party membership, with falls in some nations and increases in others (particularly newer democracies), rather than a consistent short-term erosion apparent across all societies.
3. Much of the available data on party membership has been drawn from established democracies in Western Europe, but, in light of their distinctive historical and political experiences, these probably do not represent the global picture. The survey evidence indicates that membership remains low in many postcommunist societies, but higher in some developing countries in sub-Saharan Africa, Latin America, and Asia.
4. Lastly, the impact of any change in party membership upon broader indicators of campaign activism remains unclear. In the United States, at least, there has been no significant slump evident across all of the common forms of electoral activism during the last half-century. It remains to be seen whether patterns have altered substantially elsewhere.

Yet answers to one set of questions raise others. We need to establish why there are substantial contrasts in levels of party membership across countries. Cultural explanations emphasize *supply*, in particular, the way that changes in modern lifestyles and values mean that people in postindustrial societies are less motivated to join parties and to express their interests via traditional channels. By contrast, explanations based on theories of societal modernization focus on *demand*, in particular, how changes in campaigning following the rise of television mean that party members are no longer vital for electoral success, and may well even hinder a leader's strategic pursuit of wider popularity. The next chapter explores the underlying reasons for patterns of party activism and how party organizations have altered participation through these channels.

7

Who Joins?

What causes the substantial differences in party membership and activism around the world, and the contrasts between Finland and France, Austria and Britain, not to speak of those between India and the Philippines, Uruguay and the Ukraine? As discussed in the Introduction, the process of societal modernization and the design of political institutions can be expected to influence patterns of party membership at the national level, while mobilizing agencies, social structure, and cultural attitudes are likely to prove important at the individual level.

Which Countries Have Mass Membership Parties?
National-level Models

We have already established that levels of societal modernization and human development have an important impact on patterns of electoral turnout around the world. For similar reasons, they can be expected to influence the number of people who choose to work for parties, with declining mass membership expected in the transition from developing to industrialized and postindustrial societies, despite the spread of democracy worldwide.

Theories of campaign modernization discussed earlier offer the most plausible reasons for this hypothesis. Poorer developing societies, such as India and the Dominican Republic, are characterized by low levels of literacy and minimal access to newspapers and television, so that traditional election campaigns in these countries are still based heavily upon forms of direct personal communication, such as traditional rallies, local get-out-the-vote drives, visual symbols and colorful posters, and door-to-door canvassing. In traditional campaigns, although radio remains an important form of broadcasting, party leaders need a volunteer army of helpers, neighbors, and local associations in order to contact voters and mobilize support through personal channels and social networks. Clientalism is common, with promises of local services and jobs. Elections are "up close and personal." The role of grassroots party supporters is important in elections in poorer democracies, but it may be even more critical in uncompetitive elections in developing nations such as Zimbabwe, where nondemocratic one-party regimes are seeking to legitimate their support and suppress dissident voices. In countries where leaders have difficulty reaching the mass public through television, newspapers, and radio, local party activists, who may be on the party payroll, can be vitally important in attempts to mobilize the public in symbolic elections, using threats, bribes, and intimidation where necessary.

By contrast, in middle-income industrialized societies such as South Korea, Brazil, and Mexico, greater affluence is closely associated with the spread of consumer durables, including household television sets. Broadcasting becomes the predominant form of political communication, including election advertising; growing levels of literacy, income, and education help to broaden newspaper circulation. Campaign resources mobilized by the central party leadership shift from grassroots helpers toward mediated channels of communication, particularly the bright lights of the television news studio. Mediated channels of political mobilization supplement, rather than replace, the older direct forms of electioneering, but they also bring in their wake a coterie of campaign professionals, including fund raisers, public relations experts, pollsters, and advertising agents.[1] The most recent stage in this process concerns the rise of the internet and the way that parties have adapted to this new technological environment.[2] Theories of campaign modernization suggest that many party organizations in older democracies have become more professional, financially subsidized, and media-oriented, reducing their dependence on volunteer grassroots labor for get-out-the-vote drives and fund-raising activities.[3] This pattern can be expected to influence the major parties in government and opposition most, if minor and fringe parties with limited resources remain more labor-dependent than capital-dependent. While modernization affects society in general, generating rising levels of education, literacy, and leisure, the mass media can be expected to be particularly important for parties as channels of political communication. Moreover, changes in citizens' lifestyles and political values associated with the shift from industrial to postindustrial societies mean that even if party leaders try to recruit a broader base of members and activists, (as a way to legitimate their power, for example), fewer may be willing to invest their time and energies in helping old-line party organizations when they could be engaged in more rewarding activities and more challenging forms of political participation.[4]

This suggests that party membership will be greater in poorer traditional societies than in postindustrial nations, and, in particular, that levels of party membership will be negatively related to the penetration of television. By contrast, the process of democratization, per se, is expected to have only minimal impact on *levels* of party membership (as opposed to influencing the role and powers of members in internal policy making, decision making, and leadership selection).

Table 7.1 sets out the proportion of party members and activists by levels of societal development, types of states, media systems, and cultural regions around the world. The results confirm the importance of economic development and modernization: The poorest nations have by far the highest proportion of party members, followed by medium development countries. The regional comparisons suggest that it is the less affluent countries in sub-Saharan Africa, in particular, that are driving these patterns, followed by those in Southeast Asia. Although many previous studies have generalized

TABLE 7.1. *Party membership by type of society, 1990s*

	Inactive Member	Active Member	All Members
Level of development			
Postindustrial	6.6	3.3	9.9
High development	3.7	2.6	6.3
Medium development	8.4	4.9	13.3
Low development	26.7	8.0	34.7
Type of political system			
Older democracy	6.7	3.6	10.3
Newer democracy	8.5	3.8	12.3
Semi-democracy	8.3	4.6	12.9
Non-democracy	5.2	6.1	11.3
Type of media system			
Widespread TV access	5.0	2.9	7.9
Limited TV access	10.9	6.1	17.0
Cultural region			
Catholic Europe	3.2	1.9	5.1
Central Europe	3.4	2.0	5.3
Soviet	3.4	1.9	5.3
Northern Europe	8.0	3.4	11.3
South Asia	6.5	5.0	11.4
Latin America	7.8	4.6	12.4
Anglo-American	9.6	5.8	15.4
Confucian	13.6	6.2	19.8
Africa	34.4	9.4	43.8
All	7.6	4.1	11.7

Note: For the classification of nations by level of development and type of political system, see the Appendix.

TV access: Widespread = 300 + TV sets per 1,000 population. Limited = less than 300 TV sets per 1,000 population. (World Bank)

Cultural regions: Defined by the WVS.

Source: World Values Study, early to mid-1990s in fifty-nine nations (N = 101,002).

based on the experience of Western Europe, in fact this region has lower-than-average levels of party membership; indeed, only Central and Eastern Europe rank lower worldwide. By contrast, the results suggest that the process of democratization per se does not play an important direct role in this pattern: Party members were about one tenth of the population (10.4 percent) in the older democracies, and a slightly higher proportion in all other types of political system. The highest proportion of activists are found in the non-democracies, possibly because one-party regimes in poorer developing countries may be dependent upon a large army of local supporters to maintain their control.

Table 7.1 confirms that the media system was indeed related to membership patterns: Countries with widespread television penetration have roughly half as many party members as countries with limited TV access. But this could of course be a by-product of many other features of developing societies, so multivariate analysis is needed to check this relationship. Table 7.2 analyzes aggregate levels of party membership and activism during the early to mid-1990s in fifty-nine nations by levels of human development (as measured by HDI 1990, combining education, literacy, and longevity in a single index), levels of democratization (as measured by the mean Freedom House score for political rights and civil liberties from 1990 to 1996), and the penetration of television sets and newspaper circulation. The last tests whether it is the particular features of broadcast television per se that are related to party membership, or whether it is the spread of all news media that counts. The results in Model A confirm that levels of development are strongly and significantly related to the proportion of party members in a country, in a negative direction: *More affluent countries usually have fewer members.* Levels of democratization are also related, but this time positively. Lastly, the proportion of television sets is significant and negatively associated with membership, as illustrated in Figure 7.1, with the strongest relationship in semi-democracies and newer democracies, which are often middle-income societies in the process of widening access to common consumer durables such as television sets. There is no significant relationship between levels of access to television and levels of party membership in the group of established democracies, where most major parties had established their basic organizational structures and membership bases well before the television age. In comparison, in many middle-income newer democracies in Central and Eastern Europe, Latin America, and Asia, television was already widely available in many households before the development of competitive party systems in the late 1980s and early 1990s. In the first free and fair elections, newer parties could usually reach much of the electorate more easily and efficiently through broadcasting channels than by recruiting a mass organizational base of party members to publicize their message and mobilize supporters via

TABLE 7.2. *National-level model explaining party membership*

	Model A				Model B				Model C			
	B	(s.e.)	Beta	Sig.	B	(s.e.)	Beta	Sig.	B	(s.e.)	Beta	Sig.
Development												
Level of human development	−74.05	23.28	−.707	***	−60.93	20.65	−.582	***	−13.87	22.56	−.132	
Level of democratization	1.474	.687	.396	*	1.498	.608	.402	*	.359	.566	.096	
Percent television sets	−.195	.090	−.373	*	−.267	.081	−.510	***	−.225	.084	−.430	***
Percent newspapers	.189	.103	.268		.213	.091	.303	*	.121	.095	.172	
Institutions												
District size					.001	.000	.203	***	.002	.000	.030	
Party competition					.325	.107	.354	***	.115	.108	.125	
Presidential system					−6.65	2.256	−.343	***	−3.63	2.15	−.187	
Regions												
Africa									23.23	7.64	.479	***
Asia									1.25	3.55	.043	
Central and Eastern Europe									−5.49	2.60	−.258	*
Middle East									−3.29	7.12	−.048	
North America									3.78	4.23	.095	
South America									2.62	3.62	.106	
Scandinavia									2.07	3.94	.059	
Constant	81.046				61.82				27.12			
R^2	.36				.52				.68			

Note: The table lists unstandardized OLS regression coefficients (b), standard errors (s.e.), standardized coefficients (Beta), and significance, with reported party membership as the dependent variable in fifty-nine nations. **T*$p < .05$ **$p < .01$ ***$p < .001$ Model A: Development; Model B: Development + Institutions; Model C: Development + Institutions + Regions. The models were tested for problems of multicolinearity using tolerances and variance inflation factor statistics.

Human development: Human Development Index 1990: *Human Development Report.* New York: United Nations Development Program.

Level of democratization: Freedom House Index of political rights and civil liberties, mean 1990–6. www.freedomhouse.org.

Penetration of television and newspapers: Percentage of households with television sets and newspapers. World Bank 2000.

District size: Average population size per parliamentary seat.

Party competition: Proportion of the vote for the party in first place, in elections held during the 1990s.

Presidential system. With direct presidential elections (1), parliamentary elections only (0).

Regions: Dummy variables excluding Western Europe.

Source: Party membership derived from the World Values Study, early to mid-1990s in fifty-nine nations (N = 101,002).

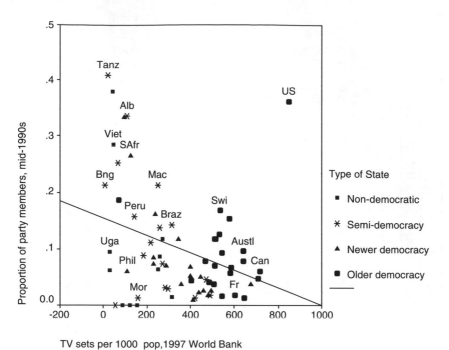

TV sets per 1000 pop,1997 World Bank

FIGURE 7.1. Party membership and access to television, mid-1990s.

traditional avenues. Finally, newspapers were found to be unrelated to levels of membership, suggesting that it is the spread of electronic broadcast media that has most impact on this process. The electronic media are probably more effective than the print media as a campaign tool in newer democracies as television allows politicians to reach a much wider mass audience and to communicate with less educated and literate populations.

Political Institutions

Yet institutional explanations suggest that the political system could also influence the structure of party organizations. In particular, the electoral system may play a role, if majoritarian single-member districts under "first past the post" promote strong linkages between elected representatives and their local constituencies, including party branch members.[5] In such a system, people may have a considerable incentive to join and work for parties, since they will thereby develop a personal connection with elected representatives in public office. Indeed, one of the classic arguments used by first-past-the-post proponents is that it promotes the accountability of officeholders to their local parties, first, and subsequently to all voters in the constituency.[6] Similar tendencies can be expected under electoral systems with a limited number of representatives in multimember districts, such as under Ireland's single transferable vote system. Under proportional representation systems with large regional or even national multimember constituencies, by contrast, the connection between party members and elected representatives can be expected to be more tenuous. We can therefore test the hypothesis that district magnitude (the number of seats per constituency) should be related to levels of party membership.

Party competition could also play a role in this process, because countries with multiple parties are likely to provide greater incentives for people to join like-minded organizations.[7] Party competition can be measured most easily as the mean proportion of votes won by the party in first place in elections during the 1990s. Lastly, the type of executive structure may also prove important; theorists argue that parties are stronger under parliamentary systems that promote unity between the legislative and executive branches, rather than in presidential systems where power is divided.[8] Accordingly, presidential systems, defined as those polities with direct elections for the prime minister or head of state, were entered into the model. Table 7.2 shows the results of the analysis in Model B. Even after continuing to control for development, the patterns of party competition and presidential systems were significantly related to the proportion of party members in a country, in the expected direction. The adjusted R^2 rises in successive models from 36 percent to 52 percent of the national-level variance in party membership.

Yet these results could always be driven by the cultural characteristics of countries, as we have already established some important differences by global region. Model C presents the full battery of factors in the regression analysis, including dummy variables for the world regions. In the final model, the variables that remain significantly associated with party membership are the level of television penetration (which continues to be negative) and the regional coefficients for sub-Saharan Africa (positive) and Central and Eastern Europe (negative). This suggests that the spread of electronic broadcasting is important for how far parties recruit members for campaigning, as suggested by theories of campaign modernization. Nevertheless, this represents only a partial explanation, which cannot fully account for exceptionally high levels of party membership claimed in South Africa and Nigeria. These preliminary findings are suggestive, but they need to be treated with caution, given the problems of survey data discussed earlier, and further evidence needs to be drawn from a much wider range of developing countries if we are to explore the reliability of these figures and to confirm the findings more fully. Moreover, so far we have not started to explore *which* parties within each country are most likely to have a mass membership base, and whether these patterns vary systematically.

Which Parties Recruit Members? Meso-level Analysis

Much of the work on party organizations suggests that certain types of parties are most likely to develop a membership based on characteristics such as their financial resources, ideological culture, and historical traditions. In particular, Duverger emphasized that it was the parties of the center-left – socialist, social democrat, and labor – that were founded as labor-intensive rather than capital-intensive organizations. If this historical legacy has continued to shape their organizational structures, these parties are most likely to have retained their mass membership bases.[9] Scarrow confirmed that prior to 1945, parties of the left were more likely to have well-established, democratic, mass membership–based organizations than other parties. Yet this pattern has some important exceptions, given what we know from official membership rolls in particular countries. In Britain, for example, the Conservatives have long been regarded as having the largest membership base in the country,[10] as did Fianna Fail in Ireland; right-wing parties in Sweden, Norway, and Denmark have also established successful mass-based organizations.

For similar reasons, we might assume that smaller parties are more likely to be based on volunteers and activists, while larger parties with richer financial resources are more likely to be able to afford the modern coterie of professional advisers, campaign consultants, and full-time paid officials.[11] In order to examine the evidence, Table 7.3 uses the pooled WVS of the early to mid-1990s to break down party membership by different types of parties. The ideological position of each party was classified based on a left-right scale using the Expert Evaluation of Party Space conducted by Huber and Inglehart.[12] The electoral size of each party was classified based on their share of votes, measured by the support that they received in the WVS survey when people were asked how they would vote if there were a general election tomorrow. Parties were categorized such that "major parties" were those that got 20 percent or more of the vote, "minor parties" 5 to 19.9 percent, and "fringe parties" less than 5 percent.

The results in Table 7.3 show that in fact there was remarkably little difference in party membership across the ideological spectrum, although, contrary to expectations, parties of the right tended to have slightly more members (especially passive members) than those of the left. But the differences proved to be relatively modest. Moreover, again somewhat surprisingly, among all those who supported a major party, 16 percent reported being members, compared with 10.5 percent and 11.5 percent respectively of those who supported minor and fringe parties. The contrast was particularly marked among passive members. This evidence remains limited, but nevertheless it does suggest that the classification of parties by ideological position and size used in this study throws remarkably little light on patterns and level of membership. Despite the initial expectations, the varia-

TABLE 7.3. *Membership by type of party (percent)*

	Inactive Member	Active Member	All Members
Party ideology			
1 Most left-wing	4.8	4.8	9.7
2	6.2	2.9	9.1
3	5.1	4.1	9.3
4	7.3	3.0	10.3
5	4.7	2.9	7.6
6	7.1	2.9	10.0
7	6.4	4.3	10.7
8	9.0	3.4	12.4
9 Most right-wing	5.7	3.7	9.4
Type of party			
Major party supporters who join	10.6	5.6	16.1
Minor party supporters who join	6.6	3.9	10.5
Fringe party supporters who join	7.5	3.9	11.5
All	7.6	4.1	11.7

Notes and sources:
Party Membership: Aggregate membership in fifty-nine nations based on the World Values Study, early to mid-1990s (N = 101,002).
Party Ideology: Parties were classified using Huber and Inglehart's Expert Survey.
Type of party: Major party (supports party with 20 percent or more of the vote), minor party (supports party with 5 to 19.9 percent of the vote), and fringe party (supports party with 0 to 4.9 percent of the vote).

tions in membership by nation, level of human development, and world region were far greater than the variations by party type. But we have not yet examined *who* is most likely to join parties and become active, a task for which individual-level survey analysis is needed.

Who Joins? Individual-level Models

Individual-level explanations focus on the structural resources, agency networks, and cultural motivations that people bring to political participation. Civic engagement models developed by Verba and colleagues stress the role of disparities in the resources that people bring to public life, including the cognitive skills derived from their educational backgrounds and the income and time resources facilitated by middle-class occupations.[13] As discussed in the previous chapter, we have already established some support for this thesis. Education and income proved to be significant predictors of electoral turnout in many, although not all, countries, and these factors can be expected to be even more important in predicting the more demanding forms of political activism such as party membership. Common branch activities – such as discussing local issues and party policies, chairing or writing minutes for branch meetings, drafting newsletters or press releases, selecting candidates, attending conferences, and arranging local fundraising events – are all facilitated by the communication skills, organizational experience, and greater leisure hours and flexible time that come with professional, managerial, and administrative careers. As we have seen, gender and age are also commonly associated with conventional modes of participation, because of the life experiences, community networks, and social skills that are related to these background characteristics. Women, in particular, have long been underrepresented as party members, as well as in party leaderships.[14] By contrast, cultural theories emphasize the importance of motivational factors. Those commonly found to be important include political interest, efficacy, and trust, all of which can be expected to boost the willingness to spend time on party work. As we have established with electoral turnout, political interest strongly increases the incentive to participate in public life and civic affairs. In addition, membership and activism is likely to be higher among those who express general confidence in political parties. Lastly, agencies are likely to be important; theories of social capital developed by Bob Putnam strongly suggest that dense networks of unions, churches, and related civic organizations are most likely to foster the conditions of party mobilization, as well as generating greater social trust.[15] In this view, face-to-face contacts and human bonds foster personal trust and feelings of mutual cooperation, so that people who work and play together in sports clubs, arts societies, workers cooperatives, and church associations are more likely to be predisposed to become active in party organizations as well.

The series of multivariate models developed in Table 7.4 use logistic regression to analyze party membership across the pooled sample of all nations during the early to mid-1990s. The analysis replicates the general approach used to analyze turnout earlier in order to facilitate comparison between these different modes of participation, even though identical variables are not always available in the different surveys. Given the importance of societal modernization, Model A first entered controls for human development, level of democratization, and the penetration of television, then the block of social *structural* variables, including age, gender, education, and income (in that order). Model B then adds two blocks of factors, the role of *mobilizing agencies* – including membership in voluntary organizations such as union and church affiliations, arts and sports clubs – and the effect of *cultural attitudes and values*, including political interest, social trust, and confidence in parties. All of the factors proved significant, and the coefficients pointed in the expected direction, with membership in a diverse range of voluntary organizations and political interest proving to be the strongest predictors of individual-level membership. After includ-

TABLE 7.4. *Individual-level model explaining party membership*

	Model A			Model B		
	B	(s.e.)	Sig.	B	(s.e.)	Sig.
Development						
Level of human development	−3.883	.232	***	−1.791	.256	***
Level of democratization	.022	.002	*	.004	.002	*
Penetration of television	.008	.002	*	.001	.002	*
Structure						
Age *(years)*	.009	.001	***	.006	.001	***
Gender *(male = 1)*	.531	.031	***	.289	.034	***
Education *(seven-pt scale)*	.086	.007	***	.075	.008	***
Class *(ten-pt scale)*	.075	.006	***	.023	.007	***
Agency						
Membership in voluntary organizations (e.g.,unions, churches, arts and sports clubs)				.367	.007	***
Culture						
Political interest				.380	.009	***
Social trust *(trusting = 1)*				.147	.036	***
Confidence in parties *(four-point scale)*				.201	.015	***
Constant	.706			−6.79		
Nagelkerke R²	*.056*			*.282*		

Note: The table lists unstandardized logistic regression coefficients, standard errors, and significance, with reported party membership as the dependent variable in fifty-nine nations.
* p < .05, ** p < .01, *** p < .001.
Human development: Human Development Index 1990: *Human Development Report*. New York: United Nations Development Program.
Level of Democratization: Mean Freedom House Index of political rights and civil liberties, 1990–6. www.freedomhouse.org.
Penetration of television: Percentage of households with television sets. World Bank 2000.
Structural factors: See Table 7.5.
Mobilizing agencies: See Table 7.6. Since memberships of all voluntary associations were highly intercorrelated, these were entered into the model as a single additive nine-point scale excluding party membership.
Cultural attitudes: See Table 7.7. The nine-point interest scale combined political discussion, interest, and salience of politics, which all also proved to be highly intercorrelated.

ing all of these factors, the overall level of variance explained by the model (shown by the R²) rises from .06 to .28, the final model providing the most satisfactory explanation of party membership. Let us consider the most plausible way to interpret these results and how these factors help to account for party work.

More information about these results can be found by examining each cluster of variables. The social background of members is illustrated in

Table 7.5, which shows that all of the standard demographic characteristics predict membership, as expected, but the relationships are not particularly strong or dramatic. That is to say, as many other studies have found, men remain more likely to join parties than women, even controlling for differences in their resources and attitudes. Party members are also more likely than average to have the cognitive skills and experience associated with higher education such as a university degree, and the advantages of a managerial and professional middle-class occupation. The age profile shows that there is a slight curvilinear pattern, with a modest peak in membership among the middle-aged, for both active and passive members. Interestingly, for those who believe that there has been a steady generational fall in support for parties, the age profile proved to be far less important than the pattern by gender, class, and education.

The distribution of party membership by agency in Table 7.6 shows even more dramatic differences, however, than the social structural variables. The World Values Study asked people whether they are active members, passive members, or not a member of a range of voluntary associa-

TABLE 7.5. *Party membership by social background, 1990s (percent)*

	Inactive Member	Active Member	All Members
Gender			
Men	9.1	5.6	14.7
Women	6.6	2.6	9.2
Age			
18–24	6.4	2.7	9.1
25–34	7.6	3.7	11.3
35–44	7.8	4.3	12.1
45–54	7.4	4.9	12.3
55–64	6.4	4.1	10.5
65+	6.7	3.3	10.0
Education			
Low education	6.9	3.4	10.3
Medium education	8.5	3.8	12.3
High education	9.5	5.8	15.3
Occupational class			
Managerial and professional	9.6	5.8	15.4
Other white-collar	6.4	3.8	10.2
Skilled manual	6.7	3.5	10.3
Unskilled manual	6.8	3.1	9.9
All	7.6	4.1	11.7

Source: World Values Study, early to mid-1990s in fifty-nine nations (N = 101,002).

TABLE 7.6. *Party membership by cultural attitudes, 1990s (percent)*

	Inactive Member	Active Member	All Members
Political interest			
Very interested	14.3	16.2	30.5
Some interest	9.2	4.4	13.6
Not very interested	6.0	1.5	7.5
Not at all interested	4.0	0.6	4.6
Confidence in parties			
Great deal	16.4	18.2	34.6
Quite a lot	11.4	8.0	19.4
Not very much	8.5	3.9	12.4
None	5.2	2.1	7.3
Discuss politics			
Frequently	11.6	11.5	23.1
Occasionally	8.0	3.3	11.3
Never	4.5	1.0	5.5
Importance of politics			
Very	13.4	14.1	27.5
Rather	10.6	5.8	16.4
Not very	6.4	2.0	8.4
Not at all	3.8	1.0	4.8
Social trust			
Trusting	9.0	5.2	14.2
Not trusting	7.1	3.7	10.8
Ideological self-placement			
Left	9.5	5.5	15.0
Center	7.3	2.9	10.2
Right	10.2	5.8	16.0
Postmaterialist attitudes			
Materialist	6.9	3.3	10.2
Mixed	8.3	4.3	12.6
Postmaterialist	8.6	5.6	14.2
All	7.6	4.1	11.7

Source: World Values Study, early to mid-1990s in fifty-nine nations (N = 101,002).

tions, such as arts and sports clubs, churches, and trade unions, as well as parties. Theories of social capital suggest that "joiners" are people who are closely bound with rich and dense networks of friends, neighbors, and colleagues through membership in community associations; and indeed, party membership proved to be closely associated with membership in all such voluntary organizations. Interestingly, there was not a significant difference among the different types of association; people who join football clubs or reading circles are just as likely to join parties as those involved in more explicitly political organizations such as trade unions, which are strongly linked to labor and social democratic parties, or churches associated with the Christian Democrats. It appears to be joining per se that matters, more than what one joins.

Lastly, cultural attitudes can be expected to play an important role in creating the motivation for people to join. As mentioned earlier, there are many rewards that draw people into becoming engaged in party life, whether process, outcome, or ideological incentives. As shown in Table 7.6, political interest, willingness to discuss politics, general confidence in parties, and the belief that politics is an important activity were all strong predictors of membership, while social trust proved to be weaker but still significant. Moreover, Inglehart's thesis of changing cultural values suggests that post-materialists are less likely to want to join old-fashioned hierarchical organizations such as parties, preferring to spend their political time and energies on more rewarding activities such as anti-globalization protest demonstrations, consumer boycotts, and community activities associated with new social movements.[16] Yet contrary to predictions in Inglehart's theories, post-materialist attitudes were found to be positively associated with membership and activism, not negatively. Lastly, ideological self-placement displayed an inverse curve, with those in the center of the political spectrum least partisan in behavior compared to those on the left and right. After the role of agencies, the cultural motivation to become engaged played the most important role in predicting the apathetic and the engaged.

Conclusions

Party channels have long been regarded as an important avenue of political participation in models of representative democracy, with parties considered the only organizations capable of aggregating as well as articulating interests. If their linkage function has decayed, as many commentators suggest, this could be a serious cause for concern for all who hold to the ideals of mass-branch party organizations. Without the membership as ballast, parties become less stable institutions, and leaders in government are less effectively tied to civic society during interelectoral periods. The previous chapter demonstrated considerable differences between countries in how many people joined parties; this study has established that membership levels are closely associated with the process of societal development, particularly the spread of television as an alternative channel of campaign communication. In traditional campaigns, parties remain reliant upon local volunteer foot soldiers, ad hoc planning, and loyal electorates. The pattern confirmed that party membership remained highest in many of the countries still using traditional campaign techniques, such as India and South Africa. In comparison, fewer joined or became active where TV broadcasting has become the predominant channel of party communications. The modern campaign is based upon a more centralized and professionalized party headquarters, televised channels of mass communication, and a more dealigned electorate. Through television, populist leaders can appeal directly to the public over the heads of rival party factions, as well as presenting a coordinated and consistent central message throughout the campaign, responding promptly to negative attacks and unexpected events. For major parties, mass organizations may have become not only increasingly redundant to leaders, but also occasionally dysfunctional, since members committed to particular ideological goals constrain and hinder the ability of leaders to maximize support across the entire electoral spectrum and to respond flexibly to new developments. In the longer term, therefore, it does seem likely that parties in long-established democracies have experienced a glacial erosion of membership as the pre-war model of electioneering has become increasingly supplemented by mediated channels of communications. Yet, in the shorter term, from 1980 to the early or mid-1990s, the survey evidence suggests that even in Western Europe there has not been a consistent further decline in party membership across all countries.

One important qualification to these conclusions should be noted: There are emerging indications that the focus on television broadcast channels may be in the process of being overtaken by a third stage, where postmodern campaigns are characterized by central control but local targeting, more fragmented and complex channels of communication, and persistent dealignment among voters.[17] In such an environment, party members may well experience a revival of importance, particularly where newer technologies allow grassroots volunteers to be deployed more effectively in strategic campaigns by party headquarters – for example, through targeted e-mail, telephone canvassing, and direct mail. Yet any postmodern campaign remains a work in progress, even in countries such as the United States and Britain that have perhaps adopted and deployed these techniques most aggressively in recent campaigns, so it remains too early to evaluate the potential impact of these developments on party organizations and political participation.

Without exploring this avenue further here, the evidence in this chapter suggests that many concerns about any sudden short-term "crisis" of party membership and activism may be exaggerated or misplaced. To summarize the key points, the evidence suggests the following general conclusions:

1. Patterns of party membership during the early to mid-1990s vary considerably cross-nationally, even within similar types of society and global regions.
2. At the national level, patterns of socioeconomic development – particularly the diffusion of access to television – are important factors driving this process. Party membership is usually highest where

television access is lowest. The reason for this pattern, it is suggested, is that parties need members in situations where traditional forms of face-to-face campaigning predominate, but parties no longer seek to recruit members so actively when they have other channels of electronic communication available to maximize electoral support.

3. The classification of party families remains limited, but the available evidence suggests that there were surprisingly few significant differences in levels of membership detectable by type of party ideology or party size.

4. At the individual level, the role of agencies and of motivational interest are far more important in explaining membership than the standard social structural differences of gender, age, class, and education. What appears to matter for party membership in most countries is less social background and personal resources per se than the social networks and political attitudes that lead people to become involved in the internal life of parties, all operating within the broader context of development.

It follows from the analysis that any positive or negative trends in levels of party membership can be expected to relate to changes in either the density and strength of social networks and voluntary associations, as social capital theories suggest, or to changes in political interest and motivation, as cultural theories emphasize. Future research monitoring trends in party membership based on subsequent waves of the World Values Study and related cross-national surveys should certainly explore these avenues. The question remains whether there are similar patterns of activism in civic society more generally and how far people are willing to become engaged through the traditional channels of unions and churches and the newer agencies of social movements and community associations. It is to these dimensions of public life that we now turn.

PART III

SOCIAL CAPITAL AND CIVIC SOCIETY

Something is happening and you don't know what it is, do you, Mr. Jones?
Bob Dylan

8

Social Capital and Civic Society

Theorists from Tocqueville and John Stuart Mill to Durkheim, Simmel, and Kornhauser have long emphasized the importance of civic society and voluntary associations as vital to the lifeblood of democracy. There is nothing particularly novel about claims for the virtues of civic associations and their capacity to perform many functions where states and the market fail. Pluralist theories popular in the 1960s emphasized the role of interest groups in aggregating and articulating public demands, providing multiple alternative channels of political participation linking citizens and the state.[1] Collaboration through a diverse range of informal organizations in the voluntary sector, such as Parent-Teacher Associations, local recycling groups, and village cooperatives, pluralists argue, provide local solutions to community problems, an alternative mechanism of governance, and a training ground for democracy. In the 1980s, social movement theorists revised and updated this approach by stressing the role of more amorphous organizations, exemplified by environmentalists, feminists, and the peace movement. These were seen as avenues of expression for post-materialist social values, especially for the younger generation, as well as organizations facilitating direct community action.[2] Work today continues to build on this foundation. But what is most striking about modern theories of civic society is the claim that typical face-to-face deliberative activities and horizontal collaboration within voluntary associations far removed from the political sphere, such as sports clubs, agricultural cooperatives, and philanthropic groups, promote interpersonal trust, fostering the capacity to work together and creating the bonds of social life that are the basis for civil society and democracy. Organized groups not only achieve certain instrumental goals, it is claimed, but in the process of doing so they also create the conditions for further collaboration, or social capital.

In order to examine the implications of social capital for democracy, the first section of this chapter reviews and summarizes the central arguments at the heart of Putnam's theory. The second section outlines the conceptual and methodological problems of measuring trends in social capital with the available empirical evidence. The third section develops an index of social capital, combining the distribution of associational activism with social trust. The next section compares the distribution of social capital around the world. The final section uses the index to examine the consequences of social capital for socioeconomic and democratic development. The conclusion considers the implications of the results for making democracies work.

Putnam's Theory of Social Capital

Theories of social capital originated in the ideas of Pierre Bourdieu and James Coleman, which emphasize the importance of social ties and shared norms to societal well-being and economic efficiency.[3] There are multiple alternative understandings of this intellectually fashionable but elusive concept. Here we shall focus on the way that Robert Putnam expanded this notion in *Making Democracies Work* (1993) and in *Bowling Alone* (2000) by linking ideas of social capital to the importance of civic associations and voluntary organizations for political participation and effective governance.[4] For Putnam, social capital is defined as *"connections among individuals – social networks and the norms of reciprocity and trustworthiness that arise from them."*[5] Most importantly, it is therefore understood as both a *structural* phenomenon (social networks) and a *cultural* phenomenon (social norms). This dual nature often creates problems associated with attempts to measure social capital that focus on one or the other dimension, but not on both.

Three core claims lie at the heart of this theory. The first is that *horizontal networks embodied in civic society, and the norms and values related to these ties, have important consequences*, both for the people in them and for society at large, producing both private goods and public goods. In particular, networks of friends, colleagues, and neighbors are commonly associated with the norms of generalized reciprocity in a skein of mutual obligations and responsibilities, so that dense bonds foster the conditions for collaboration, coordination, and cooperation that create collective goods. The shared understandings, tacit rules, agreed procedures, and social trust generated by personal contact and the bonds of friendship are believed to make it easier for people to continue to work together for mutual benefit: whether fund raising for a local hospital, sharing machinery at a local agricultural cooperative, running a childcare center or battered women's shelter, or discussing the plans of a local developer. Roladex networks can therefore be regarded as a form of investment, like financial or human capital, since social connections create further value, for both the individual and the group. Since the value of social capital exists in the relations among people, measurement needs to be at the societal level, and it is far more elusive than financial investment in company shares or factory machinery, or even educational investment in cognitive skills. For this reason, some economists such as Arrow express reservations about using the term.[6] But it seems reasonable to regard social capital as productive, analogous to physical or human capital, if it facilitates the achievement of certain common ends and engenders cooperative behavior that otherwise would not have been possible. Organizations in civic society such as unions, churches, and community groups, Putnam suggests, play a vital role in the production of social capital by bridging social cleavages, bringing together people from diverse backgrounds and values, and promoting "habits of the heart" such as tolerance, cooperation, and reciprocity, thereby contributing to a dense, rich, and vibrant social infrastructure.

Moreover, Putnam goes further than other contemporary theorists in arguing that *social capital has significant political consequences*. His theory can be understood as a two-step model of how civic society directly promotes social capital and of how, in turn, social capital (the social networks and cultural norms that arise from civic society) is believed to facilitate political participation and good governance. In particular, based on his analysis of Italian regional government, he claims that abundant and dense skeins of associational connections and rich civic societies encourage effective governance. The reasons for this relationship remain underdeveloped theoretically, but it is suggested that associations have both internal effects, instilling in their members norms and values such as collaboration and shared responsibilities, and external effects on the wider polity, as pluralists have long argued, in terms of interest articulation and aggregation.[7] In democracies rich in social capital, Putnam argues, watchful citizens are more likely to hold elected leaders accountable for their actions, and leaders are more likely to believe that their acts will be held to account. Civic society and civic norms are believed to strengthen connections between citizens and the state – for example, by encouraging political discussion and mobilizing electoral turnout. When the performance of representative government is effective, Putnam reasons, this should increase public confidence in the working of particular institutions such as the legislature and the executive, and should also maximize diffuse support for the political system.[8] Good government is believed to foster strong linkages between citizens and the states that promote the underlying conditions generating civic engagement and participatory democracy.[9] The central claim is not that the connection between social and political trust operates at the individual level, so that socially trusting individuals are also exceptionally trusting of government; and indeed, little evidence supports this contention.[10] Rather, the associations between social and political trust should be evident at the *societal* level, as social capital is a relational phenomenon that can be the property of groups, local communities, and nations, but not of individuals. *We* can be rich or poor in social capital, but *I* cannot.

Lastly, in *Bowling Alone* Putnam presents the most extensive battery of evidence that *civic society in general, and social capital in particular, have suffered substantial erosion in the postwar years in America*. Putnam considers multiple factors that may have contributed to this development, such as the pressures of time and money. But it is changes in technology and the media, particularly the rise of television entertainment as America's main source of leisure activity, that Putnam fingers as the major culprits responsible for the erosion of social connectedness and civic disengagement in the United States, with the effects being most profound among the younger generation.[11] In America during the 1950s, he argues, leisure gradually moved fro n the collective experience characteristic of the movie theatre, urban stoop, local diner, and town hall meeting to become privatized by the flickering light of the television tube. The privatization of leisure has led, he suggests, to a more deep-seated retreat from public life. Putnam is suitably cautious in extending these claims to suggest that similar trends are evident in other postindustrial societies, but by implication, if these have experienced similar secular changes in technology and the media, there should be some evidence of a parallel fall in social capital. In sum, the heart of Putnam's thesis makes certain strong claims:

1. Social networks and social norms matter for societal cooperation, coordination, and collaboration;
2. Social capital has important consequences for democracy; and
3. Social capital has declined in postwar America.

These important theoretical claims generate certain interesting hypotheses that should be open to empirical testing. Most attention in the literature has examined whether social capital has eroded over the years, in America and elsewhere. Yet we need to examine support for the logically prior question of whether any possible decline in social capital actually matters for making democracies work, and in particular, if nations rich in social capital are characterized by tolerance, engagement in democracy, and effective democratic governance. If social capital does have these consequences, *and* if it is true that social capital has been eroding during the postwar era in postindustrial societies, this thesis has important implications for the vitality of democracy. If it doesn't, then any erosion may prove of little concern politically, and the demise of social clubs such as the Elks becomes little more than a historical curiosity.

Conceptual and Methodological Problems of Measurement

Before examining any evidence, we need to pay considerable attention to the many conceptual dangers and methodological traps littering the pathway of any attempt to measure trends in social capital. There should be flashing signs posted: "Beware all who enter here." Attempts to capture this phenomenon using existing empirical data remain frustratingly elusive. Social capital may prove to be an example of a battery of sophisticated techniques being widely employed but generating more heat than light, because social scientists not have honed valid, consistent, and reliable measures of the phenomenon under investigation. The three most important problems of measurement involve excluding informal networks, including structural-but not cultural dimensions of social capital, and examining individual- but not diffuse-level effects.

Formal and Informal Networks
The most common approach following Putnam has measured social networks in structural terms (by formal associational membership) rather than in terms of more informal and intangible social bonds. In most countries, surveys monitoring longitudinal trends in association membership are often limited to one or two sectors, such as churches and unions, and data is usually unavailable prior to the 1960s or 1970s. As a result, historical-institutional studies replicating *Bowling Alone* have focused on the official records of membership in voluntary organizations such as social clubs and philanthropic societies. Yet this strategy faces multiple challenges, at progressively greater levels of difficulty.[12]

One problem is the accuracy and reliability of historical records: Perhaps even more than official party records, the membership rolls for decentralized voluntary organizations, community groups, and local associations are subject to multiple flaws; many may be incomplete; and figures may be systematically exaggerated out of organizational self-aggrandizement. Changes in the legal or financial environment may cause major shifts in record keeping – for example, following the centralization and computerization of records – producing more accurate estimates and at the same time sharp falls in the apparent membership numbers. Moreover, official records fail to distinguish between "de jure" and "de facto" membership. There is an important difference between long-standing voluntary activists involved in the day-to-day grind of maintaining the organization – unpaid shop stewards, housing cooperative managers, branch secretaries of the PTA – and the more peripheral hangers-on, irregular participants, and nominal members attracted by various secondary benefits such as receiving medical or insurance discounts, or affiliated automatically by virtue of occupation or location. The number of core activists and organizers may have remained unchanged, even if the more tangential followers who rarely attended meetings have melted away.

Even if there are reliable and consistent historical records, another related difficulty lies in the common systemic bias toward measuring the rolls of older, more bureaucratic organizations, such as unions and community groups, that have card-carrying, dues-paying members. Professional associations, labor unions, and church-related groups often have a bureaucratic form of organization characterized by official membership rules, a hierarchical and bureaucratic structure, legal recognition, written constitutions, independent funds, and full-time officials.[13] By contrast, it is far more difficult to pin down evidence for the more informal sense of belonging and identification with social movements – feminists, pacifist groups, environmentalists – where it is often difficult to know what it means to "join" even for the most committed (how many feminists who sympathize with the women's movement can be counted as card-carrying members of NOW or equivalent bodies?). The most active and demanding forms of mobilization today, exemplified by the anti-globalization protest movement at Seattle, Gothenberg, and Genoa, are characterized by loose-knit and decentralized communication, minimal formal structures of leadership, and ad hoc coalitions of disparate and autonomous activists, all committed to achieving political change, but none of whom can be captured by conventional membership rolls.[14] In poorer developing societies as well, grassroots networks of community activists coming together informally to work on local problems of schools, clean water, or food production are rarely characterized by the Weberian bureaucratic organization and formal membership.[15]

Measuring Structural but Not Cultural Dimensions

Even if we are able to overcome these initial hurdles and to establish accurate, comprehensive, and reliable records for belonging to a wide variety of traditional interest groups and new social movements, our analysis faces an even more serious difficulty. Association membership represents a proxy indicator both for the structural features of social capital (social networks) and for the cultural norms (of trust and cooperation). Macro-level trends are often examined across a variety of associations such as veterans groups, sports clubs, and college fraternities, but it is not clear whether all voluntary organizations are equally effective in generating the cultural norms of reciprocal cooperation, tolerance, and social trust, or even the bonds of friendship and collegiality, that are at the heart of social capital theory. For example, youth organizations such as the Scouts or Guides, and school-based sports clubs and arts clubs, may play particularly important roles in the formative process of socialization, stamping norms of collaboration and mutual respect in childhood, whereas professional associations and trade unions may be most effective at maintaining instrumental networks in the workplace. Much of the early work regarded the membership in formal associations as proxy indicators of social networks, yet it is possible that informal linkages such as daily meals eaten together, workplace discussions over the water cooler, and extended family ties may prove richer and denser ways to generate the social norms of mutual trust, reciprocity, and tolerance than card-carrying membership. Formal organizational affiliation is, therefore, only one indicator of community networking, and not necessarily the most important. Indeed, there could well be a trade-off involved, if people in certain cultures rely more upon close-knit extended family ties, or bonds of blood and belonging, than on more bureaucratic interest-based advocacy groups.

A related issue is that in civic organizations – the Red Cross, condo associations, organic food cooperatives – these two dimensions may go happily hand-in-hand. But, as Putnam acknowledges, there can also be sharp divergences in the functions of social networks, just as financial capital can be used to buy bread or guns. Networks can bind groups together in ways that are negative for society as a whole, reinforcing the practices of nepotism, ethnic hatred, and sectarianism. After all, the blood brotherhood of the Mafia, the tight networks of the Colombian drug cartels, and the exclusionary and racist views of the Ku Klux Klan all exemplify close-knit, mutually dependent communities. Tolerance and trust of members within the community does not necessarily mean tolerance of outsiders, sometimes just the opposite.[16] Putnam acknowledges this in distinguishing between "bridging" networks, which are socially inclusive and porous, thereby building connections between heterogeneous groups, and "bonding" networks that exclude outsiders.[17] Bonding networks can be particularly problematic in societies such as Bosnia and Somalia that are divided by deep ethnic conflicts, yet mobilized into rival organizations by populist factions and authoritarian leaders. In response to this difficulty, Putnam argues that the challenge is to channel the positive forces of social capital toward virtuous purposes and to foster "bridging" or cross-cutting inclusive networks, exemplified by youth sports clubs in South Africa and the Civic Forum in Northern Ireland, that bring together different parts of the community in a common public space.[18] For all the apparent concern about the decline of associations such as the Elks, the Boy Scouts, and the League of Women Voters, few would mourn the similar demise of the Ku Klux Klan or the Michigan Militia. What matters isn't the erosion of voluntary associations per se, but the erosion (if there has been an erosion) of those that contribute positively to civic life. But acknowledging that social networks can have positive *or* negative cultural consequences means that we need to go well beyond official membership per se to gain a better understanding of the cultural role of voluntary organizations in promoting civility, cooperation, and trust. Associations can be classified into those positive or negative for democracy by directly monitoring the values, norms, and attitudes of their members.

Individual or Diffuse-level Effects?

In addition, sociologists such as Edwards and Foley, following Coleman's conceptualization, stress that social capital is essentially context-specific; it is manifested in the social relations and social norms that exist within groups that facilitate cooperative action, but it is not necessarily transferable to other contexts.[19] For example, Coleman suggests that much of the work of the diamond trade in New York is based on relations of reciprocity and mutual trust among a close-bound community of merchants, but these norms do not persist beyond that context, so that traders are not necessarily equally trusting of members of the general public outside the market. People living in high-trust, close-knit communities, such as farmers and fishermen in northern Norway, the Amish in Pennsylvania, and members of monastic communities in Greece, are not necessarily equally trusting of their fellow man (for good reason) if visiting the Bronx, Bogotá, or Bangkok. If it is contextual, then it makes no sense to measure social capital at the individual level outside of the specific community. You and I can display high and low trust simultaneously, depending upon our location. Edwards and Foley conclude that research needs to examine diffuse aggregate or societal-level patterns of cooperation, tolerance, and civility in divergent contexts, suggesting that careful cross-national research attentive to differences in political and economic contexts is most appropriate to test the claims of the role of social capital and civic society in democracy.[20] Studies of Western public opinion by Newton and by Kaase strengthen this point.[21] Newton concluded that weak or nonexistent patterns linked social trust and political confidence at the individual level, but that a positive relationship existed between these factors at the national level, despite certain important outliers to this pattern.

Mixed Trends and Inconclusive Results
Not surprisingly, given all of these potential difficulties of conceptualization and measurement, little consensus has developed in the literature. The most detailed studies have examined whether social capital has clearly suffered a long-term decline in America, as suggested. In *Bowling Alone*, drawing upon U.S. data, Putnam demonstrates that membership rolls in many common forms of civic association that expanded during the early twentieth century subsequently faded in postwar America, including church attendance, membership in chapter-based social clubs such as the Elks and Moose, and the participation in the PTA. Based on the survey evidence available since the late 1960s and early 1970s, Putnam also shows an erosion of traditional forms of conventional political participation, such as attending public meetings, working for a political party, and signing petitions.[22]

Yet Putnam's claims have come under friendly fire from several commentators.[23] Rotolo reexamined the evidence from the General Social Survey, replicating Putnam's approach, and concluded that trends in American association membership rarely displayed a consistent linear decline from 1974 to 1994.[24] Instead, he found that some groups did experience falling membership (unions, fraternal organizations, sports-related groups, and Greek organizations), while six other groups had stable rates, and membership rose substantially in others (church-related groups, hobby clubs, literary groups, professional associations, school-related organizations, and veterans' groups). My previous work has also questioned whether there has been a steady secular slide in civic engagement in America, even in common indicators such as electoral turnout, interest in politics, and campaign activism.[25] Historical-institutional and rational-choice accounts of American associational life have also offered alternative interpretations of the thesis of civic decline.[26]

Attempts to track down parallel developments in similar postindustrial societies elsewhere has proved even more inconclusive.[27] Research has generally failed to establish evidence for a consistent secular decline in association membership in most countries. Instead, studies usually point to two patterns, namely: (1) complex and contradictory membership trends among different types of associational groups, such as trade unions, churches, and environmental organizations, and (2) persistent and stable differences in the strength and vitality of civic society in different cultural regions around the globe, such as long-standing contrasts between the Nordic region and the former Soviet states. For example, Kees Aarts presents one of the most thorough comparative studies of Western European trends in membership in traditional organizations and trade union membership from the 1950s to the 1990s, and of support for new social movements during the 1980s.[28] The study found stable differences between countries in the strength of membership, and trendless fluctuation in trends over time, rather than any general erosion of membership across Western Europe. Historical case studies in particular nations have generally confirmed a complicated and nuanced pattern. In one of the most detailed studies, Peter Hall examined trends in a wide array of indicators of social capital in Britain.[29] Membership in voluntary associations, he concluded, has been roughly stable since the 1950s, rising in the 1960s and subsiding only modestly since then. While in Britain some types of association membership have faded in popularity in recent decades, including membership in churches and parties, other groups, such as environmental organizations and charities, have expanded, so that overall the voluntary sector in Britain remains rich and vibrant. Similar case studies confirm complex trends in Sweden, Japan, and Australia, rather than a steady secular erosion of associational life and civic engagement.[30] Studies of a wide range of postcommunist and developing societies also belie the existence of any simple linkages among social networks, socioeconomic development, and good government.[31]

The comparison of social trust available in the three waves of the World Values Study also suggests a mixed picture. It is difficult to pursue the analysis further on a systematic basis, because different nations were included in different waves of the survey, but the available data suggests that trust has been falling in many countries, but apparently rising in others. The results of the comparative research conducted to date mean that the case for a widespread erosion of associational life and social trust essentially remains "unproven," based on the available evidence.[32] If association membership is flagging in postwar America, as *Bowling Alone* suggests, then particular historical events and specific institutional arrangements in the United States may best explain this pattern, rather than broad secular trends (such as changes in the mass media, the family, or the workforce).

Measuring Social Capital

These considerations lay the foundations for the criteria necessary to develop a reliable and valid measure of social capital. The arguments suggest that any measure needs to take account of both structural and cultural dimensions of social capital simultaneously, that is, the strength of social networks (measured in terms of belonging to a wide range of associational groups and social movements) and the cultural norms (measured by feelings of social trust). It also needs to gauge an informal sense of belonging as well as formal membership. And since social capital is essentially a relational phenomenon, any consistent linkage between these dimensions can be expected to operate, and needs to be measured, at the societal level. Communities with multiple and dense overlapping networks are the ones where we would expect to find the strongest culture of mutual respect, tolerance, and cooperation, as well as of civic engagement. Rich ethnographic and participant observation studies of the day-to-day inner life of particular groups and organizations offer insights into this phenomenon, although it is always difficult to generalize from these to other contexts. Societies can compare and classify detailed studies of local areas or regions, a strategy that holds certain factors constant within a country (such as the electoral system or the broad level of socioeconomic development) and isolates local variations in the dependent variables (such as the performance of Italian regional governments, or the rate of crime in American states).

Evidence in this study is drawn from the World Values Study (WVS) conducted from 1995 to 1997, aggregated at the societal level. The survey allows comparison of social capital in forty-seven nations, including a wide range of developing and industrialized societies, older and newer democracies, semi-democracies, and nondemocratic political systems, and cultural regions of the world.[33] The cross-national framework creates a more complex comparison than studies of regions within a single country, but it has the advantage of facilitating broader generalizations by varying the political systems under scrutiny. Given the claims about the role of civic society in facilitating the process of democratization, it is particularly important to compare established, transitional, and consolidating democracies. Some societies that are included are relatively homogeneous, while others are deeply divided by ethnic, nationalist, and religious conflict. The WVS allows us to compare measures of belonging to voluntary organizations and civic associations, and also provides a direct measure of personal trust, which lies at the heart of social capital theory, and multiple standard indicators of political participation and civic engagement as the dependent variables.

Measuring Association Membership

The 1995 WVS item measured association membership as follows: *"Now I am going to read off a list of voluntary organizations; for each one, could you tell me whether you are an active member, an inactive member, or not a member of that type of organization?"* The list included nine broad categories, including church or religious organizations, sports or recreational organizations, political parties, art, music, or educational organizations, labor unions, professional associations, charitable organizations, environmental organizations, and any other voluntary organization. The range covers traditional interest groups and mainstream civic associations, as well as including some new social movements. This question replicates the standard item included since 1974 in the American General Social Survey. This measure remains limited in an important regard, since it asks respondents to indicate only whether they are members of one or more associations or groups *within* each category. It therefore cannot be used to gauge whether someone belongs to several related groups within a category – several different environmental associations, say, or religious organizations. Another serious restriction is that the wording of this item has varied slightly in successive waves of the WVS; this study analyzes data only from the mid-1990s wave, rather than providing any comparison to earlier data.[34] Despite these limitations, reported membership and activism in many different types of association is arguably a more important indicator of the psychological strength of belonging and identification than payment of official dues as documented in official records. The measure allows us to analyze patterns of membership in the most common types of association, including religious-based, union, and environmental groups, that represent some of the classic linkage organizations with political parties.

Associational Activism

Since there is considerable uncertainty regarding the most appropriate empirical operationalization, several core independent variables were constructed from these items for comparison. The first measure (VOL-ANY) developed an overall summary gauge of belonging to *any* of the categories of voluntary organization (measured as a 0/1 dummy variable). This measure assumes that what matters for civic society and social capital is belonging to at least one associational category – such as a church-based, sports, or union group – and that it does not much matter which one or how actively people are involved.

It can be argued, however, that civic society is denser and stronger if people belong to multiple overlapping categories, such as churches and philanthropic groups, or unions and environmental organizations. Accordingly, in order to test this proposition, an alternative measure (VOL-ORG) summed all of the categories to estimate the mean number of associational categories of organizations that people join (using a nine-point scale). This indicator estimated the spread of multiple memberships. Overall, 40 percent were nonjoiners, unconnected to any voluntary association. About one quarter (twenty-seven percent) belonged to just one organization, while the remaining third (thirty-two percent) were multiple joiners who belonged to two or more groups. The individual-level overlap among membership in different sectors (not presented here) found that the coefficients vary in strength, although all proved to be significant.[35]

Yet what might matter is not passive belonging but more active engagement in the inner life of associations. Civic engagement may be boosted by face-to-face collaboration and deliberation, typified by regular local meetings, but not by check-paying membership among more peripheral supporters. This approach follows the arguments of Baron, Field, and Schuller that mere aggregation is insufficient: "Grossing up the numbers of organizations to which people belong tells us very little about the strength of social capital if it is not accompanied by information on two scores: what people actually do as members of an association, and how far this relates to public as well as private goods."[36] In order to examine this proposition, a third measure (VOL-ACT) was created, a scale weighting active membership, passive membership, and not belonging.

A simple correlation analysis showed that at the national level all of these measures of associational life were strongly related to each other (all correlations were significant and strong [R = 0.75 and above]). The VOL-ANY measure was eventually selected for inclusion in the final Index of social capital, as this measure incorporated the richest indicator of active engagement in associational life, and the other measures were dropped in order to simplify the construction of a single index. The subsequent analysis was double-checked using the alternative measures, and this procedure did not substantially affect the main results and findings.

Social Trust

Social trust was gauged in the 1995 WVS by the question: *"Generally speaking, would you say that most people can be trusted or that you can't be too careful in dealing with people?"* This measure remains limited for many reasons. It gives respondents the option of a simple dichotomy, whereas most modern survey items today present more subtle continuous scales. The double negative in the latter half of the question may be confusing to respondents. No social context is presented to respondents, nor can they distinguish among different categories, such as relative levels of trust in friends, colleagues, family, strangers, or compatriots. Nevertheless, this item has become accepted as the standard indicator of social or interpersonal trust, following its use as a long time series in the American GSS beginning in the early 1970s, so it will be adopted here to facilitate replication across different studies.

The Index of Social Capital

The Putnam conception of social capital was operationalized and measured by combining social networks (gauged by active membership in voluntary organizations) with the cultural norms of social trust, based on the measures presented here.[37] Weighting procedures were considered, but this did not seem appropriate because the index correlated fairly evenly across the two items, although slightly more strongly toward social trust. The index produced a mean of 2.98, a median of 2.51, and a standard deviation of 1.71. The index was slightly skewed toward the lower end of the scale; standardization procedures were initially considered and tested but eventually rejected in favor of greater ease of interpretation. The distribution in the forty-seven societies under comparison, ranked by the summary index in the final column, is shown in Table 8.1 and Figure 8.1. The results reveal striking variations across nations, in a clustered pattern, with the Nordic and Anglo-American societies highest in social capital, and the countries of South America and the Central European states at the bottom of the ranking.

Mapping the Dimensions and Distribution of Social Capital

In order to examine the consistency of the index, the two dimensions of the Putnam conceptualization of social capital are illustrated in Figure 8.2. Societies rich in both social trust and associational activism can be expected to fall into the top right quadrant, as the purest ideal type illustrating societies affluent in social capital. Those that fall into the bottom left quadrant lack both social trust and associational activism. The other quadrants represent mixed societies.

The actual spread of countries is illustrated in Figure 8.3. The graph shows some striking clusters of societies that strongly relate to cultural legacies in regions around the world. Societies richest in social capital, located in the top right-hand corner, include the Nordic nations (Norway, Sweden, and Finland) as well as Australia, West Germany, and Switzerland. The United States proves to be exceptionally high on associational activism, as others such as Curtis and colleagues have long emphasized,[38] and moderately strong on social trust. If there has been a systematic erosion of American organizational involvement, then this has been from a relatively high base, and many other strong and stable democracies manage effectively with lower levels of activism.

By contrast, many nations fall into the opposite quadrant as impoverished in social capital, including the ex-Soviet republics in Central Europe

TABLE 8.1. *Mean scores on the independent variables in forty-seven societies, mid-1990s*

Nation	Social Trust	Vol_Any	Vol_Org	Vol_Act	Social Capital
Norway	0.65	0.89	2.47	12.46	8.28
Sweden	0.57	0.92	2.57	12.59	7.26
Finland	0.48	0.97	2.48	12.01	5.91
United States	0.35	0.92	3.59	14.54	5.50
Australia	0.40	0.88	2.69	13.25	5.41
New Zealand	0.47	0.87	2.33	10.97	5.34
Germany	0.40	0.86	2.13	12.09	5.02
Taiwan	0.40	0.79	3.51	11.56	4.80
China	0.50	0.49	0.95	9.33	4.77
Switzerland	0.34	0.81	2.31	12.18	4.35
Japan	0.40	0.51	0.93	10.26	4.09
Dominican Republic	0.25	0.92	3.27	13.78	3.75
Mexico	0.26	0.83	2.90	13.31	3.73
Korea, Republic Of	0.30	0.81	2.46	12.05	3.68
India	0.33	0.54	1.55	11.3	3.67
Spain	0.29	0.58	1.39	10.97	3.21
Czech Republic	0.27	0.59	1.06	10.38	2.88
Ukraine	0.29	0.47	0.60	9.71	2.81
Chile	0.21	0.75	2.32	12.23	2.80
Slovakia	0.26	0.62	1.11	10.41	2.72
Croatia	0.23	0.80	1.67	11.22	2.70
Albania	0.24	0.68	1.05	10.35	2.58
Uruguay	0.21	0.59	1.39	10.99	2.45
Latvia	0.24	0.46	0.70	9.93	2.44
Hungary	0.22	0.49	0.82	10.27	2.41
Nigeria	0.18	0.96	3.90	13.55	2.35
Russian Federation	0.23	0.50	0.65	9.84	2.30
Bangladesh	0.20	0.63	1.53	11.57	2.29
Belarus	0.23	0.52	0.70	9.8	2.27
Bulgaria	0.24	0.25	0.35	9.49	2.23
South Africa	0.15	0.95	3.07	13.61	2.20
Ghana	0.17	1.00	6.00	13.65	2.20
Estonia	0.21	0.43	0.64	9.82	2.13
Georgia	0.21	0.28	0.45	9.64	2.11
Moldova, Republic Of	0.22	0.65	1.03	9.36	2.09
Lithuania	0.21	0.32	0.48	9.52	2.06
Romania	0.18	0.55	1.14	10.61	1.96
Argentina	0.17	0.56	1.10	10.66	1.93
Azerbaijan	0.19	0.44	0.60	9.71	1.88
Venezuela	0.13	0.63	1.87	11.67	1.81
Slovenia	0.15	0.70	1.29	10.69	1.67
Colombia	0.11	0.59	1.12	10.4	1.18

Nation	Social Trust	Vol_Any	Vol_Org	Vol_Act	Social Capital
Macedonia	0.08	0.49	1.50	10.89	0.92
Peru	0.05	0.72	2.15	11.95	0.60
Philippines	0.06	0.49	1.03	10.59	0.60
Turkey	0.05	0.30	0.50	9.69	0.53
Brazil	0.03	0.81	2.13	12.24	0.36

Note: See text for detailed explanations of these variables.

Social trust: *"Generally speaking, would you say that most people can be trusted (1) or that you can't be too careful in dealing with people? (0)"* The proportion responding 'can be trusted' in each society.

Vol_Any: The proportion of the adult population who say they belong to at least one of the nine categories of voluntary associations.

Vol_Org: The number of organizational sectors to which people belong, e.g., if they are members of a trade union, a sports club, and a political party.

Vol_Act: The organizational scale adding together whether people were active members, passive members, or not members of any of the nine categories of voluntary organizations.

Social Capital: Social trust*Vol_Act. *Source:* World Values Study.

such as Moldova, Georgia, Azerbaijan, and Russia, which clustered together with low trust and activism, along with Turkey.[39] South American nations such as Uruguay, Venezuela, and Argentina are characterized by slightly greater associational activism but equally weak bonds of interpersonal trust.[40] The Central American nations seem to be located somewhere between the United States and the South American societies; they are characterized by moderately low social trust, but greater organizational linkages. The three African nations cluster together in the bottom right-hand quadrant, as nations of joiners with extensive membership but low social trust. And in the opposite quadrant, the three societies sharing a Confucian culture (China, Japan, and Taiwan) all display moderate social trust, relatively, but low organizational involvement.[41] Japan may have what Fukuyama terms "spontaneous sociability,"[42] with a strong sense of shared norms and a culture of personal trust, but weaker institutionalized associations. The mixed societies are important theoretically; we will need to consider further the cultural and institutional factors leading to the trusting nonjoiners, and the joining mistrusters.

The patterns were confirmed by the correlation analysis in Table 8.2, which shows that Central and Eastern Europe were significantly weaker than average in civic society; Latin America was significantly more mistrusting; and the Scandinavian societies were higher than average on both dimensions. The overall distribution suggests that long-standing historical and cultural traditions function to imprint distinctive patterns on clusters of nations, despite some outliers. We can dispute the nature, origins, and

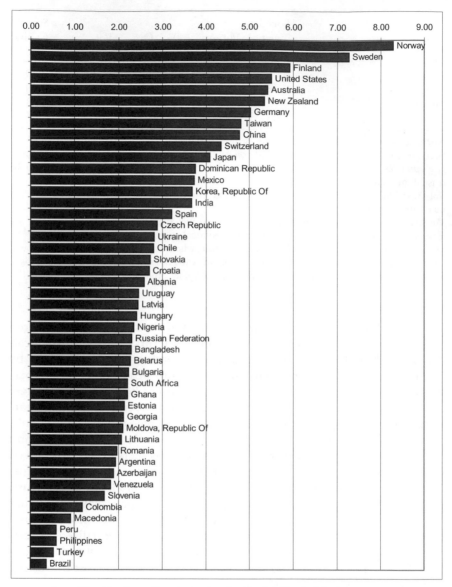

FIGURE 8.1. Distribution of societies by the Social Capital Index.

meaning of social capital, but it appears that whatever the Nordic "X" factor is, the ex-Soviet societies lack it.

For comparison, to check whether the distribution was reliable and robust or contingent upon the particular measure used, Figure 8.4 examines the pattern of social trust mapped against membership in *any* of the

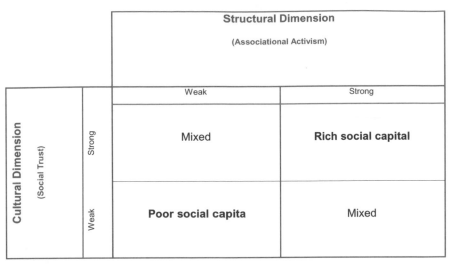

FIGURE 8.2. Typology of societies by social capital.

associational categories. The scattergram shows some minor differences that need further explanation (e.g., New Zealand), but nevertheless the overall pattern is reasonably similar. Again, the Nordic nations displayed the greatest social capital, while the societies in postcommunist Central Europe performed poorly. The fact that similar patterns are generated by two alternative (although not wholly independent) measures gives us greater confidence in the reliability and consistency of the index.

The Consequences of Social Capital

This raises the "so what?" issue. According to this evidence, social capital is not randomly distributed across the globe; instead, it produces fairly predictable patterns, and ones that appear to be closely tied to patterns of socioeconomic and democratic development. Those societies richest in social capital are all established democracies with some of the most affluent postindustrial economies in the world. To check this observation more systematically, Table 8.3 presents the correlations between the index and its component measures, and a wide range of interrelated aggregate indicators of human development. The correlations should not be taken as suggesting patterns of causation, since theoretically we would expect considerable interaction among these terms. We cannot yet unravel the direction of causality from the available cross-national data in order to claim with any confidence whether, for example, the rising living standards and educational levels associated with socioeconomic growth cause growing reservoirs of

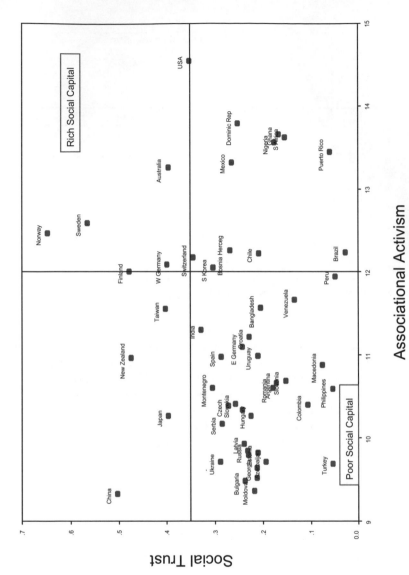

Associational Activism

FIGURE 8.3. The map of social capital (social trust and associational activism), mid-1990s.

TABLE 8.2. *Correlations between social capital and global regions*

Region		Vol_Any	Vol_Org	Vol_Act	Social Trust	Social Capital Index
Africa	R	.411	.601	.454	−.177	−.114
	Sig.	.004	.000	.001	.234	.447
Asia	R	−.021	−.019	−.088	.260	.187
	Sig.	.890	.897	.554	.078	.209
Central and	R	−.532	−.540	−.584	−.210	−.319
Eastern Europe	Sig.	.000	.000	.000	.156	.029
Middle East	R	−.260	−.162	−.164	−.223	−.213
	Sig.	.078	.277	.271	.132	.150
North America	R	.232	.282	.416	.083	.203
	Sig.	.116	.054	.004	.580	.171
South America	R	.093	.074	.173	−.377	−.300
	Sig.	.534	.621	.245	.009	.040
Scandinavia	R	.349	.180	.217	.605	.642
	Sig.	.016	.227	.144	.000	.000
Western Europe	R	.124	.048	.101	.172	.186
	Sig.	.405	.749	.499	.248	.209

Note: For the construction of the social capital measures, see Table 8.1.
Source: World Values Study, mid-1990s.

interpersonal trust, or whether trusting societies generate the underlying conditions most condusive to human development and the shift from agricultural to industrial and post/industrial societies. Historical time-series data stretching over a long period, and detailed case studies of particular developing nations, are necessary if we are to examine these issues, and to establish which comes first in this classic chicken-and-egg conundrum. Nevertheless, we can explore whether social capital and its component parts are closely linked today to many common indicators of socioeconomic development.

The results in Table 8.3 confirm that *social capital was consistently and positively associated with many indicators of socioeconomic and human development*, including levels of education, the UNDP Human Development Index (combining longevity, education, and income), per capita GDP (measured by the UNDP in purchasing power parity), and the distribution of access to the mass media (television sets, newspapers, and the internet). In short, the most affluent societies are usually the richest in social capital as well. But there is an important qualification to be made. A glance down the component measures of social capital reveals that it is social trust that is significantly related to socioeconomic development; at the same time, there is little evidence that these developmental indicators are related

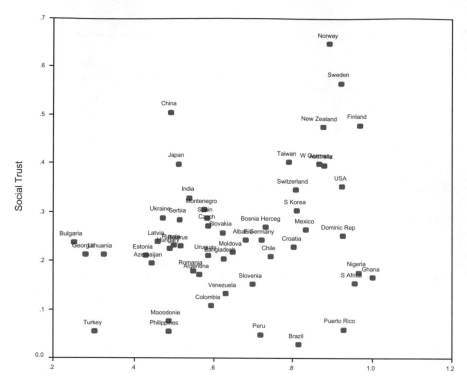

FIGURE 8.4. The alternative map of social capital (social trust and associational membership), mid-1990s.

systematically to the propensity to belong to voluntary organizations and associational activism. Social capital is associated with socioeconomic development, according to this evidence, but *this link appears to operate through social trust, not civic society.* Only one or two coefficients proved to be significant in any of the correlations between the three alternative measures of voluntary organizations and socioeconomic development.[43] This is an important finding, one that qualifies the Putnam theory and deserves to be tested in a wider range of societies with alternative indicators of development. Whether, as Fukuyama suggests,[44] trusting societies have a common set of ethical principles and internalized norms that are conducive to efficient dealings in the economic marketplace, or whether greater prosperity and economic security reduces levels of crime and grinding poverty that may cause us to fear our fellow citizens, remains an open question that cannot be explored further here.

TABLE 8.3. *Correlations between social capital and socioeconomic development*

		Vol_ Any	Vol_ Org	Vol_ Act	Social Trust	Social Capital Index
Gross educational enrollment,	R	.233	−.027	.125	**.481**	**.516**
1998 (N = 46)	Sig.	.119	.859	.409	.001	.000
Change in educational enrollment,	R	.263	−.057	.120	**.452**	**.459**
1970–98 (N = 25)	Sig.	.204	.788	.568	.023	.021
Life expectancy 1998	R	−.021	−.210	−.104	**.457**	**.457**
(N = 47)	Sig.	.888	.156	.488	.001	.001
Percent urban population, UNDP	R	−.035	−.120	−.018	.102	.141
2000 (N = 46)	Sig.	.817	.426	.908	.498	.350
Human Development Index (HDI),	R	.089	−.188	−.039	**.429**	**.467**
1975 (N = 29)	Sig.	.645	.329	.842	.020	.011
Human Development Index (HDI),	R	.102	−.127	.002	**.475**	**.499**
1998 (N = 46)	Sig.	.499	.400	.990	.001	.000
HDI Rank, 1998	R	−.145	.071	−.065	**−.503**	**−.539**
(N = 46)	Sig.	.337	.639	.667	.000	.000
GDP, 1975 (per capita GDP	R	.338	**.127**	.217	**.615**	**.657**
in PPP) (N = 32)	Sig.	.058	.489	.233	.000	.000
GDP, 1998 (per capita GDP	R	**.418**	.248	**.345**	**.666**	**.727**
in PPP) (N = 46)	Sig.	.004	.097	.019	.000	.000
Change in GDP, 1975–98	R	.284	.106	.187	**.671**	**.699**
(N = 32)	Sig.	.115	.563	.305	.000	.000
TV sets per 1,000, 1997,	R	.025	−.107	−.033	**.587**	**.577**
World Bank (N = 46)	Sig.	.871	.480	.830	.000	.000
Newspapers per 1,000, 1996,	R	.152	−.008	.061	**.744**	**.707**
UNESCO (N = 43)	Sig.	.329	.961	.697	.000	.000
Percentage of population online,	R	**.491**	**.336**	**.416**	**.698**	**.786**
2000, NUA (N = 47)	Sig.	.000	.021	.004	.000	.000

Note: For the construction of the social capital measures, see Table 8.1. Correlation significant at the 0.05 level and the 0.01 level are indicated in **bold**. The number of countries (N.) under comparison for each indicator is given in parenthesis. Aggregate data was not available for all forty-seven nations.

Sources:
Social capital measures: World Values Study, mid-1990s.
Human Development Index: UNDP, *Human Development Report 2001*. New York: UNDP/Oxford University Press.
Per capita GDP in purchasing power parity: World Bank development indicators.
Newspapers per 1,000: UNESCO, *1999 UNESCO Statistical Yearbook*. New York: UNESCO.
Percentage online: *www.NUA.com*. For details of the weighting procedure used, see Pippa Norris. 2001. *Digital Divide: Civic Engagement, Information Poverty and the Internet Worldwide*. Cambridge: Cambridge University Press.

How does social capital relate to the indicators of the political health of democracy? As noted earlier, Putnam's thesis makes certain strong claims about the beneficial consequences of social capital for democracy, generating a series of important hypotheses that are open to testing, especially using systematic cross-national evidence. Based on the arguments developed in *Making Democracy Work*, societies rich in social capital (as defined by associational networks and social trust) should be characterized by considerable reservoirs of social tolerance, relatively high levels of civic engagement – as measured by standard indicators such as interest and political discussion – and should display more effective institutions of representative democracy. If social capital does have these consequences, then any shrinkage in the pool of social capital has important implications for democracy. If not, then it may not actually matter politically (although, of course, any erosion could still have social or economic implications).

Social Capital and Social Tolerance

One of the most common claims in theories of social capital is that the face-to-face contact and bridging quality of many voluntary organizations and civic associations brings together people from different walks of life, social strata, and political backgrounds, thereby promoting tolerance of divergent lifestyles and attitudes. Social tolerance was measured in the World Values Study by the following question: "*On this list are various groups of people. Could you please sort out any that you would not like to have as neighbors?*" The list included ten categories – for example, people with a criminal record, people of a different race, drug addicts, and homosexuals. Responses were used to construct a social tolerance scale. There are many alternative measures of willingness to live and let live, to tolerate diverse lifestyles and political perspectives, but this one taps many of the most common types of narrow-mindedness and bigotry. Again, simple correlations were used to examine the relationship between social capital and social tolerance by nation, as illustrated by the scatter plot in Figure 8.5, before multivariate models were tested with controls for levels of socioeconomic development and democratization.

The results confirmed that societies rich in social capital tend to be generally more tolerant of diverse lifestyles than countries poor in social capital. The correlation was significant and moderately strong ($R = 0.35$, p. $> .01$). Moreover, in this case the relationship seemed to operate via association membership and activism, rather than via social trust (which was not significant at the conventional 0.05 level). This suggests that social interactions that generate greater understanding and empathy for others within the same organization may also have effects that spill over more widely to society at large, although the wide distribution across the line in the scatter plot suggests that many other factors can be expected to influence overall

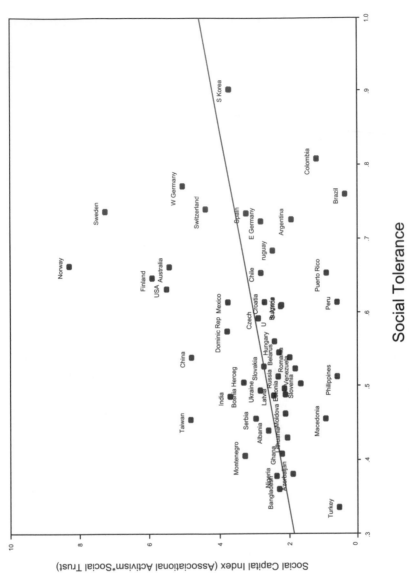

FIGURE 8.5. Social capital and social tolerance, mid-1990s.

levels of social tolerance for minority groups, such as cultural traditions, the depth of sectoral and ethnic cleavages, and historical legacies.

Social Capital and Political Culture

Multiple indicators of the political culture and system support are available in the WVS survey, including confidence in civic and political institutions, satisfaction with the performance of the current political regime, and involvement with politics. Previous studies have found that institutional confidence is multidimensional, so that people distinguish between different types and levels of organization.[45] The WVS included a four-point scaled measure tapping confidence in sixteen different types of institution, such as churches, the press, and parliament. Factor analysis with principle component analysis and varimax rotation (details not reproduced here) was used to examine the dimensions of institutional confidence at the national level. As a result, four scales were developed, measuring confidence in (1) *state institutions* (e.g., parliament, government, the civil service); (2) *private and nonprofit organizations* (e.g., the press, television, private companies, the environmental and women's movements); (3) *traditional hierarchical institutions* (the police, the army, unions); and (4) *international organizations* (e.g., the United Nations, regional agencies such as the EU).

In addition, levels of electoral turnout were compared, as one of the most important indicators of political participation, measured at the aggregate level by the number of people who voted as a proportion of the adult population (Vote/VAP) and as a proportion of the registered electorate (Vote/Reg).[46] As alternative indicators, the study compared average turnout for elections held during the 1990s, and the mean turnout for the whole postwar era.

The results in Table 8.4 suggest that, contrary to the Putnam thesis, most of the cultural indicators of institutional confidence and of electoral turnout were not consistently and significantly positively correlated at the national level with levels of social capital. The contrasts between this and previous findings on institutional confidence are probably best explained by the much wider range of societies under comparison.[47] The only important exceptions were the measure of postwar turnout (which was positive) and the indicator of support for traditional hierarchical institutions such as the army and the police (which was negative). Despite these exceptions, and the argument that social capital should promote institutional confidence and electoral participation, the evidence here does not consistently support these stronger claims.

Nevertheless, systems support can be best understood as a multidimensional phenomenon, rather than being all of one piece, and social capital was significantly related to more diffuse and weaker indicators of civic engagement. Three items were combined to create a scale of political involvement: the importance given to politics, levels of political discussion,

TABLE 8.4. *Correlations between social capital, political participation, and political culture*

		Vol_ Any	Vol_ Org	Vol_ Act	Social Trust	Social Capital Index
Electoral participation						
Turnout (Mean Vote/VAP	R	−.034	−.180	−.167	.172	.122
in 1990s)	Sig.	.821	.232	.267	.254	.419
Turnout (Mean Vote/Reg	R	.042	−.126	−.046	.125	.118
in 1990s)	Sig.	.784	.406	.759	.409	.434
Postwar turnout (Mean Vote/	R	.033	−.158	−.140	**.436**	**.374**
VAP, 1945–99)	Sig.	.826	.294	.353	.002	.010
Political culture						
Social Tolerance	R	**.370**	.142	**.312**	.280	**.347**
	Sig.	.012	.353	.037	.063	.019
Political involvement scale	R	.260	.260	.263	**.402**	**.425**
	Sig.	.082	.081	.078	.006	.003
Confidence in institutions of	R	−.006	−.030	−.036	−.175	−.152
state	Sig.	.971	.847	.813	.251	.319
Confidence in private/	R	−.013	−.164	−.180	.272	.223
nonprofit agencies	Sig.	.933	.283	.237	.070	.141
Confidence in international	R	.180	.190	.230	.201	.264
agencies	Sig.	.254	.229	.143	.203	.091
Confidence in traditional	R	**−.336**	**−.433**	**−.239**	**−.312**	**−.338**
hierarchical institutions	Sig.	.022	.003	.052	.035	.021
Evaluations of current regime	R	.142	.073	.131	.156	.181
performance (ten-point	Sig.	.365	.640	.402	.318	.246
scale from bad to good)						
Evaluations of past regime	R	−.122	−.150	−.139	−.180	−.204
performance (ten-point	Sig.	.435	.338	.376	.248	.189
scale from bad to good)						

Note: For the construction of the social capital measures, see Table 8.1. Correlations significant at the 0.05 level and the 0.01 level are indicated in **bold**.
Level of democratization: This is measured by the Freedom House Index of political rights and civil liberties, 1972–2001. www.freedomhouse.org.
Turnout: Vote as a proportion of the voting-age population (Vote/VAP) and vote as a proportion of the age-eligible electorate (Vote/REG) in elections held during the 1990s, calculated from International IDEA's *Voting Turnout Around the World, 1945–2000*. www.idea.in.
Social capital and political culture variables: World Values Study, mid-1990s.

and levels of political interest. There was a strong and significant correlation (R = .425, p. > .01) between social capital and the political involvement scale, although again it was social trust that created this relationship, not association membership. As shown in Figure 8.6, countries rich in social capital such as Norway, West Germany, and the United States displayed

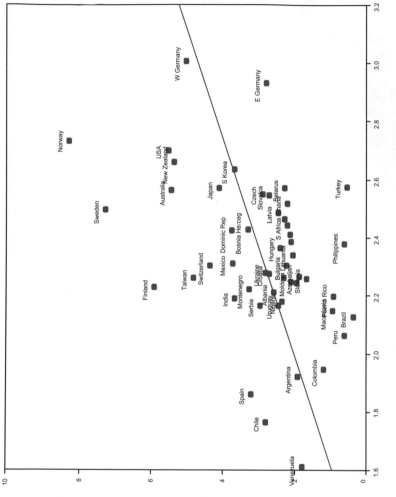

Rsq = 0.1812

Political Interest (Discuss+Interest+Politics important)

FIGURE 8.6. Social capital and political interest.

the greatest interest in political life, while citizens in Latin American states such as Colombia, Peru, and Venezuela proved to be the most disengaged. As the relationship ran primarily through social trust, not associational belonging, the results do not support the claim that belonging to voluntary organizations and community associations encourages and facilitates a broader interest in politics and public affairs.

Social Capital, Democratization, and Governance

Whether social networks and trust are essential elements of democratic societies can be measured more directly, by examining the relationship between the social capital index and the performance of democratic institutions. The latter was measured by the distribution of political rights and civil liberties using the combined fourteen-point scale derived from the 1995–6 Freedom House index, reversed so that the highest score represents the most democratic state. This measure has become the standard one used to gauge levels of democratization since the early 1970s. If social capital were essential to the broader workings of the institutions of representative democracy, as Putnam suggests, then we would expect to see a clear relationship here. The societies under comparison varied from nondemocratic states with minimal freedom, such as China, Belarus, and Nigeria, through transitional and consolidating regimes in all major regions of the world, to established Western democracies.

Recent years have seen growing attempts to gauge and measure systematic, valid, and reliable indicators of political development and the quality of democracy in a wide range of countries worldwide. We can utilize a recent study conducted for the World Bank that developed subjective perceptions of indicators of good governance, drawing on multiple surveys of experts, and assessed four dimensions based on the criteria of political stability, the rule of law, government efficiency, and levels of corruption.[48] Political stability is important, as it reflects the regular rotation of government officials, consolidation of the "rules of the game," continuity in constitutional practices, and lack of political violence. The rule of law concerns the independence and effectiveness of the judiciary and courts, levels of crime, and the enforceability of contracts. Government efficiency is gauged by perceptions of the quality of the public service and the independence of the civil service from political pressures. Lastly, perceptions of corruption reflect the success of a society in developing fair, transparent, and predictable rules for social and economic interaction. Subjective judgments may prove unreliable for several reasons, including reliance upon a small number of national "experts," or upon business leaders and academic scholars as the basis of the judgments, variations in country coverage among different indices, and possible bias toward more favorable evaluation of countries with good economic outcomes. Nevertheless, in the absence of other reliable indicators covering a wide range of nations, these measures provide some of the best available.[49] If social capital plays an important role in promoting good governance, then this should be evident in these indicators.

The correlations in Table 8.5 show that social capital was significantly associated with the indicators of democratization and good governance. Further analysis illustrated in Figure 8.7 confirms a significant relationship (R = .48, p. > .01) between levels of social capital and levels of democratization, with the pattern best captured as a curvilinear relationship showing quite a wide dispersal across the best-fitting cubic regression line. That is to say, there were similar levels of social capital among nondemocratic, semidemocratic, and newer democracies, with a few exceptions (such as Taiwan, South Korea, and Slovakia). Nevertheless, all of the older democracies (with the exception of Spain) are relatively rich in social capital, in

TABLE 8.5. *Correlations between social capital, democratization, and good governance*

		Vol_ Any	Vol_ Org	Vol_ Act	Social Trust	Social Capital Index
Democratization						
Level of democratization,	R	.237	.078	.214	**.368**	**.432**
1995	Sig.	.108	.600	.149	.011	.002
Mean level of democratization,	R	**.500**	**.375**	**.544**	**.435**	**.571**
1972–2000	Sig.	.000	.009	.000	.002	.000
Political rights, 1995	R	.185	.016	.154	**.319**	**.367**
	Sig.	.213	.915	.300	.029	.011
Civil liberties, 1995	R	.283	.143	.269	**.404**	**.483**
	Sig.	.054	.337	.067	.005	.001
Good governance						
Political stability	R	.278	.128	.140	**.676**	**.680**
	Sig.	.061	.397	.352	.000	.000
Rule of law	R	**.394**	.254	.283	**.676**	**.723**
	Sig.	.007	.088	.057	.000	.000
Government efficiency	R	**.425**	.254	.294	**.624**	**.677**
	Sig.	.003	.088	.048	.000	.000
Corruption	R	**.473**	.284	**.343**	**.631**	**.693**
	Sig.	.001	.056	.016	.000	.000

Note: For the construction of the social capital measures, see Table 8.1. Correlations significant at the 0.05 level and the 0.01 level are indicated in **bold**.
Level of democratization: This is measured by the Freedom House Index of political rights and civil liberties, 1972–2001. www.freedomhouse.org.
Turnout: Vote as a proportion of the voting-age population (Vote/VAP) and vote as a proportion of the age-eligible electorate (Vote/REG) in elections held during the 1990s, calculated from International IDEA's *Voting Turnout Around the World, 1945–2000.* www.idea.in.
Social capital and political culture variables: World Values Study, mid-1990s.

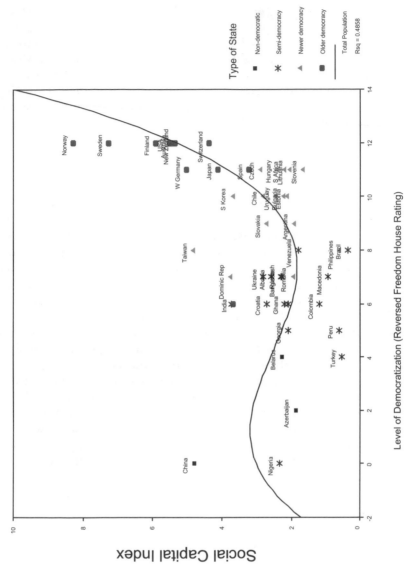

FIGURE 8.7. Social capital and democratization.

a sharp upward curve in the graph. Established democracies with the most affluent postindustrial economies are also characterized by thriving networks in civic society; but social capital fails to distinguish new democracies with widespread political rights and civil liberties, such as South Africa, Hungary, and Chile, from authoritarian regimes such as Belarius and Azerbaijan and semi-democracies such as Nigeria and Venezuela. However, the correlations with the indicators of good governance and democratization show again that it was social trust that was driving this relationship across most indicators, not associational activism.

Conclusions and Discussion

For all of the reasons already discussed, there are major difficulties in moving from the normative theory of social capital toward an examination of the systematic empirical evidence. We have to rely on existing data sources, designed for other purposes. Previous studies have focused mainly on examining trends over time within particular countries, usually studying formal association membership across different sectors such as trade unions and church-based organizations. But this strategy examines only the structural dimension of social capital. If social networks can be employed for purposes that are positive (the Red Cross) or negative (the Ku Klux Klan) for society as a whole, as they obviously can, then it is even more important to analyze the cultural norms and values associated with membership.

The cross-national comparisons developed in this study allow us to explore some of the major claims about the socioeconomic and political consequences of associational activism and social trust. Putnam's thesis suggests that communities characterized by a rich and dense network of belonging to civic associations such as environmental groups, philanthropic organizations, and sports clubs should create the "habits of the heart" that facilitate and encourage social trust, social tolerance, and civic engagement, thereby underpinning the cultural conditions promoting democracy. The results suggest four main conclusions:

1. There are two core components in Putnam's definition of social capital – social networks and social trust. When they are combined into a single index, it is true that social capital is strongly and significantly related to multiple interrelated indicators of socioeconomic development *and* to institutional indicators of democratic development.

2. But if we disentangle the twin components of Putnam's definition of social capital, what is driving this process is primarily the social trust dimension, *not* the associational network dimension. Given the ambiguities in measurement, three alternative measures of association membership and activism were employed and tested, in exploratory

analysis, but these were rarely significant across almost all indicators, no matter which measure was used.

3. Moreover, social capital and its components are not consistently related to many common measures of system support, such as institutional confidence and electoral turnout, although there is a significant relationship with social tolerance and weaker measures of political involvement.

4. Lastly, irrespective of the economic and political consequences, the most important result is perhaps the simple finding that nations cluster in fairly predictable patterns across the map of social capital. We can only speculate about the reasons for this, but the explanation probably rests on long-standing cultural traditions and historical legacies, which may relate to religious backgrounds. The map reveals that social capital is most evident in the Nordic region and in most Anglo-American democracies (characterized by high trust and high membership), and least apparent in post-Soviet Central Europe and in the South American societies (low trust and low membership). The sub-Saharan African and Asian countries under comparison fall into different quadrants as "mixed" societies on social capital.

So, in short: yes, social trust matters. It does help to make democracies work. But social trust appears to be rooted in the particular cultural histories that distinguish the major global regions, suggesting that it may not be possible to take the "X" Nordic ingredient, for example, and export this to transitional electoral democracies struggling to establish, consolidate, and institutionalize political rights and civil liberties. This study remains strictly agnostic about the causal direction behind the associations that we have uncovered. The association may be the product of culture (social trust) driving socioeconomic development and democratization, as social capital theories suggest. Or, alternatively, it could be argued that the process of societal modernization lay behind the value change (the spread of more trusting cultures). In prosperous postindustrial nations, where life is pleasant, nonbrutish, and long, people may well become more trusting of their fellow man (and woman). Or the two processes may go hand in hand. The next steps are to explore these initial findings in more detail by focusing upon changes affecting some of the traditional agencies of civic mobilization, including churches and trade unions, and the role of social movements and transnational policy networks in promoting newer forms of organizational networking, political expression, and direct-action strategies.

9

Traditional Mobilizing Agencies: Unions and Churches

Trade unions and churches are commonly regarded as central pillars of civic society, drawing citizens into public life. As Rosenstone and Hansen argue, "Citizens participate in elections and government both because they go to politics and because politics goes to them."[1] Organized labor exemplifies the traditional mobilizing agency, characterized by the older form of Weberian bureaucratic organization with formal rules and regulations, a small cadre of full-time paid officials, hierarchical mass-branch structures, broad-based rather than single-issue concerns, and clear boundaries demarcating the paid-up, card-carrying membership. The structure of religious organizations varies widely by denomination and sect, as does the role of churches, synagogues, mosques, shrines, and temples. Most Christian churches tend to have looser boundaries and more fluid criteria for affiliation than trade unions, but many Catholic and Protestant denominations display fairly traditional hierarchical structures in their religious leadership. If the process of secularization has undermined church attendance in many modern societies, and if the decline of manufacturing industry has depleted the pool of trade union members, this may have weakened these conventional channels of civic mobilization.[2]

To examine these issues, the first section of this chapter sets out the reasons why traditional mobilizing agencies can be expected to influence political participation. The second section examines cross-national levels of union density in the mid-1990s and long-term trends in union membership in postwar Western Europe. Along similar lines, the next section compares patterns of church attendance and religiosity in the mid-1990s around the world and longitudinal trends in Western Europe since the 1970s. The following section goes on to explore how far churchgoing and union membership matter for different modes of political participation, including electoral turnout, party membership, civic activism; and protest activism; and the conclusion summarizes the main findings.

The Civic Role of Mobilizing Agencies

Theories offer multiple reasons why institutions such as unions and churches can be expected to play a central role in political activism, through both indirect and direct routes.

Social Networks

Theories of civic volunteerism suggest that social institutions foster dense networks of colleagues and associates, friends and family, neighbors and compatriots, creating bonds, norms, and expectations that encourage participation, particularly for poorer communities and minority groups who might otherwise be even more marginalized politically.[3] Many American studies suggest that churches, temples, mosques, and synagogues can provide social networks and political cues, organizational skills and voluntary work, all of which encourage broader engagement in civic and community affairs.[4] Through union- and religious-sponsored organizations, members develop contacts and networks in the workplace and neighborhood that can help integrate them in their local areas.

Leadership Skills

The experience of holding office in a trade union or religious group, and voluntary work linked to these associations, can provide practical training in organizational and leadership skills such as running elections, chairing meetings, producing newsletters, and public speaking, all of which can be useful in the pursuit of elected office in local or regional government. In the United States, African-American churches have been found to be particularly important conduits of political skills, resources, and mobilization for minority groups in inner city communities.[5]

Political Awareness and Identity

The literature on interest groups, social movements, and protest politics suggests that churches and unions can also heighten political awareness and collective identity among members by generating discussion, disseminating information, and mobilizing collective action through demonstrations, political strikes, and boycotts.[6] Members may be politicized, for example, through the experience of participating in trade union demonstrations over workplace legislation, the African-American Muslim organization of the Million Man March, Christian Right protests at abortion clinics, and Catholic support for dissident movements in Latin America.[7] The traditional "two-step" notion of communication suggests that political messages spread from government, parties, and candidates to local "influentials" such as shop stewards, priests, and civic leaders, who in turn are influential among the general community.[8] The experience of belonging to a union or church may foster civic activism by developing a sense of solidarity, community, and collective identity among members.[9]

Party Linkages

Sociological accounts developed by Lipset and Rokkan emphasize the way in which unions and churches in Western Europe have played a direct role in structuring electoral politics through their formal links with party organizations.[10] In the nineteenth century, the religious cleavage between Protestants and Catholics shaped one of the major divisions in the electorate, leading to the rise of Christian Democrat parties. At the turn of the twentieth century, organized labor developed strong affiliations with parties of the left, founding labor parties to represent their interests in parliament. Lipset and Rokken's theory suggests that the party system then "froze" from the 1920s until at least the mid-1960s, so that forty years later the party system continued to reflect the predominant social cleavages of class and religion that had existed decades earlier.

Campaign Resources

Along with continuing to subsidize the regular work of party organizations, affiliated trade unions have traditionally provided many left-wing parties with a range of specific support services during election campaigns, including financial donations, the use of branch offices and facilities such as computers, printers, and telephones, and the mobilization of union staff and a voluntary army for leafleting, canvassing, direct mail production, and get-out-the-vote drives. In the 2001 British general election, for example, the Labour Party raised four million pounds in cash donations, of which three million came from trade unions.[11] Religious groups can play a similar role by contacting their members in get-out-the-vote drives, by encouraging them to support parties, and by leaving campaign literature in churches, with a significant impact in boosting turnout.[12] Religious networks can be an important source of volunteer labor and financial resources for parties and candidates; examples include the role of African American churches in Jessie Jackson's presidential bid in 1988, and the impact of evangelical Christians working for Pat Buchanan in Southern states in 1996. Of course, parties can raise funds today from many other sources, particularly from public subsidies that have become more widely available to pay for functions such as consultant services, policy research, and campaign publicity, as well as from private donations. As discussed in earlier chapters, the "professionalization" of electioneering and the rise of the "cartel" party have been widely noted phenomena in the transition from traditional to modern and postmodern campaigns.[13] Nevertheless, if parties shift from reliance upon grassroots union volunteers and party foot soldiers toward paid consultants and campaign professionals, this has important implications for patterns of campaign activism, as well as for the political role and power of trade unions.

It is unclear which of these functions remains most important, and it is difficult to establish the processes at work here. But what these accounts suggest is that for all of these different reasons – including the impact of social networks, leadership skills, political awareness, party linkages, and campaign work – people affiliated with church-based and union organizations can be expected to participate more fully in public life through the conventional channels, especially via the ballot box, but also through the more demanding forms of community involvement, party work, and protest activity.[14] For all of these reasons, any long-term erosion of mass membership in these agencies in modern societies may plausibly be expected to weaken political participation, particularly if their role and function have not been replaced by the activities of single-issue interest groups, new social movements, and ad hoc organizations.

The Decline of Union Membership?

The first issue to explore is whether modern societies have experienced a consistent and systematic long-term erosion in the mass membership underpinning these organizations, as is frequently assumed. Structural theories suggest that, although there are important variations, trade unions in postindustrial societies face common pressures in trying to maintain their grassroots membership. This view emphasizes the idea that long-term secular trends in modern societies have eroded membership in the late twentieth century. The most commonly identified factors contributing to this process – for example, in the seminal account provided by Daniel Bell – include changing class structures, new modes of production, flexible labor markets, the spread of individualist social values, the rise of white-collar and service work, increased female labor-force participation, and the falling share of the workforce employed in manufacturing industry in Western economies.[15] In particular, the well-established loss of jobs in the rust belt factories in postindustrial societies, exemplified by cutbacks at Detroit automobile production lines, Welsh coal mines, Ruhr steelworks, and Glasgow shipyards, may have reduced the number of male blue-collar workers in manufacturing production available to join trade unions.[16] Unions have traditionally drawn upon this pool, which has shrunk as a proportion of the paid workforce. The process of globalization may have undermined the bargaining power of organized labor, and thereby the benefits that they can deliver to their members, because of the competition for jobs from low-cost labor overseas, the fall of trade and tariff barriers, capital mobility, and the growing influence of multinational corporations. Structural accounts emphasize that unions can try to adapt and respond to changes in their environment, but that in the long term the labor movement is essentially attempting to run up a down escalator in trying to stanch membership losses.

The economic determinism implicit in these theories has been challenged by alternative *institutional* explanations, suggesting that legal regulations, the services that unions supply to their members, and political developments mediate the impact of secular trends, with institutions setting the constraints and shaping the options facing trade union organizations, employers' associations, and governments.[17] Organized labor has responded to the shrinkage in manufacturing industry by trying to attract new members from other sectors and from nontraditional social groups, including white-collar public sector professionals and local authority employees, such as teachers, nurses, and social workers, as well as by diversifying in order to attract more women, ethnic minorities, the young, employees in small businesses, and those in precarious employment, such as part-time, informal, and casual labor not based at the workplace. Unions have sought to develop new services and support to offer their members, for example, stressing the importance of workplace childcare facilities, flexible hours, and maternity leave policies, financial services, credit card and insurance schemes, and discounted membership fees for young people.[18] As a result of these developments, institutional accounts suggest that unions in some countries have been fairly successful in stemming their membership losses, widening their traditional recruitment base, and creating new political alliances with grassroots community organizations and NGOs sharing similar objectives.

In addition, policy initiatives and political developments can either accelerate or slow down the pace of socioeconomic change. In Central and Eastern Europe, for example, reforms brought about the end of compulsory union membership, and cuts in the public sector have also precipitated a sharp drop in membership.[19] In Latin America and Africa, substantial programs of privatization, deregulation, and the introduction of more open economies have usually proved unfavorable to union advances. In Britain, the battery of trade union laws introduced under Thatcherism ended closed shops, weakened protective legislation, and removed the legal recognition accorded to workers' organizations, contributing to a sharp decline since the early 1980s. The structure of industry within a particular country may also affect unions' organizing strength; in particular, the unionization of the workforce may reduce grievances and facilitate worker-manager communications in large firms, as well as reducing the organizational costs for unions, whereas there may be fewer incentives for unionization in small businesses.[20] The response of employers can also prove important, through the spread of centralized bargaining and the decentralization of wage negotiations. Therefore, in this account, while patterns of union growth and decline can be expected to follow broad socioeconomic trends in the shift from traditional to industrial and then to postindustrial societies, the level and pace of change in union membership can be expected to vary in particular countries according to the specific institutional contexts.

Patterns and Trends in Union Membership

In order to examine general trends, we can compare union density (membership as a proportion of wage and salary earners) both across different types of societies and across time. Union density, meaning the proportion of wage and salary earners who are union members, represents only one indicator of union strength and influence. Others include mobilizing capacity, bargaining power, organizational resources, and legal protection; nevertheless, we focus here just on mass membership levels, as this is the most relevant indicator for understanding unions as a channel of civic engagement. Figure 9.1 draws on aggregate data for ninety-one nations from the International Labour Organization (ILO) comparing levels of union density in 1995, measured by union membership as a proportion of the nonagricultural labor force, in order to standardize the comparison between industrialized and rural areas.[21] The distribution in Figure 9.1 shows the dramatic cross-national differences, with union density strongest in the mid-1990s in many of the ex-Soviet nations of Central and Eastern Europe, such as Belarus, Russia, and Hungary, in the smaller Nordic welfare states, such as Sweden and Iceland, as well as in communist China. In all of these nations, from one-half to three-quarters of the nonagricultural workforce was unionized in the mid-1990s. Most Western European and Anglo-American industrialized nations have between one-fifth and one-half of the nonagricultural workforce unionized, although countries such as the United States, France, and Spain are well below average in this regard. By contrast, many developing societies in Southeast Asia, Latin America, and Africa are ranked lowest in this comparison, including Uganda, Thailand, and Indonesia, with less than one-tenth of nonagricultural workers unionized.

Moreover, the ILO figures allow us to compare the short-term change in union membership during the decade from 1985 to 1995 in many nations. The uniformity of the fall in membership across different types of societies and world regions during this decade is vividly illustrated in Figure 9.2. In the nations where data is available from the ILO, union density shrunk in more than three-quarters (fifty-three out of sixty-three countries). The size of the fall ranged from a precipitate drop experienced in Israel and the Czech Republic to more modest but still significant erosion in countries as diverse as Kenya, Slovakia, Mexico, and New Zealand. The few countries that move contrary to this global trend, including the Philippines, Chile, Spain, and South Africa, can be explained largely as the product of the liberalization of union laws during this decade.

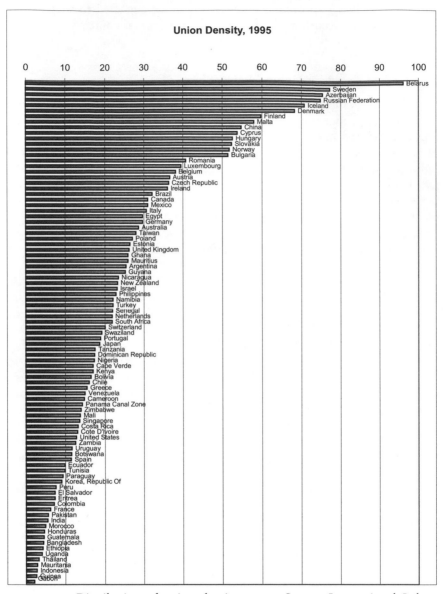

FIGURE 9.1. Distribution of union density, 1995. *Source*: International Labour Organization, *World Labour Report 1997–98*. www.ilo.org.

Yet closer examination of the longer-term annual trends in net union density across a dozen Western European nations from 1945 to 2000, where reliable data is available from Ebbinghaus and Visser, shows a more complex pattern than has been presented so far.[22] Figure 9.3 shows trends

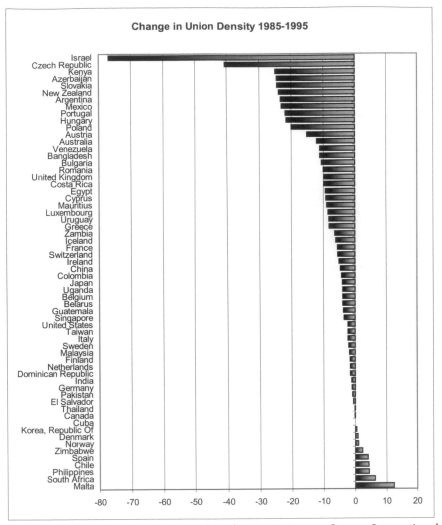

FIGURE 9.2. Percentage change in union density, 1985–95. *Source*: International Labour Organization, *World Labour Report 1997–98*. www.ilo.org.

in net union density, measured as the number of active union members (excluding pensioners and students) as a share of gainfully employed wage and salary earners (excluding the unemployed). Comparison with alternative indicators of gross union density (including pensioners and student members) confirms broadly similar trends. During the postwar era, Western Europe contained some economies that were far more heavily dependent upon agricultural production than others, such as Ireland, Portugal, and

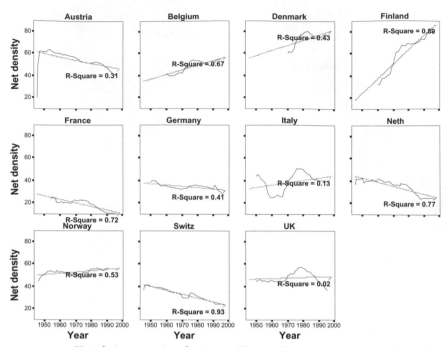

FIGURE 9.3. Trends in net union density in Western Europe 1945–2000. *Note*: Net density = active union membership (excluding pensioners, students) as a share of the gainfully employed wage and salary earners (excluding the unemployed). *Source*: Bernhard Ebbinghaus and Jelle Visser. 2000. *Trade Unions in Western Europe since 1945*. London: Macmillan.

Greece, but all of the European nations are relatively affluent postindustrial societies that have experienced a steady fall in the share of the workforce employed in manufacturing and processing industry, and a rise in the service sector of professional and managerial occupations, such as the financial, banking, and insurance industries, as well as computer software, public relations and communications, teaching and social work, and scientific and technical occupations. If union membership reflects common structural shifts in the economy, we would expect to find a fairly uniform erosion in union membership evident across Western Europe during the second half of the twentieth century.

   In fact, the comparison shows a mixed pattern of trends since 1945. A fairly steady and consistent glacial fall in union density was experienced over the last fifty years in Austria, France (from a low base), and Switzerland. Similar patterns of decline are evident in the United States, with union density down from one-fifth of all wage and salary earners in 1983 to just 14 percent in 1999.[23] Yet in the United Kingdom, the 1960s and 1970s saw a substantial rise in union density, followed by a peak in the early 1980s, before a sharp decline set in under Thatcherism during subsequent decades. The Netherlands saw a steady pattern until a sudden fall, also experienced since the 1980s. By contrast, contrary to the secular thesis, three European nations (Finland, Denmark, and Belgium) saw a significant rise in union density during the postwar era. Rather than a secular structural slide, the long-term trends suggest that institutional factors are critical to patterns of union membership; in particular, highly centralized collective bargaining and union-managed unemployment insurance schemes are associated with high levels of union density.[24] As institutional accounts emphasize, despite the short-term fall registered in the late 1980s in the ILO data, in the longer term, where unions in Western Europe have been able to deliver substantial benefits to their members in terms of pay, working conditions, and related welfare services, where they have made active efforts to mobilize the workforce, and where the regulatory legal framework facilitates their role and influence, they have held and even expanded their grassroots base.

Secularization and Religiosity

The idea that modern society leads to secularization originated in the work of Max Weber, but it was not widely discussed in the social sciences until it became popular among sociological theorists during the 1950s and 1960s.[25] Today the idea of secularization is often assumed uncritically as the conventional wisdom, although it is strongly challenged by many scholars.[26] Simply put, secularization theories suggest that modernization leads to the decline of religious beliefs, as indicated by the erosion of church attendance, denominational allegiance, and faith in religious authorities, the loss of prestige and influence of religious symbols, doctrines, and institutions, and a growing separation between church and state.[27] Modernization theories suggest that growing levels of literacy and education and wider sources of information have strengthened rational belief in scientific knowledge, expert authorities, and technological know-how, with priests, ministers, rabbis, and mullahs regarded as only one source of authority, and not necessarily the most important one, competing with the expertise of economists, physicists, and physicians.[28] The evidence supporting this thesis is clearest in Western Europe, where studies have found that many West Europeans have ceased to be regular churchgoers outside of special occasions, such as Christmas and Easter, weddings and funerals, a pattern especially evident among the young.[29] Even here, however, a distinction needs to be drawn between behavioral indicators of religiosity such as habitual attendance at church services, which has fallen, and religious values and beliefs, which may persist.[30] The United States seems to have remained exceptionally high in regular churchgoing compared to Western Europe. Elsewhere in the world, as scholars have emphasized, there is a complex picture that includes some important religious revivals and countersecular movements, such as the vigorous resurgence of Orthodox Judaism in Israel, Shinto in Japan, and fundamentalist Islamic movements in many countries in the Middle East and North Africa, and the development of new religious movements and evangelical revivals.[31] The *World Christian Encyclopedia*, which compares churches and religions around the globe and estimates trends during the twentieth century, provides the most comprehensive estimates of secularization over time based on an annual religious "mega-census" completed by ten million church leaders, clergy, and other Christian workers.[32] The study estimates that the proportion of "nonreligionists," defined as including agnostics, atheists, and other nonreligious groups, swelled from an estimated 3.2 million in 1900 (0.2 percent of the globe's population) to about 18.9 percent in 1970, then to 20.8 percent in 1980, before falling back to 15.2% by 2000, following the collapse of communism in Europe.

The most systematic evidence favoring the secularization thesis comes from trends in church attendance in European Union member states, which have been monitored regularly by the Eurobarometer from 1970 to 1998. Confirming many other studies, the evidence of trends and the best-fitting regression lines in Figure 9.4 demonstrate the consistent fall in church attendance experienced across Western Europe during the last three decades, with a fairly steep fall found in Belgium, Luxembourg, and the Netherlands, and a relatively shallow erosion over the years in Germany, France, and Ireland.[33] The disparities among nations remain stark, ranging from the strength of religiosity in Catholic Ireland to the more secular population in Protestant Denmark. Nevertheless, the United States continues to provide an important exception to Western patterns of secularization, with church attendance continuing to be as popular among Americans today as it was sixty years ago. According to Gallup polls, in 1939 about four out of ten Americans reported attending church or synagogue every week, and roughly the same proportion persisted, with minor fluctuations, until May 2001.[34] A modest fall is evident in other indicators of religiosity in the Gallup series; for example, in 2001 about two-thirds of Americans (65 percent) counted themselves members of a church or synagogue, down from almost three quarters (73 percent) in 1937. The salience of religion has also fallen slightly: In 2001 about two-thirds of Americans (64 percent) reported that religion was "very important" in their own lives, down from 75 percent in 1952. Nevertheless, it is the experience of regular church attendance, rather than religiosity per se, that can be expected to be the most important indicator for the acquisition of social networks, civic skills, and therefore for political participation, and this figure has remained stable in the United States over the years.[35]

Elsewhere in the world, the picture remains complex, and it is difficult to establish any aggregate estimates for longitudinal trends or cross-national

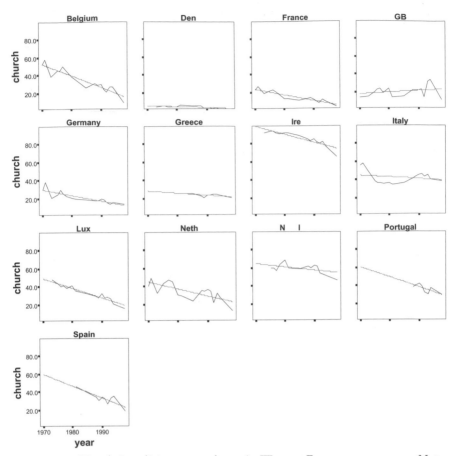

FIGURE 9.4. Trends in religious attendance in Western Europe, 1970–2000. *Note*: The percentage of the population who said they attended a religious service "at least once a week." *Source*: Eurobarometer surveys, 1970 to 2000.

comparisons in churchgoing and religious affiliation with any degree of reliability. Given different religious practices among sects and denominations – for example, differences in whether it is important to worship alone or to be part of a congregation – alternative indicators are needed for comparison. Table 9.1 presents evidence from the World Values Study comparing four indicators of religiosity, namely, the proportion of the population in different cultural regions of the world who (1) claimed to be active or passive members of church or religious organizations in the mid-1990s, (2) go to a religious service regularly (at least once a week), (3) believe in God, and (4) say that religion is "very important" in their lives. The first two indicators can be regarded as broadly behavioral, while the last two tap religious values and beliefs. The comparison shows that there

TABLE 9.1. *Indicators of religiosity by cultural region, mid-1990s (percent)*

| | Religious Behavior | | Religious Values | |
| | Member of Church or Religious Organization | Attend Religious Service at Least Once Per Week | Religion "Very Important" in Your Life | Believe in God |
Region				
Africa	75.6	50.9	76.5	98.6
Latin America	50.6	39.4	51.6	96.6
Northern Europe	47.1	13.2	15.9	71.7
Anglo-American	46.1	31.6	37.4	90.6
Catholic Europe	43.2	40.8	26.3	89.9
Central Europe	19.7	17.3	21.7	68.2
South Asia	19.1	48.8	63.9	96.2
Confucian	17.3	7.6	11.7	65.9
Ex-Soviet	13.4	6.7	21.7	75.6
All	32.9	25.1	33.6	83.1

Notes:
Member: *"Now I am going to read off a list of voluntary organizations; for each one could you tell me whether you are an active member, an inactive member, or not a member of that type of organization?"* (Proportion who are active or inactive members)
Attend: *"Apart from weddings, funerals, and christenings, about how often do you attend religious services these days?"* (percent once a week or more)
Importance: *"Please say, for each of the following, how important it is in your life. . . . Religion."* (percent 'very')
God: *"Do you believe in God?"* (percent yes)
Cultural regions: *Northern Europe*: Finland, Germany, Norway, Sweden, Switzerland, (N = 5,352); *Anglo-American*: Australia, New Zealand, United States (N = 5,884); *Catholic Europe*: Spain (N = 1,211); *Confucian*: Japan, Republic of Korea, China, Taiwan (N = 5,255); *Central Europe*: Albania, Bulgaria, Czech Republic, Hungary, Romania, Slovakia, Slovenia (N = 8,362); *Ex-Soviet*: Azerbaijan, Belarus, Croatia, Estonia, Georgia, Lithuania, Latvia, Republic of Moldova, Ukraine, Russian Federation (N = 17,943); *Latin America*: Mexico, Argentina, Brazil, Chile, Peru, Venezuela, Uruguay, Dominican Republic, Colombia (N = 13,591); *South Asia*: India, Philippines, Azerbaijan (N = 7,405); *Africa*: South Africa, Nigeria (N = 5,704).
Source: All World Values Study, pooled sample 1980–95, except for "Member" (mid-1990s only).

are substantial differences in religiosity worldwide. Overall, the African nations appear to be the most religious: About three-quarters of Africans belong to a church and say that religion is very important, half regularly attend church, and there is an almost universal belief in God. Latin America, Northern Europe, Anglo-America, and Catholic Europe prove to be moderately religious across the different indicators. Lastly, Central European and the ex-Soviet states are the least religious, although even here at least two-thirds say they believe in God.

The process of secularization is illustrated clearly in Figure 9.5, showing the strong association between levels of human development and two summary indicators of religiosity: the importance of God (measured on a ten-point scale taken as representing religious beliefs) and regularity of attendance at religious services (taken as an indicator of religious behavior). The results confirm that modern societies with higher levels of human development, characterized by widespread literacy, education, and access to multiple sources of information from the mass media, are by far the most secular, while the poorest and least developed nations, such as Bangladesh, Pakistan, Nigeria, Ghana, and India, are the most religious in their values and behavior. The wide scatter of countries in the middle of the graph shows the continuing impact of historical legacies dividing the postcommunist world from the traditional role of the Catholic Church in Latin America. The comparison also confirms that the United States remains an outlier on both measures, being far more religious than comparable postindustrial societies. Despite contemporary critiques among scholars of world religions, Weber's thesis that modernization leads more secular societies is supported by this evidence, although historical legacies continue to shape religious cultures and traditions.

The Impact of Traditional Mobilizing Agencies on Participation

The question that arises is whether the trends that we have observed have had a major impact on patterns of political participation. If union membership has fallen in particular nations, this may have important consequences for the ability of these organizations to mobilize poorer and working-class communities, both directly, in terms of the aggregation and articulation of the interests of union members, and indirectly, through their effect on voting turnout, membership in socialist parties, and protest activities such as political strikes and industrial boycotts. Radcliff and Davis compared the association between rates of union density and aggregate levels of electoral turnout in nineteen industrial democracies, and the result confirmed that the greater the share of workers represented by unions, the higher the turnout.[36] Gray and Caul present the most systematic evidence indicating that the decline of unions has had a dampening effect on electoral turnout in industrialized societies, especially for peripheral voters. Their study concluded that in industrialized societies, strong unions and strong parties of the left create the greatest incentives for working-class mobilization: "The declining levels of union density and the diminishing success and effectiveness of traditional labour-affiliated parties in industrial democracies have left many voters uninterested, uninformed, and politically inactive."[37] Whether the patterns common in Anglo-American and West European democracies hold in a wider range of nations with different historical legacies and cultural traditions, including developing societies and

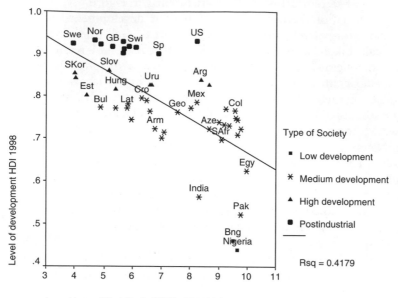

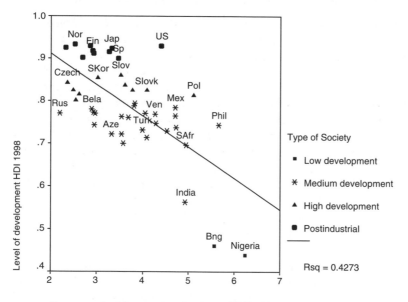

FIGURE 9.5. Indicators of religiosity and development, mid-1990s. *Sources*: Indicators of religiosity: World Values Study, mid-1990s. Human Development Index: United Nations Development Report, 1998.

postcommunist countries, remains unclear. In the same way, involvement in religious organizations has commonly been found to be strongly associated with civic engagement, as least in the United States; so again, secularization in modern societies may be expected to depress conventional forms of political participation.

Each of these organizations is based among different groups in the electorate, suggesting that there could be differential mobilizing effects. The demographic breakdown of membership in these organizations, based on the World Values Survey in the mid-1990s, is shown in Table 9.2.

TABLE 9.2. *Religious attendance and union membership by social background, mid-1990s (percent)*

	Attend Religious Service Regularly	Trade Union Member
Gender		
Men	23.0	24.4
Women	28.8	20.1
Age		
18–24	24.5	17.1
25–34	22.9	24.9
35–44	21.5	28.2
45–54	24.1	28.4
55–64	24.3	20.0
65+	28.9	11.7
Education		
High education	25.0	27.0
Medium education	22.2	24.7
Low education	30.8	14.8
Occupational class		
Managerial and professional	25.7	26.3
Other white-collar	20.9	25.9
Skilled manual	21.6	28.2
Unskilled manual	27.8	20.0
All	26.0	23.0

Note: Religious, attendance: "*Apart from weddings, funerals and christenings, about how often do you attend religious services these days?*" Attend church regularly (at least once a week).
Trade union member (active or inactive).
Source: World Values Study, mid-1990s in forty-seven nations (N-86,792).

The results suggest that religious organizations continue to prove most attractive for women, for the older generation, for those with minimal educational qualifications, and for the unskilled working class. Trade unions continue to attract more men than women, although the gender gap in membership has become fairly modest. Union membership also increases among the early to late middle-aged, and, interestingly, union membership also proves to be relatively popular among those with higher education and to be fairly evenly distributed across classes.

Tables 9.3 and 9.4 present the results of regression models for the impact of religious attendance and for union membership on four modes of political participation: voting turnout, party activism, civic activism, and protest activism. Most studies have examined the relationship between mobilizing agencies and electoral participation; but theoretically, their impact on more demanding forms of political engagement could be equally or even more important. The models include the standard controls for levels of societal development and democratization, as well as the standard demographic factors commonly associated with political participation – age, gender, education, and class – and cultural attitudes measured by political interest. The results confirm that even with the full battery of controls, both regular religious attendance and active union membership were significantly related to the four modes of political participation (although it should be noted that religiosity made protest activism less likely, not more). Moreover, union activism was a particularly strong predictor of membership in other types of civic group, as well as in political parties and forms of protest activism.

Conclusions

Many studies suggest that one reason why people become engaged in public affairs lies in the way that they are mobilized through traditional channels such as community groups, civic associations, and voluntary organizations, with trade unions and churches exemplifying this process. At the turn of the century, strong linkages developed in Western Europe between organized labor and Labour and Socialist parties, with affiliated trade unions providing an army of voluntary helpers, financial support, and local facilities for waging election campaigns. On the right, churches traditionally provided many of the same sorts of support functions for Christian Democrats. In addition, more generally, by linking members with broader community networks, providing organizational skills, and heightening political awareness, churches and unions can be expected to provide the kinds of experience that would encourage members to participate more fully in politics. Therefore, if traditional mobilizing agencies have experienced a long-term decline in popularity in modern societies, as theories of structural and secular change suggest, this could have important consequences for

TABLE 9.3. *Religious attendance and political participation, mid-1990s*

	Voting Turnout			Party Member			Civic Activism			Protest Activism		
	B	(s.e.)	Sig.	B	(s.e.)	Sig.	B	(s.e.)	Sig.	B	(s.e.)	Sig.
Development												
Level of human development	2.413	.321	***	2.214	.142	***	.040	.074		4.354	.130	***
Level of democratization	.543	.020	***	.031	.012	**	.111	.005	***	.176	.010	***
Structure												
Age (*Years*)	-.007	.001	***	.002	.001	**	-.004	.000	***	-.026	.001	***
Gender (*male = 1*)	-.224	.050	***	.258	.029	***	.087	.013	***	.257	.023	***
Education (*seven-pt scale*)	-.135	.012	***	.051	.007	***	.068	.003	***	.077	.005	***
Class (*Middle-class = 1*)	.013	.010		-.008	.006		-.025	.003	***	-.075	.005	***
Cultural attitudes												
Political Interest (nine-point scale)	.355	.013	***	.339	.007	***	.085	.003	***	.350	.006	***
Mobilizing agency												
Religious attendance (seven-point scale)	**.054**	**.013**	***	**.113**	**.007**	***	**.053**	**.003**	***	**-.013**	**.006**	*
Constant	-3.09			-3.78			-.652			1.252		
Nagelkerke R²	.164			.139								
Adjusted R²							.062			.189		
Percent correct	94.7			84.7								

Note: Voting turnout and party activism in the mid-1990s are analyzed using logistic regression, with the table listing unstandardized regression coefficients, standard errors, and significance. Civic activism and protest activism are analyzed using linear regression models. *p < .05, **p < .01, ***p < .001.
Human development: Human Development Index 1990: *Human Development Report.* New York: United Nations Development Program.
Level of democratization: Mean Freedom House Index of political rights and civil liberties, 1990–6. www.freedomhouse.org.
Mobilizing agencies: Church attendance (seven-point scale).
Cultural attitudes: See Table 7.7. The nine-point interest scale combined political discussion, interest, and the salience of politics, which all also proved to be highly intercorrelated.
Voting turnout: Yes = 1.
Party member: Inactive or active member.
Civic activism: Scale of active or passive member of sports club, arts club, environmental group, charitable group.
Protest activism: Scale of willingness to sign petition, join boycott, demonstrate, join unofficial strike, occupy building.

TABLE 9.4. *Union membership and political participation, mid-1990s*

	Voting Turnout			Party Member			Civic Activism			Protest Activism		
	B	(s.e.)	Sig.	B	(s.e.)	Sig.	B	(s.e.)	Sig.	B	(s.e.)	Sig.
Development												
Level of human development	2.245	.306	***	3.332	.138	***	.542	.067	***	4.361	.122	***
Level of democratization	.569	.020	***	.080	.012	***	.134	.005	***	.191	.009	***
Structure												
Age (*years*)	-.007	.001	***	.003	.001	***	-.003	.000	***	-.025	.001	***
Gender (*male = 1*)	-.242	.049	***	.202	.029	***	.058	.012	***	.252	.022	***
Education (*seven-pt scale*)	-.135	.012	***	.022	.007	***	.050	.003	***	.066	.005	***
Class (*ten-pt scale*)	.012	.010		-.020	.006	***	-.031	.003	***	-.080	.005	***
Cultural attitudes												
Political Interest (*nine-point scale*)	.358	.013	***	.329	.008	***	.065	.003	***	.334	.006	***
Mobilizing agency												
Trade union membership (not member = 1, passive member = 2, active member = 3)	.089	.046	*	1.060	.021	***	.710	.010	***	.528	.019	***
Constant	-3.009			-4.004			-.856			-.605		
Nagelkerke R²	.167			.223								
Adjusted R²							.145			.202		
Percent correct	94.7			85.0								

Note: Voting turnout and party activism in the mid-1990s are analyzed using logistic regression, with the table listing unstandardized regression coefficients, standard errors, and significance. Civic activism and protest activism are analyzed using linear regression models. *p < .05, **p < .01, ***p < .001.
Human development: Human Development Index 1990: *Human Development Report.* New York: United Nations Development Program. *Level of democratization:* Mean Freedom House Index of political rights and civil liberties, 1990–6. www.freedomhouse.org.
Mobilizing agencies: Union membership (three-point scale).
Cultural attitudes: See Table 7.7. The nine-point interest scale combined political discussion, interest, and the salience of politics, which all also proved to be highly intercorrelated. *Voting turnout:* Yes = 1.
Party member: Inactive or active member.
Civic activism: Scale of active or passive member of sports club, arts club, environmental group, charitable group.
Protest activism: Scale of willingness to sign petition, join boycott, demonstrate, join unofficial strike, occupy building.

civic engagement. The results of the analysis presented in this chapter suggest four major points:

1. During the postwar era, trends in net union density show divergence among different countries within Western Europe, with some experiencing slow erosion during the last fifty years, while others have expanded their memberships during the same period, and yet others have seen peaks and troughs. In short, institutional factors, such as legal regulations and the welfare services that unions provide for their members, represent more plausible explanations for changes in union density than the idea of a slow and steady secular decline in the vitality of the labor movement.

2. At the same time, ILO evidence suggests that levels of union density vary substantially around the world, owing to different historical legacies and economic structures, and that in the short term, union density did fall in many countries from the mid-1980s to the mid-1990s, while rising in only a few.

3. In terms of secularization, the evidence confirms that there was a significant decline in religious attendance during the last thirty years in Western Europe. Moreover, the Weberian thesis that modernity is associated with secularization is confirmed by the cross-national analysis: The least developed societies generally displayed the strongest religious beliefs and behavior.

4. Lastly, the analysis confirms that membership in unions and religious organizations is closely associated not only with electoral turnout, but also with indicators of party membership, belonging to other civic associations such as sports and arts clubs, and protest activism.

It follows that in countries where there has been a substantial long-term decline in church attendance and erosion in the union membership base, these developments could be expected to undermine many other common forms of civic engagement. Yet if membership in traditional mobilizing agencies has been replaced by involvement in more ad hoc types of single-issue interest groups, transnational policy networks, and new social movements, then this process could simply represent a transformation of the channels linking citizens and the state, rather than a corrosion of civic life. In order to examine this possibility, we now turn to see who belongs to the new social movements, and whether these organizations perform functions similar to those that churches and unions played in earlier times.

10

New Social Movements, Protest Politics, and the Internet

Previous chapters have focused on indicators of conventional political participation, including electoral turnout and party membership, as well as on the role of churches and unions, but it could be that in so doing we have overlooked many of the most important ways that modes of activism have been reinvented in recent decades. In particular, traditional theoretical and conceptual frameworks derived from the literature of the 1960s and 1970s, and even what we mean by "political participation," need to be revised and updated to take account of how opportunities for civic engagement have evolved and diversified over the years. The first section of this chapter outlines theories about transformations, from interest groups to new social movements, that have altered the *agencies* (collective organizations), *repertoires* (the actions commonly used for political expression), and *targets* (the political actors whom participants seek to influence). The second section examines evidence for the distribution of protest politics, including who is most likely to engage in this form of activism in different countries, and whether there is significant overlap today between conventional and protest modes. The next section analyzes environmental activists, taken as exemplifying new social movements, to see whether these participants are particularly attracted to protest politics. The following section considers the rise of the internet and the capacity of this bundle of technologies to accelerate opportunities for transnational policy advocacy in a global civic society. The conclusion considers the implications of these developments for the transformation from the politics of loyalties to the politics of choice.

The Transformation of Political Participation?

The distinctions between traditional interest groups, alternative social movements, and transnational advocacy networks are fluid and imprecise, so all of these forms of association in civic society are compared in this chapter.[1] The term "interest group" conventionally refers to more formal organizations that are focused either on particular social groups and economic sectors, such as trade unions and business and professional associations (the NAACP, the American Medical Association), or on more specific issues such as abortion, gun control, and the environment. Often traditional interest groups have well-established organizational structures and formal membership rules. Their primary orientation is toward influencing government and the policy process and providing direct services for members – for example, trade union negotiations over pay levels in industry, or the provision of informational networks for professional associations. Some develop an extensive mass membership base, while others are essentially lobbying organizations focused on insider strategies, with little need to maintain a larger constituency. New social movements, exemplified by the civil rights and antinuclear movements of the 1950s, and the environmental and women's movements of the 1970s, have more fluid and decentralized organizational structures and more open membership criteria, and tend to focus on influencing lifestyles and achieving social change through direct action and community building as much as through formal decision-making processes. Lastly, transnational advocacy networks bring together loose coalitions of such organizations under a common umbrella organization that crosses national borders.

From Interest Groups to New Social Movements?

Many believe that the channels commonly used for political activism and mobilization have been transformed during the postwar era. The issue of *agency* concerns the organizational structures through which people mobilize for political expression. Traditional interest groups that evolved with the rise of democracy in nineteenth- and early twentieth-century industrial societies usually involved regularized, institutionalized, structured, and measurable activities: People signed up and paid up to become card-carrying members of the Norwegian trade unions, the American Elks, or the British Women's Institute. Interest groups and parties typically had Weberian bureaucratic organizations, characterized by formal rules and regulations, full-time paid officials, hierarchical mass-branch structures, and clear boundaries demarcating who did, and did not, belong.[2] Our parents' and grandparents' generations often served on a local governing board or belonged to community associations – holding fund raisers, publishing newsletters, manning publicity stalls, chairing meetings, and attending socials for the Red Cross, the Parent-Teacher Association, and the Rotary Club.

Recent decades have seen the rise of new social movements and transnational advocacy networks.[3] These channels of citizen involvement are emerging as an alternative mechanism for activists, but one far more amorphous and tricky to gauge.[4] The capacity for social movements concerned

about issues such as globalization, human rights, debt relief, and world
trade to cross national borders may signal the emergence of a global civic
society.[5] Networked agencies are characterized by direct-action strategies
and internet communications, loose coalitions, relatively flat organizational
structures, and more informal modes of belonging focused on shared
concern about diverse issues and identity politics.[6] Traditional hierarchical
and bureaucratic organizations persist, but social movements may be
emerging as the most popular avenue for informal political mobilization,
protest, and expression. If this shift has occurred, it has important
implications for interpreting and measuring trends in civic engagement. In
particular, if studies are limited to traditional indicators of political participation, such as party membership, union density, and voting turnout, then
any apparent erosion of civic engagement may disguise its simultaneous
transformation into alternative movements characterized by fuzzier boundaries and informal forms of support.

From Conventional Repertoires to Protest Politics?

The question of agencies is closely related to that of *repertoires*, meaning
the ways in which people choose to express themselves politically. Much of
the traditional literature on political participation has focused extensively
upon conventional repertoires of civic engagement. Rather than a unidi-
mensional "ladder of participation," the original typology developed by
Verba and his colleagues distinguished among four main "modes" of political participation: voting, campaign activism, community organizing, and
particularized contacting activity.[7] These modes differed systematically in
their costs and benefits. Voting, for example, can be classified as one of
the most ubiquitous political activities, one that exerts diffuse pressure on
leaders, with a broad outcome affecting all citizens. Campaign work for
parties and candidates such as leafleting, attending local party meetings,
and get-out-the-vote drives also typically generates collective benefits, but
requires greater initiative, time, and effort than casting a ballot. Communal organization involves cooperation with others on some general social
issue, such as raising money for a local school or helping at an arts collective, with varying demands depending upon the level and kind of activism.
Lastly, particularized contacting, such as writing to an elected official about
a specific problem, requires high levels of information and initiative, generating individual benefits but involving little political cooperation. These
conceptual distinctions remain important, so this study has maintained this
tradition by examining the three most common repertoires of political
expression generating collective benefits: voting turnout, party campaigning, and community organizing in civic society.

The early literature also drew an important line between "conventional"
and "protest" forms of activism, and it is not clear whether this distinction
remains appropriate today. Recent decades have seen a diversification of

the types of activities used for political expression. In particular, new social movements may be adopting mixed action repertoires combining traditional acts such as voting and lobbying with a variety of alternative modes, such as internet networking, street protests, consumer boycotts, and direct action. The use of mass demonstrations in radical movements is nothing new; indeed, historically there have been periodic waves of protest and vigorous political dissent by citizens throughout Western democracies.[8] The mid-1950s saw the start of the most recent cycle of organized protest politics in established democracies, symbolized by passive resistance techniques used by the civil rights movement in the United States and the Campaign for Nuclear Disarmament in Western Europe.[9] The following decade saw the resurgence of direct action with the anti–Vietnam War demonstrations, the fashionable wave of student protest movements and social upheaval that swept the streets of Paris, Tokyo, and London, the espousal of community action by new social movements concerned about women's equality, nuclear power, and the environment, the use of economic boycotts directed against apartheid in South Africa, and the adoption by trade unions of more aggressive industrial action, including strikes, occupations, blockades, and mass demonstrations, occasionally accompanied by arson, property damage, and violence, directed against Western governments.[10] This development generated studies of "protest potential" by Barnes and Kasse, among others, examining the willingness of citizens to engage in forms of dissent such as unofficial strikes, boycotts, petitions, the occupation of buildings, mass demonstrations, and even acts of political violence.[11] The late 1980s and early 1990s saw the spread of "people power," which helped to topple the old regimes in Central and Eastern Europe, followed by the anticapitalist and anti-globalization forces of the late 1990s.

During the late 1960s and early 1970s, protests by antiwar hippies, Black Power advocates, militant workers, progressive intellectuals, students, and feminists were commonly regarded as radical politics, or even the start of violent revolutionary ferment. Today there remains a substantial difference between peaceful protests and violent political acts that harm property or people. The latter are exemplified by the long-standing ethnic-nationalist and ethnic-religious conflicts in the Middle East, Northern Ireland, Sri Lanka, Colombia, and the Basque region, and by the events surrounding the destruction of the World Trade Center and the distribution of anthrax to political and media targets through the U.S. mail. Violent terrorist activities, assassinations, hijackings, and the use of bombs for political purposes all fall into this category. Despite this distinction, because of developments in recent decades the sharp dividing line drawn in earlier studies between "conventional" electoral activity and peaceful protest has dissolved somewhat over time. Lawful street demonstrations are often used today by political parties, traditional interest groups, and unions, as well as by ordinary middle-class citizens. Studies suggest that the number of people willing to attend lawful demonstrations has risen since the mid-1970s, so that the social characteristics of the protest population have gradually "normalized."[12] Public demonstrations are used today by a multiplicity of groups ranging from Norwegian anti–fuel tax car owners to Florida retirees protesting the ballot design in Miami-Dade County, Philippino "people power" protestors intent on ousting President Estrada, local farmers critical of the McDonaldization of French culture, street theatre celebrations like the gay Mardi Gras in Sydney, and consumer boycotts such as those used against British supermarkets stocking genetically modified foods. Events at Genoa combined a mélange of mainstream charities such as Oxfam and Christian Aid, radicals such as the British Drop the Debt protestors, the German Freie ArbeiterInnen Union, and Italian anarchists such as Tute Bianchi and Ya Basta! Collective action through peaceful channels has become a generally accepted way to express political grievances, voice opposition, and challenge authorities.

Direct action strategies have also broadened to include lifestyle politics, where the precise dividing line between the "social" and the "political" breaks down even further. Such activities include volunteer work at recycling cooperatives, helping at battered women's shelters, and fund raising for a local hospital, as well as demonstrating at sites for timber logging or airport runway expansions, and protesting the use of animals in medical research. It could be argued that such activities, while having important social and economic consequences, fall outside of the sphere of the "political" per se. This conceptualization would distinguish between, for example, running the PTA fund drive (understood as a social activity) and pressuring local officials to increase public spending for education (understood as a political activity). Yet the distinction between the "public" and "private" spheres remains controversial, as the feminist literature has long emphasized.[13] Social movements often seek to reform the law or influence the policy process as well as to directly alter systematic patterns of social behavior, for example by establishing bottle bank recycling facilities, battered women's shelters, and art collectives. In many developing societies, loose and amorphous networks of community groups and grassroots voluntary associations often seek direct action within local communities over basic issues of livelihood, such as access to water, the distribution of agricultural aid, and health care, and schools.[14] The "social" and the "political" are commonly blurred around issues of identity politics, where, for example, a revivalist meeting of "born again" Christians in South Carolina, a gay and lesbian arts festival in San Francisco, and the Million Man March in Washington, D.C., can all be understood as expressions or assertions of political communities. Therefore, in general, the older definition of political participation, based on citizenship activities designed to influence government and the policy process within the nation-state, seems unduly limited today, excluding too much that is commonly understood as broadly "political." Accordingly, as well as analyzing electoral turnout, party work, and civic activism, this chapter needs to compare legitimate protest activity as a mainstream form of expression today.

The Target of Participation

This leads to a closely related and equally important question, namely, whether the *target* of participation, meaning the *actors* that participants are attempting to influence, has widened well beyond the nation-state. Traditional theories of representative democracy suggest that citizens hold elected representatives and governments to account directly through the mechanism of regular elections, and indirectly during intraelectoral periods via the news media, parties, interest groups, NGOs, and social movements in civil society. Verba, Nie, and Kim, for example, defined political participation as "*those legal activities by private citizens that are more or less directly aimed at influencing the selection of governmental personnel and/or the actions they take.*"[15] Within this model, typical *state-oriented* activities are designed to influence the institutions of representative government and the policy process, to communicate public concerns to government officials, and to pressure them to respond. These activities remain important, but today the diffusion of power resulting from both globalization and decentralization means that this represents an excessively narrow conceptualization, one that excludes some of the most common targets of civic engagement.

Non–state oriented activities are directed toward diverse actors in the public, nonprofit, and private sectors. Well-known examples include international human rights organizations, women's NGOs, transnational environmental organizations, anti-sweatshop and anti–land mines networks, the peace movement, and anti-globalization and anticapitalist forces.[16] The targets are often major multinational corporations, exemplified by consumer boycotts of Nike running shoes, McDonald's hamburgers, and California grapes, as well as by protest demonstrations directed against international agencies and intergovernmental organizations such as the World Trade Organization, the World Economic Forum in Davos, and the European Commission.[17] The process of globalization is a complex and multifaceted phenomenon, but one of the clearest political manifestations of this development is the declining autonomy of the nation-state, including the core executive, as power has shifted simultaneously toward intergovernmental organizations such as the UN and the WTO, and downward toward regional and local assemblies.[18] Moreover, the "shrinkage of the state" through initiatives such as privatization, marketization, and deregulation means that decision making has flowed away from public bodies and official government agencies that were directly accountable to elected representatives, devolving to a complex variety of nonprofit and private agencies operating at local, national, and international levels.[19] Because of these developments, it has become more difficult for citizens to use conventional state-oriented channels of participation, exemplified by national elections, as a way of challenging those in power, reinforcing the need for alternative avenues and targets of political expression and mobilization.

The Rise of Protest Politics

For all of these reasons, therefore, any conceptualization and measurement of the mainstream forms of civic engagement and political participation needs to take account of the ways in which the agencies, repertoires, and targets may have been transformed since the classic studies of the 1950s and 1960s. Not all of these developments can be examined from the available evidence, within the scope and methodology of this limited study, but we can explore the propensity to engage in protest politics and to support the environmental movement, to see whether these are distinct dimensions of political participation today compared to the channels of electoral, party, and civic activism, and to see how we can explain patterns of protest politics and support for new social movements in different countries.

One major challenge facing attempts to understand and document the extent of protest politics is that these activities are often situational rather than generic. In other words, demonstrations, occupations, and unofficial strikes are often triggered by specific events and particular circumstances, depending upon the structure of opportunities generated by particular issues, specific events, and the role of leaders, rather than reflecting the distinctive social or attitudinal profiles of citizens.[20] The American and British use of air strikes in Afghanistan triggered an outpouring of street rallies in Karachi, Jakarta, and Islamabad, but it is doubtful if residents would have displayed such propensities to protest outside of this context. In the past, specific critical events such as the American urban riots in the 1960s, reactions to the Vietnam War, the decision to site U.S. nuclear weapons at Greenham Common, and the Chernoble disaster may have had a similarly catalytic function, leading to approaches focusing on event analysis.[21] Reflecting these considerations, studies have often focused on "protest potential," or the propensity to express dissent. Yet this can be problematic: Surveys are usually better able to tap attitudes and values than actual behavior, and they are generally more reliable when reporting routine and repetitive actions ("How often do you attend church?") rather than occasional acts. Unfortunately, hypothetical questions ("Might you ever demonstrate or join in boycotts?") may well prove to be poor predictors of actual behavior. These items may prompt answers that are regarded as socially acceptable or that just tap a more general orientation toward the political system (such as approval of freedom of association or tolerance of dissent).[22] Given these limitations, this study focuses on those acts that people say they actually *have* engaged in, taken as the most accurate and reliable indicator of protest activism, and excludes those that people say they *might* engage in, or protest potential.

The first issue for analysis is whether there continues to be a distinct dimension of "protest" politics, or whether this has now become merged with other common activities such as joining unions or parties. Following the tradition established by Barnes and Kaase, protest activism is measured using five items in the World Value Survey: signing a petition, joining in boycotts, attending lawful demonstrations, joining unofficial strikes, and occupying buildings or factories. Factor analysis can be used to examine whether these activities fall into a distinct dimension compared with the others already examined here, including electoral participation, political party membership, and belonging to civic groups such as unions, religious organizations, sports and arts clubs, professional associations, charitable associations, and environmental groups.

The results of the factor analysis presented in Table 10.1 confirm that, as expected, three distinct modes of political participation emerge. All of the protest items cluster consistently together, suggesting that a citizen who would engage in one of these activities would probably engage in others as well. Civic activism emerged as another distinctive dimension, so that belonging to parties was intercorrelated with membership in unions and social clubs. Lastly, electoral turnout proved to be a third distinctive dimension of participation; as commonly emphasized, the relatively low-cost, low-benefit aspect of casting a vote means that it is atypical of the more demanding types of engagement. As the result of the analysis, a "protest activism" scale was constructed, ranging from low (0) for someone who had no experience of any of the acts to high (5) for someone who had actually engaged in all five types of protest act.

How many have experience of these different types of activity? Table 10.2 shows the frequency of protest behavior in the mid-1990s, compared to the standard indicators of conventional forms of participation, across different types of political system. Of these, the most popular protest activities across all countries were signing a petition, (28 percent of all citizens), attending a demonstration (16 percent), and joining a consumer boycott (9 percent). By contrast, industrial action was confined to a small minority (5 percent), as was occupying a building (2 percent). Among the conventional acts, discussing politics, voting, and civic activism (belonging to at least one voluntary association) all proved to be by far the most common, involving about two-thirds of the public. These acts were obviously far more common than protest politics. On the other hand, petitioning, demonstrating, and boycotting were all fairly common acts, far more so than being an active party member. The comparison across different political systems shows that these activities were consistently the most common among older democracies with the longest traditions of active citizenship; nevertheless, semi-democracies and even non-democracies were far less different than might

TABLE 10.1. *Dimensions of political participation*

	Civic Activism	Protest Activism	Voting Turnout
Belong to environmental organization	.680		
Belong to charitable organization	.647		
Belong to art, music, or educational organization	.643		
Belong to professional association	.638		
Belong to political party	.584		
Belong to sport, or recreational organization	.536		
Belong to church or religious organization	.521		
Belong to labor union	.423		
Attend a lawful demonstration		.765	
Join in boycotts		.764	
Join unofficial strike		.756	
Sign a petition		.687	
Occupy buildings or factories		.680	
Voted in election			.926
Percent Variance	20.1	19.6	7.2

Notes: Extraction method: Principal component analysis. Rotation method: Varimax with Kaiser normalization.
Protest activism: *"Now I'd like you to look at this card. I'm going to read out some different forms of political action that people can take, and I'd like you to tell me, for each one, whether you have actually done any of these things, whether you might do it, or would never, under any circumstances, do it."*
Source: World Values Survey, mid-1990s.

have been expected, based on the limited political rights and civil liberties in these countries. For example, there was almost as much political discussion and voting turnout reported in non-democracies as in older democracies, and about the same level of reported experience of demonstrations. Whether political participation in non-democracies is meaningful in terms of influencing the selection of leaders or the policy process remains an open question, one that cannot be examined here from the available data, but the similarities in levels of activism across many common modes is notable.

Moreover, the systematic survey evidence confirms the rise in protest politics that many observers and commentators believe has occurred. Protest politics is not simply a passing fad of the "hot" politics of the 1960s and early 1970s that faded with the end of the civil rights struggle, the Vietnam

TABLE 10.2. *Experience of political activism, mid-1990s (percent)*

Activity	Older Democracy	Newer Democracy	Semi-democracy	Nondemocratic	All
Discuss politics	72.3	72.2	68.2	65.6	70.0
Voting turnout	73.1	68.9	56.3	60.8	64.5
Civic activism	73.0	60.3	63.1	40.7	62.4
Signed a petition	60.7	22.6	19.4	10.0	28.5
Attended demonstrations	19.1	12.5	15.7	19.1	15.7
Joined in boycott	17.1	6.7	7.5	3.0	8.9
Active union member	8.2	5.0	4.7	3.5	5.4
Joined unofficial strike	4.8	4.4	5.6	5.2	5.0
Active party member	5.8	4.2	4.7	2.5	4.6
Occupied buildings	1.5	2.0	1.6	0.3	1.6

Notes: Protest acts (highlighted in italic): *"Now I'd like you to look at this card. I'm going to read out some different forms of political action that people can take, and I'd like you to tell me, for each one, whether you have actually done any of these things, whether you might do it, or would never, under any circumstances, do it."* Percent "have actually done."
Active party member: see Table 6.3.
Active union member: see Table 9.2.
Discuss politics: Percent "frequently" or "occasionally."
Civic activism: Active or passive member of at least one voluntary association (i.e., a sports club, arts club, environmental group, or charitable group, excluding party or union).
Voting turnout: Aggregate mean Vote/VAP, 1990s.
Source: World Values Survey, mid-1990s.

War, and the Watergate generation. Instead, the proportion of citizens engaged in protest politics has risen, and risen dramatically, during the late twentieth century. Eight nations (Britain, West Germany, the Netherlands, Austria, the United States, Italy, Switzerland, and Finland) were included in the original Political Action Survey conducted from 1973 to 1976. The protest politics items were replicated in the same countries in successive waves of the World Values Study.[23] The results of the comparisons of trends from the mid-1970s to the mid-1990s in these nations, shown in Table 10.3, confirm that experience of protest politics has risen steadily over the years. The proportion of citizens who had signed a petition in these countries doubled from 32 percent to 60 percent; the proportion who had attended a demonstration escalated from 7 percent to 19 percent; and the proportion participating in a consumer boycott tripled from 5 percent to 15

TABLE 10.3. *The rise of protest politics, mid-1970s to mid-1990s (percent)*

Activity	Mid-1970s	Early 1980s	1990	Mid-1990s
Signed petition	32	46	54	60
Demonstrated	9	14	18	17
Consumer boycott	5	8	11	15
Unofficial strike	2	3	4	4
Occupied buildings	1	2	2	2

Note: Protest activism: *"Now I'd like you to look at this card. I'm going to read out some different forms of political action that people can take, and I'd like you to tell me, for each one, whether you have actually done any of these things, whether you might do it, or would never, under any circumstances, do it."* Percent "have done."
The proportion of citizens who reported actual experience of these protest activities in eight postindustrial societies (Britain, West Germany, the Netherlands, Austria, the United States, Italy, Switzerland, and Finland). The political action survey was conducted from 1973 to 1976. Comparable figures for subsequent years for the same nations are drawn from successive waves of the World Values Study.

percent. Participation in unofficial strikes and in occupations remains confined to only a limited minority, but even here there is evidence of growing numbers.

Broader comparisons confirm that the rise of protest politics is by no means confined to postindustrial societies and established democracies. Table 10.4 shows experience engaging in demonstrations from the early 1980s to the early 1990s in the wider range of twenty-two societies for which evidence is available. The results confirm that demonstration activism became more common in seventeen nations, with particularly marked increases in South Korea, the Netherlands, and Mexico. By contrast, participation in demonstrations fell only slightly in a few places, including Argentina and Finland. Across all these societies, the proportion of citizens with experience of taking part in demonstrations rose from 14 to 20 percent of the population during this decade. Table 10.5 shows that participation through signing a petition has become even more commonplace, rising from just over a third (38 percent) to half of the population. Again, steep rises in petitioning were evident in South Korea, Mexico, and the Netherlands, as well as in Northern Ireland, Belgium, and Sweden.

The distribution of nations on the protest activism scale in Figure 10.1 compares the countries where WVS data is available for the mid-1990s. Although we might expect protest to be strongest in countries without many other opportunities for democratic participation, or that it would be most prevalent in poorer nations, the results show that it is actually strongest in established democracies and in affluent postindustrial societies. There was a strong correlation between national levels of protest activism and the

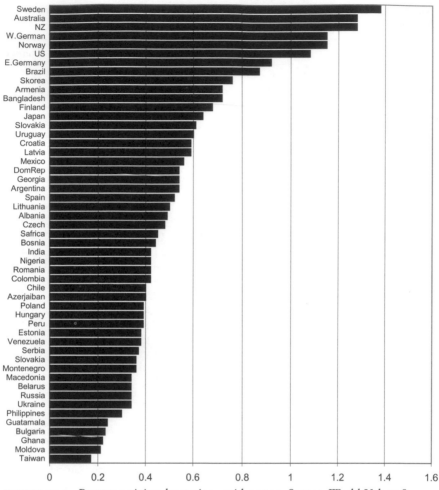

0   0.2   0.4   0.6   0.8   1   1.2   1.4   1.6

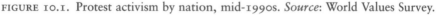

FIGURE 10.1. Protest activism by nation, mid-1990s. *Source*: World Values Survey.

UNDP Human Development Index (R = .529, sig. 001), as well as with Freedom House measures of democratization (R = .386, sig. 001). Sweden, West Germany, Norway, and Australia lead the ranking, with poorer countries such as Ghana, El Salvador, India, and Egypt lagging at the bottom of the comparison.

Dramatic events such as the anti-globalization movement disruption of international summits and the peace demonstrations triggered by the U.S. air strikes in Afghanistan suggest that willingness to engage in protest politics has increased in recent decades in many places around the world, but this perception could also reflect changes in the news media's propensity to

TABLE 10.4. *Rise in demonstration activism, early 1980s to early 1990s*
(percent)

	Early 1980s	Early 1990s	Change
South Korea	5.4	18.9	13.5
Netherlands	11.9	25.0	13.1
Mexico	7.7	20.2	12.5
Iceland	13.6	23.4	9.8
Italy	24.7	34.1	9.4
Denmark	17.8	27.0	9.2
Belgium	12.7	21.2	8.5
Canada	13.0	21.0	8.0
South Africa	6.4	13.3	6.9
Sweden	15.1	21.8	6.7
Australia	12.0	18.0	6.0
West Germany	13.8	19.5	5.7
France	25.8	31.2	5.4
Ireland	12.2	16.3	4.1
Britain	9.7	13.6	3.9
United States	12.2	15.1	2.9
Japan	6.6	9.4	2.8
Northern Ireland	17.9	17.8	−0.1
Norway	19.4	19.0	−0.4
Spain	21.8	21.2	−0.6
Finland	14.2	11.9	−2.3
Argentina	18.8	14.6	−4.2
Mean	**14.2**	**19.7**	**5.5**

Note: Protest activism: *"Now I'd like you to look at this card. I'm going to read out some different forms of political action that people can take, and I'd like you to tell me, for each one, whether you have actually done any of these things, whether you might do it, or would never, under any circumstances, do it."* Percent "have actually attended lawful demonstration."
Source: World Values Survey.

cover these events. Confirming the more anecdotal evidence, an increase in protest activism was registered in all twenty-three nations where the WVS survey was conducted in both the early 1980s and the mid-1990s, with strong gains registered in some of the developing countries such as South Africa, South Korea, and Mexico, as well as in older democracies such as Switzerland, Sweden, and West Germany. There may be more media coverage of street demonstrations, rallies, and public meetings, but these images reflect real changes in political behavior in many societies.

Who Protests?

Earlier studies have shown that during the mid-1970s, protest potential was generally highest among the younger generation, the better educated,

TABLE 10.5. *Rise in petitioning, early 1980s to early 1990s (percent)*

	Early 1980s	Early 1990s	Change
South Korea	15.7	40.6	24.9
Northern Ireland	33.0	57.9	24.9
Mexico	8.2	31.4	23.2
Belgium	21.6	44.5	22.9
Netherlands	33.1	50.1	17.0
Sweden	53.0	69.9	16.9
Canada	60.6	76.5	15.9
South Africa	17.1	31.5	14.4
Ireland	27.9	41.4	13.5
Britain	62.6	74.5	11.9
Japan	40.7	52.0	11.3
Iceland	36.7	46.6	9.9
Australia	68.7	78.6	9.9
West Germany	45.5	55.1	9.6
United States	61.2	70.1	8.9
Denmark	42.0	50.3	8.3
France	43.8	51.4	7.6
Italy	37.5	44.2	6.7
Finland	29.0	34.0	5.0
Norway	54.4	59.4	5.0
Spain	20.6	17.5	−3.1
Argentina	28.6	21.4	−7.2
Mean	**38.3**	**50.0**	**11.7**

Note: Protest activism: *"Now I'd like you to look at this card. I'm going to read out some different forms of political action that people can take, and I'd like you to tell me, for each one, whether you have actually done any of these things, whether you might do it, or would never, under any circumstances, do it."* Percent "have actually signed a petition."
Source: World Values Survey.

men, and the nonreligious; public sector professionals and students were particularly active through these channels.[24] In more recent years, however, some suggest that as protest has gone from margin to mainstream, the population willing to engage in such acts has "normalized."[25] Table 10.6 analyzes the social background of protest activists, measured by whether people had carried out at least one protest act and the mean score on the activism scale by social group, for the pooled WVS sample across all societies in the mid-1990s. The results show that one-third of the public had engaged in at least one protest act. There was a modest gender gap, as expected, with men slightly more willing to protest than women. But overall, education proved by far the best predictor of experience of protest politics, followed by social class. In a familiar pattern found in many earlier studies, 40 percent of those

TABLE 10.6. *Protest activism by social background, mid-1990s*

	Have Engaged in at Least One Protest Act (Percent)	Mean Score, Protest Activism Scale	Eta (Sig.)
Gender			
Men	36.1	.59	
Women	31.5	.47	.07***
Age			
18–24	30.6	.46	
25–34	34.4	.55	
35–44	36.4	.59	
45–54	37.5	.61	
55–64	35.2	.51	
65+	30.7	.42	.07***
Education			
High education	40.5	.70	
Medium education	33.7	.52	
Low education	24.1	.35	.15***
Occupational class			
Managerial and professional	43.7	.74	
Other white-collar	43.1	.64	
Skilled manual	32.4	.51	
Unskilled manual	25.6	.38	.13***
All	33.7	.53	

Note: For the protest activism scale, see Table 10.2. The strength (Eta) and significance of the difference in the group mean is measured by ANOVA. Sig. ***p.000.
Source: World Values Survey, mid-1990s (N = 80,583).

with high education had protested, compared to only one-quarter of those with low education. In contrast to studies in the mid-1970s, the age profile was curvilinear, reflecting common patterns found for civic activism. It was the middle-aged who proved the strongest protest activists, with a fall-off among both the youngest and the oldest cohorts. Whether this is a life-cycle effect or a generational effect is difficult to establish from cross-sectional data, but this evidence probably suggests that far from being confined to the student generation, as in the past, today protest activism has normalized as the 1960s and 1970s cohorts have aged.

Support for New Social Movements

But how does protest politics relate to the growth of new social movements? And in particular, as is often assumed, are supporters of these groups more likely to engage in demonstrations, boycotts, and petitions than in elections and party work? One difficulty facing any systematic analysis is that new social movements and transnational advocacy networks encompass a diverse mélange of organizations and causes. An estimated 700 groups attended the Social Forum in Genoa in July 2001, ranging from traditional trade unions and charities such as Oxfam and Christian Aid, to groups concerned with peaceful protests about globalization, the protection of human rights, environmentalism, the peace movement, poverty, and debt relief for developing nations, to the more radical anarchists and anticapitalist forces at the forefront of the "black block."

Here we focus on environmental activism, taken as exemplifying typical forms of participation in other new social movements. There is nothing novel about concern for wildlife, biodiversity, and preservation of natural habitats; indeed, traditional British associations in the voluntary sector that continue to campaign on these issues, founded more than a century ago, include the Royal Botanical Gardens at Kew (1840), the Royal Society for the Protection of Animals (1864), and the National Trust (1895). But the late twentieth century witnessed dramatic increases in public concern about environmental issues, membership in environmental groups, the formation of government environmental agencies, and the number of environmental regulations and international treaties, making this movement one of the most important forces in the policy process.[26] The diverse organizational structure of environmental groups, and the emphasis on "lifestyle politics" and direct action for recycling and environmental protection of local areas, exemplifies many of the defining features of the new social movements. Environmentalism encompasses a diverse coalition: ecologists and peace activists, holistic theorists and anti–nuclear power activists, feminists, animal rights activists, the organic farming movement, the soft energy movement, consumers concerned about genetically modified food, and converts from radical left groups, as well as traditional organizations seeking to preserve the countryside and wildlife habitats. There are fuzzy boundaries. Support for environmentalism includes activities as different as joining the Friends of the Earth or Greenpeace, recycling bottles and cans, boycotting nonorganic produce, signing a petition against a road development, helping to restore a local wildlife habitat, voting for a green party, or protesting against a multinational company.[27]

This study measured how far citizens had carried out a battery of five actions that cover some of the most typical forms of environmental activism, such as recycling, contributing to an environmental organization, and attending a meeting about these issues, as shown in Table 10.7. Active membership of an environmental organization, used earlier to gauge civic society, was added to this battery. Responses to all six items scaled consistently into a single dimension and proved to be highly intercorrelated (Cronbach's Alpha = 0.77). Table 10.7 shows that environmental activism

TABLE 10.7. *Environmental activism scale, mid-1990s*

Question	Percent "Yes"
Have you tried to reduce water consumption for environmental reasons?	40.8
Have you decided for environmental reasons to reuse or recycle something rather than throw it away?	34.2
Have you chosen household products that you think are better for the environment?	33.6
Are you an active or inactive member of an environmental organization?	13.8
Have you contributed to an environmental organization?	11.5
Have you attended a meeting or signed a letter or petition aimed at protecting the environment?	10.6

Note: Environmental activism: *"Which, if any, of these things have you done in the last twelve months, out of concern for the environment?"* Percent "Yes."
Voluntary organization membership: See Table 9.4.
Source: World Values Survey, mid-1990s.

varied across these items, from 40 percent of the public who said that they had tried to reduce water consumption for environmental reasons, down to 11 percent who had attended a meeting or signed a letter or petition aimed at protecting the environment. The "lifestyle" dimensions of activism all proved to be more popular and widespread than those involving more narrowly policy-oriented forms of support.

To examine who was environmentally active, Table 10.8 shows the distribution of those who have performed at least one environmental act and the mean score for groups on the scale. The results show that two-thirds claim to have performed at least one environmental act. There was a slim gender gap, with women slightly more likely to be active on these issues than men. But again, education and class proved to be far stronger predictors of activism, reflecting the well-known propensity for environmentalism to be strongest among the well-educated and among managerial and professional households. Age proved to be slightly curvilinear, with environmentalism strongest among the early middle-aged, rather than among the youngest cohort, but overall there was only a modest difference by age group.

Since the patterns that have been observed so far could be due to the types of societies included in the comparison, Table 10.9 introduces models that control for levels of human and democratic development, social structure, and cultural attitudes, as in previous chapters. The models then test for the impact of the environmental activism scale on the four dimensions of political participation examined here. The results show two important

TABLE 10.8. *Environmental activism by social background, mid-1990s*

	Have Engaged in at Least One Environmental Act (Percent)	Mean Score, Environmental Activism Scale	Eta (Sig.)
Gender			
Men	62.9	1.40	
Women	64.8	1.46	.01***
Age			
18–24	63.5	1.36	
25–34	67.1	1.51	
35–44	66.1	1.49	
45–54	68.4	1.57	
55–64	63.3	1.40	
65+	65.0	1.38	.05***
Education			
High education	70.2	1.64	
Medium education	65.2	1.45	
Low education	56.0	1.16	.12***
Occupational class			
Managerial and professional	71.9	1.73	
Other white-collar	70.4	1.67	
Skilled manual	65.6	1.41	
Unskilled manual	59.0	1.19	.13***
All	63.9	1.43	

Note: For the environmental activism scale, see Table 10.4. The strength (Eta) and significance of the difference in the group mean is measured by ANOVA. Sig. ***p.000
Source: World Values Survey, mid-1990s (N = 80,583).

and distinctive findings. First, after introducing all of these prior controls, environmental activism is *negatively* associated with voting turnout. The association is not particularly strong, but it is significant, and it does stand up to many different statistical tests. This suggests that the people who are most inclined to support environmentalism are less likely than average to cast a ballot in elections and, by contrast, that they are more likely to support protest activism such as demonstrations, petitions, strikes, and boycotts. Figure 10.2 shows the clear relationship at the societal level between the two scales of environmental activism and protest activism: Postindustrial societies such as Sweden, New Zealand, Germany, and Australia that were strong on one dimension were often strong on the other as well, with development displaying a curvilinear relationship. In these regards, the green movement could indeed be regarded as the emergence of an alternative form of politics, as many advocates claim, which may also be the case

TABLE 10.9. *Environmental activism and political participation, mid-1990s*

	Voting Turnout			Party Member			Civic Activism			Protest Activism		
	B	(s.e.)	Sig.	B	(s.e.)	Sig.	B	(s.e.)	Sig.	B	(s.e.)	Sig.
Development												
Level of human development	2.14	.300	***	-3.26	.135	***	-1.05	.088	***	.788	.047	***
Level of democratization	.576	.020	***	-.035	.012	***	.045	.007	***	.049	.004	***
Structure												
Age (*years*)	-.005	.001	***	.001	.001		-.005	.000	***	-.004	.000	***
Gender (*male = 1*)	-.239	.050	***	.263	.029	***	.122	.016	***	.068	.009	***
Education (*seven-pt scale*)	-.128	.012	***	.027	.007	***	.071	.004	***	.028	.002	***
Class (*ten-pt scale*)	.003	.010		.011	.006		-.012	.003	***	-.023	.002	***
Cultural attitudes												
Political Interest (nine-point scale)	.374	.013	***	.313	.007	***	.068	.004	***	.103	.002	***
New social movement												
Environmental activism (six-point scale)	-.191	.018	***	.350	.010	***	.459	.006	***	.114	.003	***
Constant	-2.71			-2.56			.649			-1.08		
Nagelkerke R²	.171			.178								
Adjusted R²							.174			.151		
Percent correct	94.7			84.7								

Note: Voting turnout and party activism in the mid-1990s are analyzed using logistic regression, with the table listing unstandardized regression coefficients, standard errors, and significance. Civic activism and protest activism are analyzed using linear regression models. Sig. *p < .05, **p < .01, ***p < .001.

Human development: Human Development Index 1990: *Human Development Report*. New York: United Nations Development Program.
Level of democratization: Mean Freedom House Index of political rights and civil liberties, 1990–6. www.freedomhouse.org.
New social movement: Environmental activism (six-point scale). See Table 10.4.
Cultural attitudes: See Table 7.7. The nine-point interest scale combined political discussion, interest, and the salience of politics, which all also proved to be highly intercorrelated.
Voting turnout: Yes = 1.
Party member: Inactive or active member.
Civic activism: Scale of active or passive member in church, sports club, arts club, professional, union, charitable, or other group.
Protest activism: Five-point scale of having signed petition, joined boycott, demonstrated, joined unofficial strike, or occupied building.

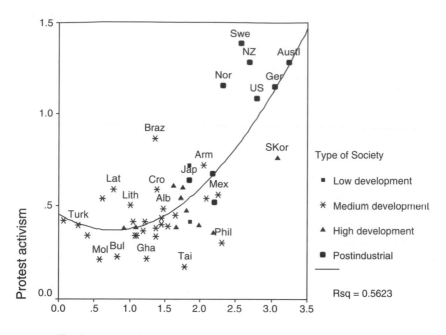

Environmental activism

FIGURE 10.2. Environmental and protest activism, mid-1990s. *Note*: Environmental activism: See Table 10.7 for details. Protest activism: See Table 10.1 for details. *Source*: World Values Survey.

with other new social movements, such as those concerned with feminism, human rights, and conflict resolution.

At the same time, environmental activism is both strongly and positively related to the conventional channels of party membership and civic activism. Indeed, environmental activism is one of the best predictors of membership in all of the other forms of community group, such as sports and arts clubs, as well as in professional associations and unions. This suggests that rather than engaging in an alternative and distinctive form of civic engagement, people who are active through recycling, green shopping, and donating to environmental groups are likely to be found among many other mainstream civic organizations.

The Role of the Internet

What is the role of the bundle of new technologies of information and communication associated with the internet in promoting an alternative channel for new social movements and direct-action politics? Protest movements have traditionally relied upon activities such as street theatre, public demonstrations, and direct action to challenge authorities. The internet has altered this dynamic by electronically promoting the diffusion of protest ideas and tactics quickly and efficiently across national borders.[28] The mobilization of transnational advocacy networks has caught policy makers off guard. The World Trade Organization meeting in Seattle in late November 1999 exemplified this process, bringing together an alliance between labor and environmental activists – the so-called turtle–teamster partnership – along with a network of consumer advocates, anticapitalists, and grassroots movements that set off a media feeding frenzy. Groups integrated the internet into their strategies; for example, the International Civil Society website provided hourly updates about the major demonstrations in Seattle to a network of almost 700 NGOs in some 80 countries, including groups of environmentalists, students, religious groups, human rights organizations, trade unions, and related movements.[29] The Seattle meeting was a particularly dramatic demonstration of the potential of this medium, but it is far from alone; other well-known examples include the anti–land mine campaign in the mid to late 1990s, the anti-globalization protests against the World Bank and IMF in Prague, protests against the EU meetings in Gothenberg and the G8 summit in Genoa, and the widespread anti–fuel tax protests that disrupted European politics in October 2000.[30]

Many environmentalists have incorporated the multimedia capabilities of the internet into their direct-action strategies. Global Forest Watch, for example, is a transnational network of scientists and local groups regularly monitoring, recording, and reporting the erosion of forests, using digital maps and web cams to publicize abuses by the timber industry and agribusiness, providing a flexible kind of regulatory process working outside of formal government structures.[31] Internet outlets can be particularly important under authoritarian regimes, where protest activities and the independent news media are severely constrained or silenced, although there are still outlets, such as web sites maintained by sympathizers of the Falun Gong in China and antistate dissidents in Cuba, that the authorities have effectively blocked and suppressed within their own borders.[32]

The Internet may serve multiple functions for all these organizations, including e-mail lobbying of elected representatives, public officials, and policy elites; networking with related associations and organizations; mobilizing organizers, activists, and members using action alerts, newsletters, and e-mails; raising funds and recruiting supporters; and communicating messages to the public via the traditional news media. The global reach and real-time speed of the internet make it particularly useful for transnational advocacy networks, exemplified by diverse campaigns such as the movement against the production and sale of land mines, demonstrators critical of the World Trade Organization meeting in Seattle, environmentalists opposing genetically modified foods, and anti-sweatshop campaigners opposed to the manufacturing conditions of Nike shoes.[33]

The potential activities for organization and mobilization involve far more than the passive reading of informational web pages. Transnational advocacy networks represent "umbrella" web sites aiming to amplify the impact of smaller like-minded NGOs. As exemplified by the Institute for Global Communications' progressive network, through the internet people can subscribe to advocacy and lobbying groups, affiliate with the organization, receive e-mailed policy newsletters and action alerts, send faxes and e-mails to decision makers, circulate electronic petitions, learn about forthcoming street demonstrations, protest events, job vacancies, and voluntary activities, as well as share effective strategies for activism, contribute short news items to the site, and participate in online discussions.[34] The IGC site, established in 1990, contains about 350,000 links in over 8,000 pages. A similar networking function is fulfilled by OneWorld.net, founded in 1995, a web site containing 15,000 pages with almost 100,000 links to progressive organizations promoting human rights and sustainable development. The web site, available in four languages, contains news and press releases about trouble spots around the globe, in-depth policy reports, selected radio and TV reports, information about volunteer jobs, opportunities to become active in a range of campaigns, and online shopping. Future developments planned for the site include a learning channel.

As illustrated by the Greenpeace site, social movements have taken advantage of many innovative features of the internet. The Greenpeace site features breaking news, streaming audio and video clips, information resources, and ways to join the organization, participate in a chat room, and subscribe to cyberactivism list-servs on such topics as biodiversity and nuclear power, and national and local branch addresses.[35] Daily counts show that www.Greenpeace.org received about 58,000 visitors in a typical week in mid-2000, up fourfold from four years earlier, with about half a million total visitors since the launch of the current site in late 1997. Domain analysis indicates that users of the web site come from all over the world, including Europe (15 percent), North America (10 percent), Australia (4 percent), South America (3 percent) and Asia (2 percent). In short, digital technologies facilitate the network of networks, which should be an environment where civic society and the public sphere flourish.

More systematic analysis of which groups and organizations have moved online, however, is far from straightforward. Others have used search engines such as InfoSeek and Yahoo! to provide a sampling frame, analyzing a random selection of American groups listed in these indexes, such as the American Civil Liberties Union, the National Organization of Women, and the Audubon Society.[36] This approach provides a representative selection of groups on the internet that are identified by these common search engines, but unfortunately this process can tell us nothing about the broader universe of interest groups and social movements. For this, we can turn to the Union of International Organizations (UIA) based in Brussels, which has published the *Yearbook of International Organizations* since 1908.[37] This source provides the most comprehensive list available of multifarious types of organization worldwide, including nonprofit associations, societies, federations, institutes, bureaus, and associations, as well as scientific and academic research centers, trade unions, business groups, and nonprofit foundations. The *Yearbook* is probably stronger on traditional interest associations with formal organizational structures than on more disparate alternative social movements, especially groups and coalitions that exist only online; nevertheless, its geographic scope and subject coverage are comprehensive. The online UIA database lists details about 55,465 international governmental organizations (IGOs) and national nongovernmental organizations (NGOs) worldwide in November 1999, including location, type, and whether the organization has established a web site. A representative sample of 468 organizations was selected from this source by a process of random selection (picking the first organization on each page of the database listed alphabetically), and the web sites were examined for those organizations found to be online.

The diverse and eclectic organizations under comparison ranged from the African Democratic League, Anti-Slavery International, and the Association for Lesbian, Gay and Bi-Sexual Psychologies to the Woodworking Association of North America, the World Copyright Organization, and the Zoo Conservation Outreach Group. Overall, from the random sample of 468 organizations, the analysis suggests that about one-quarter (109) had a web site identified by the UIA. This may seem like a relatively low proportion, but even if this is a conservative estimate (underestimating the recent proliferation of web sites by new social movements), extrapolating more generally from this sample suggests that about 12,400 interest groups are online worldwide. A systematic analysis of these groups by type, organizational structure, and sector, as well as by the contents of the web site, would require a much larger sample to prove reliable; nevertheless, a glance through the list of web sites quickly confirmed the multiplicity and variety of the groups found online: the Christian Jugglers Association and the B'nai B'rith Hillel Foundation mixed company in cyberspace, alongside the European Metalworkers' Federation, the International Potato Center, the European Board of Urology, the International Naturist Federation, the Mammal Society, the Nordic Youth Committee, and the International Chamber of Shipping. Beyond geography, there was no discernable pattern to the groups found online: The sacred and the profane coexisted, as did business associations and trade unions, the Christian right and progressive liberals. The geographic analysis established the predominance of sites for organizations headquartered in North America, Western Europe, Scandinavia, and Australia, even if their missions were broader – for example, Australian associations promoting international human rights and conflict resolution, Nordic academicians studying Middle Eastern cultures, and Virginian evangelists concerned to spread the word in Africa. The initial impression of interest groups and transnational advocacy networks on the internet, based on this comparison – and it remains only an impression – is one of tremendous diversity; a plurality of new social movements, transnational policy networks, and traditional interest groups can and do find opportunities to network, organize, and express diverse viewpoints. We need more information about who uses these web sites in many different countries as the internet grows to maturity if we are to analyze whether this represents a distinctive channel of civic activism, but the available evidence from many American and Western European surveys strongly suggests that, while the internet does facilitate political expression and mobilization, reducing the costs of information and communication, those who use these resources tend to be those who are already the most active through nonvirtual channels.[38]

Conclusions

What this chapter suggests is that there are many reasons to believe that the shift from traditional interest groups to new social movements has influenced the agencies, repertoires, and targets of political participation. It is more difficult to find systematic evidence that will allow us to analyze these issues, but the analysis presented in this chapter presents four main findings:

1. First, the factor analysis confirms that protest activism remains a consistent dimension of political participation, one that proves to be distinct from voting participation and from conventional civic activism through belonging to parties, voluntary associations, and community organizations.

2. The analysis of protest politics shows that today many of these forms of activity, such as petitions, demonstrations, and consumer boycotts, are fairly pervasive and have become increasingly popular during the 1980s. Protest politics is on the rise as a channel of political expression and mobilization.

3. Protest politics is particularly strong among the well-educated managerial and professional classes in postindustrial societies, as many others have suggested, but it has also become more "mainstream"; by the mid-1990s it was no longer confined to students and the younger generation. The social backgrounds of protest activist today generally reflect the propensity of groups to participate through conventional means as well.

4. Lastly, participation in new social movements was measured by environmental activism, which proved to be negatively related to voting

turnout, but positively linked to party membership, civic activism, and protest politics.

The internet is fostering new opportunities for civic engagement, and, as argued elsewhere, the new technology provides an environment most conducive to social movements with the organizational flexibility, resources, and technical know-how to adapt. As the network of networks, the internet provides multiple opportunities for information, communication, and mobilization, and many alternative groups and organizations have found a home there. The culture of the internet makes it favorable to new social movements, as does the social profile of users, who are among the well-educated and affluent sectors of society.[39] Therefore, before we can conclude that the vitality of civic activism is under threat, studies of conventional forms of political participation need to take into account these multiple alternative avenues for political expression. Twenty or thirty years ago, elections, parties, and interest groups were the mainstream channels for affecting the policy process within the nation-state, but today the diversification of agencies, repertoires, and targets means that energies flow through new tributaries. As a result of this process, governments face new challenges in balancing and aggregating more complex demands from multiple channels, but from the perspective of citizens this provides more diverse opportunities for engagement, which may well be healthy for representative democracy.

CONCLUSIONS

All these receive their Birth from other Things;
But from himself the Phoenix only springs:
Self-born, begotten by the Parent Flame
In which he burn'd, Another and the Same.

John Dryden, *Ovid's Metamorphoses* (1700)

Conclusions: The Reinvention of Political Activism?

There is widespread agreement among democratic theorists ranging from Jean Jacques Rousseau to James Madison, John Stuart Mill, Robert Dahl, Benjamin Barber, David Held, and John Dryzak that mass participation is essential to the lifeblood of representative democracy, although there is continued debate about how much civic engagement is either necessary or desirable.[1] Theorists advocating "strong" democracy suggest that citizen activism and deliberation are intrinsically valuable in themselves. More minimalist conceptions, proposed by Schumpeterian theorists, suggest that the essential role of citizens should be relatively limited, confined principally to the periodic election of parliamentary representatives, along with the continuous scrutiny of government actions.[2] If participation is indeed in secular decline across all modes, then this should indeed be a cause for alarm. But is the widespread concern justified? This chapter summarizes the central argument developed throughout the book, highlights the key findings, and considers the implications for understanding the evolution of democratic participation.

To recapitulate, the heart of this book examines evidence concerning three core claims. The first is that there has been a steady secular erosion of the traditional avenues of political engagement, including electoral turnout, party work, and civic activism. The second claim is that long-term processes of societal modernization and human development (including rising levels of literacy, education, and wealth) are the primary drivers shaping these changes, in a predictable curvilinear trajectory from developing to industrialized societies, although the pace of change is conditioned by the structure of the state, the role of mobilizing agencies, and the resource and motivational differences among groups and individuals. The last claim, and the one that is most difficult to prove in any systematic fashion, is that rather than eroding, political activism has been reinvented in recent decades by a diversification in the *agencies* (the collective organizations structuring political activity), the *repertoires* (the actions commonly used for political expression), and the *targets* (the political actors that participants seek to influence). The surge of protest politics, new social movements, and internet activism exemplify these changes. If the opportunities for political expression and mobilization have fragmented and multiplied over the years, like a swollen river flooding through different tributaries, democratic engagement may have adapted and evolved in accordance with the new structure of opportunities, rather than simply atrophying.

Electoral Turnout

Electoral turnout is one of the most common forms of political participation, even if atypical in terms of its relatively low costs and benefits. Chapter 3 examined the evidence for the impact of human development on postwar trends in electoral turnout. The evidence suggests three broad conclusions about postwar trends in electoral turnout around the world.

First, the study largely confirms the modernization thesis: During the last fifty years, countries with rapid human development have experienced substantial growth in electoral turnout, especially in Asia and Latin America. Modernization theories are attractive because of their claim that economic, cultural, and political changes go together in predictable ways, so that there are broadly similar trajectories, which form coherent patterns. Modernization accounts suggest that economic shifts in the production process underlie changes in the state, in particular, that rising levels of education, literacy, and wealth in the transition from rural subsistence economies to industrialized nations generate conditions favorable to expanding voting participation. When citizens are given opportunities to express their political preferences through the ballot box, then the first stage of industrialization can be expected to foster electoral turnout, as well as broader aspects of civic engagement such as the growth of party and trade union organizations. Yet there is a ceiling effect in the impact of human development. In particular, once primary and secondary education become ubiquitous throughout the population, producing the basic cognitive skills that facilitate civic awareness and access to mass communications, then further gains in the proportion of the population attending college and ever-rising levels of personal wealth, income, and leisure time do not, in themselves, produce further improvements in voting participation.

At the same time, concern that postindustrial societies are inevitably experiencing a deep secular erosion of voting participation during the last half century are greatly exaggerated. Overall, the majority of these nations saw a long-term pattern of trendless fluctuation or stability in electoral participation. Only eight postindustrial societies have experienced a significant erosion of voting turnout over successive decades since 1945. While there is good evidence for a slight short-term fall in voting participation during the 1990s across many postindustrial societies, the timing of the shift means that it cannot plausibly be attributed to the sort of glacial socioeconomic trends, such as suburbanization and secularization, that are at the heart of modernization theories. We can speculate about alternative explanations for the short-term decline. One factor could be the impact of globalization, eroding the power and autonomy of the nation-state during this era. The end of the cold war may have reduced the salience of foreign policy and defense issues in many countries. Any closure of the ideological gap in party competition, with the growth of "catch-all" campaign appeals symbolized by the "third way" politics of Clinton and Blair, could also have reduced the incentive to vote. Whatever the explanation, which requires further systematic analysis, the pattern suggests that this is a short-term phenomenon that requires us to focus more on short-term political developments than on long-term socioeconomic trends.

Despite these findings, there remain considerable variations in turnout across countries at similar levels of development today, exemplified by the stark contrasts between Switzerland and Sweden, the United States and Italy, Mexico and South Africa. The roles of political institutions and mobilizing agencies help to explain these patterns further. Rational choice theories suggest that the primary incentives facing citizens in national elections may be understood as a product of the electoral costs of registering and voting, the party choices available to electors, and the degree to which casting a ballot determines the composition of parliament and government. The costs include the time and effort required to register and to vote, any legal sanctions imposed for failure to turn out, and the frequency with which electors are called to the polls. All other things being equal, among affluent societies, turnout can be expected to be higher in political systems that reduce the costs of voting, such as those with automatic processes for maintaining the electoral register, and electoral arrangements that maximize party competition but that also maintain a strong link between voters' preferences and the outcome for parliament, for government, and for the policy agenda. The main findings about the impact of institutions on electoral turnout can be summarized as follows.

In multivariate models controlling for levels of human and political development, political institutions and legal rules proved to be strongly and significantly associated with voter turnout in national elections around the world. All other things being equal, political institutions matter; in particular, voting participation is maximized in elections using proportional representation, with small electoral districts, regular but relatively infrequent national contests, competitive party systems, and presidential contests. In terms of the legal rules, the global comparison showed that turnout was lower in countries where women had recently been enfranchised and that used literacy requirements. By contrast, the age of voting eligibility and the use of compulsory voting made no significant difference to turnout worldwide. When the comparison was limited to established democracies, the evidence shows that turnout was not strongly influenced by specific voting facilities such as the registration process, the use of transfer voting, or advance voting. In established democracies, the use of compulsory voting regulations was an important indicator of higher turnout, whereas this was not found in the broader comparison of elections worldwide. Although it cannot be proved here, the reasons for this difference probably concern the efficiency of the electoral registration process and sanctions for nonvoting, as well as cultural traditions concerning obeying the law.

Yet it is well established that even within particular political systems, some groups and individuals remain far more likely to participate than others. Some citizen's vote under almost any circumstances for largely affective reasons, such as a general sense of civic duty, or to express support for a party or cause without any hope of electoral gain. Others are motivated by more instrumental considerations and the rational tradeoff between electoral costs, electoral choices, and electoral decisiveness. Survey evidence based on pooled samples using the ISSP data in twenty-two nations provides insights into these processes. After controlling for levels of modernization and the institutional context, social structure, mobilizing agencies, and cultural attitudes still played important roles in predicting micro-level turnout. As the literature has long demonstrated, at the individual level, among all of the social background factors, age provides the strongest predictor of who votes, in a curvilinear pattern. Youngest cohorts were by far the least likely to vote, while the late middle-aged were most engaged. Moreover, this age profile of voters was evident in every country except Australia, which uses compulsory voting. Education and income also proved to be significant in the pooled model, although when broken down by country these factors proved to be important only in about half of the nations. Gender displays a more complex pattern. By itself, gender is no longer significantly related to turnout in the pooled model, but it becomes significant when interacting with other factors such as political interest and union membership. The role of mobilizing agencies was confirmed, with union membership, church attendance, and party identification all associated with higher turnout, as expected. Lastly, cultural attitudes also proved to be important influences on voting participation, particularly the impact of political interest, even with prior controls.

Party Membership

Parties serve multiple functions: simplifying and structuring electoral choices; organizing and mobilizing campaigns; articulating and aggregating disparate interests; channeling communication, consultation, and debate; training, recruiting, and selecting candidates; structuring parliamentary divisions; acting as policy think tanks; and organizing government. Not only are parties one of the main conduits of political participation, they also serve to boost and strengthen electoral turnout. If the grassroots membership is in decline, as many suspect, this could have serious implications for representative democracy. Theories of mass-branch parties offered by Duverger suggest that local activists in party organizations can act as an important conduit between citizens and elected officials, promoting internal democracy by debating party policies, electing leaders, and mobilizing electoral support. The available evidence documenting historical trends in party membership remains far more limited. The results of the analysis presented in Chapter 6 suggest a complex picture. Estimates based on official party records indicate that patterns of party membership vary considerably cross-nationally, even among Western democracies. Many established democracies have seen an erosion of party membership from the early 1980s to the early 1990s, but during this era membership has expanded in some newer democracies. The World Values Survey evidence for the mid-1990s confirms considerable cross-national variation, with the lowest membership in post-Soviet societies and far healthier party membership in newer democracies in parts of Africa and Asia. Unfortunately, because of data limitations, it is difficult to pursue this comparison in more depth, and we must await additional evidence to confirm these initial indications.

Chapter 7 went on to examine the reasons why people join parties, based on a soft version of rational choice theory. The results suggest that at the societal level, the modernization process influences cross-national differences in levels of party activism. In particular, party membership is usually highest where the diffusion of access to television remains limited. Parties need members where traditional forms of face-to-face campaigning predominate, but the usefulness of grassroots workers declines where there are multiple other channels of electronic communication available to maximize electoral support. The classification of party families remains limited, but the available evidence suggests that, contrary to expectations, there were few significant differences in levels of membership detectable by type of party ideology and by party size. At the individual level, mobilizing agencies and political interest are far more important explanations of party membership than the standard background variables of gender, age, class, and education. What matters for party membership are the social networks and political attitudes that lead citizens to become involved in the internal life of parties, all operating within the broader context of societal modernization.

Civic Society and Social Capital

Many theorists, from Tocqueville and John Stuart Mill to Durkheim, Simmel, and Kornhauser, have emphasized civic society and voluntary associations as vital to democracy. Chapter 8 explores major claims about the consequences of associational activism and social trust. Putnam's thesis suggests that communities characterized by a rich and dense network of belonging to civic associations, such as environmental groups, philanthropic organizations, and sports clubs, should create the "habits of the heart" that facilitate and encourage social trust, social tolerance, and civic engagement, thereby underpinning the cultural conditions promoting democracy.

There are two core components in Putnam's definition of social capital – social networks and social trust. When combined into a single index, social capital is strongly and significantly related to multiple interrelated indicators of socioeconomic development *and* to institutional indicators of democratic development. But if we disentangle the twin components of Putnam's definition of social capital, what is driving this process is primarily the social trust dimension, *not* the associational network dimension. Given the ambiguities in measurement, three alternative measures of associational membership and activism are employed and tested, in exploratory analysis, but these are rarely significant across almost all indicators, no matter which measure is used. Irrespective of its economic and political consequences, the most important result is perhaps the simple finding that nations cluster in fairly predictable patterns across the map of social capital. We can only speculate about the reasons for this, but the explanation probably rests on long-standing cultural traditions and historical legacies, which may relate to religious backgrounds. The map reveals that social capital is most evident in the Nordic region and in most Anglo-American democracies (characterized by high trust and high membership) and least apparent in the post-Soviet Central European and South American societies (low trust and low membership). Both the sub-Saharan African and the Asian countries under comparison fall into different quadrants as "mixed" societies on social capital.

Chapter 9 goes on to explore the role of traditional mobilizing agencies, including religious organizations and trade unions, that can foster dense networks of colleagues and associates, friends and family, neighbors and compatriots, creating social bonds, norms, and expectations that encourage participation. These organizations have long been regarded as particularly important for poorer communities and minority groups that might otherwise be more marginalized politically. Any decline in these associations is of concern if it leads to an erosion of political participation. Yet during the postwar era, trends in net union density show divergence among different countries within Western Europe. Some nations have experienced slow erosion during the last fifty years, while others have expanded their union membership base during the same period, and yet others have seen peaks and troughs. In short, institutional factors such as legal regulations and the welfare services that unions provide for their members represent more plausible explanations for changes in union density than the idea of a slow and steady secular decline in the vitality of the labor movement. At the same time, ILO evidence suggests that levels of union density vary substantially around the world, due to different historical legacies and economic structures. Moreover, in the short term the ILO data show that union density did fall in many countries from the mid-1980s to the mid-1990s, while it rose in only a few, which could be cause for concern if the trend continues. In terms of secularization, the evidence confirms a significant decline in religious attendance during the last thirty years in Western Europe. Moreover, the Weberian thesis that modernity is associated with secularization is supported by the cross-national analysis: The least developed societies generally displayed the strongest religious beliefs and behavior. Lastly, the analysis confirmed that membership in unions and religious organizations is closely associated not only with electoral turnout, but also with indicators of party membership, belonging to other civic associations such as sports and arts clubs, and protest activism.

There are many reasons to believe that the shift from traditional interest groups to new social movements has influenced the agencies, repertoires, and targets of political participation. It is more difficult to find systematic evidence that can be used to analyze these issues, but the analysis presented in Chapter 10 presents four main findings. First, the factor analysis confirms that protest activism remains a consistent dimension of political participation, which proves to be distinct from voting participation and from conventional civic activism through belonging to parties, voluntary associations, and community organizations. The analysis of protest politics shows that many of these forms of activity, such as petitions, demonstrations, and consumer boycotts, are fairly pervasive and have became increasingly popular during recent decades. Protest politics is on the rise as a channel of political expression and mobilization. Protest politics is particularly strong among the well-educated managerial and professional classes in postindustrial societies, as many others have suggested, but it has also become more "mainstream"; by the mid-1990s it was no longer confined to the younger generation. The social backgrounds of protest activists generally reflect the propensity of groups to participate through conventional means as well. Participation in new social movements is exemplified here by environmental activism. This proved to be negatively related to voting turnout, but positively linked to party membership, civic activism, and protest politics.

Many are alarmed that Western publics have become disengaged from public affairs, detached from campaigns, and bored with politics, producing, if not a crisis of democracy, then at least growing problems of legitimacy for representative government.[3] It is widely suggested that the active involvement of citizens in public affairs has been falling away over the years, potentially undermining the legitimacy of more fragile democracies, and widening the gap between citizens and the state. One does not need to subscribe to the stronger claims of "strong," "direct," or "participatory" theorists of democracy to believe that any long-term decline in electoral turnout, party membership, and associational activism is and should be a matter of genuine concern. Pollyanna-ish optimism and Panglossian sentiments should be avoided. But despite the weight of the conventional wisdom, the evidence of secular decline often remains scattered and patchy; consistent and reliable longitudinal trend data is limited; and most previous systematic research has been restricted to case studies of particular countries, particularly the United States, and comparative evidence from established democracies in Western Europe, making it hard to generalize more widely. An established democracy such as the United States, which combines both exceptionally low turnout and exceptionally strong associational activism, by definition cannot be regarded as setting the global standard.

What this broader comparison suggests is that conceptual frameworks for understanding modes of political participation than were developed in the 1950s and 1960s continue to shape our current assumptions. Yet these models were developed to account for activism at a particular time and place. The expansion of the franchise during the nineteenth and early twentieth centuries generated the rise of traditional channels for political mobilization and expression in representative government, particularly the growth of extra-parliamentary party organizations, the spread of cheap mass-circulation newspapers, and the establishment of traditional groups in civic society, exemplified by the organized labor movement, civic associations, voluntary groups, and religious organizations. By the 1940s and 1950s, these channels had settled and consolidated and were taken for granted as the major institutions linking citizens and the state within established democracies. Rising levels of human capital and societal modernization mean that today a more educated citizenry in postindustrial societies has moved increasingly from agencies of loyalty toward agencies of choice, and from electoral repertoires toward mixed-action repertoires combining electoral activities and protest politics. In postindustrial societies, the younger generations, in particular, have become less willing than their parents and grandparents to channel their political energies through traditional agencies exemplified by parties and churches, and more likely to express themselves through a variety of ad hoc, contextual, and specific activities of choice, increasingly via new social movements, internet activism, and transnational policy networks. Conventional indicators may blind us to the fact that critical citizens may be becoming less loyalist and deferential in orientation toward mass-branch parties, which evolved in the nineteenth century with the spread of the mass franchise and European democracy, at the same time that they are becoming more actively engaged via alternative mechanisms of political expression. In short, contrary to popular assumptions, the traditional electoral agencies linking citizens and the state are far from dead. And, like a phoenix, the reinvention of civic activism allows political energies to flow through diverse alternative avenues as well as conventional channels.

Appendix: Comparative Framework

		Nation	Rating of democracy, 1999–2000	Region	Human Development Index 1998, UNDP	Level of development	Name label
Older democracy	1	Australia	1.0	Asia-Pacific	929	Postindustrial	Austl
	2	Austria	1.0	W. Europe	908	Postindustrial	Aus
	3	Bahamas	1.0	S. America	844	High	Bahm
	4	Barbados	1.0	S. America	858	High	Bar
	5	Belgium	1.5	W. Europe	925	Postindustrial	Belg
	6	Canada	1.0	N. America	935	Postindustrial	Can
	7	Costa Rica	1.5	S. America	797	Medium	CRica
	8	Cyprus	1.0	W. Europe	886	Postindustrial	Cyp
	9	Denmark	1.0	Scandinavia	911	Postindustrial	Den
	10	Dominica	2.0	S. America	793	Medium	Dom
	11	Finland	1.0	Scandinavia	917	Postindustrial	Fin
	12	France	1.5	W. Europe	917	Postindustrial	Fr
	13	Germany	1.5	W. Europe	911	Postindustrial	Ger
	14	Greece	2.0	W. Europe	875	Postindustrial	Greece
	15	Iceland	1.0	Scandinavia	927	Postindustrial	Ice
	16	India	2.5	Asia-Pacific	563	Medium	India
	17	Ireland	1.0	W. Europe	907	Postindustrial	Ire
	18	Israel	1.5	Middle East	883	Postindustrial	Isr
	19	Italy	1.5	W. Europe	903	Postindustrial	Ita
	20	Jamaica	2.0	S. America	735	Medium	Jam
	21	Japan	1.5	Asia-Pacific	924	Postindustrial	Jap
	22	Kiribati	1.0	Asia-Pacific	.	.	Kiri
	23	Luxembourg	1.0	W. Europe	908	Postindustrial	Lux
	24	Malta	1.0	W. Europe	865	Postindustrial	Malta
	25	Mauritius	1.5	Africa	761	Medium	Maur
	26	Netherlands	1.0	W. Europe	925	Postindustrial	Neth
	27	New Zealand	1.0	Asia-Pacific	903	Postindustrial	NZ
	28	Norway	1.0	Scandinavia	934	Postindustrial	Nor
	29	Portugal	1.0	W. Europe	864	Postindustrial	Por
	30	Saint Lucia	1.0	S. America	728	Medium	StL
	31	San Marino	1.5	W. Europe	.	High	SMar

	Nation	Rating of democracy, 1999–2000	Region	Human Development Index 1998, UNDP	Level of development	Name label
	32 Solomon Islands	1.5	Asia-Pacific	614	Medium	Sol
	33 Spain	1.5	W. Europe	899	Postindustrial	Sp
	34 St. Vincent & Grenadine	1.5	S. America	738	Medium	StV
	35 Sweden	1.0	Scandinavia	926	Postindustrial	Swe
	36 Switzerland	1.0	W. Europe	915	Postindustrial	Swi
	37 Trinidad & Tobago	1.5	S. America	793	Medium	Tri
	38 United Kingdom	1.5	W. Europe	918	Postindustrial	UK
	39 United States	1.0	N. America	929	Postindustrial	US
Newer democracy	1 Andorra	1.0	W. Europe	.	High	And
	2 Argentina	2.5	S. America	837	High	Arg
	3 Belize	1.0	S. America	777	Medium	Beli
	4 Benin	2.5	Africa	411	Low	Ben
	5 Bolivia	2.0	S. America	643	Medium	Bol
	6 Botswana	2.0	Africa	593	Medium	Bots
	7 Bulgaria	2.5	C&E Europe	772	Medium	Bul
	8 Cape Verde	1.5	Africa	688	Medium	CVerd
	9 Chile	2.0	S. America	826	High	Chil
	10 Czech Republic	1.5	C&E Europe	843	High	Czech
	11 Dominican Republic	2.5	S. America	729	Medium	DomR
	12 Ecuador	2.5	S. America	722	Medium	Ecu
	13 El Salvador	2.5	S. America	696	Medium	ElSal
	14 Estonia	1.5	C&E Europe	801	High	Est
	15 Fiji	2.5	Asia-Pacific	769	Medium	Fiji
	16 Grenada	1.0	S. America	785	Medium	Gren
	17 Guyana	2.0	S. America	709	Medium	Guy
	18 Hungary	1.5	C&E Europe	817	High	Hung
	19 Korea, Republic of	2.0	Asia-Pacific	854	High	SKor
	20 Latvia	1.5	C&E Europe	771	Medium	Lat
	21 Liechtenstein	1.0	W. Europe	.	High	Liech
	22 Lithuania	1.5	C&E Europe	789	Medium	Lith
	23 Marshall Islands	1.0	Asia-Pacific	.	.	Mar
	24 Micronesia, Fed Stat	1.5	Asia-Pacific	.	.	Mic
	25 Mongolia	2.5	Asia-Pacific	628	Medium	Mong
	26 Namibia	2.5	Africa	632	Medium	Nam
	27 Nauru	2.0	Asia-Pacific	.	Medium	Nau
	28 Palau	1.5	Asia-Pacific	.	.	Pal
	29 Panama Canal Zone	1.5	S. America	776	Medium	Pan
	30 Papua New Guinea	2.5	Asia-Pacific	542	Medium	Pap

	Nation	Rating of democracy, 1999–2000	Region	Human Development Index 1998, UNDP	Level of development	Name label
31	Philippines	2.5	Asia-Pacific	744	Medium	Phil
32	Poland	1.5	C&E Europe	814	High	Pol
33	Romania	2.0	C&E Europe	770	Medium	Rom
34	Sao Tome & Principe	1.5	Africa	547	Medium	STom
35	Slovakia	1.5	C&E Europe	825	High	Slovk
36	Slovenia	1.5	C&E Europe	861	High	Slov
37	South Africa	1.5	Africa	697	Medium	SAfr
38	St. Kitts & Nevis	1.5	S. America	798	Medium	StK
39	Taiwan	2.0	Asia-Pacific	.	High	Tai
40	Thailand	2.5	Asia-Pacific	745	Medium	Thai
41	Tuvalu	1.0	Asia-Pacific	.	.	Tuv
42	Uruguay	1.5	S. America	825	High	Uru
43	Vanuatu	2.0	Asia-Pacific	623	Medium	Van
Semi-democracy 1	Albania	4.5	C&E Europe	713	Medium	Alb
2	Antigua and Barbuda	3.0	S. America	833	High	Ant
3	Armenia	4.0	C&E Europe	721	Medium	Arm
4	Bangladesh	3.5	Asia-Pacific	461	Low	Bng
5	Brazil	3.5	S. America	747	Medium	Braz
6	Burkina Faso	4.0	Africa	303	Low	Burk
7	Central African Republic	3.5	Africa	371	Low	CAR
8	Colombia	4.0	S. America	764	Medium	Col
9	Croatia	4.0	C&E Europe	795	Medium	Cro
10	Gabon	4.5	Africa	592	Medium	Gab
11	Georgia	3.5	C&E Europe	762	Medium	Geo
12	Ghana	3.0	Africa	556	Medium	Gha
13	Guatemala	3.5	S. America	619	Medium	Guat
14	Guinea-Bissau	4.0	Africa	331	Low	G-Biss
15	Honduras	3.0	S. America	653	Medium	Hon
16	Indonesia	4.0	Asia-Pacific	670	Medium	Indonesi
17	Jordan	4.0	Middle East	721	Medium	Jor
18	Kuwait	4.5	Middle East	836	High	Kuw
19	Lesotho	4.0	Africa	569	Medium	Les
20	Liberia	4.5	Africa	.	Low	Lib
21	Macedonia	3.0	C&E Europe	763	Medium	Mac
22	Madagascar	3.0	Africa	483	Low	Mada
23	Malawi	3.0	Africa	385	Low	Mala
24	Mali	3.0	Africa	380	Low	Mali
25	Mexico	3.5	N. America	784	Medium	Mex
26	Moldova, Republic of	3.0	C&E Europe	700	Medium	Mol
27	Monaco	1.5	W. Europe	.	High	Mon
28	Morocco	4.5	Middle East	589	Medium	Mor
29	Mozambique	3.5	Africa	341	Low	Moz
30	Nepal	3.5	Asia-Pacific	471	Low	Nep
31	Nicaragua	3.0	S. America	631	Medium	Nic

	Nation	Rating of democracy, 1999–2000	Region	Human Development Index 1998, UNDP	Level of development	Name label
	32 Nigeria	3.5	Africa	439	Low	Nigeria
	33 Paraguay	3.5	S. America	736	Medium	Para
	34 Peru	4.5	S. America	737	Medium	Peru
	35 Russian	4.5	C&E Europe	771	Medium	Rus
	36 Senegal	4.0	Africa	416	Low	Sene
	37 Seychelles	3.0	Africa	786	Medium	Sey
	38 Sierra Leone	4.0	Africa	252	Low	SLeo
	39 Sri Lanka	3.5	Asia-Pacific	733	Medium	SLan
	40 Suriname	3.0	S. America	766	Medium	Sur
	41 Tanzania	4.0	Africa	415	Low	Tanz
	42 Tonga	4.0	Asia-Pacific	.	.	Tong
	43 Turkey	4.5	Middle East	732	Medium	Turk
	44 Ukraine	3.5	C&E Europe	744	Medium	Ukr
	45 Venezuela	4.0	S. America	770	Medium	Ven
	46 Western Samoa	2.0	Asia-Pacific	711	Medium	Sam
	47 Zambia	4.5	Africa	420	Low	Zam
Non-democratic	1 Afghanistan	7.0	Middle East	.	Low	Afg
	2 Algeria	5.5	Africa	683	Medium	Alg
	3 Angola	6.0	Africa	405	Low	Ang
	4 Azerbaijan	5.0	Asia-Pacific	722	Medium	Aze
	5 Bahrain	6.5	Middle East	820	High	Bah
	6 Belarus	6.0	C&E Europe	781	Medium	Bela
	7 Bhutan	6.5	Asia-Pacific	483	Low	Bhu
	8 Bosnia and Herzegovina	5.0	C&E Europe	.	.	Bos
	9 Brunei Darussalam	6.0	Asia-Pacific	848	High	Bru
	10 Burundi	6.0	Africa	321	Low	Burun
	11 Cambodia	6.0	Asia-Pacific	512	Medium	Camb
	12 Cameroon	6.5	Africa	528	Medium	Came
	13 Chad	5.5	Africa	367	Low	Chad
	14 China	6.5	Asia-Pacific	706	Medium	China
	15 Comoros	5.0	Africa	510	Medium	Comor
	16 Congo, Democratic Republic of	6.5	Africa	430	Low	CongDR
	17 Congo, Republic of	5.5	Africa	507	Medium	ConR
	18 Cote D'Ivoire	5.5	Africa	420	Low	CD'Ivo
	19 Cuba	7.0	S. America	783	Medium	Cuba
	20 Djibouti	5.0	Africa	447	Low	Dji
	21 Egypt	5.5	Middle East	623	Medium	Egy
	22 Equatorial Guinea	7.0	Africa	555	Medium	Equ
	23 Eritrea	6.0	Africa	408	Low	Erit
	24 Ethiopia	5.0	Africa	309	Low	Ethi

	Nation	Rating of democracy, 1999–2000	Region	Human Development Index 1998, UNDP	Level of development	Name label
25	Gambia	6.0	Africa	396	Low	Gam
26	Guinea	5.5	Africa	394	Low	Guin
27	Haiti	5.0	S. America	440	Low	Hait
28	Iran	6.0	Middle East	709	Medium	Iran
29	Iraq	7.0	Middle East	583	Medium	Iraq
30	Kazakhstan	5.5	C&E Europe	754	Medium	Kaz
31	Kenya	5.5	Africa	508	Medium	Ken
32	Korea, North	7.0	Asia-Pacific	.	Low	NKor
33	Kyrgyzstan	5.0	C&E Europe	706	Medium	Kyr
34	Laos	6.5	Asia-Pacific	484	Low	Laos
35	Lebanon	5.5	Middle East	735	Medium	Leb
36	Libya Arab Jamahiriy	7.0	Middle East	760	Medium	Libya
37	Malaysia	5.0	Asia-Pacific	772	Medium	Malay
38	Maldives	5.5	Asia-Pacific	725	Medium	Mald
39	Mauritania	5.5	Africa	451	Low	Maur
40	Myanmar	7.0	Asia-Pacific	585	Medium	Bur
41	Niger	5.0	Africa	293	Low	Niger
42	Oman	6.0	Middle East	730	Medium	Om
43	Pakistan	6.0	Asia-Pacific	522	Medium	Pak
44	Qatar	6.0	Middle East	819	High	Qua
45	Rwanda	6.5	Africa	382	Low	Rwan
46	Saudi Arabia	7.0	Middle East	747	Medium	SAra
47	Singapore	5.0	Asia-Pacific	881	Postindustrial	Sing
48	Somalia	7.0	Africa	.	Low	Som
49	Sudan	7.0	Africa	477	Low	Sud
50	Swaziland	5.5	Africa	655	Medium	Swazi
51	Syrian Arab Republic	7.0	Middle East	660	Medium	Syr
52	Tajikistan	6.0	C&E Europe	663	Medium	Taj
53	Togo	5.0	Africa	471	Low	Togo
54	Tunisia	5.5	Middle East	703	Medium	Tun
55	Turkmenistan	7.0	C&E Europe	704	Medium	Turkm
56	Uganda	5.0	Africa	409	Low	Uga
57	United Arab Emirates	5.5	Middle East	810	High	UAE
58	Uzbekistan	6.5	C&E Europe	686	Medium	Uzb
59	Viet Nam	7.0	Asia-Pacific	671	Medium	Viet
60	Yemen	5.5	Middle East	448	Low	Yem
61	Yugoslavia	5.0	C&E Europe	.	High	Yug
62	Zimbabwe	5.5	Africa	555	Medium	Zim
191		Total All				

Notes and Sources:
Level of human development
All countries are classified based on the 1998 rankings of the Human Development Index from the United Nations Development Programme: *Human Development Report 2000*. New York: Oxford University Press.

Postindustrial societies are defined as those societies with a Human Development Index of .864 and above, ranked 1–28 by the UNDP (excluding Hong Kong).

Other high development societies includes all those ranked 29–46, with an HDI from .861 through .801.

Medium human development follows the UNDP classification, including all nations with an HDI between .798 and .507.

Low human development follows the UNDP classification, including all nations with an HDI between .484 and .252.

Classification of political systems

Older democracies = thirty-nine nation-states with average Freedom House ratings of political rights and civil liberties of 2.0 or less for 1999–2000 (plus India, rated at 2.5) and with at least twenty years' continuous experience of democracy (1980–2000) based on the mean Freedom House rating (1972–99).

Newer democracies = forty-three nation-states with average Freedom House ratings of political rights and civil liberties of 2.5 or less for 1999–2000 and with less than twenty years' continuous experience of democracy (1980–2000) based on the mean Freedom House rating (1972–99).

Semi-democracies = forty-seven nation-states with average Freedom House ratings of political rights and civil liberties from 3.0 to 4.5 for 1999–2000.

Non-democracies = sixty-two nation-states with average Freedom House ratings of political rights and civil liberties of 5.0 or more for 1999–2000.

For details, see *Freedom Around the World*. www.freedomhouse.org.

Notes

Preface

1 For a skeptical look at this thesis, see Stephen Earl Bennett. 2001. "Were the halcyon days really golden? An analysis of American attitudes towards the political system, 1945–1965." In *What Is It about Government that Americans Dislike?*, ed. John R. Hibbing and Elizabeth Theiss-Morse. Cambridge: Cambridge University Press.

2 Seymour Martin Lipset. 1996. *American Exceptionalism: A Double Edged Sword.* New York: Norton; Seymour Martin Lipset. 1990. *Continental Divide: The Values and Institutions of Canada and the United States.* New York: Routledge.

3 Gabriel Almond. 1988. "Separate tables: Schools and sects in political science." *PS: Political Science*, 21(4): 828–842.

4 Adam Przeworski and Henry Teune. 1970. *The Logic of Comparative Social Inquiry.* New York: Wiley.

1. The Decline and Fall of Political Activism?

1 Ronald Inglehart claims that there is also a shift in the "why" (if the left-right issues of the economy have been replaced by concern about the postmaterialist quality of life issues), but this argument is not pursued in depth here. For details, see Ronald Inglehart. 1997. *Modernization and Postmodernization: Cultural, Economic and Political Change in Forty-three Societies.* Princeton, NJ: Princeton University Press.

2 For a discussion about these debates, see David Held. 1987. *Models of Democracy.* Stanford, CA: Stanford University Press.

3 Joseph A. Schumpeter. 1952. *Capitalism, Socialism and Democracy*, 4th ed. London: George Allen and Unwin.

4 Details are from the International IDEA database *Voter Turnout from 1945 to 2000.* www.indea.int. See the Appendix for the detailed classification of all nations.

5 On the fall in turnout in postindustrial societies, see Mark Gray and Miki Caul. 2000. "Declining voter turnout in advanced industrial democracies, 1950 to 1997." *Comparative Political Studies*, 33(9): 1091–1122.

6 On trends in party membership, see Peter Mair. 2001. "Party membership in twenty European democracies 1980–2000." *Party Politics*, 7(1): 5–22; Susan Scarrow. 2001. "Parties without members?" In *Parties without Partisans*, ed. Russell J. Dalton and Martin Wattenberg. New York: Oxford University Press.

7 For a summary of the partisan dealignment theory and evidence, see Russell J. Dalton and Martin Wattenberg, Eds. 2001. *Parties without Partisans*. New York: Oxford University Press.

8 C. Kerr. 1983. *The Future of Industrial Societies: Convergence or Continuing Diversity?* Cambridge, MA: Harvard University Press; L. Griffin, H. McCammon, and C. Bosko. 1990. "The unmaking of a movement? The crisis of U.S. trade unions in comparative perspective." In *Changes in Societal Institutions*, ed. M. Hallinan, D. Klein, and J. Glass. New York: Plenum. For the alternative view, that institutional arrangements affect levels of union density, see Bernhard Ebbinghaus and Jelle Visser. 1999. "When institutions matter: Union growth and decline in Western Europe, 1950–1995." *European Sociological Review*, 15(2): 135–158; and S. Blashke. 2000. "Union density and European integration: Diverging convergence." *European Journal of Industrial Relations*, 6(2): 217–236; International Labour Organization. 1997. *World Employment Report 1996–97*. Geneva: ILO. www.ilo.org/public/english/bureau/inf/pkits/wlr97.htm.

9 Steve Bruce. 1996. *Religion in the Modern World: From Cathedrals to Cults*. Oxford: Oxford University Press; Sheena Ashford and Noel Timms. 1992. *What Europe Thinks: A Study of Western European Values*. Aldershot: Dartmouth; Wolfgang Jagodzinski and Karel Dobbelaere. 1995. "Secularization and church religiosity." In *The Impact of Values*, ed. Jan W. van Deth and Elinor Scarbrough. Oxford: Oxford University Press; L. Voye. 1999. "Secularization in a context of advanced modernity." *Sociology of Religion*, 60(3): 275–288. For the counterargument, see Peter L. Berger, Ed. 1999. *The Desecularization of the World*. Washington, DC: Ethics and Public Policy Center; Rodney Stark. 1999. "Secularization, RIP." *Sociology of Religion*, 60(3): 249–273.

10 For a discussion about the evidence for the diversity of trends across many postindustrial societies, see Robert Putnam, Ed. 2002. *Democracies in Flux. The Evolution of Social Capital in Contemporary Societies*. New York: Oxford University Press; Jan Willem Van Deth, Ed. 1997. *Private Groups and Public Life: Social Participation, Voluntary Associations and Political Involvement in Representative Democracies*. London: Routledge; J. E. Curtis, E. G. Grabb, and D. E. Baer. 1992. "Voluntary association membership in fifteen countries – a comparative analysis." *American Sociological Review*, 57(2): 139–152.

11 Robert Putnam. 2000. *Bowling Alone: The Collapse and Revival of American Community*. New York: Simon and Schuster, p. 46.

12 On trends in trust in American government, see John R. Hibbing and Elizabeth Theiss-Morse, Eds. 2001. *What Is It about Government that Americans Dislike?* Cambridge: Cambridge University Press; Joseph S. Nye. 1997. "Introduction: The decline of confidence in government." In *Why People Don't Trust Government*, ed. Joseph S. Nye, Philip D. Zelikow, and David C. King. Cam-

bridge, MA: Harvard University Press. For other nations, see Hans-Dieter Klingeman. 1999. "Mapping political support in the 1990s: A global analysis." In *Critical Citizens: Global Support for Democratic Governance*, ed. Pippa Norris. Oxford: Oxford University Press.

13 See the discussion in Susan Pharr and Robert Putnam, Eds. 2000. *Disaffected Democracies*. Princeton, NJ: Princeton University Press; and Pippa Norris, Ed. 1999. *Critical Citizens: Global Support for Democratic Governance*. Oxford: Oxford University Press.

14 See Larry Diamond. 2002. "Consolidating democracies." In *Comparing Democracies 2: Elections and Voting in Global Perspective*, ed. Lawrence LeDuc, Richard G. Niemi, and Pippa Norris. London: Sage. Freedom House estimates that in 2000–01 there were 120 electoral democracies around the world, and the highest proportion of people (40.7 percent) living under freedom since the survey started in 1980. See Freedom House. 2000. *Freedom Around the World, 2000–2001*. www.freedomhouse.org.

15 Andrew Reynolds, Ed. 2002. *The Architecture of Democracy*. Oxford: Oxford University Press. For the issue of reversal, see Marc Plattner and Larry Diamond. 2001. "High anxiety in the Andes." *Journal of Democracy*, 12(2) (special Issue). On public opinion in Latin America, see Roderic Ai Camp. 2001. *Citizen Views of Democracy in Latin America*. Pittsburgh: University of Pittsburgh Press; Marta Lagos. 2001. "Between stability and crisis in Latin America." *Journal of Democracy*, 12(1): 137–145.

16 On UK turnout, see Paul Whiteley. 2001. "Turnout." In *Britain Votes 2001*, ed. Pippa Norris. Oxford: Oxford University Press. In September 2001, the British Labour Party's annual report showed that they had 311,000 members, a drop of 50,000 during the previous year. The Conservative Party's annual report noted that it had 325,500 members in September 2001, down from an estimated 400,000 in 1997.

17 For details of these results, see the International IDEA database *Voter Turnout from 1945 to 2000*. www.indea.int. For more recent election results, see www.electionworld.org.

18 Voting turnout here is measured by votes cast as a proportion of the voting-age population (Vote/VAP), as explained further in Chapter 3. Details are from the International IDEA database *Voter Turnout from 1945 to 2000*. www.indea.int.

19 Adam Przeworski and Henry Teune. 1970. *The Logic of Comparative Social Inquiry*. New York: Wiley–Interscience.

20 Sidney Verba, Norman Nie, and Jae-on Kim. 1978. *Participation and Political Equality: A Seven-Nation Comparison*. New York: Cambridge University Press, Table 3.2, pp. 58–59.

21 Sidney Verba, Kay Schlozman, and Henry E. Brady. 1995. *Voice and Equality: Civic Voluntarism in American Politics*. Cambridge, MA: Harvard University Press.

22 Ibid., Figure 3.4, p. 80. For a discussion of some of the reasons for this phenomenon, see, for example, Seymour Martin Lipset. 1996. *American Exceptionalism: A Double Edged Sword*. New York: Norton.

23 Adam Przeworski and Henry Teune. 1970. *The Logic of Comparative Social Inquiry*. New York: Wiley–Interscience.

24 These countries are ranked as equally "free" according to the 2000–01 Freedom House assessments of political rights and civil liberties. Freedom House. 2000. *Freedom in the World 2000–2001.* www.freedomhouse.org.

25 The main differences are the exclusion of Hungary and Poland (ranked by UNDP as highly developed), Mexico and Turkey (both ranked as medium developed), and the inclusion of Singapore as postindustrial. Hong Kong is included in the UNDP list but excluded from this study, as a dependent territory. See the Appendix for the detailed classification of all nations.

26 Societies are defined based on the annual ratings provided by Freedom House since 1972. The *level of freedom* is classified according to the combined mean score for political rights and civil liberties in Freedom House's 1972–2000 annual surveys, *Freedom Around the World.* www.freedomhouse.org.

27 Daniel Lerner. 1958. *The Passing of Traditional Society: Modernizing the Middle East.* New York: Free Press; Seymour Martin Lipset. 1959. "Some social requisites of democracy: Economic development and political legitimacy." *American Political Science Review,* 53: 69–105; Seymour Martin Lipset. 1960. *Political Man: The Social Basis of Politics.* New York: Doubleday; W. W. Rostow. 1961. *The Stages of Economic Growth.* Cambridge: Cambridge University Press; Karl W. Deutsch. 1964. "Social mobilization and political development." *American Political Science Review,* 55: 493–514. For an updated version of this thesis, see Seymour Martin Lipset, Kyoung-Ryung Seong, and John Charles Torres. 1993. "A comparative analysis of the social requisites of democracy." *International Social Science Journal,* 45(2): 154–175.

28 Including issues raised in Peter Mair. 1997. *Party System Change.* Oxford: Oxford University Press; Peter Mair. 2001. "Party membership in twenty European democracies 1980–2000." *Party Politics,* 7(1): 7–21.

29 Robert Putnam. 2000. *Bowling Alone: The Collapse and Revival of American Community.* New York: Simon and Schuster.

30 Samuel Barnes and Max Kaase. 1979. *Political Action: Mass Participation in Five Western Democracies.* Beverley Hills, CA: Sage. See also Alan Marsh. 1977. *Protest and Political Consciousness.* Beverly Hills, CA: Sage.

2. Theories of Political Activism

1 Daniel Bell. 1999. *The Coming of Post-Industrial Society: A Venture in Social Forecasting.* New York: Basic Books; Russell Dalton. 1998. *Citizen Politics: Public Opinion and Political Parties in Advanced Western Democracies,* 2nd ed. Chatham, NJ: Chatham House; Ronald Inglehart. 1997. *Modernization and Postmodernization.* Princeton, NJ: Princeton University Press.

2 G. Bingham Powell, Jr. 1986. "American turnout in comparative perspective." *American Political Science Review,* 80: 17–43; Robert Jackman. 1987. "Political institutions and voter turnout in industrialized democracies." *American Political Science Review,* 81: 405–423.

3 Steven J Rosenstone and John Mark Hansen. 1993. *Mobilization, Participation and Democracy in America.* New York: Macmillan.

4 Robert Putnam. 1995. *Making Democracy Work.* Princeton, NJ: Princeton University Press; Robert Putnam. 2000. *Bowling Alone: The Collapse and Revival of American Community.* New York: Simon and Schuster; Robert Putnam, Ed.

2002. *Democracies in Flux: The Evolution of Social Capital in Contemporary Societies*. New York: Oxford University Press.

5 Sidney Verba, Kay Schlozman, and Henry E. Brady. 1995. *Voice and Equality: Civic Voluntarism in American Politics*. Cambridge, MA: Harvard University Press.

6 Daniel Lerner. 1958. *The Passing of Traditional Society: Modernizing the Middle East*. New York: Free Press; Seymour Martin Lipset. 1959. "Some social requisites of democracy: Economic development and political legitimacy." *American Political Science Review*, 53: 69–105; Seymour Martin Lipset. 1960. *Political Man: The Social Basis of Politics*. New York: Doubleday; W. W. Rostow. 1961. *The Stages of Economic Growth*. Cambridge: Cambridge University Press; Karl W. Deutsch. 1964. "Social mobilization and political development." *American Political Science Review*, 55: 493–514; Daniel Bell. 1999. *The Coming of Post-Industrial Society: A Venture in Social Forecasting*. New York: Basic Books.

7 For updated versions of this thesis, see Seymour Martin Lipset, Kyoung-Ryung Seong, and John Charles Torres. 1993. "A Comparative analysis of the social requisites of democracy." *International Social Science Journal*, 45(2): 154–175.

8 G. O'Donnell, Philippe Schmitter, and Lawrence Whitehead. 1987. *Transitions from Authoritarian Rule*. Baltimore: Johns Hopkins University Press.

9 Peter L. Berger, Ed. 1999. *The Desecularization of the World*. Washington, DC: Ethics and Public Policy Center.

10 Ronald Inglehart. 1977. *The Silent Revolution: Changing Values and Political Styles among Western Publics*. Princeton, NJ: Princeton University Press; Ronald Inglehart. 1990. *Culture Shift in Advanced Industrial Society*. Princeton, NJ: Princeton University Press; Ronald Inglehart. 1997. *Modernization and Postmodernization*. Princeton, NJ: Princeton University Press.

11 Alex Inkeles. 1983. *Exploring Individual Modernity*. New York: Columbia University Press; Anthony Giddens. 1990. *The Consequences of Modernity*. Stanford, CA: Stanford University Press.

12 Daniel Bell. 1999. *The Coming of Post-Industrial Society: A Venture in Social Forecasting*. New York: Basic Books.

13 See, for example, the summary of the core features of industrial societies in Ronald Inglehart. 1997. *Modernization and Postmodernization*. Princeton, NJ: Princeton University Press, p. 18.

14 Daniel Bell. 1999. *The Coming of Post-Industrial Society: A Venture in Social Forecasting*. New York: Basic Books.

15 Richard Brody. 1978. "The puzzle of political participation in America." In *The New American Political System*, ed. Anthony King. Washington, DC: American Enterprise Institute.

16 See, for example, Sidney Verba, Kay Schlozman, and Henry E. Brady. 1995. *Voice and Equality: Civic Voluntarism in American Politics*. Cambridge, MA: Harvard University Press.

17 Russell J. Dalton, Scott C. Flanagan, Paul A. Beck, and James E. Alt. 1984. *Electoral Change in Advanced Industrial Democracies: Realignment or Dealignment?* Princeton, NJ: Princeton University Press; Mark Franklin, Tom Mackie, and Henry Valen. 1992. *Electoral Change: Responses to Evolving*

Social and Attitudinal Structures in Western Countries. New York: Cambridge University Press; Russell J. Dalton and Martin Wattenberg, Eds. 2001. *Parties without Partisans.* New York: Oxford University Press. For the argument that postindustrial societies have not experienced a consistent secular decline in the role of social class in structuring voting behavior, however, see Geoffrey Evans. 1999. *The Decline of Class Politics?* Oxford: Oxford University Press; and Jeff Manza, M. Hout, and Clem Brooks. 1995. "Class voting in capitalist democracies since World War II – dealignment, realignment or trendless fluctuation?" *Annual Review of Sociology,* 21: 137–162.

18   Sidney Verba, Kay Schlozman, and Henry E. Brady. 1995. *Voice and Equality: Civic Voluntarism in American Politics.* Cambridge, MA: Harvard University Press, p. 71.

19   Sidney Verba, Norman Nie, and Jae-on Kim. 1978. *Participation and Political Equality: A Seven-Nation Comparison.* New York: Cambridge University Press, p. 21.

20   Richard Topf. 1995. "Beyond electoral participation." In *Citizens and the State,* eds. Hans-Dieter Klingemann and Dieter Fuchs. Oxford: Oxford University Press.

21   Bernhard Wessels. 1997. "Organizing capacity of societies and modernity." In *Private Groups and Public Life: Social Participation, Voluntary Associations and Political Involvement in Representative Democracies,* ed. Jan W. van Deth. London: Routledge.

22   Russell Dalton. 1996. *Citizen Politics,* 2nd ed. Chatham, NJ: Chatham House, Chapter 4.

23   Sidney Tarrow. 2000. "Mad cows and social activists: Contentious politics in the trilateral democracies." In *Disaffected Democracies,* ed. Robert D. Putnam and Susan J. Pharr. Princeton, NJ: Princeton University Press, p. 279.

24   Ronald Inglehart. 1997. *Modernization and Postmodernization.* Princeton, NJ: Princeton University Press, p. 296; see also Ronald Inglehart. 1977. *The Silent Revolution: Changing Values and Political Styles among Western Publics.* Princeton, NJ: Princeton University Press; Ronald Inglehart. 1990. *Culture Shift in Advanced Industrial Society.* Princeton, NJ: Princeton University Press.

25   Ivor Crewe. 1981. "Electoral participation." In *Democracy at the Polls,* ed. David Butler, Howard Penniman, and Austin Ranney. Washington, DC: American Enterprise Institute; Richard Flickinger and Donley Studlar. 1992. "The disappearing voters? Exploring declining turnout in Western European elections." *West European Politics,* 15: 1–16; Mark N. Franklin. 1996. "Electoral participation." In *Comparing Democracies: Elections and Voting in Global Perspective,* ed. Lawrence LeDuc, Richard G. Niemi, and Pippa Norris. Thousand Oaks, CA: Sage; Mark Franklin. 2000. "Understanding cross-national turnout differences: What role for compulsory voting?" *British Journal of Political Science,* 29: 205–216.

26   Raymond E. Wolfinger and Steven J. Rosenstone. 1980. *Who Votes?* New Haven, CT: Yale University Press, p. 88.

27   Arend Lijphart. 1999. *Patterns of Democracy.* New Haven, CT: Yale University Press, pp. 284–286; G. Bingham Powell, Jr. 1980. "Voting turnout in thirty democracies: Partisan, legal and socioeconomic influences." In *Electoral Participation: A Comparative Analysis,* ed. Richard Rose. London: Sage.

28 M. D. Martinez and D. Hill. 1999. "Did motor voter work?" *American Politics Quarterly*, 27(3): 296–315.

29 Jeff A. Karp and Susan Banducci. 1999. "The impact of proportional representation on turnout: Evidence from New Zealand." *Australian Journal of Political Science*, 34(3): 363–377.

30 Sidney Verba, Norman Nie, and Jae-on Kim. 1978. *Participation and Political Equality: A Seven-Nation Comparison*. New York: Cambridge University Press, Chapter 6.

31 Steven J. Rosenstone and John Mark Hansen. 1993. *Mobilization, Participation and Democracy in America*. New York: Macmillan, p. 5.

32 See the discussion in Kay Lawson, ed. 1980. *Political Parties and Linkage: A Comparative Perspective*. New Haven, CT: Yale University Press; Kay Lawson and Peter H. Merkl, eds. 1988. *When Parties Fail: Emerging Alternative Organizations*. Princeton, NJ: Princeton University Press.

33 E. E. Schattschneider. 1942. *Party Government*. New York: Rinehart.

34 See, for example, Alan Ware. 1996. *Political Parties and Party Systems*. Oxford: Oxford University Press.

35 For case studies assessing the impact of this process on British political parties, see Patrick Seyd and Paul Whiteley. 1992. *Labour's Grass Roots: The Politics of Party Membership*. Oxford: Oxford University Press; Paul Whiteley, Patrick Seyd, and Jeremy Richardson. 1994. *True Blues: The Politics of Conservative Party Membership*. Oxford: Clarendon Press.

36 Herbert Kitschelt. 1994. *The Transformation of European Social Democracy*. New York: Cambridge University Press.

37 Russell J. Dalton and Martin Wattenberg, eds. 2001. *Parties without Partisans*. New York: Oxford University Press.

38 Martin Wattenberg. 2000. "The decline of party mobilization." In *Parties without Partisans*, ed. Russell J. Dalton and Martin Wattenberg. New York: Oxford University Press. See also Mark Gray and Miki Caul. 2000. "Declining voter turnout in advanced industrial democracies, 1950 to 1997: The effects of declining group mobilization." *Comparative Political Studies*, 33(9): 1091–1122. On trends in party membership, see Peter Mair. 2001. "Party membership in twenty European democracies 1980–2000." *Party Politics*, 7(1): 5–21; Susan Scarrow. 2000. "Parties without members?" In *Parties without Partisans*, ed. Russell J. Dalton and Martin Wattenberg. New York: Oxford University Press. On partisan dealignment, see Russell J. Dalton. 2000. "The decline of party identifications." In *Parties without Partisans*, ed. Russell J. Dalton and Martin Wattenberg. New York: Oxford University Press.

39 Mark Gray and Miki Caul. 2000. "Declining voter turnout in advanced industrial democracies, 1950 to 1997: The effects of declining group mobilization." *Comparative Political Studies*, 33(9): 1091–1122.

40 Sami Borg. 1995. "Electoral participation." In *The Impact of Values*, ed. Jan W. van Deth and Elinor Scarbrough. Oxford: Oxford University Press.

41 For American accounts of this process, see John Aldrich. 1996. *Why Parties? The Origins and Transformation of Political Parties in America*. Chicago: University of Chicago Press; Robert Huckfelt and John Sprague. 1995. *Citizens, Politics and Social Communication: Information and Influence in an Election Campaign*. New York: Cambridge University Press.

42   Robert Putnam. 1995. *Making Democracy Work*. Princeton, NJ: Princeton University Press; Robert Putnam. 2000. *Bowling Alone: The Collapse and Revival of American Community*. New York: Simon and Schuster; Robert Putnam, ed. 2002. *Democracies in Flux: The Evolution of Social Capital in Contemporary Societies*. New York: Oxford University Press.

43   Peter Hall. 1999. "Social capital in Britain." *British Journal of Political Science*, 29: 417–461; Jan Willem van Deth. 2000. "Interesting but irrelevant: Social capital and the saliency of politics in Western Europe." *European Journal of Political Research*, 37: 115–147; see also contributors in Robert Putnam, Ed. 2002. *Democracies in Flux: The Evolution of Social Capital*. New York: Oxford University Press.

44   See the arguments in Robert A. Dahl. 1971. *Polyarchy: Participation and Opposition*. New Haven, CT: Yale University Press.

45   For a discussion of the conceptual distinctions and theoretical frameworks in the literature, as well as the structure, function, and organization of interest groups and new social movements, see Jeffrey Berry. 1984. *The Interest Group Society*. Boston: Little Brown; Jack L. Walker. 1991. *Mobilizing Interest Groups in America*: Ann Arbor: University of Michigan Press; Sidney Tarrow. 1994. *Power in Movement*. Cambridge: Cambridge University Press; Charles Tilly. 1978. *From Mobilization to Revolution*. Reading, MA: Addison-Wesley; Doug McAdam, John D. McCarthy, and Mayer N. Zald, Eds. 1996. *Comparative Perspectives on Social Movements*. New York: Cambridge University Press.

46   Russell J. Dalton and Manfred Kuechler, Eds. 1990. *Challenging the Political Order: New Social and Political Movements in Western Democracies*. New York: Oxford University Press.

47   Joseph N. Cappella and Kathleen H. Jamieson. 1997. *Spiral of Cynicism*. New York: Oxford University Press.

48   Pippa Norris. 2000. *A Virtuous Circle: Political Communications in Postindustrial Democracies*. New York: Cambridge University Press.

49   For further evidence supporting this argument, see Marc Hooghe. 2001. "Television and the erosion of social capital: Disentangling the causal mechanisms." Paper presented at the annual meeting of the American Political Science Association, San Francisco, August 30–September 2, 2001; Kees Arts and Holli A. Semetko. 2001. "The divided electorate: Media use and political involvement." Paper presented at the annual meeting of the American Political Science Association, San Francisco, August 30–September 2, 2001.

50   Sidney Verba, Kay Schlozman, and Henry E. Brady. 1995. *Voice and Equality: Civic Voluntarism in American Politics*. Cambridge, MA: Harvard University Press.

51   Ray Wolfinger and Steven Rosenstone. 1980. *Who Votes?* New Haven, CT: Yale University Press.

52   Nancy Burns, Kay Lehman Schlozman, and Sidney Verba. 2001. *The Private Roots of Public Action*. Cambridge, MA: Harvard University Press, p. 35.

53   Michel Crozier, Samuel P. Huntington, and Joji Watanuki. 1975. *The Crisis of Democracy: Report on the Governability of Democracies to the Trilateral Commission*. New York: New York University Press.

54   Robert D. Putnam, Susan J. Pharr, and Russell J. Dalton. "Introduction: What's troubling the trilateral democracies." In *Disaffected Democracies*, ed. Robert

D. Putnam and Susan J. Pharr. Princeton, NJ: Princeton University Press, p. 6.

55 Jack Citrin. 1974. "Comment: The political relevance of trust in government." *American Political Science Review*, 68: 973–988; Jack Citrin and Donald Green. 1986. "Presidential leadership and trust in government." *British Journal of Political Science*, 16: 431–453; Russell J. Dalton. 1996. *Citizen Politics*, 2nd ed. Chatham, NJ: Chatham House.

56 Jack Citrin and Donald Green. 1986. "Presidential leadership and trust in government." *British Journal of Political Science*, 16: 431–453; Amy Fried and Douglas B. Harris. 2001. "On red capes and charging bulls: How and why conservative politicians and interest groups promoted public anger." In *What Is It about Government that Americans Dislike?*, ed. John R. Hibbing and Elizabeth Theiss-Morse. Cambridge: Cambridge University Press.

3. Mapping Turnout

1 Frances Fox Piven and Richard Cloward. 2000. *Why Americans Still Don't Vote: And Why Politicians Want It That Way.* Boston: Beacon Press; Ruy A. Teixeira. 1992. *The Disappearing American Voter.* Washington, DC: Brookings Institution. It should be noted, however, that even in the U.S. the claim of steadily declining turnout since 1972 has been challenged as an artificial product of the rise in the number of ineligible voters (due to increased numbers of resident aliens and of felons in prison or on probation), swelling the size of the voting-age population. See Michael P. McDonald and Samuel L. Popkin. 2001. "The myth of the vanishing voter." *American Political Science Review*, 95(4): 963–974.

2 Warren Miller and Merrill Shanks. 1996. *The Changing American Voter.* Ann Arbor: University of Michigan Press, Part II. For trends from 1788 to 1996, see Harold W. Stanley and Richard Niemi. 1995. *Vital Statistics on American Politics.* Washington, DC: CQ Press, Figure 3-1.

3 Robert Putnam. 2000. *Bowling Alone: The Collapse and Revival of American Community.* New York: Simon and Schuster.

4 On Western European trends from 1945 to 1989, see Richard Topf. 1995. "Electoral participation." In *Citizens and the State*, ed. Hans-Dieter Klingemann and Dieter Fuchs. Oxford: Oxford University Press. See also Rudy B. Andweg. 1996. "Elite-mass linkages in Europe: Legitimacy crisis or party crisis?" In *Elitism, Populism and European Politics*, ed. Jack Hayward. Oxford: Clarendon Press.

5 See Figure 1 and Figure 15 in International IDEA. 1997. *Voter Turnout from 1945 to 1998: A Global Report.* Stockholm: International IDEA, www.intidea.se. The slippage in global elections was from turnout of 68 percent in the 1980s down to 64 percent in the 1990s. The classification of thirty-six established democracies used in the IDEA study follows the definition in Arend Lijphart. 1999. *Patterns of Democracy.* New Haven, CT: Yale University Press. The measure of turnout is based on votes cast as a proportion of the voting-age population.

6 Peter Mair. 2001. "In the aggregate: Mass electoral behaviour in Western Europe, 1950–2000." In *Comparative Democracy*, ed. Hans Keman. London: Sage.

7   Mark Gray and Miki Caul. 2000. "Declining voter turnout in advanced indus-
     trialized democracies, 1950 to 1997." *Comparative Political Studies*, 33(9):
     1091–1122. The difference in the size of the estimates relates to slightly dif-
     ferent countries under comparison, with Gray and Caul comparing eighteen
     established democracies, and the fact that the estimates by Gray and Caul are
     based on a comparison of the average turnout in the first two elections held
     during the 1950s with the last two elections held during the mid-1990s, whereas
     Mair compares mean turnout by decade. See also similar patterns reported in
     Martin Wattenberg. 2000. "The decline of party mobilization." In *Parties
     without Partisans*, ed. Russell J. Dalton and Martin Wattenberg. New York:
     Oxford University Press.

8   Butler and Ranney compared the mean turnout in referendum elections and in
     parliamentary general elections from 1945 to 1993 in a dozen established
     democracies and found that turnout was on average twelve percentage points
     lower in referendums. David Butler and Austin Ranney. 1994. *Referendums
     around the World*. Washington, DC: AEI Press, Table 2-1. In the case of ref-
     erendums and initiatives in the United States, Magelby and Cronin have found
     that the mean drop-off is about fifteen percentage points. Thomas Cronin.
     1989. *Direct Democracy: The Politics of Initiative, Referendum and Recall*.
     Cambridge, MA: Harvard University Press, pp. 226–228; David Magelby.
     1984. *Direct Legislation: Voting on Ballot Propositions in the United States*.
     Baltimore: Johns Hopkins University Press, pp. 83–87.

9   Cees van der Eijk, Mark Franklin et al. 1996. *Choosing Europe? The Euro-
     pean Electorate and National Politics in the Face of the Union*. Ann Arbor:
     University of Michigan Press; Pippa Norris. 2000. "Blaming the messenger?
     Political communications and turnout in EU elections." In *Citizen Participa-
     tion in European Politics* (Demokratiutredningens skrift nr 32). Stockholm:
     Statens Offentliga Utredningar. For details of turnout in elections to the
     European parliament, see http://europa.eu.int.

10   International IDEA. 1997. *Voter Turnout from 1945 to 1998: A Global Report*.
     Stockholm: International IDEA, www.int-idea.se; E. Ochoa. 1987. "The rapid
     expansion of voter participation in Latin America: Presidential elections
     1845–1986." In *Statistical Abstract of Latin America*, Vol. 25, ed. J. W. Wilkie
     and D. Lorey. Los Angeles: UCLA Latin American Center.

11   For a fuller discussion of modernization theories, see Daniel Bell. 1999. *The
     Coming of Post-Industrial Society: A Venture in Social Forecasting*. New York:
     Basic Books; Alex Inkeles. 1983. *Exploring Individual Modernity*. New York:
     Columbia University Press; Anthony Giddens. 1990. *The Consequences of
     Modernity*. Stanford, CA: Stanford University Press.

12   For an overview of the literature, see Ross E. Buckhart and Michael S. Lewis-
     Beck. 1994. "Comparative democracy: The economic development thesis."
     American Political Science Review, 88(4): 903–910.

13   G. Bingham Powell. 1982. *Contemporary Democracies: Participation, Stabil-
     ity and Violence*. Cambridge, MA: Harvard University Press, p. 121.

14   Sidney Verba, Kay Lehman Schlozman, and Henry E. Brady. 1995. *Voice and
     Equality: Civic Volunteerism in American Politics*. Cambridge, MA: Harvard
     University Press, pp. 358–360.

15   D. Lerner. 1958. *The Passing of Traditional Society*. Glencoe, IL: Free Press.

16 Ronald Inglehart. 1977. *The Silent Revolution: Changing Values and Political Styles among Western Publics.* Princeton, NJ: Princeton University Press; Ronald Inglehart. 1990. *Culture Shift in Advanced Industrial Society.* Princeton, NJ: Princeton University Press; Ronald Inglehart. 1997. *Modernization and Postmodernization.* Princeton, NJ: Princeton University Press.

17 Alex Inkeles. 1983. *Exploring Individual Modernity.* New York: Columbia University Press; Anthony Giddens. 1990. *The Consequences of Modernity.* Stanford, CA: Stanford University Press.

18 Daniel Bell. 1973. *The Coming of Post-Industrial Society: A Venture in Social Forecasting.* New York: Basic Books.

19 Robert W. Jackman. 1987. "Political institutions and voter turnout in industrialized democracies." *American Political Science Review,* 81: 405–423.

20 Ronald Inglehart. 1997. *Modernization and Postmodernization.* Princeton, NJ: Princeton University Press, p. 296.

21 Robert Putnam. 2000. *Bowling Alone: The Collapse and Revival of American Community.* New York: Simon and Schuster; Mark Gray and Miki Caul. 2000. "Declining voter turnout in advanced industrialized democracies, 1950 to 1997." *Comparative Political Studies,* 33(9): 1091–1122; Martin Wattenberg. 2001. "The decline of party mobilization." In *Parties without Partisans,* ed. Russell J. Dalton and Martin Wattenberg. New York: Oxford University Press.

22 IDEA, *Voter Turnout from 1945 to 1998,* www.int-idea.se. It should be noted that the author is most grateful to International IDEA for use of the data set. Turnout in the most recent elections (2000) were updated from the IFES election guide available at www.ifes.org/eguide/turnout2000.htm. The estimates of the voting-age populations in the most recent elections were updated with population data from the World Bank.

23 For example, Teixeira compares turnout as a proportion of the legally eligible electorate, although this measure of turnout excludes most blacks before 1870, most women before 1920, and aliens, felons, and illegal immigrants throughout. Ruy A. Teixeira. 1992. *The Disappearing American Voter.* Washington, DC: Brookings Institution, Table 1.3, p. 9.

24 Andrew Blais, Louis Massicotte, and A. Yoshinaka. 2001. "Deciding who has the right to vote: A comparative analysis of election laws." *Electoral Studies,* 20(1): 41–62. See also Richard S. Katz. 1997. *Democracy and Elections.* Oxford: Oxford University Press.

25 For details, see "What if the vote were flawless?" *The Miami Herald,* December 2, 2000. www.Herald.com.

26 Michael P. McDonald and Samuel L. Popkin. 2000. "The myth of the vanishing voter." Paper presented at the 2000 convention of the American Political Science Association, Washington, D.C.

27 The mean figures for Vote/VAP and Vote/Registered in the 1990s in these countries for comparison are as follows:

	Vote/Reg	*Vote/VAP*	*Difference*
Kuwait	82.5	20.6	61.8
US	64.3	46.9	17.4
UK	74.6	72.3	2.2
All	70.8	64.5	6.4

28 Estimates of Vote/VAP and Vote/Registered were fairly strongly correlated (R = 0.66, sig. = 0.01 level). Since both measures were included in the International IDEA database, models were replicated and checked using both indicators, so the choice of measure did not make a critical difference to the interpretation of the results.

29 Robert Putnam. 2000. *Bowling Alone: The Collapse and Revival of American Community.* New York: Simon and Schuster.

30 Ruy A. Teixeira. 1992. *The Disappearing American Voter.* Washington, DC: Brookings Institution, Table 1.3, p. 9.

31 Robert Putnam. 2000. *Bowling Alone: The Collapse and Revival of American Community.* New York: Simon and Schuster.

32 For a fuller discussion of long-term historical trends in America, see Walter Dean Burnham. 1982. *The Current Crisis in American Politics.* New York: Oxford University Press; Walter Dean Burnham. 1987. "The turnout problem." In *Elections American Style*, ed. James Reichley. Washington, DC: Brookings Institution; Frances Fox Piven and Richard Cloward. 2000. *Why Americans Still Don't Vote.* New York: Pantheon.

33 Michael P. McDonald and Samuel L. Popkin. 2000. "The myth of the vanishing voter." Paper presented at the 2000 convention of the American Political Science Association, Washington, D.C.

34 In the 2000 race, 103,814,206 votes were cast for president, and the U.S. Bureau of the Census estimates that the U.S. population over eighteen years old on November 1, 2000, totaled 205,576,000, producing turnout as a percentage of the voting-age population of 50.5 percent. See http://www.census.gov/population/estimates. These estimates are subject to revision in the light of the 2000 census results. For a discussion and breakdown by state, see Martin P. Wattenberg. 2001. "Getting out the vote." *Public Perspective*, Jan./Feb.: 16–17.

35 It could be argued that the use of significance tests for aggregate turnout data is inappropriate and too restrictive, since the data is not based on a representative sample of the population. Nevertheless, significance tests are standard in estimates of changes in turnout rates over time, even with aggregate data. See, for example, Michael P. McDonald and Samuel L. Popkin. 2000. "The myth of the vanishing voter." Paper presented at the 2000 convention of the American Political Science Association, Washington, D.C.

36 For a detailed account of the democratization process in Latin America, see Merilee S. Grindle. 2000. *Audacious Reforms: Institutional Invention and Democracy in Latin America.* Baltimore: Johns Hopkins University Press.

37 For a discussion of the reasons for these developments, see Michael Bratton and Nicholas van de Walle. 1997. *Democratic Experiments in Africa.* New York: Cambridge University Press.

38 See Richard Rose, William Mishler, and Christian Haerpfer. 1998. *Democracy and Its Alternatives: Understanding Post-Communist Societies.* Oxford: Polity.

4. Do Institutions Matter?

1 Charles Edward Merriam. 1924. *Non-Voting: Causes and Methods of Control.* Chicago: University of Chicago Press; Harold Foote Gosnell. 1930. *Why*

Europe Votes. Chicago: University of Chicago Press; Herbert Tingsten. 1937. *Political Behavior: Studies in Election Statistics*. Reprinted Totowa, NJ: Bedminster Press (1963).

2 G. Bingham Powell. 1980. "Voting turnout in thirty democracies: Partisan, legal and socioeconomic influences." In *Electoral Participation: A Comparative Analysis*, ed. Richard Rose. London: Sage; G. Bingham Powell. 1982. *Contemporary Democracies: Participation, Stability and Violence*. Cambridge, MA: Harvard University Press; G. Bingham Powell. 1986. "American voter turnout in comparative perspective." *American Political Science Review*, 80(1): 17–43.

3 Robert W. Jackman and Ross A. Miller. 1995. "Voter turnout in the industrial democracies during the 1980s." *Comparative Political Studies*, 27: 467–492. See also Richard Katz. 1997. *Democracy and Elections*. Oxford: Oxford University Press.

4 Andre Blais and A. Dobrzynska. 1998. "Turnout in electoral democracies." *European Journal of Political Research*, 33(2): 239–261.

5 Mark Franklin, Cess van der Eijk, and Erik Oppenhuis. 1996. "The institutional context: Turnout." In *Choosing Europe? The European Electorate and National Politics in the Face of Union*, ed. Cees van der Eijk and Mark Franklin. Ann Arbor: University of Michigan Press.

6 Raymond Wolfinger and Steven Rosenstone. 1980. *Who Votes?* New Haven, CT: Yale University Press; M. D. Martinez and D. Hill. 1999." Did motor voter work?" *American Politics Quarterly*, 27(3): 296–315.

7 Jeff A. Karp and Susan Banducci. 1999. "The impact of proportional representation on turnout: Evidence from New Zealand." *Australian Journal of Political Science*, 34(3): 363–377.

8 Richard Katz. 1997. *Democracy and Elections*. New York: Oxford University Press, Table 13.2.

9 See Richard Rose, Ed. 2000. The *International Encyclopedia of Elections*. Washington, DC: CQ Press.

10 Sarah Birch. 1997. "Ukraine: The perils of majoritarianism in a new democracy." In *The International IDEA Handbook of Electoral System Design*, ed. Andrew Reynolds and Ben Reilly. Stockholm: International Institute for Democracy and Electoral Assistance; Sarah Birch and Andrew Wilson. 1999. "The Ukranian parliamentary elections of 1998." *Electoral Studies*, 18(2): 276–282; Sarah Birch. 1998. "Electoral reform in Ukraine: The 1988 parliamentary elections." *Representation*, 35(2/3): 146–154.

11 See the discussion in Anthony Heath and Bridget Taylor. 1999. "New sources of abstention?" In *Critical Elections: British Parties and Voters in Long-term Perspective*, ed. Geoffrey Evans and Pippa Norris. London: Sage.

12 Maurice Duverger. 1954. *Political Parties*. London: Methuen; Douglas Rae. 1971. *The Political Consequences of Electoral Laws*. New Haven, CT: Yale University Press. For a good discussion and overview, see Arend Lijphart. 1994. *Electoral Systems and Party Systems*. Oxford: Oxford University Press; Andre Blais and Louis Massicotte. 2001. "Electoral participation." In *Comparing Democracies 2: Elections and Voting in Global Perspective*, ed. Lawrence LeDuc, Richard G. Niemi, and Pippa Norris. London: Sage.

13 G. Bingham Powell. 1986. "American voter turnout in comparative perspective." *American Political Science Review*, 80(1): 17–43; Robert W. Jackman.

1987. "Political institutions and voter turnout in industrialized democracies." *American Political Science Review*, 81: 405–423; Robert W. Jackman and Ross A. Miller. 1995. "Voter turnout in industrial democracies during the 1980s." *Comparative Political Studies*, 27: 467–492; Andre Blais and A. Dobrzynska. 1998. "Turnout in electoral democracies." *European Journal of Political Research*, 33(2): 239–261; A. Ladner and H. Milner. 1999. "Do voters turn out more under proportional than majoritarian systems? The evidence from Swiss communal elections." *Electoral Studies*, 18(2): 235–250.

14 See the discussion in Andre Blais and A. Dobrzynska. 1998. "Turnout in electoral democracies." *European Journal of Political Research*, 33(2): 239–261.

15 Andrew Reynolds and Ben Reilly. 1997. *The International IDEA Handbook of Electoral System Design*. Stockholm: International IDEA, Annex A.

16 For a discussion, see Robert Dahl. 1998. *On Democracy*. New Haven, CT: Yale University Press.

17 For a discussion about this in the context of Britain and the United States, see Bruce Cain, John Ferejohn, and Morris Fiorina. 1987. *The Personal Vote*. Cambridge, MA: Harvard University Press.

18 See, for example, the discussion of role orientations of MEPs and MPs in different electoral systems in Richard S. Katz. 1999. "Role orientations in Parliament." In *The European Parliament, the National Parliaments, and European Integration*, ed. Richard S. Katz and Bernhard Wessels. Oxford: Oxford University Press.

19 Mark Franklin, Cess van der Eijk, and Erik Oppenhuis. 1996. "The institutional context: Turnout." In *Choosing Europe? The European Electorate and National Politics in the Face of Union*, ed. Cees van der Eijk and Mark Franklin. Ann Arbor: University of Michigan Press.

20 Mark Franklin. 2001. "Electoral participation." In *Comparing Democracies 2: Elections and Voting in Global Perspective*, ed. Lawrence LeDuc, Richard G. Niemi, and Pippa Norris. London: Sage; Arend Lijphart. 2000. "Turnout." In *The International Encyclopedia of Elections*, ed. Richard Rose. Washington, DC: CQ Press.

21 Anthony King. 1997. *Running Scared*. New York: Free Press, p. 157.

22 Maurice Duverger. 1954. *Political Parties*. London: Methuen.

23 Arend Lijphart. 1999. *Patterns of Democracy*. New Haven, CT: Yale University Press, pp. 168–170.

24 Andrew Blais and Kenneth Carty. 1990. "Does proportional representation foster voter turnout?" *European Journal of Political Research*, 18: 167–181.

25 J. M. Colomer. 1991. "Benefits and costs of voting." *Electoral Studies*, 10(4): 313–325.

26 Andre Blais and R. K. Carty. 1990. "Does proportional representation foster voter turnout?" *European Journal of Political Research*, 18(2): 167–181.

27 Robert W. Jackman. 1987. "Political institutions and voter turnout in industrialized democracies." *American Political Science Review*, 81(2): 405–424.

28 For a discussion of this party type, see Giovanni Sartori. 1976. *Parties and Party Systems*. Cambridge: Cambridge University Press; T. J. Pempel. 1990. *Uncommon Democracies*. Ithaca, NY: Cornell University Press.

29 Karl Reif and Hermann Schmitt. 1980. "Nine national second order elections." *European Journal of Political Research*, 8: 3–44.

30 For a fuller discussion of the nature of presidential systems, see Arend Lijphart,
    Ed. 1992. *Parliamentary versus Presidential Government*. Oxford: Oxford
    University Press.
31 Richard Topf. 1995. "Electoral participation." In *Citizens and the State*, ed.
    Hans-Dieter Klingemann and Dieter Fuchs. Oxford: Oxford University Press,
    pp. 43–45; Warren Miller and Merrill Shanks. 1996. *The Changing American
    Voter*. Ann Arbor: University of Michigan Press.
32 Andre Blais and A. Dobrzynska. 1998. "Turnout in electoral democracies."
    European Journal of Political Research, 33(2): 246.
33 Florian Grotz. 2000. "Age of voting." In *The International Encyclopedia of
    Elections*, ed. Richard Rose. Washington, DC: CQ Press.
34 Andrew Blais, Louis Massicotte, and A. Yoshinaka. 2001. "Deciding who has
    the right to vote: A comparative analysis of election laws." *Electoral Studies*,
    20(1): 41–62. See also Richard S. Katz. 1997. *Democracy and Elections*.
    Oxford: Oxford University Press.
35 See Michael P. McDonald and Samuel L. Popkin. 2000. "The myth of the
    vanishing voter." Paper presented at the 2000 convention of the American
    Political Science Association, Washington, D.C.
36 For details, see Richard Katz. 1997. *Democracy and Elections*. New York:
    Oxford University Press, Tables 13.1 and 13.2.
37 For details, see Wilma Rule. 2000. "Women's enfranchisement," and Stefano
    Bartolini. 2000. "Franchise expansion." Both in *The International Encyclope-
    dia of Elections*, ed. Richard Rose. Washington, DC: CQ Press.
38 Pippa Norris. 2001. "Women's turnout." In *Voter Participation from 1945 to
    2000*. Stockholm: International IDEA.
39 Wolfgang Hirczy. 1994. "The impact of mandatory voting laws on turnout: A
    quasi experimental approach." *Electoral Studies*, 13(1): 64–76; Arend Lijphart.
    1997. "Unequal participation: Democracy's unresolved dilemma." *American
    Political Science Review*, 91: 1–14; Wolfgang Hirczy. 2000. "Compulsory
    voting." In *The International Encyclopedia of Elections*, ed. Richard Rose.
    Washington, DC: CQ Press.
40 I am most grateful for help received in identifying the countries that use com-
    pulsory voting from Gillian Evans, Lisa Hill, Marian Sawer, Ian McAllister, and
    Wolfgang Hirczy.
41 Ian McAllister. 1986. "Compulsory voting, turnout and party advantage in
    Australia." *Politics*, 21(1): 89–93.
42 One difficulty in analyzing the systematic effects of mandatory voting regula-
    tions concerns significant differences among alternative reference sources in the
    particular countries classified as using these laws. In such cases, the rule was
    adopted that the use of compulsory voting requirements had to be confirmed
    in at least three independent sources for classification in this study. These
    sources included the detailed report provided in a private communication by
    Gillian Evans and Lisa Hill at the Australian National University; *The Inter-
    national Encyclopedia of Elections*, ed. Richard Rose. Washington, DC: CQ
    Press; Inter-Parliamentary Union. *Chronicle of Parliamentary Elections*, annual
    volumes 1995–9. Geneva: IPU; the list published by the Australian Electoral
    Commission as provided by IFES (1996) at
    www.aec.gov.au/voting/compulsory%5Fcountries.htm; the *CIA World Fact-*

book 2000, www.cia.gov/cia/publications/fields/suffrage.html; and the tables provided in Richard Katz. 1997. *Democracy and Elections*. Oxford: Oxford University Press, Tables 13.1 and 13.2. Reference was also made to the electoral laws and constitutions compiled by IFES at www.IFES.org.

43 Ivor Crewe. "Electoral participation." In *Democracy at the Polls*, ed. Austin Ranney and David Butler. Washington, DC: AEI Press; G. Bingham Powell, Jr. 1986. "American voter turnout in comparative perspective." *American Political Science Review*, 80(1): 17–43; Robert W. Jackman. 1987. "Political institutions and voter turnout in industrialized democracies." *American Political Science Review*, 81: 405–423; Robert W. Jackman and Ross A. Miller. 1995. "Voter turnout in industrial democracies during the 1980s." *Comparative Political Studies*, 27: 467–492. Andre Blais and A. Dobrzynska. 1998. "Turnout in electoral democracies." *European Journal of Political Research*, 33(2): 239–261; Mark Franklin, Cess van der Eijk, and Erik Oppenhuis. 1996. "The institutional context: Turnout." In *Choosing Europe? The European Electorate and National Politics in the Face of Union*, ed. Cees van der Eijk and Mark Franklin. Ann Arbor: University of Michigan Press; Arend Lijphart. 1997. "Unequal participation: Democracy's unresolved dilemma." *American Political Science Review*, 91: 1–14.

44 Raymond E. Wolfinger and Steven J. Rosenstone. 1980. *Who Votes?* New Haven, CT: Yale University Press. For a more recent study, see Mark J. Fenster. 1994. "The impact of allowing day of registration voting on turnout in U.S. elections from 1960 to 1992." *American Politics Quarterly*, 22: 74–87.

45 Stephen Knack. 1995. "Does 'motor voter' work? Evidence from state-level data." *Journal of Politics*, 57: 796–811; M. D. Martinez and D. Hill. 1999." Did motor voter work?" *American Politics Quarterly*, 27(3): 296–315.

46 Craig Leonard Brians and Bernard Grofman. 1999. "When registration barriers fall, who votes? An empirical test of a rational choice model." *Public Choice*, 21: 161–176.

47 Raymond E. Wolfinger, David P. Glass, and Peverill Squire. 1990. "Predictors of electoral turnout: An international comparison." *Policy Studies Review*, 9: 551–574.

48 Richard S. Katz. 1997. *Democracy and Elections*. Oxford: Oxford University Press, Tables 13.1 and 13.2.

49 The mean Vote/VAP in the 1990s was the same (72 percent) in the countries classified by Katz as using automatic and those using application registration procedures, and the mean Vote/Reg in the 1990s was slightly higher (78.1 percent) in countries with application procedures than in those with automatic processes (75.1 percent).

50 The best discussion of the administrative arrangements for registration and balloting found around the world can be found at www.ACE.org, developed by International IDEA and IFES. For further details, see Michael Maley. 2000. "Absentee voting." In *The International Encyclopedia of Elections*, ed. Richard Rose. Washington, DC: CQ Press. See also entries by Andre Blais and Louis Massicotte.

51 Mark Franklin. 2001. "Electoral participation." In *Comparing Democracies 2: Elections and Voting in Global Perspective*, ed. Lawrence LeDuc, Richard G. Niemi, and Pippa Norris. London: Sage.

5. Who Votes?

1 John P. Katosh and Michael W. Traugott. 1981. "Consequences of validated and self-reported voting measures." *Public Opinion Quarterly*, 45: 519–535; Kevin Swaddle and Anthony Heath. 1989. "Official and reported turnout in the British general election of 1987." *British Journal of Political Science*, 19(4): 537–551; H. E. Andersson and D. Granberg. 1997. "On the validity and reliability of self-reported vote: Validity without reliability." *Quality and Quantity*, 31(2): 127–140. In the 2000 NES, for example, 76.1 percent claimed that "they were sure they had voted," compared to 50.5 percent who had actually voted, based on votes cast as a proportion of the voting-age population.

2 It should be noted that the difference between the actual and reported turnout in Table 5.1 is larger than usual in two nations, Canada and Latvia. There are many possible explanations for this discrepancy, and it may be that respondents are recalling previous voting in local, state, or regional elections rather than in the previous general election.

3 For comparison, as far as possible the institutional factors were selected to replicate the analysis used in Chapter 4. However, Table 5.2 had to drop the political institutions and legal rules with too few cases providing variance in the subset of twenty-two countries in the ISSP survey, namely, predominant party systems, presidential contests, and literacy requirements. Voting facilities were also excluded, since they failed to prove significant in the earlier analysis presented in Table 4.5 once institutional controls were entered.

4 Arend Lijphart. 1994. *Electoral Systems and Party Systems: A Study of Twenty-seven Democracies, 1945–1990*. Oxford: Oxford University Press; Andrew Reynolds and Ben Reilly. 1997. *The International IDEA Handbook of Electoral System Design*. Stockholm: International Institute for Democracy and Electoral Assistance.

5 This includes the introduction of the additional member system for the Scottish Parliament, the Welsh Assembly, and the London Assembly; the supplementary vote for the London mayor; the regional list system for European elections; and the single transferable vote for the new Northern Ireland Assembly. For details, see Lord Jenkins. 1998. *The Report of the Independent Commission on the Voting System*. London: The Stationery Office, Cm.4090–1.

6 Anthony King. 1997. *Running Scared: Why America's Politicians Campaign Too Much and Govern Too Little*. New York: Martin Kessler Books.

7 Stephen White, Richard Rose, and Ian McAllister. 1997. *How Russia Votes*. Chatham, NJ: Chatham House, Chapter 7.

8 Warren E. Miller and J. Merrill Shanks. 1996. *The New American Voter*. Cambridge, MA: Harvard University Press, Chapters 3–5.

9 Robert Putnam. 2000. *Bowling Alone: The Collapse and Revival of American Community*. New York: Simon and Schuster.

10 Richard Topf. 1995. "Electoral Participation." In *Citizens and the State*, ed. Hans-Dieter Klingemann and Dieter Fuchs. Oxford: Oxford University Press, p. 47.

11 International IDEA. 1999. *Youth Voter Participation*. Stockholm: International IDEA.

12 Herbert Tingsten. 1937. *Political Behavior: Studies in Election Statistics.*
    Reprinted Totowa, NJ: Bedminster Press (1963); Gabriel A. Almond and Sidney
    Verba. 1963. *The Civic Culture: Political Attitudes and Democracy in Five
    Nations.* Princeton, NJ: Princeton University Press.

13 Sidney Verba, Norman Nie, and Jae-on Kim. 1978. *Participation and Political
    Equality: A Seven-Nation Comparison.* New York: Cambridge University Press.

14 Carol Christy. 1987. *Sex Differences in Political Participation: Processes of
    Change in Fourteen Nations.* New York: Praeger; David DeVaus and Ian
    McAllister. 1989. "The changing politics of women: Gender and political
    alignments in eleven nations." *European Journal of Political Research,*
    17: 241–262; Margaret Conway, Gertrude A. Steuernagel, and David Ahern.
    1997. *Women and Political Participation.* Washington, DC: CQ Press, p. 79;
    Kay Lehman Schlozman, Nancy Burns, and Sidney Verba. 1994. "Gender and
    pathways to participation: The role of resources." *Journal of Politics,* 56:
    963–990.

15 CAWP. 2000. "Sex differences in voting turnout." www.cawp.org.

16 Pippa Norris. 2002. "Women's power at the ballot box." In *IDEA Voter
    Turnout from 1945 to 2000: A Global Report on Political Participation,* 3rd
    ed. Stockholm: International IDEA.

17 Seymour Martin Lipset. 1960. *Political Man.* New York: Doubleday.

18 See, for example, Raymond E. Wolfinger and Steven J. Rosenstone. 1980. *Who
    Votes?* New Haven, CT: Yale University Press, Chapter 2; Sidney Verba and
    Norman Nie. 1972. *Participation in America: Political Democracy and Social
    Equality.* New York: Harper and Row.

19 Ruy A. Teixeira. 1992. *The Disappearing American Voter.* Washington, DC:
    Brookings Institution, pp. 66–67.

20 Sidney Verba, Kay Schlozman, and Henry E. Brady. 1995. *Voice and Equality:
    Civic Voluntarism in American Politics.* Cambridge, MA: Harvard University
    Press, p. 190.

21 Sidney Verba, Norman Nie, and Jae-on Kim. 1978. *Participation and Political
    Equality: A Seven-Nation Comparison.* New York: Cambridge University Press,
    pp. 75–77.

22 Sidney Verba, Norman Nie, and Jae-on Kim. 1978. *Participation and Political
    Equality: A Seven-Nation Comparison.* New York: Cambridge University Press,
    p. 19; G. Bingham Powell. 1986. "American voter turnout in comparative per-
    spective." *American Political Science Review,* 80(1): 17–43.

23 Frances Fox Piven and Richard Cloward. 2000. *Why Americans Still Don't
    Vote: And Why Politicians Want It That Way.* Boston: Beacon Press.

24 Anthony Heath and Bridget Taylor. 1999. "New sources of abstention." In
    Critical Elections: British Parties and Voters in Long-term Perspective, ed.
    Geoffrey Evans and Pippa Norris. London: Sage; Charles Pattie and Ron
    Johnston. 1998. "Voter turnout at the British general election of 1992:
    Rational choice, social standing or political efficacy?" *European Journal of
    Political Research,* 33: 263–283; Kevin Swaddle and Anthony Heath. 1989.
    "Official and reported turnout in the British general election of 1987." *British
    Journal of Political Science,* 19(4): 537–551.

25 Richard Topf. 1995. "Electoral participation." In *Citizens and the State,* ed.
    Hans-Dieter Klingemann and Dieter Fuchs. Oxford: Oxford University Press.

26 Stephen White, Richard Rose, and Ian McAllister. 1997. *How Russia Votes.* Chatham, NJ: Chatham House, Chapter 7.

27 Pippa Norris. 2000. *A Virtuous Circle.* Cambridge: Cambridge University Press.

28 International IDEA. 2001. *Campaign Finance Handbook.* Stockholm: International IDEA.

29 Steven J. Rosenstone and John Mark Hansen. 1995. *Mobilization, Participation and Democracy in America.* New York: Macmillan. See also C. A. Cassel. 1999. "Voluntary associations, churches and social participation theories of turnout." *Social Science Quarterly,* 80(3): 504–517.

30 Robert Putnam. 2000. *Bowling Alone: The Collapse and Revival of American Community.* New York: Simon and Schuster.

31 Sidney Verba, Kay Lehman Schlozman, and Henry Brady. 1995. *Voice and Equality: Civic Voluntarism in American Politics.* Cambridge, MA: Harvard University Press.

32 John Aldrich. 1995. *Why Parties?* Chicago: University of Chicago Press; Martin P. Wattenberg. 1996. *The Decline of American Political Parties: 1952–1994.* Cambridge, MA: Harvard University Press.

33 K. Q. Hill and J. E. Leighley. 1996. "Political parties and class mobilization in contemporary United States elections." *American Journal of Political Science,* 40(3): 787–804.

34 G. Bingham Powell. 1980. "Voting turnout in thirty democracies: Partisan, legal and socioeconomic influences." In *Electoral Participation: A Comparative Analysis,* ed. Richard Rose. London: Sage.

35 It should be noted that the ISSP survey measured only whether people had a party affiliation, not the strength of party identification, which is the more standard measure used for analysis. The size of the gap is therefore perhaps all the more remarkable.

36 Gabriel Almond and Sidney Verba. 1963. *The Civic Culture: Political Attitudes and Democracy in Five Nations.* Princeton, NJ: Princeton University Press.

37 Gabriel Almond and Sidney Verba. 1963. *The Civic Culture: Political Attitudes and Democracy in Five Nations.* Princeton, NJ: Princeton University Press; Samuel Barnes and Max Kaase. 1979. *Political Action: Mass Participation in Five Western Democracies.* Beverley Hills, CA: Sage.

38 Pippa Norris, Ed. 1999. *Critical Citizens: Global Support for Democratic Governance.* Oxford: Oxford University Press.

39 Jack Citrin and Donald Green. 1986. "Presidential leadership and trust in government." *British Journal of Political Science,* 16: 431–453; Jack Citrin. 1974. "Comment: The political relevance of trust in government." *American Political Science Review,* 68: 973–988.

40 Geraint Parry, George Moyser, and Neil Day. 1992. *Political Participation and Democracy in Britain.* Cambridge: Cambridge University Press.

41 Jack Citrin and Donald Green. 1986. "Presidential leadership and trust in government." *British Journal of Political Science,* 16: 431–453.

42 See Sidney Verba and Norman Nie. 1972. *Participation in America: Political Democracy and Social Equality.* New York: Harper and Row; Sidney Verba, Kay Lehman Schlozman, and Henry Brady. 1995. *Voice and Equality: Civic Voluntarism in American Politics.* Cambridge, MA: Harvard University Press.

6. Mapping Party Activism

1   V. O. Key. 1964. *Politics, Parties and Pressure Groups*. New York: Crowell.
2   See the conclusions in Russell J. Dalton and Martin P. Wattenberg. 2001. *Parties without Partisans: Political Change in Advanced Industrial Democracies*. Oxford: Oxford University Press.
3   Kay Lawson and Peter Merkl, Eds. 1988. *When Parties Fail: Emerging Alternative Organizations*. Princeton, NJ: Princeton University Press.
4   The most comprehensive recent reviews of the evidence are available in Hermann Schmitt and Soren Holmberg. 1995. "Political parties in decline?" In *Citizens and the State*, ed. Hans-Dieter Klingemann and Dieter Fuchs. Oxford: Oxford University Press; Russell J. Dalton and Martin P. Wattenberg. 2001. *Parties without Partisans: Political Change in Advanced Industrialized Democracies*. Oxford: Oxford University Press.
5   See, in particular, Peter Mair and Ingrid van Biezen. 2001. "Party membership in twenty European democracies 1980–2000." *Party Politics*, 7(1): 7–22; Susan Scarrow. 2001. "Parties without members?" In *Parties without Partisans*, ed. Russell J. Dalton and Martin Wattenberg. New York: Oxford University Press.
6   See Eric Shaw. 1994. *The Labour Party since 1945*. Oxford: Blackwell.
7   John H. Aldrich. 1995. *Why Parties? The Origin and Transformation of Party Politics in America*. Chicago: University of Chicago Press.
8   Angelo Panebianco. 1988. *Political Parties: Organization and Power*. Cambridge: Cambridge University Press.
9   See, for example, Anthony Heath, Roger Jowell, and John Curtice. 2001. *The Rise of New Labour*. Oxford: Oxford University Press; Stefano Bartolini. 2000. *The Political Mobilization of the European Left, 1860–1980*. Cambridge: Cambridge University Press; Herbert Kitschelt. 1994. *The Transformation of European Social Democracy*. Cambridge: Cambridge University Press.
10 For general discussions, see Angelo Panebianco. 1988. *Political Parties: Organization and Power*. Cambridge: Cambridge University Press; Peter Mair. 1997. *Party System Change*. Oxford: Oxford University Press; Alan Ware. 1996. *Political Parties and Party Systems*. Oxford: Oxford University Press; Pippa Norris. 2001. *A Virtuous Circle: Political Communications in Post-industrial Societies*. Cambridge: Cambridge University Press.
11 Maurice Duverger. 1954. *Political Parties*. New York: Wiley; Leon Epstein. 1980. *Political Parties in Western Democracies*. New Brunswick, NJ: Transaction Books.
12 Paul Whiteley, Pat Seyd, and Jeremy Richardson. 1994. *True Blues: The Politics of Conservative Party Membership*. Oxford: Clarendon Press, p. 84. Others have often divided incentives into material (e.g., being given a government job), solidary (e.g., the social benefits of membership), and purposive (the achievement of programmatic and ideological goals). See Peter B. Clark and James Q. Wilson. 1961. "Incentive systems: A theory of organizations." *Administrative Science Quarterly*, 6: 129–166.
13 Maurice Duverger. 1954. *Political Parties*. New York: Wiley.
14 See John H. Aldrich. 1995. *Why Parties? The Origin and Transformation of Party Politics in America*. Chicago: University of Chicago Press.
15 For a discussion, see K. Heidar. 1994. "The polymorphic nature of party membership." *European Journal of Political Research*, 25(1): 61–86; Per Selle.

1991. "Membership in party organizations and the problems of decline of parties." *Comparative Political Studies*, 23(4): 459–477.

16 See Susan Scarrow. 1994. "The paradox of enrollment: Assessing the costs and benefits of party memberships." *European Journal of Political Research*, 25(1): 41–60.

17 Walter Bagehot. 1964. (1867) *The English Constitution*. London: C. A. Watts.

18 Considerable dispute continues regarding how far local campaigns can activate voters; on the United States, see Paul Allen Beck, Russell J. Dalton, A. A. Haynes, and Robert Huckfeldt. 1997. "Presidential campaigning at the grassroots." *Journal of Politics*, 59(4): 1264–1275; Robert Huckfeldt and John Sprague. 1992. "Political parties and electoral mobilization: Political structure, social structure and the party canvass." *American Political Science Review*, 86(1): 70–86. On Britain, see David Denver, Gordon Hands, and Simon Henig. 1998. "Triumph of targeting? Constituency campaigning in the 1997 election." In *British Elections and Parties Review, 8: The 1997 General Election*, ed. David Denver, Justin Fish, Philip Cowley, and Chouln Pattie. London: Frank Cass; Paul Whiteley and Patrick Seyd. 1994. "Local party campaigning and electoral mobilization in Britain." *Journal of Politics*, 56(1): 242–252.

19 For a series of case studies, see David Swanson and Paolo Mancini. 1996. *Politics, Media and Modern Democracy*. New York: Praeger; Richard Gunther and Anthony Mughan, Eds. 2000. *Democracy and the Media*. Cambridge: Cambridge University Press. See also Kay Lawson. 1980. *Political Parties and Linkage: A Comparative Perspective*. New Haven, CT: Yale University Press; Kay Lawson and Peter Merkl, Eds. 1988. *When Parties Fail: Emerging Alternative Organizations*. Princeton, NJ: Princeton University Press; Susan Scarrow. 1996. *Parties and Their Members: Organizing for Victory in Britain and Germany*. Oxford: Oxford University Press; Alan Ware. 1987. *Political Parties: Electoral Change and Structural Response*. Oxford: Blackwell.

20 Otto Kirchheimer. 1966. "The transformation of Western European party systems." In *Political Parties and Political Development*, ed. J. La Palombara and M. Weiner. Princeton, NJ: Princeton University Press. See also Angelo Panebianco. 1988. *Political Parties: Organization and Power*. Cambridge: Cambridge University Press.

21 Leon Epstein. 1980. *Political Parties in Western Democracies*. New Brunswick, NJ: Transaction Books.

22 Richard S. Katz and Peter Mair. 1995. "Changing models of party organization and party democracy: The emergence of the cartel party." *Party Politics*, 1(1): 5–28; Richard S. Katz and Peter Mair. 1996. "Cadre, catch-all or cartel? A rejoinder." *Party Politics*, 2(4): 525–534.

23 On the growth and mobilization of socialist and social democratic parties, see Stefano Bartolini. 2000. *The Political Mobilization of the European Left, 1860–1980*. Cambridge: Cambridge University Press; Herbert Kitschelt. 1994. *The Transformation of European Social Democracy*. Cambridge: Cambridge University Press.

24 On the United States, see Steven Rosenstone and John Mark Hansen. 1993. *Mobilization, Participation and Democracy in America*. New York: Macmillan, pp. 170–173. On Britain, see David Denver and Gordon Hands. *Modern Constituency Electioneering: Local Campaigning in the 1992 General Election*. London: Frank Cass.

25 See Scott Mainwaring and Timothy Scully. 1995. *Building Democratic Institutions: Party Systems in Latin America.* Stanford, CA: Stanford University Press.

26 See Michael Bratton and Nicolas van de Walle. 1997. *Democratic Experiments in Africa.* Cambridge: Cambridge University Press; Michelle Kuenzi and Gina Lambright. 2001. "Party system institutionalization in thirty African countries." *Party Politics,* 7(4): 437–468.

27 See Herbert Kitschelt, Zdenka Mansfeldova, Radoslaw Markowski, and Gabor Toka. 1999. *Post-Communist Party Systems.* Cambridge: Cambridge University Press; Sten Berglund and Jan A. Dellenbrant. 1994. *The New Democracies in Eastern Europe: Party Systems and Political Cleavages.* Aldershot: Edward Elgar; Peter Kopecky. 1995. "Developing party organizations in East-Central Europe." *Party Politics,* 1: 515–534; Paul Lewis. 1996. *Party Structure and Organization in East-Central Europe.* Aldershot: Edward Elgar; Dietrich Rueschemeyer, Marilyn Rueschemeyer, and Bjorn Wittrock. 1998. *Participation and Democracy: East and West.* New York: M. E. Sharpe; Ingrid van Biezen. 2000. "On the internal balance of party power: Party organizations in new democracies." *Party Politics,* 6(4): 395–417; K. Grabow. 2001. "The reemergence of the cadre party? Organizational patterns of Christian and Social Democrats in unified Germany." *Party Politics,* 7(1): 23–43.

28 For a typology, see Juan Linz and Alfred Stepan. 1996. *Problems of Democratic Transition and Consolidation.* Baltimore: Johns Hopkins University Press.

29 T. J. Pempel. 1990. *Uncommon Democracies: The One-Party Dominant Regimes.* Ithaca, NY: Cornell University Press.

30 See Larry Diamond and Richard Gunther. 2001. *Political Parties and Democracy.* Baltimore: Johns Hopkins University Press.

31 Richard Katz and Peter Mair, Eds. 1994. *How Parties Organize: Change and Adaptation in Party Organizations in Western Democracies.* London: Sage, Table 1.1. See also Peter Mair. 1997. *Party System Change.* Oxford: Oxford University Press.

32 Peter Mair and Ingrid van Biezen. 2001. "Party membership in twenty European democracies 1980–2000." *Party Politics,* 7(1): 7–21.

33 Susan Scarrow. 2001. "Parties without members?" In *Parties without Partisans,* ed. Russell J. Dalton and Martin Wattenberg. New York: Oxford University Press, p. 88.

34 Ibid.

35 Knut Heidar. 1994. "The polymorphic nature of party membership." *European Journal of Political Research,* 25: 61–88; Patrick Seyd, and Paul Whiteley. 1992. *Labour's Grass Roots: The Politics of Labour Party Membership.* Oxford: Clarendon Press; Paul Whiteley, Patrick Seyd, and Jeremy Richardson. 1994. *True Blues: The Politics of Conservative Party Membership.* Oxford: Clarendon Press.

36 A. C. Tan. 1997. "Party change and party membership decline: An exploratory analysis." *Party Politics,* 3(3): 363–377; A. C. Tan. 1998. "The impact of party membership size: A cross-national analysis." *Journal of Politics,* 60(1): 188–198.

37 Anders Widfeldt. 1995. "Party membership and party representativeness." In *Citizens and the State,* ed. Hans-Dieter Klingemann and Dieter Fuchs. Oxford: Oxford University Press.

38 Anders Widfeldt. "Losing touch? The political representativeness of Swedish parties, 1985–1994." *Scandinavian Political Studies*, 22(4): 307–326.

39 A detailed case study of British Conservative membership in a sample of constituency associations reported that the difference between the claimed official membership and the actual level of membership documented in the survey ranged from an overestimate of 69 percent to an underestimate of 194 percent. See Paul Whiteley, Pat Seyd, and Jeremy Richardson. 1994. *True Blues: The Politics of Conservative Party Membership*. Oxford: Clarendon Press, p. 22.

40 For a discussion of some of the reasons, see See Herbert Kitschelt, Zdenka Mansfeldova, Radoslaw Markowski, and Gabor Toka. 1999. *Post-Communist Party Systems*. Cambridge: Cambridge University Press; Sten Berglund and Jan A. Dellenbrant. 1994. *The New Democracies in Eastern Europe: Party Systems and Political Cleavages*. Aldershot: Edward Elgar; Stephen White, Richard Rose, and Ian McAllister. 1997. *How Russia Votes*. Chatham, NJ: Chatham House.

41 See, for example, R. B. Mattes, A. Gouws, and H. J. Kotze. 1995. "The emerging party system in the new South Africa." *Party Politics*, 1(3): 381–395.

42 Pippa Norris. 2000. *A Virtuous Circle: Political Communications in Post-Industrial Societies*. Cambridge: Cambridge University Press, Chapter 13.

43 For a general discussion of these trends, see Steven J. Rosenstone and John Mark Hansen. 1993. *Mobilization, Participation and Democracy in America*. New York: Macmillan. The temporary increase in donations that occurred in 1976 may have been caused by the new campaign finance reforms regulated by the Federal Election Commission.

7. Who Joins?

1 There is a large literature on these topics. For summaries, see David Swanson and Paolo Mancini. 1996. *Politics, Media and Modern Democracy*. New York: Praeger; Pippa Norris. 1999. *A Virtuous Circle: Political Communications in Post-Industrial Societies*. Cambridge: Cambridge University Press; David Farrell and Paul Webb. 2001. "Political parties as campaign organizations." In *Parties without Partisans*, ed. Russell J. Dalton and Martin Wattenberg. New York: Oxford University Press.

2 Pippa Norris. 2001. *Digital Divide: Information Poverty, Civic Engagement and the Internet Worldwide*. Cambridge: Cambridge University Press.

3 The theory of cartel parties is developed in Richard S. Katz and Peter Mair. 1995. "Changing models of party organization and party democracy: The emergence of the cartel party." *Party Politics*, 1(1): 5–28. For a critical review of the evidence for these claims, see J. Pierre, L. Svasand, and A. Widfeldt. 2000. "State subsidies to political parties: Confronting rhetoric with reality." *West European Politics*, 23(3): 1–24.

4 Ronald Inglehart. 1997. *Modernization and Post-Modernization*. Princeton, NJ: Princeton University Press, Chapter 10.

5 Bruce Cain, John Ferejohn, and Morris Fiorina. 1987. *The Personal Vote: Constituency Service and Electoral Independence*. Cambridge, MA: Harvard University Press.

6 Pippa Norris. "The twilight of Westminster?" *Political Studies*, 2001. 49(5): 877–900.

7   Juan Linz, Ed. 1994. *The Failure of Presidential Democracy*. Baltimore: Johns Hopkins University Press.
8   See Scott Mainwaring and Timothy Scully. 1995. *Building Democratic Institutions: Party Systems in Latin America*. Stanford, CA: Stanford University Press.
9   See Stefano Bartolini. 2000. *The Political Mobilization of the European Left, 1860–1980*. Cambridge: Cambridge University Press; Herbert Kitschelt. 1994. *The Transformation of European Social Democracy*. Cambridge: Cambridge University Press.
10 See Paul Whiteley, Pat Seyd, and Jeremy Richardson. 1994. *True Blues: The Politics of Conservative Party Membership*. Oxford: Clarendon Press.
11 Fritz Plassner, Christian Scheucher, and Christian Senft. 1999. "Is there a European style of political marketing?" In *The Handbook of Political Marketing*, ed. Bruce I. Newman. Thousand Oaks, CA: Sage.
12 Jon Huber and Ronald Inglehart. 1995. "Expert interpretations of party space and party locations in forty-two societies." *Party Politics*, 1(1): 73–111.
13 Sidney Verba, Kay Schlozman, and Henry E. Brady. 1995. *Voice and Equality: Civic Voluntarism in American Politics*. Cambridge, MA: Harvard University Press.
14 Joni Lovenduski and Pippa Norris, Eds. 1993. *Gender and Party Politics*. London: Sage; Inter-Parliamentary Union. 1997. *Men and Women in Politics* (Reports and Documents Series 28). Geneva: IPU; Inter-Parliamentary Union. 2000. *Participation of Women in Public Life*. Geneva: IPU.
15 Robert Putnam. 2000. *Bowling Alone: The Collapse and Revival of American Community*. New York: Simon and Schuster.
16 Ronald Inglehart. 1997. *Modernization and Post-Modernization*. Princeton, NJ: Princeton University Press, Chapter 10.
17 For a discussion, see Pippa Norris. 1999. *A Virtuous Circle: Political Communications in Post-Industrial Democracies*. Cambridge: Cambridge University Press.

8. Social Capital and Civic Society

1   See the discussions in Jeffrey Berry. 1984. *The Interest Group Society*. Boston: Little Brown; and Jack L. Walker. 1991. *Mobilizing Interest Groups in America*: Ann Arbor: University of Michigan Press.
2   Sidney Tarrow. 1994. *Power in Movement*. Cambridge: Cambridge University Press; Charles Tilly. 1978. *From Mobilization to Revolution*. Reading, MA: Addison-Wesley; Doug McAdam, John D. McCarthy, and Mayer N. Zald, Eds. 1996. *Comparative Perspectives on Social Movements*. New York: Cambridge University Press; Russell J. Dalton and Manfred Kuechler, Eds. 1990. *Challenging the Political Order: New Social and Political Movements in Western Democracies*. New York: Oxford University Press.
3   Pierre Bourdieu. 1970. *Reproduction in Education, Culture and Society*. London: Sage; James S. Coleman. 1988. "Social capital in the creation of human capital." *American Journal of Sociology*, 94: 95–120; James S. Coleman. 1990. *Foundations of Social Theory*. Cambridge, MA: Belknap. For a discussion of the history of the concept, see also the Introduction in Stephen

Baron, John Field, and Tom Schuller, Eds. 2000. *Social Capital: Critical Perspectives*. Oxford: Oxford University Press.

4   The seminal works are Robert D. Putnam. 1993. *Making Democracy Work: Civic Traditions in Modern Italy*. Princeton, NJ: Princeton University Press; Robert D. Putnam. 1996. "The strange disappearance of civic America." *The American Prospect*, 7(24): 34–48. Robert D. Putnam. 2000. *Bowling Alone: The Collapse and Revival of American Community*. New York: Simon and Schuster. More recent comparative research is presented in Susan Pharr and Robert Putnam, Eds. 2000. *Disaffected Democracies: What's Troubling the Trilateral Countries?* Princeton, NJ: Princeton University Press; Robert D. Putnam, Ed. 2002. *Democracies in Flux: The Evolution of social capital in contemporary societies*. New York: Oxford University Press.

5   Robert D. Putnam. 2000. *Bowling Alone: The Collapse and Revival of American Community*. New York: Simon and Schuster, p. 19. Putnam also offers a related definition: "By 'social capital' I mean features of social life – networks, norms and trust – that enable participants to act together more effectively to pursue shared objectives." Robert D. Putnam. 1996. "The strange disappearance of civil America." *The American Prospect*, 7(24): 34–48.

6   See Kenneth J. Arrow. 2000. "Observations on social capital." In *Social Capital: A Multifaceted Perspective*, ed. Partha Dasgupta and Ismail Serageldin. Washington, DC: World Bank.

7   Robert Putnam. 1993. *Making Democracy Work: Civic Traditions in Modern Italy*. Princeton, NJ: Princeton University Press, pp. 89–90.

8   Susan Pharr and Robert Putnam, Eds. 2000. *Disaffected Democracies: What's Troubling the Trilateral Countries?* Princeton, NJ: Princeton University Press.

9   Robert D. Putnam. 1993. *Making Democracy Work: Civic Traditions in Modern Italy*. Princeton, NJ: Princeton University Press.

10 For a discussion see Kenneth Newton and Pippa Norris. 2000. "Confidence in public institutions: Faith, culture or performance?" In *Disaffected Democracies: What's Troubling the Trilateral Countries?*, ed. Susan Pharr and Robert Putnam. Princeton, NJ: Princeton University Press; Kenneth Newton. 2001. "Trust, social capital, civic society, and democracy." *International Political Science Review*, 22(2): 201–214.

11 Robert Putnam. 2000. *Bowling Alone: The Collapse and Revival of American Community*. New York: Simon and Schuster, p. 246. See also Robert Putnam. 1995. "Tuning in, tuning out: The strange disappearance of social capital in America." *PS: Political Science and Politics*, 28(4): 664–683; Pippa Norris. 1996. "Did television erode social capital? A reply to Putnam." *PS: Political Science and Politics*, 29(3): 474–480.

12 See, for example, Frank R. Baumgartner and Jack L. Walker. 1988. "Survey research and membership in voluntary associations." *American Journal of Political Science*, 32(4): 908–928; Francis Fukuyama. 1995. *Trust: The Social Virtues and the Creation of Prosperity*. New York: Free Press.

13 For a discussion of this distinction and a typology of associations, see Mark E. Warren. 2001. *Democracy and Association*. Princeton, NJ: Princeton University Press.

14 Russell J. Dalton and Manfred Kuechler, Eds. 1990. *Challenging the Political Order: New Social and Political Movements in Western Democracies*. New

York: Oxford University Press; Margaret E. Keck and Kathryn Sikkink. 1998. *Activists beyond Borders: Advocacy Networks in International Politics.* Ithaca, NY: Cornell University Press; J. Smith, C. Chatfield, and R. Pagnucco, Eds. 1997. *Transnational Social Movements and Global Politics: Solidarity beyond the State.* Syracuse, NY: Syracuse University Press; H. Kriesi, D. D. Porta, and Dieter Rucht, Eds. 1998. *Social Movements in a Globalizing World.* London: Macmillan.

15 Jonathan Baker. 1999. *Street Level Democracy: Political Settings at the Margins of Global Power.* West Hartford, CT: Kumarian Press.

16 A. Portess and P. Landholt. 1996. "The downside of social capital." *The American Prospect*, 26: 18–21.

17 Robert D. Putnam. 2002. "Introduction." In *Democracies in Flux: The Evolution of Social Capital in Contemporary Societies*, ed. Robert D. Putnam. New York: Oxford University Press.

18 See C. McCall and A. Williamson. 2001. "Governance and democracy in Northern Ireland: The role of the voluntary and community sector after the agreement." *Governance*, 14 (3): 363–383.

19 Bob Edwards and Michael W. Foley. 1998. "Civil society and social capital beyond Putnam." *American Behavioral Scientist*, 42(1): 124–139.

20 See also Kenneth Newton and Pippa Norris. 2000. "Confidence in public institutions: Faith, culture or performance?" In *Disaffected Democracies: What's Troubling the Trilateral Countries?*, ed. Susan Pharr and Robert Putnam. Princeton, NJ: Princeton University Press; Kenneth Newton. 2001. "Trust, social capital, civic society, and democracy." *International Political Science Review*, 22(2): 201–214.

21 Ibid. See also Max Kaase. 1999. "Interpersonal trust, political trust and non-institutionalized political participation in Western Europe." *West European Politics*, 22(3): 1–23; Jan van Deth. 2000. "Interesting but irrelevant: Social capital and the saliency of politics in Western Europe." *European Journal of Political Research*, 37: 115–147.

22 Robert Putnam. 2000. *Bowling Alone: The Collapse and Revival of Community in America.* New York: Simon and Schuster, p. 27.

23 See Carl Everett Ladd. 1996. "The data just don't show erosion of America's social capital." *The Public Perspective*, 7(4); Theda Skopol. 1996. "Unravelling from above." *The American Prospect*, 25: 20–25; Michael Schudson. 1996. "What if civic life didn't die?" *The American Prospect*, 25: 17–20.

24 Thomas Rotolo. 1999. "Trends in voluntary association participation." *Nonprofit and Voluntary Sector Quarterly*, 28(2): 199–212.

25 Pippa Norris. 2000. *A Virtuous Circle: Political Communications in Postindustrial Societies.* Cambridge: Cambridge University Press, Chapter 13.

26 Theda Skopol and Morris P. Fiorina, Eds. 1999. *Civic Engagement in American Democracy.* Washington, DC: Brookings Institution.

27 For comparative work, see Jan Willem Van Deth, Ed. 1997. *Private Groups and Public Life: Social Participation, Voluntary Associations and Political Involvement in Representative Democracies.* London: Routledge; Jan Willem van Deth and F. Kreuter. 1998. "Membership of voluntary associations." In *Comparative Politics: The Problem of Equivalence*, ed. Jan. W. van Deth. London: Routledge, pp. 135–155; Jan van Deth. 2000. "Interesting but irrele-

vant: Social capital and the saliency of politics in Western Europe." *European Journal of Political Research*, 37:115–147.

28 Kees Aarts. 1995. "Intermediate organizations and interest representation." In *Citizens and the State*, ed. Hans-Dieter Klingemann and Dieter Fuchs. Oxford: Oxford University Press.

29 Peter Hall. 2000. "Social capital in Britain." In *Democracies in Flux: The Evolution of Social Capital in Contemporary Societies*, ed. Robert D. Putnam. New York: Oxford University Press; Peter Hall. 1999. "Social Capital in Britain." *British Journal of Political Science*, 29(3): 417–61. See also William L. Maloney, Graham Smith, and Gerry Stoker. 2000. "Social capital and associational life." In *Social Capital: Critical Perspectives*, ed. Stephen Baron, John Field, and Tom Schuller. Oxford: Oxford University Press.

30 See Bo Rothstein. 2000. "Sweden." In *Democracies in Flux: the Evolution of Social Capital in Contemporary Societies*, ed. Robert D. Putnam. New York: Oxford University Press.

31 Partha Dasgupta and Ismail Serageldin, Eds. 2000. *Social Capital: A Multifaceted Perspective*. Washington, DC: World Bank.

32 See ibid.

33 For details of the classification, see Appendix A.

34 Unfortunately, the questions used to monitor belonging to voluntary associations in different waves of the WVS survey were equivalent but not identical, and the wording varied as follows:

1980 WVS: *"Please look carefully at the following list of voluntary organizations and activities and say which, if any, do you belong to?"*

Early 1990 WVS: *"Please look carefully at the following list of voluntary organizations and activities and say . . . a) which, if any, do you belong to? b) Which, if any, are you currently doing unpaid voluntary work for?"*

Mid-1990s WVS *"Now I am going to read off a list of voluntary organizations; for each one, could you tell me whether you are an active member, an inactive member or not a member of that type of organization?"*

The change in wording makes it difficult to compare *activism* among all waves, and the wording in 1995 may generate different response rates as well. I am grateful to Ron Inglehart for providing these details.

35 Variations among different sectors, and the reasons why people join, are discussed in detailed elsewhere. See ibid.

36 Stephen Baron, John Field, and Tom Schuller, eds. 2000. *Social Capital: Critical Perspectives*. Oxford: Oxford University Press, p. 27.

37 Because this index is a conceptual measure based on theoretical considerations, factor analysis and reliability tests, which are often employed to test the consistency of scaled items, would be inappropriate techniques.

38 James E. Curtis, Edward G. Grabb, and Douglas E. Baer. 1992. "Voluntary association membership in fifteen countries: A comparative analysis." *American Sociological Review*, 57(2): 139–152.

39 For a detailed study of Russia using alternative measures of social capital, see Richard Rose. 2000. "Uses of social capital in Russia: Modern, pre-modern, and anti-modern." *Post-Soviet Affairs*, 16(1): 33–57. See also Richard Rose, William Mishler, and Christopher Haerpfer. 1997. "Social capital in civic and

stressful societies." *Studies in Comparative International Development*. 32(3): 85–111.

40   For details about recent trends in social trust from the *Latinobarometro*, see Marta Laros. "An alarm call for Latin American democrats." *The Economist*, 28 July 2001. See also Roderic A. Camp. 2001. *Citizens Views of Democracy in Latin America*. Pittsburgh: University of Pittsburgh Press.

41   For a discussion of the cases of China and Taiwan, see T. J. Shi. 2001. "Cultural values and political trust: A comparison of the People's Republic of China and Taiwan." *Comparative Politics*, 3(4): 401–412.

42   F. Fukuyama. 1992. *The End of History and the Last Man*. New York: Free Press, p. 159.

43   The exception concerns the consistently significant association between voluntary organizations and the distribution of online access, the latter measured by the proportion of the population estimated to use the internet. It may be that the density of voluntary organizations encourages the spread of the internet, but this relationship is probably driven more strongly by the extreme North-South divide in internet access and the prevalence of the Nordic and Anglo-American societies online, all "joining" societies. For details, see Pippa Norris. 2001. *Digital Divide: Civic Engagement, Information Poverty, and the Internet Worldwide*. Cambridge: Cambridge University Press.

44   F. Fukuyama. 1995. *Trust: The Social Virtues and the Creation of Prosperity*. New York: Free Press.

45   Pippa Norris, Ed. 1999. *Critical Citizens: Global Support for Democratic Governance*. Oxford: Oxford University Press.

46   Data was derived from International IDEA. *Voting Turnout around the World 1945–2000*. Stockholm: IDEA.

47   See Kenneth Newton and Pippa Norris. 2000. "Confidence in public institutions: Faith, culture or performance?" In *Disaffected Democracies: What's Troubling the Trilateral Countries?*, ed. Susan Pharr and Robert Putnam. Princeton, NJ: Princeton University Press. This work examined the impact of social trust (not social capital), and it considered a narrower range of seventeen affluent postindustrial societies and established democracies, not forty-seven nations worldwide.

48   Daniel Kaufman, Aart Kraay, and Pablo Zoido-Lobaton. 1999. *Governance Matters* (Policy Research Working Paper 2196). Washington, DC: World Bank.

49   It should be noted that none of the indicators that were selected included measures of freedom of the press or media access.

9. Traditional Mobilizing Agencies: Unions and Churches

1   Steven J. Rosenstone and John Mark Hansen. 1993. *Mobilization, Participation and Democracy in America*. New York: Macmillan.

2   For a summary of the debate about secularization theory, see W. H. Swatos and K. J. Christiano. 2001. "Secularization theory: The course of a concept." *Sociology of Religion*, 60(3): 209–228. For trends in trade union membership, see Michael Wallerstein. 1989. "Union organization in advanced industrial democracies." *American Political Science Review*, 83(2): 481–501; Michael Waller-

stein and B. Western. 2000. "Unions in decline? What has changed and why." *Annual Review of Political Science*, 3: 355–377.

3 Sidney Verba, Kay Schlozman, and Henry E. Brady. 1995. *Voice and Equality: Civic Voluntarism in American Politics*. Cambridge, MA: Harvard University Press.

4 See Nancy Burns, Kay Lehman Schlozman, and Sidney Verba. 2001. *The Private Roots of Public Action*. Cambridge, MA: Harvard University Press, Chapter 9; Robert Wuthnow. 1999. "Mobilizing civic engagement: The changing impact of religious involvement." In *Civic Engagement in American Democracy*, ed. Theda Skocpol and Morris P. Fiorina. Washington, DC: Brookings Institution; P. A. Djupe and J. T. Grant. 2001. "Religious institutions and political participation in America." *Journal for the Scientific Study of Religion*, 40(2): 303–314; B. D. McKenzie. 2001. "Self-selection, church attendance, and local civic participation." *Journal for the Scientific Study of Religion*, 40(3): 479–488.

5 Y. Alex-Assensoh and A. B. Assensoh. 2001. "Inner-city contexts, church attendance, and African-American political participation." *Journal of Politics*, 63(3): 886–901.

6 On social movements and political consciousness, see, for example, Sidney Tarrow. 1992. *Power in Movement*. Cambridge: Cambridge University Press. On the role of these organizations in protest politics, see Samuel Barnes and Max Kaase. 1979. *Political Action: Mass Participation in Five Western Democracies*. Beverley Hills, CA: Sage. See also Alan Marsh. 1977. *Protest and Political Consciousness*. Beverly Hills, CA: Sage.

7 R. McVeigh and D. Sikkink. 2001. "God, politics, and protest: Religious beliefs and the legitimation of contentious tactics." *Social Forces*, 79(4): 1425–1458.

8 See Zlimu Katz and Paul F. Lazarsfeld. 1955. *Personal Influence*. Glencoe, IL: Free Press.

9 Jan Willem van Deth, Ed. 1997. *Private Groups and Public Life: Social Participation, Voluntary Associations and Political Involvement in Representative Democracies*. London: Routledge; Carole Uhlaner. 1989. "Rational turnout: The neglected role of groups." *American Journal of Political Science*, 33: 390–422.

10 Seymour M. Lipset and Stein Rokkan, Eds. 1967. *Party Systems and Voter Alignments*. New York: Free Press.

11 Justin Fisher. 2001. "Campaign finance." In *Britain Votes 2001*, ed. Pippa Norris. Oxford: Oxford University Press, Tables 1 and 2.

12 Clyde Wilcox and I. Sigelman. 2001. "Political mobilization in the pews: Religious contacting and electoral turnout." *Social Science Quarterly*, 82(3): 524–535.

13 Richard Katz and Peter Mair. 1995. "Changing models of party organization and party democracy: The emergence of the cartel party." *Party Politics*, 1(1): 5–28. See, however, the critique by Ruud Koole. 1996. "Cadre, catch-all or cartel? A comment on the notion of the cartel party." *Party Politics*, 2: 507–523.

14 C. A. Cassel. 1999. "Voluntary associations, churches, and social participation theories of turnout." *Social Science Quarterly*, 80(3): 504–517; B. Radcliff and

P. Davis. 2000. "Labor organization and electoral participation in industrial democracies." *American Journal of Political Science*, 44(1): 132–141.

15 Daniel Bell. 1999. *The Coming of Post-Industrial Society*. New York: Basic Books.

16 L. Griffin, H. McCammon, and C. Bosko. 1990. "The unmaking of a movement? The crisis of U.S. trade unions in comparative perspective." In *Changes in Societal Institutions*, ed. M. Hallinan, D. Klein, and J. Glass. New York: Plenum.

17 See Bernhard Ebbinghaus and Jelle Visser. 1999. "When institutions matter: Union growth and decline in Western Europe, 1950–1995." *European Sociological Review*, 15(2): 135–158; and Sabine Blashke. 2000. "Union density and European integration: Diverging convergence." *European Journal of Industrial Relations*, 6(2): 217–236; Bruce Western. 1994. "Institutionalized mechanisms for unionization in sixteen OECD countries: An analysis of social survey data." *Social Forces*, 73(2): 497–519.

18 International Confederation of Free Trade Unions. 1998. "European trade unions step up organizing activities." www.iftu.org.

19 International Labour Organization. 1997. *World Employment Report 1996–97*. Geneva: ILO. www.ilo.org/public/english/bureau/inf/pkits/wlr97.htm.

20 Barry T. Hirsch and John T. Addison. 1986. *The Economic Analysis of Unions: New Approaches and Evidence*. London: Allen and Unwin.

21 It should be noted that union density can also be compared as a proportion of wage and salary earners, but data on this is less complete from ILO sources, and the available comparisons show that this does not make a substantial difference to the relative rankings of union density in different countries, although it does change the size of the estimates. For details, see International Labour Organization. 1997. *World Employment Report 1996–97*. Geneva: ILO. www.ilo.org/public/english/bureau/inf/pkits/wlr97.htm.

22 Bernhard Ebbinghaus and Jelle Visser. 2000. *Trade Unions in Western Europe since 1945*. London: Macmillan.

23 U.S. Census. "Labor union membership by sector." *Statistical Abstract of the United States*, www.census/gov, Table 712. For a discussion, see L. Griffin, H. McCammon, and C. Bosko. 1990. "The unmaking of a movement? The crisis of U.S. trade unions in comparative perspective." In *Changes in Societal Institutions*, ed. M. Hallinan, D. Klein, and J. Glass. New York: Plenum.

24 Bruce Western. 1994. "Institutionalized mechanisms for unionization in sixteen OECD countries: An analysis of social survey data." *Social Forces*, 73(2): 497–519.

25 Max Weber. 1930. *The Protestant Ethic and the Spirit of Capitalism*. New York: Scribner. For a discussion, see Steve Bruce, Ed. 1992. *Religion and Modernization*. Oxford: Oxford University Press.

26 O. Tschannen. 1991. "The secularization paradigm." *Journal for the Scientific Study of Religion*, 30: 395–415.

27 W. H. Swatos and K. J. Christiano. 2001. "Secularization theory: The course of a concept." *Sociology of Religion*, 60(3): 209–228.

28 Daniel Bell. 1999. *The Coming of Post-Industrial Society*. New York: Basic Books.

29 Steve Bruce. 1996. *Religion in the Modern World: From Cathedrals to Cults.* Oxford: Oxford University Press; Sheena Ashford and Noel Timms. 1992. *What Europe Thinks: A Study of Western European Values.* Aldershot: Dartmouth; Wolfgang Jagodzinski and Karel Dobbelaere. 1995. "Secularization and church religiosity." In *The Impact of Values,* ed. Jan W. van Deth and Elinor Scarbrough. Oxford: Oxford University Press; L. Voye. 1999. "Secularization in a context of advanced modernity." *Sociology of Religion,* 60(3): 275–288.

30 R.Stark and W. S. Bainbridge. 1985. "A supply-side reinterpretation of the "secularization" of Europe." *Journal for the Scientific Study of Religion,* 33: 230–252.

31 See Samuel P. Huntington. 1996. *The Clash of Civilizations and the Remaking of World Order.* New York: Simon and Schuster; Peter L. Berger, Ed. 1999. *The Desecularization of the World.* Washington, DC: Ethics and Public Policy Center; Rodney Stark. 1999. "Secularization, RIP." *Sociology of Religion.* 60(3): 249–273; W. H. Swatos, Jr., Ed. 1989. *Religious Politics in Global and Comparative Perspective.* New York: Greenwood Press.

32 David B. Barrett, George T. Kurian, and Todd M. Johnson. 2001. *World Christian Encyclopedia: A Comparative Survey of Churches and Religions in the Modern World.* Oxford: Oxford University Press. For details, see Table 1.1. See also Philip M. Parker. 1997. *Religious Cultures of the World: A Statistical Reference.* Westport, CT: Greenwood Press; David B. Barrett and Todd M. Johnson. 2001. *World Christian Trends AD 30–2200.* Pasedena, CA: William Carey Library; Global Evangelization Movement. 2001. *Status of Global Mission 2001,* www.gem-werc.org.

33 For further discussion, see Anthony M. Abela. 1993. "Post-secularisation: The social significance of religious values in four Catholic European countries." *Melita Theolgica,* 44: 39–58; Karel Dobbelaere. 1993. "Church involvement and secularization: Making sense of the European case." In *Secularization, Rationalism and Sectarism,* ed. E. Barker, J. A. Beckford, and K. Dobbelaere. Oxford: Clarendon Press; Karel Dobbelaere and Wolfgang Jagodzinski. 1995. "Religious cognitions and beliefs." In *The Impact of Values,* ed. Jan W. van Deth and Elinor Scarbrough. Oxford: Oxford University Press.

34 The Gallup Organization. *"Did you, yourself, happen to attend church or synagogue in the last seven days, or not?"* 1939 41% Yes. 2001 41% Yes. www.gallup.com/poll/indicators/indreligion.asp. For a more detailed analysis see Robert Wuthnow. 1999. "Mobilizing civic engagement: The changing impact of religious involvement." In *Civic Engagement in American Democracy,* ed. Theda Skocpol and Morris P. Fiorina. Washington, DC: Brookings Institution.

35 For a detailed discussion, see Andrew Greeley. 1980. *Religious Change in America.* Cambridge, MA: Harvard University Press; Andrew Greeley. 1995. "The persistence of religion." *Cross Currents,* 45(Spring): 24–41; Karel Dobbelaere. 1995. "Religion in Europe and North America." In *Values in Western Societies,* ed. Ruud de Moor. Tiburg: Tilburg University Press.

36 B. Radcliff and P. Davis. 2000. "Labor organization and electoral participation in industrial democracies." *American Journal of Political Science,* 44(1): 132–141.

37 On the relationship between unions and turnout in postindustrial societies, see Mark Gray and Miki Caul. 2000. "Declining voter turnout in advanced industrial democracies, 1950 to 1997." *Comparative Political Studies*, 33(9): 1091–1122.

10. New Social Movements, Protest Politics, and the Internet

1 For discussions of the conceptual distinctions and theoretical frameworks in the literature, as well as of the structure, function, and organization of interest groups and new social movements, see Jeffrey Berry. 1984. *The Interest Group Society*. Boston: Little Brown; Jack L. Walker. 1991. *Mobilizing Interest Groups in America*. Ann Arbor: University of Michigan Press; Sidney Tarrow. 1994. *Power in Movement*. Cambridge: Cambridge University Press; Charles Tilly. 1978. *From Mobilization to Revolution*. Reading, MA: Addison-Wesley; Doug McAdam, John D. McCarthy, and Mayer N. Zald, Eds. 1996. *Comparative Perspectives on Social Movements*. New York: Cambridge University Press.

2 Jeffrey Berry. 1984. *The Interest Group Society*. Boston: Little Brown; Jack L. Walker. 1991. *Mobilizing Interest Groups in America*. Ann Arbor: University of Michigan Press; Terry Nichols Clarke and Michael Rempel. 1997. *Citizen Politics in Post-Industrial Societies: Interest Groups Transformed*. Boulder, CO: Westview Press.

3 Sidney Tarrow. 1994. *Power in Movement*. Cambridge: Cambridge University Press; Charles Tilly. 1978. *From Mobilization to Revolution*. Reading, MA: Addison-Wesley; Doug McAdam, John D. McCarthy, and Mayer N. Zald. Eds. 1996. *Comparative Perspectives on Social Movements*. New York: Cambridge University Press; Russell J. Dalton and Manfred Kuechler, Eds. 1990. *Challenging the Political Order: New Social and Political Movements in Western Democracies*. New York: Oxford University Press.

4 Margaret E. Keck and Kathryn Sikkink. 1998. *Activists beyond Borders: Advocacy Networks in International Politics*. Ithaca, NY: Cornell University Press; J. Smith, C. Chatfield, and R. Pagnucco, Eds. 1997. *Transnational Social Movements and Global Politics: Solidarity beyond the State*. Syracuse, NY: Syracuse University Press; H. Kriesi, D. D. Porta, and Dieter Richt, Eds. 1998. *Social Movements in a Globalizing World*. London: Macmillan.

5 James Rosenau. 1990. *Turbulance in World Politics: A Theory of Change and Continuity*. Princeton: Princeton University Press; Ronnie Lipschutz. 1996. *Global Civic Society and Global Environmental Governance*. Albany, NY: State University of New York Press.

6 Mayer Zald and John McCarthy, Eds. 1987. *Social Movements in an Organizational Society*. New Brunswick, NJ: Transaction Books; Anthony Oberschall. 1993. *Social Movements: Ideologies, Interests and Identities*. New Brunswick, NJ: Transaction Books; David Meyer and Sidney Tarrow, Eds. 1998. *The Social Movement Society: Contentious Politics for a New Century*. Lanham, MD: Rowman and Littlefield; Enrique Larana, Hank Johnston, and Joseph R. Gudfield, Eds. 1994. *New Social Movements: From Ideology to Identity*. Philadelphia: Temple University Press; Douglas McAdam, John D. McCarthy, and Mayer N. Zald. 1996. *Com-*

parative Perspectives on Social Movements. New York: Cambridge University Press.

7   Sidney Verba, Norman H. Nie, and Jae-on Kim. 1971. The Modes of Democratic Participation: A Cross-National Analysis. Beverly Hills, CA: Sage; Sidney Verba and Norman Nie. 1972. Participation in America: Social Equality and Political Participation. New York: Harper Collins; Sidney Verba, Norman Nie, and Jae-on Kim. 1978. Participation and Political Equality: A Seven-Nation Comparison. New York: Cambridge University Press.

8   Charles Tilly, Louise Tilly, and Richard Tilly. 1975. The Rebellious Century. Cambridge, MA: Harvard University Press.

9   Frank Parkin. 1968. Middle Class Radicalism. New York: Praeger.

10 Barbara Epstein. 1991. Political Protest and Cultural Revolution: Nonviolent Direct Action in the 1970s and 1980s. Berkeley: University of California Press.

11 Samuel Barnes and Max Kaase. 1979. Political Action: Mass Participation in Five Western Democracies. Beverly Hills, CA: Sage. See also Alan Marsh. 1977. Protest and Political Consciousness. Beverly Hills, CA: Sage; Charles Adrian and David A. Apter. 1995. Political Protest and Social Change: Analyzing Politics. New York: New York University Press.

12 Peter Van Aelst and Stefaan Walgrave. 2001. "Who is that (wo)man in the street? From the normalization of protest to the normalization of the protester." European Journal of Political Research, 39: 461–486.

13 See Carole Pateman. 1988. The Sexual Contract. Cambridge: Polity Press; Anne Phillips. 1991. Engendering Democracy. Cambridge: Polity Press.

14 See Jonathan Baker. 1999. Street-Level Democracy: Political Settings at the Margins of Global Power. Connecticut: Kumarian Press.

15 Sidney Verba, Norman Nie, and Jae-on Kim. 1978. Participation and Political Equality: A Seven-Nation Comparison. New York: Cambridge University Press, p. 46. See also Sidney Verba, Kay Schlozman, and Henry E. Brady. 1995. Voice and Equality: Civic Voluntarism in American Politics. Cambridge, MA: Harvard University Press, p. 38.

16 Saskia Sassen. 1999. Globalization and Its Discontents. New York: New Press; Margaret Keck and Kathryn Sikkink. 1998. Activists beyond Borders: Advocacy Networks in International Politics. Ithaca, NY: Cornell University Press; Michael Edwards and John Gaventa, Eds. 2001. Global Citizen Action. Boulder, CO: Lynne Reinner; Peter Evans. 2000. "Fighting marginalization with transnational networks: Counter-hegemonic globalization." Contemporary Sociology, 29(1): 230–241.

17 Margaret E. Keck and Kathryn Sikkink. 1998. Activists beyond Borders: Advocacy Networks in International Politics. Ithaca, NY: Cornell University Press.

18 For a discussion, see David Held. 1999. Global Transformations: Politics, Economics and Culture. London: Polity Press; Joseph S. Nye and John Donahue, Eds. 2001. Governance in a Globalizing World. Washington, DC: Brookings Institution; Daniele Archibugi, David Held, and Martin Kohler. 1998. Reimagining Political Community: Studies in Cosmopolitan Democracy. Stanford, CA: Stanford University Press.

19 Harvey B. Feigenbaum, J. Henig, and C. Hamnett. 1998. Shrinking the State: The Political Underpinnings of Privatization. Cambridge: Cambridge University Press.

20 M. Kent Jennings, Jan W. van Deth, et al. 1989. *Continuities in Political Action: A Longitudinal Study of Political Orientations in Three Western Democracies.* New York: Walter de Gruyter.

21 Dieter Rucht, Ruud Koopmans, and Friedhelm Neidhart, Eds. 1998. *Acts of Dissent: New Developments in the Study of Protest.* Berlin: Edition Sigma.

22 For a fuller discussion, see Samuel Barnes and Max Kaase. 1979. *Political Action: Mass Participation in Five Western Democracies.* Beverly Hills, CA: Sage; Christopher A. Rootes. 1981. "On the future of protest politics in Western democracies: A critique of Barnes, Kaase et al., *Political Action.*" *European Journal of Political Research,* 9: 421–432.

23 It should be noted that not every nation was included in every wave of the WVS survey, so the average figures across all eight nations are presented here; but further examination suggests that this process did not influence the substantive findings.

24 J. Craig Jenkins and Michael Wallace. 1996. "The generalized action potential of protest movements: The new class, social trends, and political exclusion explanations." *Sociological Forum,* 11(2): 183–207.

25 Peter Van Aelst and Stefaan Walgrave. 2001. "Who is that (wo)man in the street? From the normalization of protest to the normalization of the protester." *European Journal of Political Research,* 39: 461–486.

26 Russell Dalton. 1994. *The Green Rainbow: Environmental Interest Groups in Western Europe.* New Haven, CT: Yale University Press; Christopher Rootes. 1999. *Environmental Movements: Local, National and Global.* London: Frank Cass.

27 Pippa Norris. 1997. "We're all green now: Public opinion and environmentalism in Britain." *Government and Opposition,* 32(3): 320–339.

28 This section draws on analysis developed in more detail in Pippa Norris. 2001. *Digital Divide: Civic Engagement, Information Poverty, and the Internet Worldwide.* Cambridge: Cambridge University Press. See also Jeffrey M. Ayres. 1999. "From the streets to the Internet: The cyber-diffusion of contention." *Annals of the American Academy of Political and Social Science,* 566: 132–143; Jessica Matthews. 1997. "Power shifts." *Foreign Affairs,* January/February.

29 Sylvia Ostry. 2000. "Making sense of it all: A post-mortem on the meaning of Seattle." In *Seattle, the WTO, and the Future of the Multilateral Trading System,* ed. Roger B. Porter and Pierre Sauve. Cambridge, MA: Center for Business and Government, John F. Kennedy School of Government; Steve Cisler. 1999. "Showdown in Seattle: Turtles, teamsters and tear gas." *First Monday,* 4(2), www.firstmonday.dk/issues/issue4 12/cisler/index.html.

30 See Sylvia Ostry. 2000. "Making sense of it all: A post-mortem on the meaning of Seattle." In *Seattle, the WTO, and the Future of the Multilateral Trading System,* ed. Roger B. Porter and Pierre Sauve. Cambridge, MA: Center for Business and Government, John F. Kennedy School of Government; Margaret E. Keck and Kathryn Sikkink. 1998. *Activists beyond Borders: Advocacy Networks in International Politics.* Ithaca, NY: Cornell University Press; Maxwell A. Cameron, Ed. 1998. *To Walk without Fear: The Global Movement to Ban Landmines.* Oxford: Oxford University Press; J. Zelwietro. 1998. "The politi-

cization of environmental organizations through the internet." *Information Society*, 14(1): 45–55.

31 Allen Hammond and Jonathan Lash. 2000. "Cyber-activism: The rise of civil accountability and its consequences for governance." *IMP: The Magazine on Information Impacts*, May, www.cisp.org/imp/may_2000/05_00hammond.htm.

32 Mamoun Fandy. 1999. "Cyberresistance: Saudi Opposition between globalization and localization." *Comparative Studies in Society and History*, 41(1): 124–147; William J. Drake, Shanthi Kalathil, and Taylor C. Boas. 2000. "Dictatorships in the digital age: Some considerations on the internet in China and Cuba." *IMP: The Magazine on Information Impacts*, October, www.cisp.org/imp; Taylor C. Boas. 2000. "The dictator's dilemma? The internet and U.S. policy toward Cuba." *The Washington Quarterly*, 23(3): 57–67.

33 Howard Frederick. 1992. "Computer communications in cross-border coalition-building: North American NGO networking against NAFTA." *Gazette*, 50: 217–242; Margaret E. Keck and Kathryn Sikkink. 1998. *Activists beyond Borders: Advocacy Networks in International Politics*. Ithaca, NY: Cornell University Press; J. Zelwietro. 1998. "The politicization of environmental organizations through the internet." *Information Society*, 14(1): 45–55.

34 The Institute for Global Communications can be found at *www.igc.org*. One World net can be located at www.OneWorld.org. For the range of volunteer activities and activist organizations available online, see also http://www.serviceleader.org/vv/forvols.html.

35 http://www.greenpeace.org.

36 See, for example, Kevin A. Hill and John E. Hughes. 1998. *Cyberpolitics: Citizen Activism in the Age of the Internet*. Lanham, MD: Rowan and Littlefield, Chapter 6; Richard Davis. 1999. *The Web of Politics*. Oxford: Oxford University Press, Chapter 3.

37 Union of International Organizations, http://www.uia.org.

38 For details, see Chapters 10 and 11 in Pippa Norris. 2001. *Digital Divide: Civic Engagement, Information Poverty, and the Internet Worldwide*. Cambridge: Cambridge University Press.

39 Ibid.

11. Conclusions

1 See the discussion in David Held. 1987. *Models of Democracy*. Stanford, CA: Stanford University Press.

2 Joseph A. Schumpeter. 1952. *Capitalism, Socialism and Democracy*, 4th ed. London: George Allen and Unwin.

3 For a detailed review of the "crisis of the state" literature discussing these claims, see Pippa Norris. 1999. *Critical Citizens: Global Support for Democratic Governance*. Oxford: Oxford University Press.

Selected Bibliography

Aarts, Kees. 1995. "Intermediate organizations and interest representation." In *Citizens and the State*, ed. Hans-Dieter Klingemann. Oxford: Oxford University Press.

Abramson, Paul R. 1983. *Political Attitudes in America: Formation and Change*. San Francisco, CA: W. H. Freeman.

Abramson, Paul R. and Ronald Inglehart. 1995. *Value Change in Global Perspective*. Ann Arbor: University of Michigan Press.

Aelst, Peter Van and Stefaan Walgrave. 2001. "Who is that (wo)man in the street? From the normalization of protest to the normalization of the protester." *European Journal of Political Research*, 39: 461–486.

Aldrich, John H. 1993. "Rational choice and turnout." *American Journal of Political Science*, 37: 246–278.

1995. *Why Parties? The Origin and Transformation of Party Politics in America*. Chicago: University of Chicago Press.

Alex-Assensoh, Y. and A. B. Assensoh. 2001. "Inner-city contexts, church attendance, and African-American political participation." *Journal of Politics*, 63(3): 886–901.

Almond, Gabriel A. 1980. "The intellectual history of the civic culture concept." In *The Civic Culture Revisited*, ed. Gabriel A. Almond and Sidney Verba. Boston: Little, Brown.

Almond, Gabriel A. and G. Bingham Powell. 1978. *Comparative Politics: System, Process, and Policy*. Boston: Little, Brown.

Almond, Gabriel A. and Sidney Verba. 1963. *The Civic Culture: Political Attitudes and Democracy in Five Nations*. Princeton, NJ: Princeton University Press.

Almond, Gabriel and Sidney Verba, Eds. 1980. *The Civic Culture Revisited*. Boston: Little, Brown.

Aminzade, Ronald R. et al., Eds. 2001. *Silence and Voice in the Study of Contentious Politics*. New York: Cambridge University Press.

Anderson, Christopher J. and Christine A. Guillory. 1997. "Political institutions and satisfaction with democracy." *American Political Science Review*, 91(1): 66–81.

Anderson, Christopher J. 1995. *Blaming the Government: Citizens and the Economy in Five European Democracies*. New York: M. E. Sharpe.

Andersson, H. E. and D. Granberg. 1997. "On the validity and reliability of self-reported vote: Validity without reliability." *Quality and Quantity*, 31(2): 127–140.

Archibugi, Daniele, David Held, and Martin Kohler, Eds. 1998. *Re-imagining Political Community: Studies in Cosmopolitan Democracy.* Stanford, CA: Stanford University Press.

Ashford, Sheena and Noel Timms. 1992. *What Europe Thinks: A Study of Western European Values.* Aldershot: Dartmouth.

Ayala, L. J. 2000. "Trained for democracy: The differing effects of voluntary and involuntary organizations on political participation." *Political Research Quarterly*, 53(1): 99–115.

Baker, Jonathan. 1999. *Street Level Democracy: Political Settings at the Margins of Global Power.* West Hartford, CT: Kumarian Press.

Barber, Benjamin. 1984. *Strong Democracy.* Berkeley: University of California Press.

Barnes, Samuel and Max Kaase. 1979. *Political Action: Mass Participation in Five Western Democracies.* Beverly Hills, CA: Sage.

Barnes, Samuel and Janos Simon, Eds. 1998. *The Post-Communist Citizen.* Budapest: Erasmus Foundation.

Baron, Stephen, John Field, and Tom Schuller, Eds. 2000. *Social Capital: Critical Perspectives.* Oxford: Oxford University Press.

Bartolini, Stefano. 2000. *The Political Mobilization of the European Left, 1860–1980.* Cambridge: Cambridge University Press.

Basanez, Miguel, Ronald Inglehart, and Alejandro Moreno. 1998. *Human Values and Beliefs: A Cross Cultural Sourcebook.* Ann Arbor: University of Michigan Press.

Beck, Paul Allen, Russell J. Dalton, A. A. Haynes, and Robert Huckfeldt. 1997. "Presidential campaigning at the grassroots." *Journal of Politics*, 59(4): 1264–1275.

Bell, Daniel. 1999. *The Coming of Post-Industrial Society: A Venture in Social Forecasting.* New York: Basic Books.

Bennett, Lance W. and Robert M. Entman, Eds. 2000. *Mediated Politics: Communication and the Future of Democracy.* New York: Cambridge University Press.

Bennett, Stephen E., Richard S. Flickinger, and Stacy L. Rhine. 2000. "Political talk over here, over there, over time." *British Journal of Political Science*, 30(1): 99–119.

Berger, Peter L., Ed. 1999. *The Desecularization of the World.* Washington, DC: Ethics and Public Policy Center.

Berglund, Sten and Jan A. Dellenbrant. 1994. *The New Democracies in Eastern Europe: Party Systems and Political Cleavages.* Aldershot: Edward Elgar.

Berry, Jeffrey. 1984. *The Interest Group Society.* Boston: Little, Brown.

Blais, Andre. 2000. *To Vote or Not to Vote? The Merits and Limits of Rational Choice Theory.* Pittsburgh: University of Pittsburgh Press.

Blais, Andre and R. Kenneth Carty. 1990. "Does proportional representation foster voter turnout?" *European Journal of Political Research*, 18(2): 167–181.

Blais, André and A. Dobrzynska. 1998. "Turnout in electoral democracies." *European Journal of Political Research*, 33(2): 239–261.

Blashke, S. 2000. "Union density and European integration: Diverging convergence." *European Journal of Industrial Relations*, 6(2): 217–236.

Blondel, Jean, Richard Sinnott, and Palle Svensson. 1998. *People and Parliament in the European Union: Participation, Democracy and Legitimacy.* Oxford: Oxford University Press.

Bourdieu, Pierre. 1970. *Reproduction in Education, Culture and Society.* London: Sage.

Bratton, Michael and Nicolas van de Walle. 1997. *Democratic Experiments in Africa.* Cambridge: Cambridge University Press.

Brehm, John and Wendy Rahn. 1997. "Individual-level evidence for the causes and consequences of social capital." *American Journal of Political Science,* 41(3): 999–1023.

Brody, Richard. 1978. "The puzzle of political participation in America." In *The New American Political System,* ed. Anthony King. Washington, DC: American Enterprise Institute.

Bruce, Steve. 1996. *Religion in the Modern World: From Cathedrals to Cults.* Oxford: Oxford University Press.

Budge, Ian. 1996. *The New Challenge of Direct Democracy.* Oxford: Polity Press.

Budge, Ian and Kenneth Newton. 1997. *The Politics of the New Europe.* Harlow, Essex: Addison Wesley Longman.

Burnham, Walter Dean. 1980. "The appearance and disappearance of the American voter." In *Electoral Participation: A Comparative Analysis,* ed. Richard Rose. Beverly Hills, CA: Sage.

Butler, David and Austin Ranney, Eds. 1994. *Referendums around the World: The Growing Use of Democracy?* Washington, DC: American Enterprise Institute.

Cappella, Joseph N. and Kathleen H. Jamieson. 1997. *Spiral of Cynicism.* New York: Oxford University Press.

Carothers, Thomas. 1999. *Aiding Democracy Abroad: The Learning Curve.* Washington, DC: Carnegie Endowment.

Cassel, C. A. 1999. "Voluntary associations, churches and social participation theories of turnout." *Social Science Quarterly,* 80(3): 504–517.

Cheles, Luciano, Ronnie Ferguson, and Michalina Vaughan. 1995. *The Far Right in Western and Eastern Europe.* New York: Longman.

Christy, Carol. 1987. *Sex Differences in Political Participation: Processes of Change in Fourteen Nations.* New York: Praeger.

Citrin, Jack. 1974. "Comment: The political relevance of trust in government." *American Political Science Review,* 68: 973–988.

Citrin, Jack and Donald Green. 1986. "Presidential leadership and trust in government." *British Journal of Political Science,* 16: 431–453.

Clarke, Harold D., Nitish Dutt, and Allan Kornberg. 1993. "The political economy of attitudes toward polity and society in Western European democracies." *The Journal of Politics,* 55(4): 998–1021.

Clarke, Harold D., Euel W. Elliott, William Mishler, Marianne C. Stewart, Paul F. Whiteley, and Gary Zuk. 1992. *Controversies in Political Economy.* Boulder, CO: Westview Press.

Clarke, Terry Nichols and Michael Rempel. 1997. *Citizen Politics in Post-Industrial Societies: Interest Groups Transformed.* Boulder, CO: Westview Press.

Coleman, James S. 1988. "Social capital in the creation of human capital." *American Journal of Sociology,* 94: 95–120.

1990. *Foundations of Social Theory.* Cambridge, MA: Belknap Press.

Colomer, J. M. 1991. "Benefits and costs of voting." *Electoral Studies*, 10(4): 313–325.
Conway, Margaret, Gertrude A. Steuernagel, and David Ahern. 1997. *Women and Political Participation*. Washington, DC: CQ Press.
Cox, Gary. 1988. "Closeness and turnout: A methodological note." *Journal of Politics*, 50: 768–775.
Craig, Stephen C. 1993. *The Malevolent Leaders: Popular Discontent in America*. Boulder, CO: Westview Press.
Craig, Stephen C. and Michael A. Maggiotto. 1981. "Political discontent and political action." *Journal of Politics*, 43: 514–522.
Crepaz, Marcus. 1990. "The impact of party polarization and post-materialism on voter turnout." *European Journal of Political Research*, 18(2): 183–205.
Crewe, Ivor. 1981. "Electoral participation." In *Democracy at the Polls*, ed. David Butler, Howard Penniman, and Austin Ranney. Washington, DC: American Enterprise Institute.
Crewe, Ivor and David T. Denver. 1985. *Electoral Change in Western Democracies: Patterns and Sources of Electoral Volatility*. New York: St. Martin's Press.
Crozier, Michel, Samuel P. Huntington, and Joji Watanuki. 1975. *The Crisis of Democracy: Report on the Governability of Democracies to the Trilateral Commission*. New York: New York University Press.
Curtis, J. E., E. G. Grabb, and D. E. Baer. 1992. "Voluntary association membership in fifteen countries – a comparative analysis." *American Sociological Review*, 57(2): 139–152.
Dahl, Robert A. 1971. *Polyarchy: Participation and Opposition*. New Haven, CT: Yale University Press.
    1982. *Dilemmas of Pluralist Democracy*. New Harven, CT: Yale University Press.
    1989. *Democracy and Its Critics*. New Haven, CT: Yale University Press.
Dalton, Russell J. 1993. "Citizens, Protest and Democracy," special issue of *The Annals of Political and Social Sciences* (July).
    1996. *Citizen Politics*, 2nd ed. Chatham, NJ: Chatham House.
    2000. "Citizen attitudes and political behavior." *Comparative Political Studies*, 33(6–7): 912–940.
Dalton, Russell J., Scott C. Flanagan, Paul A. Beck, and James E. Alt. 1984. *Electoral Change in Advanced Industrial Democracies: Realignment or Dealignment?* Princeton, NJ: Princeton University Press.
Dalton, Russell J. and Manfred Kuechler, Eds. 1990. *Challenging the Political Order: New Social and Political Movements in Western Democracies*. New York: Oxford University Press.
Dalton, Russell J. and Martin Wattenberg, Eds. 2001. *Parties without Partisans*. New York: Oxford University Press.
Dasgupta, Partha and Ismail Serageldin, Eds. 2000. *Social Capital: A Multifaceted Perspective*. Washington, DC: World Bank.
De Winter, L. and J. Ackaert. 1998. "Compulsory voting in Belgium: A reply to Hooghe and Pelleriaux." *Electoral Studies*, 17(4): 425–428.
DeVaus, David and Ian McAllister. 1989. "The changing politics of women: Gender and political alignments in eleven nations." *European Journal of Political Research*, 17: 241–262.

Diamond, Larry and Richard Gunther. 2001. *Political Parties and Democracy.* Baltimore: Johns Hopkins University Press.

Djupe, P. A. and J. T. Grant. 2001. "Religious institutions and political participation in America." *Journal for the Scientific Study of Religion,* 40(2): 303–314.

Downs, Anthony. 1957. *An Economic Theory of Voting.* New York: Harper.

Duch, Raymond. 1998. "Participation in the new democracies of Central and Eastern Europe: Cultural versus rational choice explanations." In *The Post-Communist Citizen,* ed. Samuel Barnes and Janos Simon. Budapest: Erasmus Foundation.

Duverger, Maurice. 1954. *Political Parties.* New York: Wiley.

Easton, David. 1965. *A Framework for Political Analysis.* Englewood Cliffs, NJ: Prentice-Hall.

   1965. *A Systems Analysis of Political Life.* New York: Wiley.

   1975. "A reassessment of the concept of political support." *British Journal of Political Science,* 5: 435–457.

Ebbinghaus, Bernhard and Jelle Visser. 1999. "When institutions matter: Union growth and decline in Western Europe, 1950–1995." *European Sociological Review,* 15(2): 135–158.

   2000. *Trade Unions in Western Europe since 1945.* London: Macmillan.

Edwards, Bob and Michael W. Foley. 1998. "Civil society and social capital beyond Putnam." *American Behavioral Scientist,* 42(1): 124–139.

Edwards, Michael and John Gaventa, Eds. 2001. *Global Citizen Action.* Boulder, CO: Lynne Rienner.

Eijk, Cees van der, Mark Franklin, et al. 1996. *Choosing Europe? The European Electorate and National Politics in the Face of the Union.* Ann Arbor: University of Michigan Press.

Epstein, Leon. 1980. *Political Parties in Western Democracies.* New Brunswick, NJ: Transaction Books.

Evans, Geoffrey. 1999. *The Decline of Class Politics?* Oxford: Oxford University Press.

Evans, Peter. 2000. "Fighting marginalization with transnational networks: Counter-hegemonic globalization." *Contemporary Sociology,* 29(1): 230–241.

Farah, Barbara G., Samuel H. Barnes, and Felix Heunis. 1979. "Political dissatisfaction." In *Political Action: Mass Participation in Five Western Democracies,* ed. Samuel H. Barnes and Max Kaase. Beverly Hills, CA: Sage.

Flickinger, Richard and Donley Studlar. 1992. "The disappearing voters? Exploring declining turnout in Western European elections." *West European Politics,* 15: 1–16.

Foley, Michael and Bob Edwards. 1998. "Beyond Tocqueville: Civil society and social capital in comparative perspective." *American Behavioral Scientist,* 42(1): 5–20.

Fox Piven, Frances. 1992. *Labour Parties in Postindustrial Societies.* Oxford: Oxford University Press.

Fox Piven, Frances and Richard Cloward. 1988. *Why Americans Don't Vote.* New York: Pantheon.

   2000. *Why Americans Still Don't Vote: And Why Politicians Want It That Way.* Boston: Beacon Press.

Franda, Marcus. 2002. *Launching into Cyberspace: Internet Development and Politics in Five World Regions.* Boulder, CO: Lynne Rienner.

Franklin, Mark. 1996. "Electoral participation." In *Comparing Democracies: Elections and Voting in Global Perspective,* ed. Lawrence LeDuc, Richard G. Niemi, and Pippa Norris. Thousand Oaks, CA: Sage.

——— 2000. "Understanding cross-national turnout differences: What role for compulsory voting?" *British Journal of Political Science,* 29: 205–216.

Franklin, Mark, Tom Mackie, and Henry Valen. 1992. *Electoral Change: Responses to Evolving Social and Attitudinal Structures in Western Countries.* New York: Cambridge University Press.

Freedom House. 2001. *Freedom in the World: The Annual Survey of Political Rights and Civil Liberties, 2000–2001.* New York: Freedom House.

Fukuyama, Francis. 1995. *Trust: The Social Virtues and the Creation of Prosperity.* New York: Free Press.

Gibson, Rachel and Stephen J. Ward, Eds. 2000. *Reinvigorating Government: UK Politics and the Internet.* Aldershot, Hampshire: Ashgate.

Gosnell, H. F. 1927. *Why Europe Votes.* Chicago: University of Chicago Press.

Gray, Mark and Miki Caul. 2000. "Declining voter turnout in advanced industrialized democracies, 1950 to 1997." *Comparative Political Studies,* 33(9): 1091–1122.

Greenwood, Justin and Mark Aspinwall, Eds. 1998. *Collective Action in the European Union: Interests and the New Politics of Associability.* London: Routledge.

Gunter, Richard and Anthony Mughan. 2000. *Democracy and the Media: A Comparative Perspective.* New York: Cambridge University Press.

Hall, Peter. 1999. "Social capital in Britain." *British Journal of Political Science,* 29: 417–461.

Halman, L. and Neil Nevitte, Eds. 1996. *Political Value Change in Western Democracies.* Tilberg: Tilberg University Press.

Hayes, B. C. and Clive Bean. "Political efficacy: A comparative study of the United States, West Germany, Great Britain and Australia." *European Journal of Political Research,* 23(3): 261–280.

Heath, Anthony, Roger Jowell, and John Curtice. 2001. *The Rise of New Labour.* Oxford: Oxford University Press.

Heath, Anthony and Bridget Taylor. 1999. "New sources of abstention?" In *Critical Elections: British Parties and Voters in Long-term Perspective,* ed. Geoffrey Evans and Pippa Norris. London: Sage.

Heidar, K. 1994. "The polymorphic nature of party membership." *European Journal of Political Research,* 25(1): 61–86.

Held, David. 1987. *Models of Democracy.* Stanford, CA: Stanford University Press.

Held, David, Anthony McGrew, David Goldblatt, and Jonathan Perraton. 1999. *Global Transformations.* Stanford, CA: Stanford University Press.

Hibbing, John R. and Elizabeth Theiss-Morse. 2001. *What Is It about Government That Americans Dislike?* Cambridge: Cambridge University Press.

Hill, K. Q. and J. E. Leighley. 1996. "Political parties and class mobilization in contemporary United States elections." *American Journal of Political Science,* 40(3): 787–804.

Hill, Kevin A. and John E. Hughes. 1998. *Cyberpolitics: Citizen Activism in the Age of the Internet*. Lanham, MD: Rowan and Littlefield.

Hirczy, Wolfgang. 1994. "The impact of mandatory voting laws on turnout: A quasi experimental approach." *Electoral Studies*, 13(1): 64–76.

1995. "Explaining near-universal turnout: The case of Malta." *European Journal of Political Research*, 27: 467–492.

Hirschman, Albert O. 1970. *Exit, Voice and Loyalty*. Cambridge, MA: Harvard University Press.

Huckfeldt, Robert and John Sprague. 1992. "Political parties and electoral mobilization: Political structure, social structure and the party canvass." *American Political Science Review*, 86(1): 70–86.

Institute for Democracy and Electoral Assistance. 1997. *The International IDEA Handbook of Electoral System Design*. Stockholm: International Institute for Democracy and Electoral Assistance.

Institute for Democracy and Electoral Assistance. *Voter Turnout from 1945 to 2000*. Stockholm: International IDEA.

International Labour Organization. *Yearbook of Labour Statistics* (annual). Geneva: ILO.

Inglehart, Ronald. 1977. *The Silent Revolution: Changing Values and Political Styles among Western Publics*. Princeton, NJ: Princeton University Press.

1990. *Culture Shift in Advanced Industrial Society*. Princeton, NJ: Princeton University Press.

1997. *Modernization and Postmodernization: Cultural, Economic and Political Change in forty-three Societies*. Princeton, NJ: Princeton University Press.

Jackman, Robert W. 1987. "Political institutions and voter turnout in industrialized democracies." *American Political Science Review*, 81: 405–423.

Jackman, Robert W. and Ross A. Miller. 1995. "Voter turnout in industrial democracies during the 1980s." *Comparative Political Studies*, 27: 467–492.

Jagodzinski, Wolfgang and Karel Dobbelaere. 1995. "Secularization and church religiosity." In *The Impact of Values*, ed. Jan W. van Deth and Elinor Scarbrough. Oxford: Oxford University Press.

Jennings, M. Kent and Jan van Deth. 1989. *Continuities in Political Action*. Berlin: Walter de Gruyter.

Kaase, Max and Kenneth Newton. 1995. *Beliefs in Government*. New York: Oxford University Press.

Karp, Jeff A. and Susan Banducci. 1999. "The impact of proportional representation on turnout: Evidence from New Zealand." *Australian Journal of Political Science*, 34(3): 363–377.

Katz, Richard and Peter Mair, Eds. 1994. *How Parties Organize: Change and Adaptation in Party Organizations in Western Democracies*. London: Sage.

Katz, Richard S. 1997. *Democracy and Elections*. New York: Oxford University Press.

Katz, Richard S. and Peter Mair. 1992. "The membership of political parties in European democracies, 1960–1990." *European Journal of Political Research*, 22: 329–345.

1995. "Changing models of party organization and party democracy: The emergence of the cartel party." *Party Politics*, 1(1): 5–28.

1996. "Cadre, catch-all or cartel? A rejoinder." *Party Politics*, 2(4): 525–534.

Katz, Richard S. and Peter Mair, Eds. 1992. *Party Organizations: A Data Handbook on Party Organizations in Western Democracies, 1960–1990*. London: Sage.

Keck, Margaret E. and Kathryn Sikkink. 1998. *Activists beyond Borders – Advocacy Networks in International Politics*. Ithaca, NY: Cornell University Press.

Kent Jennings, M., Jan W. van Deth, et al. 1989. *Continuities in Political Action: A Longitudinal Study of Political Orientations in Three Western Democracies*. New York: Walter de Gruyter.

Key, V. O. 1964. *Politics, Parties and Pressure Groups*. New York: Crowell.

Kim, J., R. O. Wyatt, and E. Katz. 1999. "News, talk, opinion, participation: The part played by conversation in deliberative democracy." *Political Communication*, 16(4): 361–385.

King, J. D. 1994. "Political culture, registration laws and voter turnout in the American states." *Publius: The Journal of Federalism*, 24: 115–127.

Kirchheimer, Otto. 1966. "The transformation of Western European party systems." In *Political Parties and Political Development*, ed. J. La Palombara and M. Weiner. Princeton, NJ: Princeton University Press.

Kitschelt, Herbert. 1986. "Political opportunity structures and political protest: Anti-nuclear movements in four democracies." *British Journal of Political Science*, 16(1): 57–86.

1994. *The Transformation of European Social Democracy*. Cambridge: Cambridge University Press.

Kitschelt, Herbert, Zdenka Mansfeldova, Radoslaw Markowski, and Gabor Toka. 1999. *Post-Communist Party Systems*. Cambridge: Cambridge University Press.

Klingemann, Hans-Dieter and Dieter Fuchs. 1995. *Citizens and the State*. Oxford: Oxford University Press.

Kluegel, James R. and David S. Mason. 1999. "Political involvement in transition: Who participated in Central and Eastern Europe?" *International Journal of Comparative Sociology*, 40(1): 41–60.

Knack, S. 2001. "Election-day registration: The second wave." *American Politics Research*, 29(1): 65–78.

Koopman, R. 1996. "New social movements and changes in political participation in Western Europe." *West European Politics*, 19(1): 28–50.

Kriesi, Hanspetar, et al. 1995. *New Social Movements in Western Europe: A Comparative Analysis*. Minneapolis: University of Minnesota Press.

Kriesi, H., D. Della Porta, and Dieter Riucht, Eds. 1998. *Social Movements in a Globalizing World*. London: Macmillan.

Kuenzi, Michelle and Gina Lambright. 2001. "Party system institutionalization in thirty African countries." *Party Politics*, 7(4): 437–468.

Ladd, Everett C. 1996. "The data just don't show erosion of America's social capital." *The Public Perspective*, 7(4).

Ladner, A. and H. Milner. 1999. "Do voters turn out more under proportional than majoritarian systems? The evidence from Swiss communal elections." *Electoral Studies*, 18(2): 235–250.

Lane, Jan-Erik and Svante Ersson. 1990. "Macro and micro understanding in political science: What explains electoral participation?" *European Journal of Political Research*, 18(4): 457–465.

Lane, Jan-Erik, David McKay, and Kenneth Newton, Eds. 1997. *Political Data Handbook*, 2nd ed. Oxford: Oxford University Press.

Lawson, Kay. 1980. *Political Parties and Linkage: A Comparative Perspective.* New Haven, CT: Yale University Press.

Lawson, Kay and Peter Merkl, Eds. 1988. *When Parties Fail: Emerging Alternative Organizations.* Princeton, NJ: Princeton University Press.

Levy, Margaret and David Olson. 2000. "The battles in Seattle." *Politics & Society*, 28(3): 309–329.

Lewis-Beck, Michael and Brad Lockerbie. 1989. "Economics, votes and protests: Western European cases." *Comparative Political Studies*, 22: 155–177.

Lijphart, Arend. 1994. *Electoral Systems and Party Systems: A Study of Twenty-Seven Democracies, 1945–1990.* Oxford: Oxford University Press.

1997. "Unequal participation: democracies' unresolved dilemma." *American Political Science Review*, 91: 1–14.

1999. *Patterns of Democracy.* New Haven, CT: Yale University Press.

Linz, Juan J. and Alfred C. Stepan. 1996. *Problems of Democratic Transition and Consolidation: Southern Europe, South America and Post-Communist Europe.* Baltimore: Johns Hopkins University Press.

Lipschutz, Ronnie D. 1996. *Global Civil Society and Global Environmental Governance: The Politics of Nature from Place to Planet.* Albany: State University of New York Press.

Lipset, Seymour M. 1959. "Some social requisites of democracy, economic development and political legitimacy." *American Political Science Review*, 53: 69–105.

1960. *Political Man: The Social Basis of Politics.* New York: Doubleday.

1993. "A comparative analysis of the social requisites of democracy." *International Social Science Journal*, 136(2): 155–175.

1994. "The social requisites of democracy revisited." *American Sociological Review*, 59: 1–22.

1996. *American Exceptionalism: A Double Edged Sword.* New York: Norton.

Lipset, Seymour M. and Stein Rokkan, Eds. 1967. *Party Systems and Voter Alignments.* New York: Free Press.

Lipset, Seymour M. and William C. Schneider. 1987. *The Confidence Gap: Business, Labor, and Government in the Public Mind*, rev. ed. Baltimore: Johns Hopkins University Press.

Lockerbie, Brad. 1993. "Economic dissatisfaction and political alienation in Western Europe." *European Journal of Political Research*, 23: 281–293.

Lovenduski, Joni and Pippa Norris. 1993. *Gender and Party Politics.* Thousand Oaks, CA: Sage.

Mackie, Thomas and Richard Rose. 1991. *The International Almanac of Electoral History.* Washington, DC: Congressional Quarterly.

Maier, Charles S. 1994. "Democracy and its discontents." *Foreign Affairs*, 73(4): 48–65.

Mainwaring, Scott and Timothy Scully. 1995. *Building Democratic Institutions: Party Systems in Latin America.* Stanford, CA: Stanford University Press.

Mair, Peter. 1997. *Party System Change.* Oxford: Oxford University Press.

2001. "In the aggregate: Mass electoral behaviour in Western Europe, 1950–2000." In *Comparative Democracy*, ed. Hans Keman. London: Sage.

2001. "Party membership in twenty European democracies 1980–2000." *Party Politics*, 7(1): 5–22.

Marsh, Alan. 1977. *Protest and Political Consciousness*. Beverly Hills, CA: Sage.

1990. *Political Action in Europe and the USA*. London: Macmillan.

Martinez, M. D. and D. Hill. 1999. "Did motor voter work?" *American Politics Quarterly*, 27(3): 296–315.

Mattes, R. B., A. Gouws and H. J. Kotze. 1995. "The emerging party system in the new South Africa." *Party Politics*, 1(3): 381–395.

McAdam, Doug, John D. McCarthy, and Mayer N. Zeld. 1996. *Comparative Perspectives on Social Movements*. Cambridge: Cambridge University Press.

McAllister, Ian. 1986. "Compulsory voting, turnout and party advantage in Australia." *Politics*, 21(1): 89–93.

McKenzie, B. D. 2001. "Self-selection, church attendance, and local civic participation." *Journal for the Scientific Study of Religion*, 40(3): 479–488.

McVeigh, R. and D. Sikkink. 2001. "God, politics, and protest: Religious beliefs and the legitimation of contentious tactics." *Social Forces*, 79(4): 1425–1458.

Merriam, Charles Edward. 1924. *Non-Voting: Causes and Methods of Control*. Chicago: University of Chicago Press.

Milbrath, Lester and M. L. Goel. 1977. *Political Participation: How and Why Do People Get Involved in Politics?* 2nd ed. New York: University Press of America.

Miller, Arthur H. 1974a. "Political issues and trust in government, 1964–1970." *American Political Science Review*, 68: 951–972.

1974b. "Rejoinder to 'Comment' by Jack Citrin: Political discontent or ritualism?" *American Political Science Review*, 68: 989–1001.

Miller, William L., Stephen White, and Paul Heywood. 1998. *Values and Political Change in Postcommunist Europe*. New York: St. Martin's Press.

Morlino, Leonardo. 1998. *Democracy between Consolidation and Crisis: Parties, Groups, and Citizens in Southern Europe*. Oxford: Oxford University Press.

Muller, Edward N. 1979. *Aggressive Political Participation*. Princeton, NJ: Princeton University Press.

Murphy, C. 1994. *International Organizations and International Change: Global Governance since 1850*. Cambridge: Cambridge University Press.

Nagler, Jack. 1991. "The effects of registration laws and education on US voter turnout." *American Political Science Review*, 85: 1393–1405.

Newton, Kenneth. 2001. "Trust, social capital, civic society, and democracy." *International Political Science Review*, 22(2): 201–214.

Norris, Pippa. 1996. "Did television erode social capital? A reply to Putnam." *PS: Political Science and Politics*, 29(3): 474–480.

2000. "Blaming the messenger? Political communications and turnout in EU elections." In *Citizen Participation in European Politics* (Demokratiutredningens skrift nr 32). Stockholm: Statens Offentliga Utredningar.

2000. *A Virtuous Circle: Political Communication in Post-Industrial Democracies*. New York: Cambridge University Press.

2001. "Women's power at the ballot box." In *IDEA Voter Turnout from 1945 to 2000: A Global Report on Political Participation*, 3rd ed. Stockholm: International IDEA.

2001. *Digital Divide: Civic Engagement, Information Poverty and the Internet Worldwide*. New York: Cambridge University Press.

Norris, Pippa, Ed. 1998. *Passages to Power*. Cambridge: Cambridge University Press.

1999. *Critical Citizens: Global Support for Democratic Governance*. Oxford: Oxford University Press.

Ochoa, E. 1987. "The rapid expansion of voter participation in Latin America: Presidential elections 1845–1986." In *Statistical Abstract of Latin America*, Vol. 25, ed. J. W. Wilkie and D. Lorey. Los Angeles: UCLA Latin American Center.

Oppenhuis, Eric. 1995. *Voting Behavior in Europe: A Comparative Analysis of Electoral Participation and Party Choice*. Amsterdam: Het Spinhuis.

Pacek, Alexander and Benjamin Radcliffe. 1995. "Turnout and the left-of-center parties: A cross-national analysis." *British Journal of Political Science*, 25: 137–143.

Panebianco, Angelo. 1988. *Political Parties: Organization and Power*. Cambridge: Cambridge University Press.

Parry, Geraint, George Moyser, and Neil Day. 1992. *Political Participation and Democracy in Britain*. Cambridge: Cambridge University Press.

Pattie, Charles and Richard Johnston. 1998. "Voter turnout at the British general election of 1992: Rational choice, social standing or political efficacy?" *European Journal of Political Research*, 33(2): 263–283.

Pempel, T. J. 1990. *Uncommon Democracies: The One-Party Dominant Regimes*. Ithaca, NY: Cornell University Press.

Pérez-Liñán, Aníbal. 2001. "Neoinstitutional accounts of voter turnout: Moving beyond industrial democracies." *Electoral Studies*, 20(2): 281–297.

Pharr, Susan and Robert Putnam, Eds. 2000. *Disaffected Democracies: What's Troubling the Trilateral Countries?* Princeton, NJ: Princeton University Press.

Powell, G. Bingham, Jr. 1980. "Voting turnout in thirty democracies: Partisan, legal and socioeconomic influences." In *Electoral Participation: A Comparative Analysis*, ed. Richard Rose. London: Sage.

1982. *Contemporary Democracies: Participation, Stability and Violence*. Cambridge, MA: Harvard University Press.

1986. "American turnout in comparative perspective." *American Political Science Review*, 80: 17–43.

2000. *Elections as Instruments of Democracy*. New Haven, CT: Yale University Press.

Preiser, S., S. Janas, and R. Theis. 2000. "Political apathy, political support and political participation." *International Journal of Psychology*, 35(3): 74–84.

Przeworski, Adam, Michael E. Alvarez, Jose Antonio Cheibub, and Fernando Limongi. 2000. *Democracy and Development*. Cambridge: Cambridge University Press.

Przeworski, Adam and Henry Teune. 1970. *The Logic of Comparative Social Inquiry*. New York: Wiley–Interscience.

Putnam, Robert D. 1995. *Making Democracy Work*. Princeton, NJ: Princeton University Press.

1995. "Tuning in, tuning out: The strange disappearance of social capital in america." *P.S.: Political Science and Politics*, 28(4): 664–683.

1996. "The strange disappearance of civic America." *The American Prospect*, 24: 34–48.

2000. *Bowling Alone: The Collapse and Revival of American Community*. New York: Simon and Schuster.

Putnam, Robert D., Ed. 2002. *Democracies in Flux: The Evolution of Social Capital*. New York: Oxford University Press.

Radcliff, B. and P. Davis. 2000. "Labor organization and electoral participation in industrial democracies." *American Journal of Political Science*, 44(1): 132–141.

Rose, Richard. 1997. "Voter turnout: A global survey." In *IDEA Voter Turnout from 1945 to 1997: A Global Report on Political Participation*, 2nd ed. Stockholm: International IDEA.

Rose, Richard, Ed. 1980. *Electoral Participation: A Comparative Analysis*. London: Sage.

Rosenstone, Steven J. and John Mark Hansen. 1993. *Mobilization, Participation and Democracy in America*. New York: Macmillan.

Rotolo, Thomas. 1999. "Trends in voluntary association participation." *Nonprofit and Voluntary Sector Quarterly*, 28(2): 199–212.

Rucht, Dieter, R. Koopmans, and F. Niedhart. 1998. *Acts of Dissent: New Developments in the Study of Protest*. Berlin: Sigma.

Rueschemeyer, Dietrich, Marilyn Rueschemeyer, and Bjorn Wittrock, Eds. 1998. *Participation and Democracy, East and West: Comparisons and Interpretations*. Armonk, NY: M. E. Sharp.

Scarrow, Susan. 1994. "The paradox of enrollment: Assessing the costs and benefits of party memberships." *European Journal of Political Research*, 25(1): 41–60.

1996. *Parties and Their Members: Organizing for Victory in Britain and Germany*. Oxford: Oxford University Press.

2001. "Parties without members?" In *Parties without Partisans*, ed. Russell J. Dalton and Martin Wattenberg. New York: Oxford University Press.

Schlozman, Kay Lehman, Nancy Burns, and Sidney Verba. 1994. "Gender and pathways to participation: The role of resources." *Journal of Politics*, 56: 963–990.

Schmitt, Herman and Sören Holmberg. 1995. "Political parties in decline?" In *Citizens and the State*, ed. Hans-Dieter Klingemann and Dieter Fuchs. Oxford: Oxford University Press.

Schumpeter, Joseph A. 1952. *Capitalism, Socialism and Democracy*, 4th ed. London: George Allen and Unwin.

Selle, Per. 1991. "Membership in party organizations and the problems of decline of parties." *Comparative Political Studies*, 23(4): 459–477.

Sen, Amartya. 1999. *Development as Freedom*. New York: Anchor.

Seyd, Patrick and Paul Whiteley. 1992. *Labour's Grass Roots: The Politics of Labour Party Membership*. Oxford: Clarendon Press.

Shah, D. V., N. Kwak, and R. L. Holbert. 2001. " 'Connecting' and 'disconnecting' with civic life: Patterns of Internet use and the production of social capital." *Political Communication*, 18(2): 141–162.

Shaw, Eric. 1994. *The Labour Party Since 1945*. Oxford: Blackwell.

Skocpol, Theda and Morris P. Fiorina, Eds. 1999. *Civic Engagement in American Democracy*. Washington, DC: Brookings/Russell Sage Foundation.

Smith, J., C. Chatfield, and R. Pagnucco, Eds. 1997. *Transnational Social Movements and Global Politics: Solidarity beyond the State.* Syracuse, NY: Syracuse University Press.

Smith, Jackie. 1998. "Global civil society? Transnational social movement organization and social capital." *American Behavioral Scientist,* 42(1): 93–107.

Sousa, D. J. 1993. "Organized labor in the electorate, 1960–1988." *Political Research Quarterly,* 46(4): 741–758.

Stark, Rodney. 1999. "Secularization, RIP." *Sociology of Religion,* 60(3): 249–273.

Swaddle, K. and Anthony Heath. 1989. "Official and reported turnout in the British general election of 1987." *British Journal of Political Science,* 19(4): 537–551.

Swanson, David and Paolo Mancini. 1996. *Politics, Media and Modern Democracy.* New York: Praeger.

Tan, A. C. 1997. "Party change and party membership decline: An exploratory analysis." *Party Politics,* 3(3): 363–377.

1998. "The impact of party membership size: A cross-national analysis." *Journal of Politics,* 60(1): 188–198.

Tarrow, Sidney. 1992. *Power in Movement.* Cambridge: Cambridge University Press.

2000. "Mad cows and social activists: Contentious politics in the trilateral democracies." In *Disaffected Democracies,* ed. Robert D. Putnam and Susan J. Pharr. Princeton, NJ: Princeton University Press.

Teixeira, Ruy. A. 1992. *The Disappearing American Voter.* Washington, DC: Brookings.

Thomassen, Jacques. 1990. "Economic crisis, dissatisfaction and protest." In *Continuitites in Political Action,* ed. M. Kent Jennings, Jan w. van Deth, et al. New York: Walter de Gruyter.

Tingsten, Herbert. 1937. *Political Behavior: Studies in Election Statistics.* Reprinted Totowa, NJ: Bedminster Press (1963).

Topf, Richard. 1995. "Electoral participation." In *Citizens and the State,* ed. Hans-Dieter Klingemann and Dieter Fuchs. Oxford: Oxford University Press.

United Nations Development Program. 2000. *Human Development Report 2000: Human Rights and Human Development.* New York: UNDP/Oxford University Press.

van Deth, Jan Willem. 2000a. "Interesting but irrelevant: Social capital and the saliency of politics in Western Europe." *European Journal of Political Research,* 37: 115–147.

2000b. "Political interest and apathy: The decline of a gender gap?" *Acta Politica,* 35(2): 247–274.

van Deth, Jan Willem, Ed. 1997. *Private Groups and Public Life: Social Participation, Voluntary Associations and Political Involvement in Representative Democracies.* London: Routledge.

van Deth, Jan Willem and F. Kreuter. 1998. "Membership of voluntary associations." In *Comparative Politics: The Problem of Equivalence,* ed. Jan. W. van Deth. London: Routledge.

Verba, Sidney and Norman Nie. 1972. *Participation in America: Political Democracy and Social Equality.* New York: Harper and Row.

Verba, Sidney, Norman Nie, and Jae-on Kim. 1978. *Participation and Political Equality: A Seven-Nation Comparison.* New York: Cambridge University Press.

Verba, Sidney, Kay Schlozman, and Henry E. Brady. 1995. *Voice and Equality: Civic Voluntarism in American Politics*. Cambridge, MA: Harvard University Press.

Wallerstein, Michael. 1989. "Union organization in advanced industrial democracies." *American Political Science Review*, 83(2): 481–501.

Wallerstein, Michael and B. Western. 2000. "Unions in decline? What has changed and why." *Annual Review of Political Science*, 3: 355–377.

Ware, Alan. 1996. *Political Parties and Party Systems*. Oxford: Oxford University Press.

Warren, Mark E. 2001. *Democracy and Association*. Princeton, NJ: Princeton University Press.

Wattenberg, Martin. 1996. *The Decline of American Political Parties: 1952–1994*. Cambridge, MA: Harvard University Press.

Weatherford, Stephen M. 1984. "Economic 'stagflation' and public support for the political system." *British Journal of Political Science*, 14: 187–205.

   1987. "How does government performance influence political support?" *Political Behavior*, 9: 5–28.

   1991. "Mapping the ties that bind: Legitimacy, representation and alienation." *Western Political Quarterly*, 44: 251–276.

   1992. "Measuring political legitimacy." *American Political Science Review*, 86: 149–166.

Webb, Paul, Ed. *Political Parties in Advanced Industrial Democracies*. Oxford: Oxford University Press.

Weil, Frederick D. 1989. "The sources and structure of legitimation in Western democracies. A consolidated model tested with time-series data in six countries since World War II." *American Sociological Review*, 54: 682–706.

Wessels, Bernhard. 1997. "Organizing capacity of societies and modernity." In *Private Groups and Public Life: Social Participation, Voluntary Associations and Political Involvement in Representative Democracies*, ed. Jan W. van Deth. London: Routledge.

Western, B. 1993. "Postwar unionization in eighteen advanced capitalist countries." *American Sociological Review*, 58: 226–282.

   1994. "Institutionalized mechanisms for unionization in sixteen OECD countries: An analysis of social survey data." *Social Forces*, 73(2): 497–519.

White, Stephen, Richard Rose, and Ian McAllister. 1997. *How Russia Votes*. Chatham, NJ: Chatham House.

Whiteley, Paul. 1995. "Rational choice and political participation: Evaluating the debate." *Political Research Quarterly*, 48: 211–233.

Whiteley, Paul and Patrick Seyd. 1994. "Local party campaigning and electoral mobilization in Britain." *Journal of Politics*, 56(1): 242–252.

Whiteley, Paul, Patrick Seyd, and Jeremy Richardson. 1994. *True Blues: The Politics of Conservative Party Membership*. Oxford: Clarendon Press.

Widfeldt, Anders. 1995. "Party membership and party representativeness." In *Citizens and the State*, ed. Hans-Dieter Klingemann and Dieter Fuchs. Oxford: Oxford University Press.

   1999. "Losing touch? The political representativeness of Swedish parties, 1985–1994." *Scandinavian Political Studies*, 22(4): 307–326.

   1999. *Linking Parties with People? Party Membership in Sweden 1960–1997*. Aldershot: Ashgate.

Wilcox, Clyde and I. Sigelman. 2001. "Political mobilization in the pews: Religious contacting and electoral turnout." *Social Science Quarterly*, 82(3): 524–535.

Wilkins, K. G. 2000. "The role of media in public disengagement from political life." *Journal of Broadcasting and Electronic Media*, 44(4): 569–580.

Wolfinger, Ray and Steven Rosenstone. 1980. *Who Votes?* New Haven, CT: Yale University Press.

Wright, James D. 1976. *The Dissent of the Governed*. New York: Academic Press.

Index